Using the
National
Gifted
Education
Standards
for Teacher Preparation

Second Edition

Using the
National
Gifted
Education
Standards
for Teacher Preparation

Susan K. Johnsen, Ph.D., Joyce VanTassel-Baska, Ed.D., Ann Robinson, Ph.D.,
Alicia Cotabish, Ed.D., Debbie Dailey, Ed.D., Jennifer Jolly, Ph.D.,
Jane Clarenbach, J.D., and Cheryll M. Adams, Ph.D.

A Service Publication of the

NATIONAL ASSOCIATION FOR
Gifted Children

Council for
Exceptional
Children
The voice and vision of special education

tag The Association *for the Gifted*
Council for Exceptional Children

PRUFROCK PRESS INC.
WACO, TEXAS

Library of Congress Cataloging-in-Publication Data

Johnsen, Susan K.
Using the national gifted education standards for teacher preparation programs / by Susan K. Johnsen, Ph.D., Joyce VanTassel-Baska, Ed.D., Ann Robinson, Ph.D., Alicia Cotabish, Ed.D., Debbie Dailey, Ed.D., Jennifer Jolly, Ph.D., Jane Clarenbach, J.D., and Cheryll M. Adams, Ph.D. -- Second Edition.
    1 online resource.
"A Service Publication of the National Association for Gifted Children and The Association for the Gifted-Council for Exceptional Children."
Includes bibliographical references.
Description based on print version record and CIP data provided by publisher; resource not viewed.
ISBN 978-1-61821-476-8 (Paperback)
ISBN 978-1-61821-477-5 (ebook)
ISBN 978-1-61821-478-2 (epub)
1. Gifted children--Education--United States--Standards. 2. Universities and colleges--Curricula--United States--Planning. I. Title.
LC3993.9 .J63 2016
371.95--dc23
                        2015031626

Edited by Lacy Compton

Cover and layout design by Raquel Trevino

ISBN-13: 978-1-61821-476-8

Printed in the United States of America.

At the time of this book's publication, all facts and figures cited are the most current available. All telephone numbers, addresses, and websites URLs are accurate and active. All publications, organizations, websites, and other resources exist as described in the book, and all have been verified. The authors and Prufrock Press Inc. make no warranty or guarantee concerning the information and materials given out by organizations or content found at websites, and we are not responsible for any changes that occur after this book's publication. If you find an error, please contact Prufrock Press Inc.

Prufrock Press Inc.
P.O. Box 8813
Waco, TX 76714-8813
Phone: (800) 998-2208
Fax: (800) 240-0333
http://www.prufrock.com

TABLE OF CONTENTS

FOREWORD

Informed standards are the foundation of quality teacher preparation programs. Standards define the destination, suggest routes, and provide landmarks to creating programs that graduate effective gifted education teachers who then positively influence our high-ability students. The Council for the Accreditation of Educator Preparation (CAEP) views the NAGC-CEC Teacher Preparation Standards in Gifted Education as the benchmark of excellence.

This guidebook provides the map to using the NAGC-CEC standards to build an effective teacher preparation program, including information on providing quality clinical experiences and measuring the outcomes of those experiences. You will find information on how the 2006 and 2013 teacher preparation standards differ and the research base used in creating the standards. The guidebook was written by teacher educators who are among the best in the field of gifted education.

There are two important new sections in this updated guide. One addresses creating partnerships with K–12 schools, parents, and the community at large. Gifted education is a collaborative effort, and providers need to be strategic in sharing the value of and the specifics of effective gifted education strategies. The other new section discusses how to work with our general education colleagues to incorporate gifted education into general education teacher preparation courses. This is crucially important considering the general education teacher is typically the gateway to gifted education assessments and services or, in many cases, is the primary provider of advanced coursework.

Finally, information is provided on preparing a program report for CAEP program review. This section includes examples of quality elements, as well as areas of concern that can assist programs as they apply to become nationally recognized.

We are seeing increased attention to the connection between developing high levels of giftedness and talent in all student populations and the success of the nation. This guidebook will assist schools and districts in supporting that talent development by graduating superior gifted educators.

George Betts
NAGC President
2015–2017

ACKNOWLEDGMENTS

Although the authors are responsible for the content, this book incorporates the 2013 teacher preparation standards and builds on the previous guidebook that resulted from the combined efforts of numerous colleagues who contributed to the standards' development and their application to higher education settings. Of particular note is Jane Clarenbach at the National Association for Gifted Children (NAGC) who provides ongoing assistance to universities seeking national recognition; Cheryll Adams, chair of the NAGC Professional Standards Committee and representative from The Association for the Gifted on the Council for Exceptional Children's Knowledge and Skills Subcommittee; the boards of the National Association for Gifted Children and The Association for the Gifted; and the authors of the first guidebook—Susan K. Johnsen, Joyce VanTassel-Baska, and Ann Robinson. We also want to thank Lacy Compton, Prufrock Press, for her fine editorial work on this guidebook. We especially appreciate faculty from higher education institutions who so generously contributed examples of coursework and assessments and who believe that these teacher preparation standards will improve the quality of gifted education for Pre-K–12 students.

CHAPTER 1

INTRODUCTION AND BACKGROUND

SUSAN K. JOHNSEN AND JOYCE VANTASSEL-BASKA

Introduction

Since the national teacher preparation standards in gifted education were first released in 2006, two important events have occurred in the area of standards development. First, the National Council for Accreditation of Teacher Education's (NCATE) Specialty Areas Studies Board (SASB; 2004) developed guidelines recommending that Specialized Professional Associations (SPAs; i.e., teaching specialty areas such as social studies, gifted education, science, special education) reduce the number of their teacher preparation standards to 7 and the number of elements to 28 to facilitate both the preparation of program reports and the review process. Second, the Interstate Teacher Assessment and Support Consortium (InTASC, 2013) released the Model Core Teaching Standards "as a resource for states, districts, professional organizations, teacher education programs, teachers, and others as they develop policies and programs to prepare, license, support, evaluate, and reward today's teachers" (p. 5). These two events precipitated a review by the National Association for Gifted Children (NAGC) and the Council for Exceptional Children (CEC) of the Teacher Preparation Standards in Gifted and Talented Education (2013 Teacher Preparation Standards) and a consequent revision to realign the 2006 Teacher Preparation Standards in Gifted and Talented Education (2006 Teacher Preparation

Standards) with the new guidelines and InTASC standards (for the complete development process, see pages 6–13).

With the release of the 2013 Teacher Preparation Standards, NAGC's Professional Standards Committee (PSC) decided to update the teacher preparation resources in order to help not only universities realign their programs to the new standards, but also provide guidance to others involved in professional learning and development such as public and private Pre-K–12 schools, state departments of education, professional associations, and community organizations. The authors have revised the guide, *Using the National Gifted Education Standards for University Teacher Preparation Programs* (Johnsen, VanTassel-Baska, & Robinson, 2008), and updated previous chapters related to the rationale for standards, the development process, the 2013 Teacher Preparation Standards and their relationship to the 2006 Teacher Preparation Standards, and the research base for the standards. Similar to the previous guide, this revised edition provides specific examples and ways for integrating the standards within the Educator Preparation Provider's (EPP) conceptual framework, courses at both the undergraduate and graduate levels, key assessments that operationalize the standards for candidates, and clinical experiences. Moreover, it provides a new chapter that describes how to develop a SPA program report for national recognition status as part of the accreditation process administered now by the Council for Accreditation of Educator Preparation (CAEP), with particular emphasis on developing rubrics to evaluate teacher candidate performance. (*Note.* NCATE merged with the Teacher Education Accreditation Council [TEAC] in 2013 to form CAEP, which is now the national accreditor for teacher preparation programs. Readers will note references to both organizations.)

Another new chapter within this guide focuses on how to develop partnerships with preservice teacher education programs, Pre-K–12 schools, other educator preparation providers, and community organizations. Specific examples of partnership activities are discussed that highlight the integration of gifted education standards within general education teacher preparation courses, support for new teachers, accountability, continuous improvement, and interrelationships among various entities that promote Pre-K–12 gifted students' learning. Also included in this revised guidebook are the new Advanced Standards in Gifted Education and how they might be used for developing programs for educators who already have their initial certificates in gifted education.

This guidebook concludes with a discussion of challenges and a rich set of resources in the appendices, including sample course syllabi, a bibliography of the research literature related to the field of gifted education, and an alignment of the 2013 Teacher Preparation Standards with the NAGC Pre-K–Grade 12 Gifted Education Programming Standards.

Rationale for Standards

According to InTASC (2013), standards serve three major functions: They provide a common vision of where educators need to go, they set a level of performance that needs to be met, and they provide a way of assessing progress so that each teacher has the support and opportunity to meet the standards. The standards therefore provide educators with meaningful outcomes to assess in optimizing candidates' knowledge, skills, and dispositions.

Standards have benefits particular to the field of gifted education. In order to ensure equity and systematic talent search and programming, it is essential that practicing teachers and candidates are educated in the relevant theory, research, pedagogy, and management techniques important for developing and sustaining classroom-based opportunities specifically designed for gifted learners. Educators must "develop a deep understanding of the critical concepts and principles of their discipline and, by completion, are able to use discipline-specific practices flexibly to advance the learning of all students toward attainment of college and career-readiness standards" (CAEP, 2013, Standard 1, p. 2). Standards therefore assist candidates and practicing teachers in having specific content knowledge and pedagogical skills in gifted education so that they are able to develop gifted learners' talents for high-level functioning in the 21st century.

Because gifted education is not federally mandated, these standards are able to provide a structure that creates consistency across states, universities, and schools involved in teacher preparation, development, licensure, and evaluation. This consistency ensures that each gifted learner receives a challenging curriculum and the pedagogical supports needed to master it effectively.

Standards also are able to provide a curriculum template for the development of courses and other professional learning opportunities so that candidates and practicing teachers are able to develop their knowledge and pedagogical skills systematically. In the case of candidates who want to be gifted educators, they need to learn how to develop, deliver, and differentiate curriculum for gifted learners, often within an inclusive classroom. The sophistication and complexity of the instructional practices that work in such a setting need time to be developed. Standards are able to provide guidance about what practices are effective, how they might be implemented, and resources needed for improving instruction to deepen learning for gifted and talented students.

Standards also offer a focus and a direction for new research efforts that link seminal ideas about teaching with ways of studying their effects on gifted and talented students' learning. Standards, then, provide criteria for selecting problems for which solutions may be found and function as consensus-building agents within and across institutions.

The systemic reform movement in education displays many of the features just described. It causes educators to reconstruct their reality based on new views of teaching and learning, as well as new assumptions about the nature of learners. It calls for a coordinated response in schools to the major problems of student achievement and alienation. It suggests that schools have to be reorganized as collegial and collaborative learning communities and that classrooms have to focus on maximum competency standards designed to create competent adults in the society. It also suggests that teacher preparation institutions need to partner with Pre-K–12 learning communities in working together toward learning how candidates impact student learning.

Differences Between the 2013 and 2006 NAGC-CEC Teacher Preparation Standards in Gifted and Talented Education

The 2013 Teacher Preparation Standards are closely aligned to the 2006 NAGC-CEC Teacher Preparation Standards. As mentioned previously, the 2013 Teacher Preparation Standards were revised to align with the InTASC standards and to meet the SASB recommendations (i.e., reduction to 7 standards and 28 elements). Although the content of the standards and the elements are not substantially changed (see Table 1.1), the following differences should be noted:

1. *Reduction of standards.* Formerly, the 10 standards included Foundations (Standard 1), Development and Characteristics of Learners (Standard 2), Individual Learning Differences (Standard 3), Instructional Strategies (Standard 4), Learning Environments and Social Interactions (Standard 5), Language and Communication (Standard 6), Instructional Planning (Standard 7), Assessment (Standard 8), Professional and Ethical Practice (Standard 9), and Collaboration (Standard 10). These were integrated into seven standards: Learner Development and Individual Learning Differences (formerly Standards 2 and 3), Learning Environments (formerly Standards 5 and 6), Curricular Content Knowledge (formerly Standard 7), Assessment (formerly Standard 8), Instructional Planning and Strategies (formerly Standards 4 and 7), Professional Learning and Ethical Practice (formerly Standards 1 and 9), and Collaboration (formerly Standard 10). (See Table 1.1 for a comparison between the 2013

and the 2006 standards; for a reverse comparison [i.e., 2006 standards are aligned to the 2013 standards], see Appendix A.)

2. *Reduction of elements.* As the 77 elements from the former standards were reduced to 28 and placed into the new 7 standards, they were reviewed for redundancy and clarity. Elements were eliminated if they were redundant and closely related elements were combined. Elements focused on what the candidate needed to know and be able to do instead of student performance. Elements were not only kept general to incorporate the knowledge and skills from the former elements but were also restated so that the content of the element was clearly conveyed.

3. *Rewritten narratives.* To ensure that gifted educators understood each of the standards and their corresponding elements, narratives were crafted that elaborated the required foundational knowledge and skills required and incorporated the detail in the former elements. For example, with the Assessment Standard, the types of assessments were elaborated to include quantitative, qualitative, formal, and informal assessments of behavior, learning, achievement, and environments.

4. *Updated research base.* The research base for the former standards was updated to ensure that the standards and each of the elements were supported by the latest research regarding effective practices with students. This research included literature/theory-based, research-based (i.e., empirical), and practice-based research. Any elements that were not supported by research were discarded.

5. *Alignment of language to InTASC standards.* In developing the titles for the revised standards, CEC and NAGC used the language from the 2011 InTASC Model Core Teaching Standards (see Table 1.2). This common language provides opportunities for teacher educators to collaborate not only within the field of gifted education but also across other teacher preparation disciplines.

It should be noted that Standard 3, Curricular Content Knowledge, was contained only within elements of Standard 7 in the former standards. Its change to a stand-alone standard stresses the importance of developing the gifted candidates' understanding of both general and specialized curricula. This firm foundation of the role of central concepts, structures of the discipline, and tools of inquiry allows the candidate to understand how to organize knowledge, integrate cross-disciplinary skills, and develop meaningful learning progressions for gifted and advanced learners. This understanding is the first step toward developing specialized content domains that incorporate advanced, accelerated, conceptually challenging, in-depth, distinctive, and/or complex content.

6.   *Alignment to the NAGC Pre-K–Grade 12 Gifted Programming Standards.*
     Since 2006, the National Association for Gifted Children revised and
     aligned its 1998 Program Standards to reflect the principles contained
     in the NAGC-CEC Teacher Preparation Standards. The program
     standards for Pre-K to grade 12 gifted education programs and services
     were therefore updated to incorporate more diversity, special educa-
     tion, technology, and differentiation. The result was the development
     of the 2010 NAGC Pre-K–Grade 12 Gifted Education Programming
     Standards. The programming standards, along with the 2006 NAGC-
     CEC Teacher Preparation Standards, were considered in revising and
     developing the 2013 teacher preparation standards, providing continu-
     ity and cohesion across all of the standards in gifted education.

The 2013 NAGC-CEC Teacher Preparation Standards in Gifted and Talented Education

The Development Process

The Council for Exceptional Children, The Association for the Gifted
(CEC-TAG), and the National Association for Gifted Children (NAGC), the
two major professional organizations that provide leadership in the field of
gifted education, were involved in the development of the 2013 NAGC-CEC
Teacher Preparation Standards. These initial standards for teachers of students with gifts and talents used the CEC process for standards development
and were aligned to the 2006 NAGC-CEC Teacher Knowledge and Skill
Standards for Gifted Education. CEC-TAG and NAGC initiated a review process in 2011 to realign the 2006 NAGC-CEC Teacher Preparation Standards
and its knowledge base and research, guided by the SASB 2004 guidelines
and the 2011 release of the InTASC Model Core Teaching Standards. The
Professional Standards and Practices Standing Committee (CEC-PSPSC)
and the Knowledge and Skills Subcommittee (CEC-KSS) of the Council
for Exceptional Children and the NAGC Professional Standards Committee
(NAGC-PSC) provided oversight for the process. During the realignment
process, a wide range of stakeholders and experts was consulted during numerous meetings and conference calls over a 2-year period. Each meeting offered
the opportunity to provide input, typically asking participants to comment on
the most recent draft of the standards or to add to a list of research support

Table 1.1

Comparison of 2013 NAGC-CEC to 2006 NAGC-CEC Teacher Preparation Standards in Gifted and Talented Education

2013 NAGC-CEC Teacher Preparation Standards in Gifted and Talented Education	2006 NAGC-CEC Teacher Preparation Standards in Gifted and Talented Education
Standard 1. Learning Development and Individual Learning Differences	
1.1 Influences on learning	GT1K.5: Impact of dominant culture GT1K6: Factors that enhance/inhibit GT2.K2: Culture/environmental effects GT2K3: Role of families GT3K1: Influences of diversity GT3K4: Beliefs, traditions, and values influences on relationships GT3S1: Integrate perspectives in planning instruction GT6K2: Impact of diversity
1.2 Differences in development	GT2K4: Advanced milestones GT2.K1: Cognitive/affective development GT2K5: Differences with general GT3K2: Academic/affective GT3K3: Idiosyncratic learning patterns
Standard 2. Learning Environments	
2.1 Creation of engaging environments	GT5K2: Social/emotional development influences on relationships GT5S3: Safe environments for independence/interdependence/positive relationships GT5S4: Intercultural experiences GT5S5: Social interaction/coping skills to address personal/social issues, including discrimination
2.2 Facilitation and adaptation of environments	GT5S1: Opportunities that promote self-awareness/peer relations/intercultural/leadership GT5S2: Environments that promote self-awareness, self-efficacy, leadership, learning
2.3 Adjustment of language and communication	GT5K1: Stereotypes/discrimination GT6K1: Forms and methods GT6K2: Impact of diversity GT6K3: Implications of culture, behavior, language GT6S1: Resources/strategies to enhance advanced communication
2.4 Continuum of services	GT10S4: Families, general and special educators, school staff in comprehensive program
Standard 3. Curricular Content Knowledge	
3.1 Organization of knowledge, skills, and progressions	GT7K1: Theories/research models that form basis of curriculum and instruction GT7K3: Curriculum emphases within domains GT7S3: Scope and sequence

Table 1.1, *Continued*

2013 NAGC-CEC Teacher Preparation Standards in Gifted and Talented Education	2006 NAGC-CEC Teacher Preparation Standards in Gifted and Talented Education
3.2 Design of learning and performance modifications	GT7S5: Advanced, conceptually challenging, in-depth, distinctive, complex curricula
3.3 Differentiation of materials using assessments	GT4S4: Preassess learning in domains and adjust using assessment GT7K2: Differences between differentiated and general curriculum
3.4 Modification of general and specialized curriculum	GT7S5: Advanced, conceptually challenging, in-depth, distinctive, complex curricula
Standard 4. Assessment	
4.1 Use of technically sound instruments that minimize bias in identification	GT1K4: Conceptions/identification GT8K1: Identification GT8K3: Uses and limitations of assessments for documenting growth GT8S1: Nonbiased and equitable GT8S2: Technically adequate for identification/placement
4.2 Differentiation of assessments and interpretation of results	GT8S3: Differentiated and curriculum-based for use in instruction
4.3 Collaboration in using multiple assessment information	GT4S4: Preassess learning in domains and adjust using assessment GT8K2: Multiple assessments in different domains for identifying GT8K3: Uses and limitations of assessments for documenting growth GT8S1: Nonbiased and equitable GT8S4: Alternative assessments and technologies to evaluate learning GT10K1: Culturally responsive GT10S1: Concerns of families
4.4 Use of assessments for long- and short-range goals	GT4S4: Preassess learning in domains and adjust using assessment GT8S3: Differentiated and curriculum-based for use in instruction GT5S2: Environments that promote self-awareness, self-efficacy, leadership, learning
4.5 Student's assessment of own learning	GT8S3: Differentiated and curriculum-based for use in instruction
Standard 5. Instructional Planning and Strategies	
5.1 Principles of practice and repertoire of instructional strategies	GT4K1: Resources/differentiation GT4K2: Effective strategies GT4S1: Pedagogical content knowledge GT4S2: Apply higher level thinking and metacognitive models to content areas

Table 1.1, *Continued*

2013 NAGC-CEC Teacher Preparation Standards in Gifted and Talented Education	2006 NAGC-CEC Teacher Preparation Standards in Gifted and Talented Education
5.1 Principles of practice and repertoire of instructional strategies	GT4S3: Explore, develop, and research areas of interest GT4S5: Pace curriculum and instruction consistent with needs GT7S4: Resources/strategies/product options that respond to differences
5.2 Application of technologies	GT4S7: Assistive technologies GT6S2: Advanced oral/written tools, including assistive technologies GT7S1: Instructional plans aligned to standards GT7S2: Design learning plans GT7S4: Resources/strategies/product options that respond to differences
5.3 Collaboration in use of strategies	GT4S1: Pedagogical content knowledge GT7S4: Resources/strategies/product options that respond to differences GT10K1: Culturally responsive GT10S1: Concerns of families
5.4 Use of advanced knowledge and skills across environments	GT4S3: Explore, develop, and research areas of interest GT4S6: Challenging, multicultural curriculum GT7S6: Academic/career guidance
5.5 Strategies for affective development	GT4S1: Pedagogical content knowledge GT7S4: Resources/strategies/product options that respond to differences
Standard 6. Professional Learning and Ethical Practice	
6.1 Ethical principles and standards	GT1K1: Historical foundations GT1K2: Key philosophy/research GT1K3: Laws and policies GT9K2: Relevant organizations and publications GT1K7: Key issues and trends GT9S4: Laws, policies, standards GT9S6: Professional organizations
6.2 Current issues and foundational knowledge	GT9K1: Personal/cultural frames of reference, including bias GT9S4: Laws, policies, standards
6.3 Respect for diversity	GT9S3: Encourage/model respect
6.4 Lifelong learning	GT9S1: Personal skills and limitations GT9S5: Continuous research-supported professional development GT9S7: Reflect on personal practice
6.5 Advance profession through advocacy and mentoring	GT10S3: Advocate for benefit

Table 1.1, *Continued*

2013 NAGC–CEC Teacher Preparation Standards in Gifted and Talented Education	2006 NAGC–CEC Teacher Preparation Standards in Gifted and Talented Education
Standard 7. Collaboration	
7.1 Elements of effective collaboration	GT10S2: Stakeholders outside school setting GT10S4: Families, general and special educators, school staff in comprehensive program GT10S5: Families, community, and professionals in assessment
7.2 Collaborative resource to others	GT10S6: Provide school personnel with in information about characteristics
7.3 Collaboration to promote students	GT10K1: Culturally responsive GT10S1: Concerns of families GT10S2: Stakeholders outside school setting GT10S4: Families, general and special educators, school staff to plan comprehensive program GT10S5: Families, community, and professionals in interpreting assessments

Table 1.2

Comparison of 2013 NAGC–CEC Teacher Preparation Standards in Gifted and Talented Education to the 2011 InTASC Standards

2013 NAGC–CEC Teacher Preparation Standard in Gifted and Talented Education	2011 InTASC Standards
Standard 1: Learner Development and Individual Learning Differences	Standard 1: Learner Development Standard 2: Learning Differences
Standard 2: Learning Environments	Standard 3: Learning Environments
Standard 3: Curricular Content Knowledge	Standard 4: Content Knowledge Standard 5: Application of Content
Standard 4: Assessment	Standard 6: Assessment
Standard 5: Instructional Planning and Strategies	Standard 7: Planning for Instruction Standard 8: Instructional Strategies
Standard 6: Professional Learning and Ethical Practice	Standard 9: Professional Learning and Ethical Practice
Standard 7: Collaboration	Standard 10: Leadership and Collaboration

for each standards area. The timeline and description of activities are outlined below:

1. *Information about the realignment process was presented to NAGC-PSC at NAGC's Annual Conference in November 2009.* The Professional Standards Committee was informed of the need to reduce the number of standards to 7 and the number of elements to 28 to conform to NCATE's Specialty Area Studies Board recommendations. This realignment needed to occur by fall of 2013 when the revised standards needed to be submitted for approval to NCATE (now CAEP). The NAGC-PSC recommended that the revision follow the CEC realignment process.

2. *The standards were reduced from 10 to 7 at the CEC Annual Conference in April 2010.* The CEC-KSS and the CEC-PSPSC identified seven standards that aligned to CEC's Common Core initial licensure standards.

3. *CEC's Initial Level Special Educator Preparation Standards were realigned at the CEC Annual Conference, April 2011.* CEC-KSS began the realignment process of CEC's Initial Level Special Educator Preparation Standards to meet SASB recommendations and to incorporate the new InTASC standards. To ensure that knowledge and skills from the previous standards are included, no substantive changes are made to the content.

4. *CEC-KSS reviewed the realigned CEC Initial Level Special Educator Preparation Standards at its fall meeting in October 2011, and CEC-PSPSC reviewed the realigned standards at its meeting in Washington, DC, in January 2012.*

5. *The NAGC-PSC reviewed the 7 standards and began the realignment process of key elements of the 2006 Teacher Preparation Standards in January 2012.* The NAGC-PSC reviewed the draft CEC Initial Level Special Educator Preparation Standards and members began realigning the elements to the seven standards. The realignment process included these steps:
   » The elements from the 2006 NAGC-CEC standards were placed into the seven realigned CEC Initial Level Special Educator Preparation Standards.
   » Elements were eliminated if they were redundant or were combined with closely related elements.
   » Each element was reviewed to ensure that it related to what a teacher does, rather than what a student does.
   » Elements were kept general but needed to convey the element clearly.

> » Elements were reviewed to ensure they did not include specific methods or strategies.
> » When not important to a given element, subjective qualifiers, such as "appropriate" or "effective," were avoided.
> » Long and partial lists were removed unless there were only a few inclusive items.
> » Parenthetical information was removed.
> » Examples were removed when the meaning of the element was clear without them.
> » Terminology was used consistently across the elements.
> » Elements were updated using current professional literature.
> » Narratives were written that incorporated the elements and explanatory content.

6. *The CEC Initial Level Special Educator Preparation Standards were approved at the CEC Annual Conference in April 2012 by CEC-KSS, CEC-PSPC, and the CEC Board.*

7. *The CEC Initial Level Special Educator Preparation Standards were approved by NCATE in the fall of 2012.*

8. *At the CEC-KSS fall meeting in October 2012, and at the NAGC-PSC meeting in November 2012, workgroup leaders reviewed the NAGC-CEC Teacher Preparation Standards in Gifted and Talented Education, reviewed realigned elements, and completed draft narratives.* They coordinated the literature review among the NAGC-PSC members.

9. A *survey was sent to NAGC-PSC members and other stakeholders in the fall of 2012.* The draft narrative, standards, and elements of the realigned NAGC-CEC Teacher Preparation Standards in Gifted and Talented Education were sent to NAGC-PSC members and other stakeholders for their review to ensure that the 2006 knowledge and skills were represented in the newly aligned standards.

10. *The survey results were reviewed by the NAGC-PSC in January 2013.* Comments from surveys were integrated into the standards and narrative paragraphs. NAGC-PSC members then reviewed the literature independently to ensure that it had been updated and was complete.

11. *The NAGC-CEC Teacher Preparation Standards were approved by the CEC-PSPC in February 2013.*

12. *NAGC posted the NAGC-CEC Teacher Preparation Standards on its website and NCATE posted them on its website for public comment in April 2013.*

13. *The workgroup leaders reported that the NAGC-CEC Teacher Preparation Standards were approved by CEC's KSS and PSPC in May 2013.*

14. *The NAGC-PSC reviewed the public comments in June 2013.* The committee received 34 additional public comments submitted for the realigned standards. NAGC-PSC members reviewed these independently and suggested final changes along with any other research updates.

15. *The NAGC Board and the CEC Board approved the final standards in summer 2013.*

16. *The final standards and updated research base was submitted to CAEP in August 2013.*

17. *CAEP Board of Directors approved the NAGC-CEC Teacher Preparation Standards in December 2013.*

Throughout the entire process, NAGC and CEC were diligent in ensuring that the realigned standards did not eliminate any of the substantive knowledge and skills that are relevant to effective practice in gifted education and continued to emphasize diversity. CAEP provides teacher preparation programs with an 18-month transition period to begin using the revised standards. Programs seeking national recognition must use the 2013 standards beginning with programs reviewed in the spring of 2016.

Introduction to the 2013 NAGC-CEC Teacher Preparation Standards

The 2013 NAGC-CEC Teacher Preparation Standards define knowledge about gifted and talented students, content, pedagogy, collaboration, and professional and ethical principles for teachers of gifted and talented students. The Council for the Accreditation of Educator Preparation (2013) defined content knowledge as describing the "depth of understanding of critical concepts, theories, skills, processes, principles, and structures that connect and organize ideas within a field" (p. 4). Pedagogical knowledge includes

> core activities of teaching, such as figuring out what students know; choosing and managing representations of ideas; appraising, selecting, and modifying textbooks; . . . deciding among alternative courses of action and analyzing the subject matter knowledge and insight entailed in these activities. (CAEP, 2013, p. 5)

Both content and pedagogical knowledge are based on a thorough understanding of learners—their development and individual differences. In the case of gifted and talented students, this knowledge is used to accelerate and enrich learning experiences so that each learner can develop and reach his or her potential.

The standards begin with a gifted professional's understanding of individual learning differences, focusing on how language, culture, economic status, family background, and/or disability impacts the learning of individuals with gifts and talents. Based on these understandings, gifted education professionals respond to learners' individual needs.

Standard 2 emphasizes the nature of multiple learning environments for gifted learners. This includes creating safe, inclusive, and culturally responsive environments for all learners. These environments provide the framework for a continuum of services that respond to an individual's gifts, talents, motivations, and cultural and linguistic differences.

Standards 3, 4, and 5 focus on gifted education professionals' knowledge and implementation of the learning process. Standard 3 emphasizes educators' knowledge and use of core and specialized curricula to advance learning for individuals with gifts and talents. Standard 4 concentrates on assessment, both for identifying individuals with gifts and talents and also the types of assessment used to differentiate and accelerate instruction. Standard 5 focuses on the selection, adaption, and planned use of a variety of evidence-based instructional strategies to advance learning of gifted and talented individuals.

Standard 6 emphasizes the use of foundational knowledge of the field and professional ethical principles, as well as national Pre-K–Grade 12 gifted education programming standards to inform gifted education practice, to engage in lifelong learning, and to advance the profession.

Finally, Standard 7 focuses on gifted education professionals' collaboration with families, other educators, related-service providers, individuals with gifts and talents, and personnel from community agencies in culturally responsive ways to address the needs of individuals with gifts and talents across a range of learning experiences. A glossary for key terms in the standards may be found in Figure 1.1.

NAGC-CEC Teacher Preparation Standards in Gifted and Talented Education

Standard 1: Learner Development and Individual Learning Differences

Beginning gifted education professionals understand the variations in learning and development in cognitive and affective areas between and among individuals

Acceleration: Acceleration practices may include grade-based acceleration that shortens the number of years an individual is in the Pre-K–12 system and/or subject-based acceleration that brings advanced content and skills earlier than expected for age or grade level (Rogers, 2002).

Bias: Bias may occur not only within quantitative assessments that do not have technical adequacy but also from barriers within identification procedures such as low teacher expectations, exclusive definitions, and a focus on deficits rather than strengths (Ford, 1998; Ryser, 2011).

Differentiated assessment: The practice of varying assessments in such a way that it reflects differentiation in the curriculum and/or the instruction. Differentiated assessment implies that as students experience differences in their learning, they should experience differences in their assessment. For example, students with gifts and talents may require off-level/above-grade-level tests to accurately assess their level of ability or achievement.

Differentiated curriculum: Adaptation of content, process, and product to meet a higher level of expectation appropriate for advanced learners. Curriculum can be differentiated through acceleration, complexity, depth, challenge, and creativity (VanTassel-Baska & Wood, 2008).

Differentiated instruction: Multiple ways to structure a lesson so that each student is challenged at an appropriate level. Differentiated instruction may include such features as learner centeredness; planned assignments and lessons based on preassessment; and flexible grouping, materials, resources, and pacing (Tomlinson & Hockett, 2008).

Diversity: Differences among groups of people and individuals based on ethnicity, race, socioeconomic status, gender, exceptionalities, language, religion, sexual orientation, and geographical area (Matthews & Shaunessy, 2008)

Technical adequacy: This term refers to the psychometric properties of an assessment instrument. Instruments with technical adequacy demonstrate validity for the identified purpose, reliability in providing consistent results, and minimized bias, and have been normed on a population matching the census data (Johnsen, 2008).

FIGURE 1.1. Glossary for 2013 NAGC-CEC Teacher Preparation Standards in Gifted and Talented Education.

with gifts and talents and apply this understanding to provide meaningful and challenging learning experiences for individuals with exceptionalities.

1.1	Beginning gifted education professionals understand how language, culture, economic status, family background, and/or area of disability can influence the learning of individuals with gifts and talents.
1.2	Beginning gifted education professionals use understanding of development and individual differences to respond to the needs of individuals with gifts and talents.

Historically, gifted education professionals have placed the learning needs of the individual at the center of gifted education instruction. Gifted education professionals have altered instructional practices to optimize learning for individuals with gifts and talents. Development of expertise begins with a thorough understanding of and respect for similarities and differences in all areas of human growth and development. Like all educators, beginning gifted education professionals first respect individuals with gifts and talents within the context of human development and individual learning differences. Not only do beginning gifted education professionals understand advanced developmental milestones of individuals with gifts and talents from early childhood through adolescence, but they also understand how exceptionalities can interact with development and learning, and create developmentally appropriate learning environments to provide relevant, meaningful, and challenging learning experiences for individuals with gifts and talents.

Beginning gifted education professionals understand the variation in characteristics between and among individuals with and without gifts and talents. They know exceptionalities can interact with multiple domains of human development to influence an individual's learning in school, community, and throughout life. Moreover, they understand that the beliefs, traditions, and values across and within cultures can influence relationships among and between students, their families, and the school community. Furthermore, these experiences of individuals with exceptionalities can influence the individual's ability to learn, interact socially, and live as fulfilled contributing members of the community. Educators of the gifted understand the phenomenon of underachievement and how it manifests itself in males and females. They understand techniques for reversing underachievement.

Beginning gifted education professionals are active and resourceful in seeking to understand how the primary language, culture, family, and areas of disability interact with the gifts and talents to influence the individual's academic and social abilities, attitudes, values, interests, and career and postsecondary options. These learning differences and their interactions provide the foundation upon which beginning gifted education professionals differentiate instruction to provide developmentally meaningful and challenging learning for individuals with exceptionalities.

Standard 2: Learning Environments

Beginning gifted education professionals create safe, inclusive, and culturally responsive learning environments so that individuals with gifts and talents become effective learners and develop social and emotional well-being.

2.1	Beginning gifted education professionals create safe, inclusive, culturally responsive learning environments that engage individuals with gifts and talents in meaningful and rigorous learning activities and social interactions.

2.2	Beginning gifted education professionals use communication and motivational and instructional strategies to facilitate understanding of subject matter and to teach individuals with gifts and talents how to adapt to different environments and develop ethical leadership skills.
2.3	Beginning gifted education professionals adjust their communication to an individual's language proficiency and cultural and linguistic differences.
2.4	Beginning gifted education professionals demonstrate understanding of the multiple environments that are part of a continuum of services for individuals with gifts and talents, including the advantages and disadvantages of various settings and teach students to adapt to these environments.

Like all educators, beginning gifted education professionals develop safe, inclusive, culturally responsive learning environments for all students. They also collaborate with colleagues in general education and other specialized environments that develop students' gifts and talents, engaging gifted students in meaningful learning activities that enhance independence, interdependence, and positive peer-relationships.

Beginning gifted education professionals modify learning environments for individual needs and risk taking. Knowledge regarding the interaction of an individual's language, family, culture, areas of disability, and other significant contextual factors with an individual's gifts and talents guides the beginning gifted educator in modifying learning environments, and provides for the maintenance and generalization of acquired skills across environments and subjects. They adjust their communication methods to an individual's language proficiency. They value and are responsive to cultural and linguistic differences and avoid discrimination, stereotyping, and deficit views of differences.

Beginning gifted education professionals structure environments to encourage self-awareness, self-regulation, self-efficacy, self-direction, personal empowerment, leadership, and self-advocacy of individuals with gifts and talents, and directly teach them how to adapt to the expectations and demands of differing environments.

Standard 3: Curricular Content Knowledge

Beginning gifted education professionals use knowledge of general[1] and specialized curricula[2] to advance learning for individuals with gifts and talents.

---

1 As used, "general" or the core curricula means the general academic content of the curricula including math, reading, English/language arts, science, social studies, and the arts.
2 As used, "specialized curricula" means the content of specialized interventions that are designed to address the unique needs of individuals with gifts and talents.

3.1	Beginning gifted education professionals understand the role of central concepts, structures of the discipline, and tools of inquiry of the content areas they teach, and use their understanding to organize knowledge, integrate cross-disciplinary skills, and develop meaningful learning progressions within and across grade levels.
3.2	Beginning gifted education professionals design appropriate learning and performance modifications for individuals with gifts and talents that enhance creativity, acceleration, depth, and complexity in academic subject matter and specialized domains.
3.3	Beginning gifted education professionals use assessments to select, adapt, and create materials to differentiate instructional strategies and general and specialized curricula to challenge individuals with gifts and talents.
3.4	Beginning gifted education professionals understand that individuals with gifts and talents demonstrate a wide range of advanced knowledge and performance levels and modify the general or specialized curriculum appropriately.

The professional knowledge base in general education clearly indicates that educators' understanding of the central concepts and structure of the discipline and tools of inquiry related to the academic subject-matter content areas they teach makes a significant difference in student learning.

Within the general curricula, beginning gifted education professionals demonstrate in their planning and teaching a solid foundation of understanding of the theories, central concepts and principles, structures of the discipline, and tools of inquiry of the academic subject-matter content areas they teach so they are able to organize knowledge, integrate cross-disciplinary skills, develop meaningful learning progressions, and collaborate with educators in:

* using and interpreting assessments to select, adapt, and create materials to differentiate instructional strategies and general and specialized curricula to challenge individuals with gifts and talents;
* teaching the content of the general or specialized curriculum to individuals with gifts and talents across advanced performance levels; and
* designing appropriate learning and performance modifications for individuals with gifts and talents in academic subject matter and specialized content domains that incorporate advanced, conceptually challenging, in-depth, distinctive, and/or complex content.

Additionally, beginning gifted education professionals use a variety of specialized curricula to individualize meaningful and challenging learning for individuals with exceptionalities.

Standard 4: Assessment

Beginning gifted education professionals use multiple methods of assessment and data sources in making educational decisions about identification of individuals with gifts and talents and student learning.

4.1	Beginning gifted education professionals understand that some groups of individuals with gifts and talents have been underrepresented in gifted education programs and select and use technically sound formal and informal assessments that minimize bias in identifying students for gifted education programs and services.
4.2	Beginning gifted education professionals use knowledge of measurement principles and practices to differentiate assessments and interpret results to guide educational decisions for individuals with gifts and talents.
4.3	Beginning gifted education professionals collaborate with colleagues and families in using multiple types of assessment information to make identification and learning progress decisions and to minimize bias in assessment and decision making.
4.4	Beginning gifted education professionals use assessment results to develop long- and short-range goals and objectives that take into consideration an individual's abilities and needs, the learning environment, and other factors related to diversity.
4.5	Beginning gifted education professionals engage individuals with gifts and talents in assessing the quality of their own learning and performance and in setting future goals and objectives.

Beginning gifted education professionals understand measurement theory and practice for addressing issues of validity, reliability, norms, bias, and interpretation of assessment results.

Beginning gifted education professionals understand the policies and ethical principles of measurement and assessment related to gifted education referral/nomination, identification, program planning, differentiated instruction, learning progress, and services for individuals with gifts and talents, including individuals with culturally, linguistically, and economically diverse backgrounds.

Beginning gifted education professionals understand the appropriate use and limitations of various types of assessments and collaborate with families and other colleagues to ensure nonbiased, meaningful assessments and decision making.

Beginning gifted education professionals select and use quantitative and qualitative assessment information to support a wide variety of decisions within gifted education. They conduct formal and informal assessments of behavior, learning, achievement, and environments to differentiate the learning experiences and document the growth of individuals with gifts and talents. Moreover, they differentiate assessments to identify above-level performances and to accelerate and enrich the general curriculum.

Beginning gifted education professionals use available technologies routinely to support their assessments and employ a variety of assessments such as performance-based assessment, portfolios, and computer simulations. Using these data, beginning gifted education professionals make multiple types of assessment decisions, including strategic adaptations and modifications in response to an individuals' constellation of social, linguistic, and learning factors in ways to minimize bias. They also use the results of assessments to identify above-level performance, develop long-range instructional plans anchored in both general and specialized curricula and translate these plans into carefully selected short-range goals and objectives to differentiate and accelerate instruction. Moreover, beginning gifted education professionals engage individuals with gifts and talents in assessing the quality of their own learning and performance and in providing feedback to guide them in setting future goals.

Like their general education colleagues, beginning gifted education professionals regularly monitor the learning progress of individuals with gifts and talents in both general and specialized content and make instructional adjustments based on these data.

Standard 5: Instructional Planning and Strategies

Beginning gifted education professionals select, adapt, and use a repertoire of evidence-based instructional strategies[3] to advance the learning of individuals with gifts and talents.

5.1	Beginning gifted education professionals know principles of evidence-based, differentiated, and accelerated practices and possess a repertoire of instructional strategies to enhance the critical and creative thinking, problem-solving, and performance skills of individuals with gifts and talents.
5.2	Beginning gifted education professionals apply appropriate technologies to support instructional assessment, planning, and delivery for individuals with gifts and talents.
5.3	Beginning gifted education professionals collaborate with families, professional colleagues, and other educators to select, adapt, and use evidence-based strategies that promote challenging learning opportunities in general and specialized curricula.
5.4	Beginning gifted education professionals emphasize the development, practice, and transfer of advanced knowledge and skills across environments throughout the lifespan leading to creative, productive careers in a multicultural society for individuals with gifts and talents.
5.5	Beginning gifted education professionals use instructional strategies that enhance the affective development of individuals with gifts and talents.

---

3   Instructional strategies, as used throughout this document, include interventions used in general or core and specialized curricula.

In the selection, development, and adaptation of learning experiences for individuals with gifts and talents, beginning gifted education professionals consider an individual's abilities, interests, learning environments, and cultural and linguistic factors to achieve positive learning results in general and special curricula. Understanding these factors, curriculum models, and the implications of being recognized as gifted and talented guides the educator's development of scope and sequence plans; selection, adaptation, and creation of learning activities; pace of instruction; and use of differentiated evidence-based instructional strategies.

Beginning gifted education professionals possess a repertoire of evidence-based strategies to differentiate and accelerate the curriculum for individuals with gifts and talents. They select, adapt, and use these strategies to promote challenging learning opportunities in general and special curricula and to modify learning environments to enhance self-awareness, self-regulation, and self-efficacy for individuals with gifts and talents. They enhance 21st-century student outcomes, such as critical and creative thinking, problem solving, collaboration, and performance skills in specific domains and allow individuals with gifts and talents opportunities to explore, develop, or research their areas of interest or talent.

Beginning gifted education professionals also emphasize the development, practice, and transfer of advanced knowledge and skills across environments throughout the lifespan leading to creative, productive careers in society for individuals with gifts and talents. Moreover, beginning gifted education professionals facilitate these actions in a collaborative context that includes individuals with gifts and talents, families, professional colleagues, and personnel from other agencies as appropriate. They are familiar with alternative and augmentative communication systems and are comfortable using technologies to support language and communication, instructional planning, and differentiated instruction for individuals with exceptionalities.

Standard 6: Professional Learning and Ethical Practice

Beginning gifted education professionals use foundational knowledge of the field and professional ethical principles and programming standards[4] to inform gifted education practice, to engage in lifelong learning, and to advance the profession.

6.1	Beginning gifted education professionals use professional ethical principles and specialized program standards to guide their practice.

---

4   NAGC (2010).

6.2	Beginning gifted education professionals understand how foundational knowledge, perspectives, and historical and current issues influence professional practice and the education and treatment of individuals with gifts and talents both in school and society.
6.3	Beginning gifted education professionals model respect for diversity, understanding that it is an integral part of society's institutions and impacts learning of individuals with gifts and talents in the delivery of gifted education services.
6.4	Beginning gifted education professionals are aware of their own professional learning needs, understand the significance of lifelong learning, and participate in professional activities and learning communities.
6.5	Beginning gifted education professionals advance the profession by engaging in activities such as advocacy and mentoring.

Beginning gifted education professionals practice in multiple roles and complex situations across wide age and developmental ranges that requires ongoing attention to legal matters and serious consideration of professional and ethical issues. Ethical principles and Program Standards guide beginning gifted education professionals. These principles and standards provide benchmarks by which gifted education professionals practice and professionally evaluate each other.

Beginning gifted education professionals understand gifted education as an evolving and changing discipline based on philosophies, evidence-based principles and theories, policies, historical points of view that continue to influence the field of gifted education and the education of and services for individuals with gifts and talents and their families in both school and society. Beginning gifted education professionals understand how these factors influence professional practice, including assessment, instructional planning, services, and program evaluation.

Beginning gifted education professionals understand the aspects of human diversity and equity as related to academic diversity. They understand aspects of human diversity and equity regarding individuals identified as gifted and talented, as well as those who have the potential of being identified gifted and talented.

Beginning gifted education professionals are sensitive to the aspects of diversity of individuals with gifts and talents and their families, how human diversity can influence families, cultures, and schools, and how these complex issues can each interact with the delivery of gifted education services. Of special significance is the growth in the number and prevalence of English language learners (ELL) and economically disadvantaged (ED) students and the provision of effective gifted education services for ELL and ED learners with exceptionalities and their families. Beginning gifted education professionals also understand historical relationships of gifted education services related to diversity and equity and the organization of schools, school systems, and education-related agencies within the culture in which they practice.

Beginning gifted education professionals also understand the relationships of the organization of gifted education services to the organization of schools, school systems, and education-related agencies within cultures in which they practice. They are aware of how their own and others' attitudes, behaviors, and ways of communicating can influence their practice, and use this knowledge as a foundation to inform their own personal understandings and philosophies of special education.

Beginning gifted education professionals engage in professional activities and participate actively in professional learning communities that benefit individuals with gifts and talents, their families, colleagues, and their own professional growth. They view themselves as lifelong learners, regularly reflect on and adjust their practice, and develop and use personalized professional development plans. They plan and engage in activities that foster their professional growth and keep them current with evidence-based practices and know how to recognize their own skill limits and practice within them. They place particular emphasis on professional activities that focus on human diversity and academic diversity in all of its manifestations. Moreover, educators of the gifted embrace their special role as advocates for individuals with gifts and talents. They promote and advocate for the learning and well-being of individuals with gifts and talents across multiple and varied settings through diverse learning experiences.

Standard 7: Collaboration

Beginning gifted education professionals collaborate with families, other educators, related-service providers, individuals with gifts and talents, and personnel from community agencies in culturally responsive ways to address the needs of individuals with gifts and talents across a range of learning experiences.

7.1	Beginning gifted education professionals apply elements of effective collaboration.
7.2	Beginning gifted education professionals serve as a collaborative resource to colleagues.
7.3	Beginning gifted education professionals use collaboration to promote the well-being of individuals with gifts and talents across a wide range of settings, experiences, and collaborators.

One of the significant changes in education over the past several decades is the rapid growth of collaborative educational teams to address the educational needs of students. The diversity of the students, complexity of curricular demands, growing influence of technology, and the rising targets for learner outcomes in the 21st century has created the demand for teams of educators collaborating together to ensure all students are effectively learning challenging curricula.

Beginning gifted education professionals embrace their role as a resource to colleagues and use the theory and elements of collaboration across a wide range of contexts and collaborators. They use culturally responsive behaviors that promote effective communication and collaboration with individuals with gifts and talents, their families, school personnel, and community members. They collaborate with their general education and other special education colleagues to create learning environments that meaningfully include individuals with gifts and talents, and that foster cultural understanding, safety and emotional well-being, positive social interactions, and active engagement. Additionally, beginning gifted education professionals use collaboration to facilitate differentiated assessment and instructional planning to advance learning of individuals with gifts and talents across a wide range of settings and different learning experiences. They routinely collaborate with other educators in developing mentorships, internships, and vocational programming experiences to address the needs of individuals with gifts and talents. Gifted education professionals have long recognized the positive significance of the active involvement of individuals with gifts and talents and their families in the education process, and gifted education professionals involve individuals with gifts and talents and their families collaboratively in all aspects of the education of individuals with gifts and talents.

Knowledge Base for the Seven Standards

Teachers in gifted education are members of a profession that has a strong research base and formal body of knowledge that distinguishes them from other professional educators and from laypersons. This research has been organized into three categories:

1. *Literature/Theory-based.* Knowledge or skills that are based on theories or philosophical reasoning. They include knowledge and skills derived from sources such as position papers, policy analyses, and descriptive reviews of the literature (CEC, 2010).

2. *Research-based.* Knowledge or skills that are based on peer-reviewed studies that use appropriate research methodologies to address questions of cause and effect, and that researchers have independently replicated and found to be effective (CEC, 2010).

3. *Practice-based.* Knowledge and skills that are derived from a number of sources. Practices based on a small number of studies or nomination procedures, such as promising practices, are usually practice-based. Practice-based knowledge or skills also include those derived primarily from model and lighthouse programs. Practice-based knowledge and skills include professional wisdom. These practices have been used so widely with practical evidence of effectiveness that there is an implicit professional assumption that the practice is effective. Practice-based knowledge and skills also include "emerging practice," practices that arise from teachers' classroom experiences validated through some degree of action research (CEC, 2010).

Using these definitions, the NAGC-PSC updated the research base by identifying recent citations in each category for each standard. Special efforts were made to include articles that addressed diverse populations. The following summaries of annotated references for each of the standards are meant to be representative, not exhaustive, and are not intended to endorse a particular theory, model, test, method, strategy, or material (for a complete list of references related to the following sections, see Appendix B).

Research Summary for Standard 1: Learner Development and Individual Learning Differences

Gifted students have varied affective and cognitive characteristics. Theories distinguish gifted students from other nonidentified students in their cognitive abilities (Cattell, 1971; Gagné, 2005; Guilford, 1967). In terms of affective development, gifted students are at least as well adjusted socially and emotionally as their nonidentified peers (Cross, 2011). Gifted individuals experience life in a different way with heightened sensitivities (Tieso, 2007) and more reports of perfectionism (Nugent, 2000; Siegle & Schuler, 2000). Because asynchronous development of gifted students may contribute to social or emotional problems (Silverman, 1997), the affective needs of gifted students should be addressed (Cross, 2011; Hébert, 2011).

Gifted students' learning and achievement can be influenced by diverse issues including the student's identity (Ford, Moore, & Milner, 2005), race (Good, Aronson, & Inzlicht, 2003), gender (Benbow, Lubinski, Shea, & Eftekhari-Sanjani, 2000; Callahan & Hébert, 2014; Kerr & Kurpius, 2004; Stormont, Stebbins, & Holliday, 2001), sexual orientation (Peterson & Rischar, 2000), culture and language (Ogbu, 1995), family background (Peterson, 2002; Renzulli & Park, 2002), poverty (Stormont et al., 2001), and/or having a disability (Lovecky, 2003; Foley Nicpon, Allmon, Sieck, & Stinson, 2011;

Stormont et al., 2001). Students with learning disabilities can experience negative school experiences, such as difficulty with teacher and student relationships (Coleman, 2001). Learning disabilities coupled with hyperactivity disorder or attention deficit disorder can disguise appropriate educational needs, affecting the students' learning experience at school (Baum & Olenchak, 2002; Kalbfleisch, 2014). Other concerns such as underachievement can be influenced by the level of appropriate challenge in the classroom (Kanevsky & Keighley, 2003), teachers' personality and organization (Peters, Grager-Loidl, & Supplee, 2000), motivation/self-regulation (Clinkenbeard, 2014; McCoach & Siegle, 2003), and/or social, cultural, and psychological factors in the life of the diverse gifted student (Grantham, 2004; Reis, Colbert, & Hébert, 2005).

Because of these issues, gifted students' advanced cognitive abilities (Gottfried, Gottfried, & Guerin, 2006), and their need for talent development, teachers need to look into alternative assessment procedures (Kirschenbaum, 2004) and specialized curriculum and instructional strategies (Castellano & Pinkos, 2005; Matthews & Matthews, 2004; Renzulli & Richards, 2000) to provide intellectual challenge in their classrooms and support the affective growth of these students (Neihart, 2007). Educators should foster the development of cognitive strategies (Hong & Aqui, 2004) and higher order thinking skills (Friedman & Lee, 1996; VanTassel-Baska, Bass, Ries, Poland, & Avery, 1998), and encourage deliberate training in specific talent areas (Ericcson & Charness, 1994). Fostering a classroom environment that values different cultures (Ford et al., 2005; Harmon, 2002), provides access to mentors (Callahan & Dickson, 2014; Hébert & Neumeister, 2000) and gives students a voice in their learning process (Kanevsky & Keighley, 2003) decreases underachievement and creates a supportive learning environment.

Educators of gifted and talented students need to understand the diversity among gifted and talented learners and how their characteristics interact with a variety of internal and external influences to impact their cognitive and affective learning and development. Using this knowledge, they need to be able to tailor gifted instruction to provide meaningful learning experiences

Research Summary for Standard 2: Learning Environments

Educators of the gifted understand the role of language and communication in talent development and the role that it plays for English language learners in the school setting. Educators of the gifted strive to provide a continuum of learning environments that value diversity, emotional well-being, positive social interactions, and engagement both in the present and in the future. Cultural, linguistic, and socioeconomic factors all influence verbal and nonverbal construction of concepts among gifted students (Gonzales, 2005).

Socioeconomic and linguistic differences can affect verbal performance. Linguistic differences may put English language learners at a disadvantage, because many teachers perceive language abilities as an important characteristic of giftedness (Fernández, Gay, Lucky, & Gavilan, 1998). Bilingual gifted education classrooms are important in influencing the gifted Hispanic students' confidence in their academic abilities and their assimilation in the program (Shaunessy, McHatton, Hughes, Brice, & Ratliff, 2007). Educators should use research-based strategies for instructing English learners (Kitano & Pederson, 2002) and view multilingualism as a strength (Valdes, 2002). Parents and teachers of multilingual students, particularly English language learners, can keep open communication by providing information about gifted students and advocacy at parent workshops (Stephens, 1999; Strip & Hirsch, 2001).

Ways that educators can promote verbal development in gifted students is through training in private speech (Daugherty & White, 2008), analogical reasoning (Castillo, 1998), leadership (Leshnower, 2008), public speaking (Choi, 1998), writing (Frey, 2000), self-advocacy (Frey, 1998), empathy (Ingram, 2003), and by differentiating the curriculum (Smutny, 2001; VanTassel-Baska, Zuo, Avery, & Little, 2002).

Working in groups with other gifted students can yield academic benefits (Kulik & Kulik, 1992), as well as enhance self-confidence and communication skills (VanTassel-Baska, Feng, Quek, & Struck, 2004). Working under a successful mentor in their area of interest can foster personal growth (Hébert & Neumeister, 2000; Siegle & McCoach, 2005), leadership skills (Bonner, Jennings, Marbley, & Brown, 2008), and higher levels of learning (Betts, 2004).

Summer programs (Cooper, 2001), early college entrance programs (Assouline, Colangelo, VanTassel-Baska, & Lupkowski-Shoplik, 2015), talent searches (Olszewski-Kubilius, 2004, 2014), competitions (Barbeau & Taylor, 2009), problem-based learning (Gallagher & Stepien, 1996), differentiated teaching/learning activities (Schillereff, 2001), independent play (Christophersen & Mortweet, 2003), independent study (Betts, 2004; Johnsen & Goree, 2015), and the International Baccalaureate program (Kyburg, Hertberg-Davis, & Callahan, 2007; Poelzer & Feldhusen, 1997) are other learning situations that support self-efficacy, creativity, and lifelong learning for gifted students.

Research Summary for Standard 3: Curricular Content Knowledge

Gifted educators possess a solid foundation of the theories, central concepts and principles, structure of the discipline, and tools of inquiry of the academic subject-matter content areas they teach so they are able to organize knowledge, integrate cross-disciplinary skills, develop meaningful learning progressions, and collaborate with educators (VanTassel-Baska, Avery, Little, & Hughes, 2000). Based on this knowledge, they know how to design curriculum in specific domains and how the organization of the content may vary across domains (VanTassel-Baska & Stambaugh, 2006). Teachers design specialized curricular units that remove the learning ceiling (Roberts & Roberts, 2005) and enhance the general curriculum for gifted and talented students by incorporating acceleration (Assouline, Colangelo, VanTassel-Baska, & Lupkowski-Shoplik, 2015; Stamps, 2004), depth and complexity (Kaplan, 2005), critical thinking (Paul & Elder, 2002), creative thinking (Renzulli & Reis, 2003), and problem solving (Gallagher & Stepien, 1996; Schillereff, 2001). They also know how to select and develop resources and materials for high-ability learners (Avery & Zuo, 2003; Riley, 2005) and use curriculum units designed specifically for gifted and talented students (Feng, VanTassel-Baska, Quek, Bai, & O'Neill, 2005).

Using preassessments and ongoing and summative assessments, the teacher is able to differentiate instruction that challenges gifted and talented students (Firmender, Reis, & Sweeny, 2012). This assessment knowledge enables the teacher to develop a learning profile that develops each student's talents and needs (Rogers, 2002; Tomlinson, 2004). Specific strategies may include the use of multiple menus (Renzulli, Leppien, & Hays, 2000), curriculum compacting (Renzulli & Reis, 2004), and independent study (Winebrenner & Brulles, 2012).

Special attention needs to be given to curriculum that is responsive not only to culture, but also to economic backgrounds (Angelelli, Enright, & Valdés, 2002; Coates et al., 2003). For example, in economically disadvantaged urban settings, students who received curricular modifications incorporating problem solving, primary concepts of the discipline, contextual assessments, and personally relevant curriculum made more gains in problem solving, creativity, and social skills than comparison groups (Moon & Callahan, 2001). Moreover, students who participated in an afterschool enrichment reading program that encouraged multicultural materials in their area of interest and incorporated structured read-alouds, discussion groups, and self-choice made significant gains in reading fluency and were more confident in reading books at their instructional level (Reis, 2009). Understanding general and specialized curriculum and how it interacts with individual students' needs enhances the learning trajectories of gifted and talented students.

Research Summary for Standard 4: Assessment

For gifted educators, assessments are vital for decision making when working with gifted students in terms of identification, monitoring academic process, and adjusting instruction.

Researchers have suggested using multiple measures and alternative assessments in the identification process (Johnsen, 2011). Different groups of children who have different areas of gifts and talents require different assessments (Reid, Romanoff, Algozzine, & Udall, 2000). Specific assessments have been designed that measure creativity (Hunsaker & Callahan, 1995; Torrance, 1984), music and dance (Baum, Owen, & Oreck, 1996; Oreck, Owen, & Baum, 2003), visual arts (Clark, 2004), leadership (Oakland, Falkenberg, & Oakland, 1996), domain-specific areas, and general intelligence. Unfortunately, a content analysis of program data from 20 programs showed a lack of match between identification procedures and program services (VanTassel-Baska, 2004). Schools' identification procedures should be examined for validity and improved based upon evaluations (Feldhusen, Asher, & Hoover, 2004; Lohman, 2006).

Assessments suggested for identification of gifted students, particularly those from culturally and linguistically backgrounds, include dynamic assessment (Kanevsky, 2000; Kirschenbaum, 1998), peer nomination (Cunningham, Callahan, Plucker, Roberson, & Rapkin, 1998), nonverbal tests (Naglieri & Ford, 2003), alternative screenings (Reid et al., 2000), performance assessment (VanTassel-Baska, Johnson, & Avery, 2002), problem-based tasks (Tomlinson, Callahan, & Lelli, 1997), observations (Johnsen, 2011) and other qualitative methods (Johnsen, 2008). When identifying minority students, teachers need to be trained to look for factors other than "schoolhouse giftedness" (Baldwin, 2002; Masten & Plata, 2000). Artiles and Zamora-Duran (1997) presented guidelines for assessing student language proficiency in order to gauge whether a more comprehensive assessment is necessary. Ford (2004) explored test bias among racially and culturally diverse students and encouraged the use of sound, equitable principles and practices when using traditional or alternative tests that minimize bias.

Another way that assessments are used in the classroom is to document academic growth. These assessments include curriculum-based assessments (Feng et al., 2005; VanTassel-Baska, Bass, Ries, Poland, & Avery, 1998), portfolios (Johnsen, 2008; Siegle, 2002) and performance-based assessments (VanTassel-Baska, 2002). The results of these assessments can be used to adjust instruction, including placement in appropriate group learning settings (Winebrenner & Brulles, 2012), or provide opportunities for academic acceleration (Assouline, Colangelo, VanTassel-Baska, & Lupkowski-Shoplik, 2015). Involving students in assessing their own work helps them set short- and long-term goals in their areas of strengths and weaknesses.

Research Summary for Standard 5:
Instructional Planning and Strategies

Curriculum and instructional planning is a central part of gifted education. Different theories and research models forming the basis of curriculum development and instructional practice include acceleration (Rogers, 2002; Steenbergen-Hu & Moon, 2010; Swiatek, 2000), autonomous learning (Betts, 2004), the Integrated Curriculum Model (VanTassel-Baska & Stambaugh, 2006), the Parallel Curriculum Model (Tomlinson et al., 2008), layered curriculum (Kaplan, 2005), the Purdue Three-Stage Model (Moon, Feldhusen, & Dillon, 1994), the Schoolwide Enrichment Model (Renzulli & Reis, 2003), the Triarchic Model (Sternberg, Torff, Grigorenko, 1998), and Talents Unlimited (Schlichter & Palmer, 1993).

These and other models emphasize the need for considering students' interests (Moon et al., 1994; Renzulli & Reis, 2008), environmental and natural catalysts (Gagné, 2005), curriculum differentiation (Kaplan, 2005; Tomlinson & Cunningham-Eidson, 2003), challenge (Tomlinson et al., 2008), and the development of higher level thinking skills (Anderson & Krathwohl, 2001; Elder & Paul, 2004).

When designing a differentiated curriculum, it is essential to align national, state or provincial, and/or local curricular standards with the differentiated curriculum (Johnsen, 2012; VanTassel-Baska & Stambaugh, 2006). These standards may include the Common Core State Standards in English Language Arts and Mathematics (National Governors Association Center for Best Practices [NGA] & Council of Chief State School Officers [CCSSO], 2010a, 2010b), Next Generation Science Standards (NGSS Lead States, 2013), and/or the National Association for Children Pre-K–Grade 12 Gifted Education Programming Standards (NAGC, 2010). Specific curricula have been designed for gifted students and include affective education (Nugent, 2005), leadership (Parker & Begnaud, 2003), domain-specific studies (Gavin & Adelson, 2014; VanTassel-Baska, Avery, Little, & Hughes, 2000; VanTassel-Baska & Stambaugh, 2006), and the arts (Clark, 2004; Rostan, Pariser, & Gruber, 2002).

Differentiation of curriculum in the classroom can have several distinguishing features from general curricula. Examples are acceleration (Assouline, Colangelo, VanTassel-Baska, & Lupkowski-Shoplik, 2015; Rogers, 2002), enrichment (Renzulli & Reis, 2008), curriculum compacting (Reis, Westberg, Kulikowich, & Purcell, 1998), problem-based learning (Gallagher & Stepien, 1996; VanTassel-Baska & Stambaugh, 2006), ability grouping (Byers, Whitsell, & Moon, 2004; Gentry, 2014; Rogers, 2002), multiple menus (Renzulli, Leppien, & Hays, 2000), modular and supplementary materials (Johnson, Boyce, & VanTassel-Baska, 1995), independent study (Betts & Neihart, 1986;

Johnsen & Goree, 2015), tiered lessons (Tomlinson, 2002) and the use of specific curriculum models (Tomlinson et al., 2008; VanTassel-Baska & Little, 2003). Specific instructional strategies should encourage metacognitive thinking (Paul & Elder, 2002; VanTassel-Baska et al., 2000), higher-level thinking in content areas (Anderson & Krathwohl, 2001; Coates et al., 2003; Elder & Paul, 2003; Steiner & Carr, 2003), and research so that gifted students are able to explore their areas of interest and develop their talents (Hébert, 1993; Johnsen & Goree, 2015).

Preassessment can help educators adjust instruction for a positive educational experience since the pace of delivery of instruction should be consistent with the individual students' progress (Johnsen, 2005; Rogers, 2002; VanTassel-Baska, 2004; Winebrenner & Brulles, 2012). Gifted students report learning more in a homogenous grouping environment than in heterogeneous groups (Byers et al., 2004; Rogers, 2002). Educators should also integrate academic and career guidance (Horowitz, Subotnik, & Matthews, 2009; Kerr & Sodano, 2003) into learning plans for gifted students, particularly those from diverse backgrounds (Boothe & Stanley, 2004; Ford, Tyson, Howard, & Harris, 2000). Differentiated curricula results in increased student engagement, enhanced reasoning skills, and improved habits of mind (VanTassel-Baska et al., 2000).

Technology can be used in differentiating instructional strategies for the gifted. Students can pursue their own individual interests (Berger, 2003) by accessing resources using the Internet, e-mail, chat rooms, online journals, instant messaging, distance learning, virtual field trips (Siegle, 2004), telementoring (VanTassel-Baska & Stambaugh, 2006), and computer-based advanced classes (Ravaglia, Suppes, Stillinger, & Alper, 1995).

It is important to consider gifted students' cultural, linguistic, and intellectual differences when developing a culturally responsive curriculum (Boothe & Stanley, 2004; Granada, 2002; Hertzog, 2005). Multicultural literature can be used to build respect across individual students' cultures (Ford et al., 2000) and improve standardized test scores (Uresti, Goertz, & Bernal, 2002). By engaging gifted individuals from diverse backgrounds in challenging curricula, they are more likely to qualify for gifted programming (Lee & Olszewski-Kubilius, 2009), enhance their self-confidence and improve their communication skills (VanTassel-Baska, Feng, Quek, & Struck, 2004), understand differing points of view and cultures (VanTassel-Baska et al., 2004), and reduce underachievement (Ford, 1996; Ford et al., 2000).

Research Summary for Standard 6:
Professional Learning and Ethical Practice

Educators need to understand the foundational knowledge of the field that informs state and federal definitions, policies, rules, regulations, and ultimately classroom practices (Robinson & Jolly, 2014). The conception of giftedness tends to parallel the theoretical development of intelligence from Galton's (1865) general laws of distribution and Spearman's (1927) general intellectual ability, to the more recent theories that includes Cattell's (1963) fluid and crystallized intelligence, Guilford's (1967) information processing model, Gardner's (1983) multiple intelligences, Sternberg's (1985) triarchic model of intelligence, and Carroll's (1993) three-stratum model of narrow, broad, and single general abilities. As theoretical conceptions grew, the definition of giftedness expanded from a focus on general intelligence to a variety of categories that include specific academic aptitude, leadership, creativity, and the arts (Marland, 1972; No Child Left Behind, 2002; U.S. Congress, Public Law 91-230, 1970; U.S. Department of Education, 1993). Although most states use the federal definition, researchers continue to examine other definitions that encompass school reform, the developmental nature of giftedness, domain-specific giftedness, and sociocultural context influences (Gagné, 1985; NAGC, 2010; Renzulli, 1978). The majority of researchers and practitioners view the concept of giftedness as a more dynamic rather than static construct with interventions required to fully develop above-average ability into exceptional performance or expertise (Gagné, 1985; NAGC, 2010).

Because no federal law mandates gifted education, variations among conceptions, definitions, state mandates, and preparation of school personnel influence assessment and services to gifted and talented students. Identification of gifted students may be influenced by teachers' preconceived notions of giftedness such as gender stereotypes (Siegle & Powell, 2004), academic achievement (Hunsaker, Finley, & Frank, 1997), socioeconomic background (Hunsaker et al., 1997), verbal ability, and social skills (Neumeister, Adams, Pierce, Cassady, & Dixon, 2007). Teachers need professional development to understand all aspects of giftedness, particularly students from underrepresented groups (Briggs, Reis, & Sullivan, 2008).

Teachers' biases may also affect their teaching of gifted minority students. A study of gifted African American students described their ineffective teachers as the ones who had a lack of understanding about their culture, resulting in low academic expectations (Harmon, 2002). Ford and Trotman (2001) discussed desired multicultural characteristics and competencies of those who teach diverse gifted students. These characteristics include culturally relevant pedagogy, equity pedagogy, a holistic teaching philosophy, a communal philosophy, respect for students' primary language, culturally congruent instructional practices, culturally sensitive assessment, student-family-teacher relationships, and teacher diversity. Overall, teachers with gifted education training demonstrated greater teaching skills and developed more positive classroom climates (Eyre et al., 2002).

Professionally, gifted education teachers should learn to discriminate between caring and confidential conversations in a school setting (Keller, 1999), exhibit qualified employee behaviors in the workplace (Morehead, 1998), and be familiar with the code of ethics of their profession (CEC, 2010). Also, teachers of the gifted should be familiar with state identification policies and the legal framework in which gifted services are to be provided (Gallagher, 2002). Educators of the gifted should diligently improve their practice through research-supported professional development and reflection in order to correct any misconceptions about gifted students and programs and become effective teachers (Callahan, Cooper, & Glascock, 2003; Garet, Porter, Desimone, Birman, & Yoon, 2001; Gubbins et al., 2002). Knowledge in best practices of the field leads to higher student achievement (Gentry, 1999). Organizations dedicated to the field of gifted education include the National Association for Gifted Children and the Council for Exceptional Children. Both support professional development and advocate appropriate governmental policies for gifted students. Publications in the field of gifted education include *Gifted Child Quarterly, Gifted Child Today, Gifted Education International, Journal for the Education of the Gifted, Journal of Advanced Academics, Journal of Creative Behavior, Parenting for High Potential, Roeper Review*, and *Teaching for High Potential*. Given the importance of gifted education, professionals must confront problems that create inequity in educational outcomes (Kitano, 2003) and find ways of shaping educational reforms to benefit all students (Gallagher, 2004). As long as gifted education is not protected by federal and state mandates, vigorous advocacy and organized collaboration among gifted educators, administration, and parents is essential for change to occur (Grantham, 2003; Hertzog, 2003).

Research Summary for Standard 7: Collaboration

Collaboration among educators of gifted and talented students, families, other professionals, the community, and related service providers promotes the well-being of gifted and talented students across a range of learning experiences and facilitates successful transitions among levels of their schooling process.

Overall, parents can detect early signs of giftedness in their young children (Hertzog & Bennett, 2004; Pletan, Robinson, Berninger, & Abbot, 1995); however, they may be reluctant to seek educational options for intellectual stimulation for their gifted children from the school (Hertzog & Bennett, 2004; Olszewski-Kubilius & Lee, 2004). Although parent education programs may be a way to disseminate information about gifted children (Matthews & Menna, 2003; Stephens, 1999), content relevancy, teaching techniques, teacher characteristics, and practical considerations may influence their effectiveness (Pearl, 1997). Parents and teachers need to work together in assessing and developing programs (Matthews & Menna, 2003; Strip & Hirsch, 2001).

Teachers can work with parents and work together in developing and implementing appropriate services for gifted children and maintaining current knowledge about best practices in the field (Landrum, 2003). Teachers need to collaborate with the surrounding area to provide service learning and other types of learning opportunities so that students feel more connected and committed to their schools and communities (Terry, 2003). For example, mentors within the school setting can be a critical factor in motivating students to take advanced courses (Hébert & Neumeister, 2000), while mentors from the community can influence the identification of a career and understanding of the importance of networks (Siegle & McCoach, 2005). Partnerships may be formed with museums (Melber, 2003) and with neighboring colleges and/or universities to provide dual credit options for gifted students (Olszewski-Kubilius & Lee, 2004). Collaboration with schools and companies overseas can allow for studying aboard, which may broaden gifted students' perspectives in families, schools, and communities (Limburg-Weber, 1999/2000).

Specialized types of collaboration are needed for gifted students from special populations (Pereles, Omdal, & Baldwin, 2009). For example, teachers need to collaborate with special education teachers in providing appropriate services to gifted students with learning disabilities and/or physical impairments within a Response to Intervention framework (Coleman & Hughes, 2009). Educators and families must also recognize and remove social and institutional obstacles for gifted minority students, so that they might receive services (Williams & Baber, 2007). Teachers tended to nominate fewer minorities and minority parents were less likely to request an evaluation of their child for possible placement in the gifted program (Olszewski-Kubilius & Thomson, 2010). Gifted minority students themselves may resist academic success because of their fear of "acting White" (Ogbu, 1994).

The research shows that the absence of appropriate academic experiences can contribute to underachievement (Grantham, 2004; Reis, Colbert, & Hébert, 2005). However, positive collaboration among schools, families, communities, and service providers of the gifted can lead to personal growth and development, career choice, overall academic achievement benefits, and social integration of economically disadvantaged gifted students.

CHAPTER 2

DEVELOPING PARTNERSHIPS

ALICIA COTABISH AND DEBBIE DAILEY

Introduction

The practitioner nature of education creates opportunities to nurture aspiring candidates to develop, practice, and demonstrate the content and pedagogical knowledge and skills that promote student learning (CAEP, 2013). Preparing gifted educators is no different. Educator Preparation Providers (EPPs) are challenged with imparting an understanding of the field as an evolving and changing discipline that requires certain responsibilities, actions, and instructional practices that benefit high-ability and promising learners. Teacher education begins with preservice teacher preparation, continues through induction, mentoring, professional development, and lifelong learning. Candidates' practica opportunities typically take place in school-based situations, but other related experiences such as virtual situations can enhance clinical experiences.

The responsibility for teacher education typically has been divided between EPPs and schools, rather than shared between these systems, creating a missed opportunity. Partnership reform efforts begin at the EPP level, extend across Pre-K–12 and the community at large, and reflect organizational accountability and expansion of leadership roles among all partners involved in teacher preparation. Figure 2.1 highlights the symbiotic relationship between EPPs and school-based agencies, including the larger community (CAEP, 2013).

FIGURE 2.1. Cyclical collaborative partnerships between EPP, Pre-K–12, and community at large.

Goals for partnerships should be developed and include key features assumed to be related to teacher preparation quality (U.S. Department of Education [USDOE], 2006). Recognition of common similarities and differences make it easier to facilitate a shared mission. An assessment should be conducted to understand areas of mutual self-interest for the partners, so both will feel vested in the partnership.

Figure 2.2 provides a framework for establishing partnership goals for teacher preparation according to features assumed to be related to teacher preparation quality. The figure centers around four goals: (a) characteristics of high-quality preservice teacher preparation, and changes to the content and structure of the preservice teacher preparation programs; (b) contribution of the partnership between EPPs and schools/districts, and their roles in teacher preparation; (c) organizational changes and relationships among partners; and (d) efforts to institutionalize partnerships.

Goal 1, characteristics of high-quality teacher preparation programs, is grounded in strong content preparation and includes extensive clinical experiences involving the integration of technology. Related features of this goal

Suggested Partnership Goals for Teacher Preparation and Other Related Features	
Goal Considerations for Evaluating Partnerships Between EPPs and Partners	
	Features Assumed to be Related to Teacher Preparation Quality
1. Characteristics of high-quality preservice teacher preparation, and changes to the content and structure of the preservice teacher-preparation programs	
Strong content preparation, extensive clinical experience, and integration of technology	• Number and types of courses required • Program models • Continuous program quality review • Training in using best practices in teaching and instructional materials development • Induction program • Entry requirements • Amount and quality of clinical training and field experience • Training in using technology • Performance on teacher assessments • Program accreditation • Academic degrees in content areas • Quality of undergraduate education
2. Contribution of partnership between EPPs and schools/ districts, and schools' and districts' roles in teacher preparation	
Support for new teachers	• Expanded interaction between school district personnel and faculty to support clinical experiences and professional development • Support for new teachers through mentoring and other supports • Initiatives related to parental involvement • Improved strategies for EPP recruitment and retention
3. Organizational changes and relationships among partners	
Shared accountability for preparing teachers	• Development and expansion of leadership roles between EPP and partnering entity • Shared responsibility for accountability and increased collaboration with school personnel

FIGURE 2.2. Adapted from "Suggested Partnership Goals for Teacher Preparation and Other Related Features" in U.S. Department of Education, 2006, *Partnerships for Reform: Changing Teacher Preparation Through the Title II HEA Partnership Program: Final Report* (Exhibit 6), Washington, DC: U.S. Department of Education.

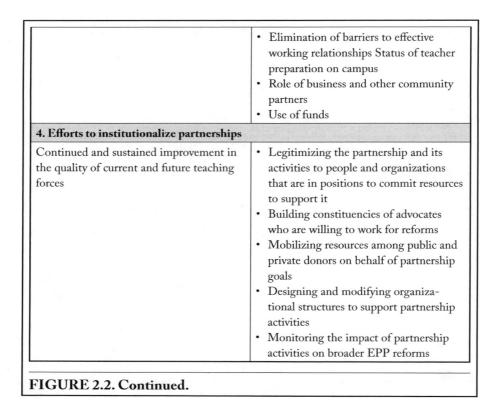

	• Elimination of barriers to effective working relationships Status of teacher preparation on campus
	• Role of business and other community partners
	• Use of funds
4. Efforts to institutionalize partnerships	
Continued and sustained improvement in the quality of current and future teaching forces	• Legitimizing the partnership and its activities to people and organizations that are in positions to commit resources to support it
	• Building constituencies of advocates who are willing to work for reforms
	• Mobilizing resources among public and private donors on behalf of partnership goals
	• Designing and modifying organizational structures to support partnership activities
	• Monitoring the impact of partnership activities on broader EPP reforms

FIGURE 2.2. Continued.

focus on evolving continuous improvement through the quantity and quality of courses and their instructors; teacher candidate training and professional development using best practices in teaching, instructional materials, and technology; embedded learning experiences including quality clinical and field experiences; and assessments that ensure teacher candidates' performance.

Goal 2 focuses on increasing support for new teachers. Developing partnerships between EPPs and Pre-K–12 schools and other community-based situations can encourage, support, and inform teacher preparation (National Council for Accreditation of Teacher Education [NCATE], 2010) and improve strategies for EPP recruitment and retention. Building partnerships that include robust clinical experiences can raise and assure candidate quality and demonstrate that teacher preparation affects outcomes that impact Pre-K–12 student learning and development (NCATE, 2010). Effective teachers develop these abilities by mastering their profession's knowledge base, skills, and dispositions. However, mastery and fluency of practice largely emerge through "expertly mentored experiences in the field and through pedagogically designed approximations of practices such as case studies and simulations that allow candidates to study and observe practice and test their skills in controlled situations" (NCATE, 2010, p. 27).

Goal 3 captures the transformative nature of shared accountability between partners. In particular, partnerships can lead to changes in course content, their alignment to state and teacher preparation standards, professional development, and/or instructional practices of teacher candidates (Zeichner, 2010). Among others, collaborative partnership activities can involve clinical experiences, professional development, and redesigning methods of instruction and assessing teacher education candidates. These types of partnerships can often be facilitated through discussions with partnership districts and involve advisory committees that reflect all stakeholders (USDOE, 2006). At institutions where teacher induction programs are not well established, partnerships can fill a distinct need. Other partnerships can undertake activities designed to improve the academic content knowledge of teacher candidates.

Goal 4, efforts to institutionalize partnerships, centers on continuous and sustained improvement in the quality of teaching and teacher preparation. The goal includes five tenets focused on organizational support, advocacy, mobilizing resources, evolving organizational structures that support partnership activities, and monitoring the impact of the partnership activities and their impact on broader EPP reforms.

In concert, the four goals provide a framework for evaluating ongoing relationships between EPPs and their partners. The key features of each can provide direction to continuous improvement in teacher preparation quality and will most likely

> affect the role and responsibilities of K–12 school teachers (i.e., cooperating or clinical teachers) . . . The overall result is that each partner should experience change in ways that improve the preparation, recruitment, and retention of qualified teachers in partner schools. (USDOE, 2006, pp. 1–2).

EPP Accreditation and the Clinical Partnership Perspective

In November 2010, the National Council for the Accreditation of Teacher Education, now the Council for the Accreditation of Educator Preparation, which is the national accreditor of teacher preparers, released a major report on the importance of field experiences and clinical practice. The report of the Blue Ribbon Panel on Clinical Preparation for Improved Learning (NCATE, 2010) suggested that field experiences and clinical practice should serve as the primary and central focus for all teacher preparation programs. The Executive Summary from the report stated:

> The education of teachers in the United States needs to be turned upside down. To prepare effective teachers for 21st century classrooms, teacher education must shift away from a norm which emphasizes academic preparation and coursework loosely linked to school-based experiences. Rather, it must move to programs that are fully grounded in clinical practice and interwoven with academic content and professional courses. (p. ii)

The 2010 NCATE Blue Ribbon panel proposed partnerships that are strategic in meeting partners' needs by defining common work, shared responsibility, authority, and accountability. The report concluded that clinical experiences were critically important to teacher preparation but that the research, to date, does not tell us what specific experiences or sequence of experiences are most likely to result in more effective beginning teachers (National Research Council [NRC], 2010).

In response to the 2010 NCATE panel's recommendation, the newly formed CAEP recognized the importance of the EPP-school partnership relationship in the creation of CAEP Accreditation Standard 2—Clinical Partnerships and Practice. CAEP Standard 2 states, "The provider ensures that effective partnerships and high-quality clinical practice are central to preparation so that candidates develop the knowledge, skills, and professional dispositions necessary to demonstrate positive impact on all P–12 students' learning and development" (CAEP, 2013, p. 7). Specifically, the intent and rationale for Standard 2 is:

> Educator preparation providers (EPPs) seeking accreditation should have strong collaborative partnerships with school districts and individual school partners, as well as other community stakeholders, in order to pursue mutually beneficial and agreed upon goals for the preparation of education professionals. These collaborative partnerships are a shared endeavor meant to focus dually on the improvement of student learning and development and on the preparation of teachers for this goal. The partners shall work together to determine not only the values and expectations of program development, implementation, assessment, and continuous improvement, but also the division of responsibilities among the various partnership stakeholders. At a minimum, the district and/or school leadership and the EPP should

be a part of the partnership; other partners might include business and community members. (CAEP, n.d., para. 2)

The Blue Ribbon report also identified important dimensions of clinical practice. CAEP drew from the panel's recommendations to structure the three components of Standard 2 around (a) constructing partnerships for clinical preparation; (b) selecting, preparing, evaluating, and supporting clinical educators; and (c) designing clinical experiences that demonstrate candidates' developing effectiveness and positive impact on all students' learning and development. Specifically, the three components of Standard 2 were developed and are defined as follows:

> **2.1 Partnerships for Clinical Preparation:** Partners co-construct mutually beneficial P–12 school and community arrangements, including technology-based collaborations, for clinical preparation and share responsibility for continuous improvement of candidate preparation.
> **2.2 Clinical Educators:** Partners co-select, prepare, evaluate, support, and retain high-quality clinical educators, both provider- and school-based, who demonstrate a positive impact on candidates' development and P–12 student learning and development.
> **2.3 Clinical Experiences:** The provider works with partners to design clinical experiences of sufficient depth, breadth, diversity, coherence, and duration to ensure that candidates demonstrate their developing effectiveness and positive impact on all students' learning and development. (CAEP, n.d., para. 2–4)

Although the three components of Standard 2 are grounded in clinical partnerships and experiences, CAEP (2013) acknowledged a lack of a clinical system being in place:

> Until the research base for clinical practices and partnerships is more definitive, "wisdom of practice" dictates that the profession move more forcefully into deepening partnerships; into clarifying and, where necessary, improving the quality of clinical educators who prepare the field's new practitioners and into delivering field and clinical experiences that contribute to the development of effective educators. (p. 8)

Providing Evidence to Support the Three Components

CAEP requires evidence supported by a quality design of data collection, analysis, and reporting that highlights program impact. The organization provides guidance to EPPs for each standard and their related components. Although these recommendations guide the EPPs at large, they should be considered when developing partnerships at the programmatic level (e.g., gifted education licensure programs).

Component 2.1. Evidence for this component is viewed as a ". . . shared responsibility for continuous improvement of preparation, expectations for candidates, coherence across clinical and academic components and accountability for the results in P–12 learning" (CAEP, 2013, p. 6). CAEP recommends that EPPs consider the following evidence (McKee, 2014):

- description of partnerships (e.g., MOU) along with documentation that partnership is being implemented as described;
- orientations of clinical educators;
- schedules of joint meetings between partners and purpose/topics covered in meetings;
- field experience handbooks (section(s) specific to component);
- documentation of stakeholder involvement;
- budgets/expenditures list; and
- evidence that placements, observational instruments, and evaluations are co-constructed by partners.

Component 2.2. In terms of this component, high-quality evidence demonstrating that clinical educators are coselected, prepared, evaluated, supported, and retained is required (CAEP, 2013). CAEP recommends that EPPs consider the following evidence (McKee, 2014):

- a table of clinical educator and clinical placement characteristics that shows coselection and also shares adherence to criterion selection model;
- criterion selection form for clinical educators;
- professional disposition evaluation;
- performance evaluations;
- surveys of clinical educators, candidates, employers, and/or human resources directors;
- interviews of clinical educators, candidates, employers, and/or human resources directors;
- records of counseling out of clinical educators;
- clinical educators training/coaching; and
- joint sharing of curriculum development/design/redesign between EPP and clinical site.

Component 2.3. This component requires a narrative of both the description and documentation of clinical experiences (CAEP, 2013). EPP examples of evidence might include at least 2 years of data on candidates' progressive development of teaching skills and their impact on Pre-K–12 student learning (to be available at the time the self-study is submitted for accreditation review); use of technology to enhance learning experiences; a chart of candidate experiences in diverse settings; field experience evaluations; internship and/or student teaching evaluations; and video clips with evidence of reliable assessments (McKee, 2014). CAEP examples cited include:

* work samples from Pre-K–12 student work;
* candidate portfolio examples of assessments with analysis;
* applications of Pre-K–12 student learning data in teacher evaluations for the purposes of program evaluation and accreditation rather than for evaluation of individual teacher performance;
* scope and sequence matrix that charts depth, breadth, and diversity of clinical experience;
* examples of tasks created by candidates, student responses, and candidate reflections;
* "teachers of record" for alternative preparation—state student growth and Value-Added Models (VAMs) apply; and
* provider studies—case studies conducted by the EPP.

In conclusion, CAEP aims to guide models of teacher preparation and development. CAEP Standard 2 serves as a framework for clinical practice that is grounded in the demonstration of candidate knowledge and supported by vehicles for communicating professional understandings among EPPs and their partnering agencies. Within EPPs, these understandings should be strongly supported at the program level. In specialized teacher preparation programs, such as university-based gifted education programs, teacher preparation should be supported by relevant learning experiences that involve a variety of stakeholders including EPPs, Pre-K–12 schools, and the community at large. Although these types of partnerships are not uncommon, the unique learning needs of both gifted education teacher candidates and Pre-K–12 gifted students require special consideration when developing and implementing differentiated learning experiences that are appropriate for high-ability learners.

The Clinical Experience in Gifted Education: Expanding Our Partnership Perspective

The need for clinical experiences in a program of study in gifted education is critical to ensuring that candidates are capable of demonstrating the skills delineated in each of the seven NAGC-CEC Teacher Preparation Standards in gifted education. The 2013 NAGC-CEC Teacher Preparation Standards in Gifted Education require candidates to be proficient in gifted learner development and be attuned to individual learning differences, apply curriculum planning and curriculum strategies, be effective in providing learning environments that are conducive to the learning needs of diverse learners, emphasize appropriate collaboration skills, demonstrate professionalism at a high level, attend to individual differences and concomitant learning needs through instructional planning and strategies, and select and apply multiple differentiated formal and informal assessments that minimize bias.

Such clinical experiences require regular practice in working with gifted learners during and after the formal coursework has been taken. Candidates need to have experiences in classrooms with diverse learners who represent the various populations of interest delineated in the standards. They also will require experiences with school personnel and families where their advocacy skills can be tapped. In order to enhance this specialized clinical learning environment, partnerships with schools and other appropriate agencies that can provide the specialized learning environment need to be considered. Typically, practicum/clinical placements include local school programs for gifted students, university-based Saturday and summer programs, and other settings conducive to working with gifted students. Although the clinical experience for gifted education candidates has remained rooted in specialized placements, the call for increased collaboration and partnerships between EPPs and applicable stakeholders (e.g., schools, districts, parents, school-based agencies, and the community at large) requires the field of gifted education to revisit the topic and possibly update our thinking about collaborative efforts and partnership activities.

In addition to university gifted education faculty, EPP stakeholders often include college and university faculty and clinical educators. Pre-K–12 gifted program stakeholders encompass teachers of the gifted; school counselors and administrators; specialty program personnel, including special education professionals; and parents and students. Community partners are inclusive of local businesses and corporations including nonprofit organizations and other community members, entities, and organizations. Figure 2.3 highlights the interrelated nature of partner relationships and provides example activities that promote Pre-K–12 gifted students' learning.

Partner	Possible Partnership Activities
Community at Large Local Businesses and Corporations Nonprofit Organizations General Community Population	• Coteach/mentor in practicum/clinical experiences in Saturday and university-based summer programs • Provide mentoring/shadowing experiences to Pre-K–12 and gifted program candidates • Contribute human and financial resources to Pre-K–12 and EPP • Participate in local gifted affiliate organization
Education Preparation Provider (EPP) University Faculty Gifted Program Faculty Other Clinical Educators Other Education Professionals	• Facilitate clinical experiences between Pre-K–12 and EPP through Pre-K–12 placement, Saturday programming option, and/or university-based summer programs • Develop partnerships with community at large to provide coteaching/mentoring opportunities to gifted program candidates
Pre-K–12 Gifted Program Stakeholders Teachers of the Gifted and Pre-K–12 Teachers School Counselor(s) and Administrator(s) Specialty Program and Special Education Personnel Parents and Students	• Create gifted education advisory board inclusive of stakeholders • Organize and utilize district/school gifted education affiliate organization • Develop partnership and mentorship opportunities with community • Increase communication efforts with stakeholders and community by utilizing social media platforms • Participate in the development of IEPs • Judge competitions (e.g., DI, science fair, history day, robotics)

FIGURE 2.3 Partnership example activities to promote Pre-K-12 gifted students' learning.

The importance of ongoing partnerships between the EPP gifted and talented program, Pre-K–12 schools, and the community at large cannot be overstated. Although each of the partnership agencies has a personal responsibility to develop and negotiate collaborative activities between one another, EPP gifted programs are in a unique position to facilitate specialized learning experiences for gifted education candidates. In particular, university-based EPPs benefit from existing community relationships, particularly with businesses, corporations, and nonprofit organizations. Universities are a central part of a local community, and typically possess leveraging power with community stakeholders.

University-based gifted program faculty are better positioned than Pre-K–12 schools and individual businesses to tap human resources (e.g., across the university campus and across the larger business community) and secure additional financial resources (through grants, contracts and existing relationships in the community) that can contribute to or enhance existing specialized teaching environments that are necessary for gifted education candidates. For example, a university located in central Arkansas recently created a clinical gifted education practicum option that is an engineering-focused Science, Technology, Engineering, and Mathematics (STEM) summer academy for gifted and high-ability students entering grades 4 through 6. A small university foundation grant provided the seed money that was necessary to support the program's engineering instructional materials. The university's practicum experience required gifted education candidates to teach differentiated engineering content in a summer program that was supported by professional development focused on content and differentiation. To provide a more authentic learning experience to gifted education candidates and high-ability students, program personnel approached a local paper-product manufacturing facility to garner financial and human resource support. Program faculty prioritized their requests into two categories: (a) *financial support* consisting of a monetary contribution to offset program costs for local gifted and promising learners—making it a no-cost summer learning experience for students and increasing access for low-income, high-ability learners; and (b) *human resource support* consisting of the manufacturing facility's engineers—enabling a coteaching experience between the gifted education candidates and the facility's engineers. In support of the initiative, the facility's manager made a surprising request of program faculty—provide the engineering-focused professional development component aligned to the summer program as a no-cost option to inservice gifted and talented teachers located in the local school district. Ultimately, the partnership resulted in a collaborative learning experience that involved a specialized setting (engineering-focused STEM academy housed at a university) cotaught by a local manufacturing facility's engineers and gifted education candidates, involving local school districts' inservice gifted and talented teachers as a no-cost learning experience for gifted and promising learners (including low-income learners).

Logistics of Gifted Education Clinical Experiences

Contact time in a practicum setting may be variable, based on several factors, including prior experience, the quality of available contexts, and the candidate's capacity to schedule the placement. The practicum should be a minimum of 40 hours of contact time in the classroom working with gifted learners and up to 100 hours of time spent on developing the full range of skills required (Johnsen et al., 2008). Multiple placements may be considered if the practicum is to be conducted over multiple semesters. Credit hours for a practicum may range from 2–3 hours, depending on the number of hours expended by the candidate. Grading, ideally, should be pass/fail based on a rubric developed to capture teaching and instructional behaviors appropriate for gifted learners.

During the practicum, the candidate should meet regularly with the university supervisor to encourage discussion on key issues and problems encountered in the school/specialized setting. Use of the NAGC-CEC Teacher Preparation Standards as a basis for these discussions ensures that candidates are reaching mastery in the skills required. In a school placement setting spanning a semester or longer, the use of monthly seminars for a small group of candidates interspersed with an online discussion board forum provide the ongoing contact deemed desirable to maintaining dialogue and discussion with candidates during this phase of their program. To involve school faculty, the university supervisor, on-site administrator (e.g., gifted education school-based mentor), and teacher candidate should meet regularly face-to-face or through VOIP online mechanisms such as Skype or Google Hangouts to discuss mastery in the skills, and progress toward meeting the NAGC-CEC Teacher Preparation Standards.

Practica in gifted education may vary considerably in the actual activities that candidates may accomplish. However, at a minimum, candidates would prepare and teach a unit of study they have developed in their curriculum class; collect pre- and postunit assessment data to inform students' differentiated instructional needs and to demonstrate candidate impact on student learning; keep a daily log of reflections on classroom interactions, concerns, and issues during the implementation of the unit; and visit three other classrooms during the practicum experience to observe other teachers in their work with gifted learners (Johnsen et al., 2008).

In a school-based setting, supervision of the practicum experience would be collaborative between the university supervisor and an onsite administrator who is in charge of the district's or school's gifted program. A structured observation form that emphasizes the standards-based skills and their underlying indicators would be employed to assist in the observation process. Ideally, the university supervisor and onsite administrator would observe the candidate on three occasions each using a structured form, discuss the observation at the conclusion of each observation, and offer ideas for improving practice. Although the structure of the practicum experience is much like the ones found in general education, the expectations differ in several ways. Framed by the 2013 NAGC-CEC Teacher Preparation Standards, the university supervisor would indicate the degree (extent and quality) that teacher candidates demonstrate proficiency in gifted learner development and individual learning differences, apply curriculum planning and strategies, provide learning environments conducive to the learning needs of diverse learners, emphasize appropriate collaboration skills, demonstrate professionalism at a high level, attend to individual differences and concomitant learning needs through instructional planning and strategies, and select and apply multiple differentiated formal and informal assessments that minimize bias.

Use of Technology to Facilitate Clinical Experiences for Gifted Education Candidates

CAEP recently acknowledged the unique nature of providing online clinical/practicum experiences to teacher candidates. Although the organization aims to guide models of teacher preparation and development, they have openly stated that they have delayed guidance on the subject while they review newly emergent research and investigate evolving best practices (A. Cotabish, CAEP Standards Committee meeting notes, September 5, 2014). With the increased demand for universities to provide online programming options for their students, we felt that it was necessary to provide an example of how one university gifted program is using technology to conduct its clinical/practicum experience for gifted education candidates.

At a university located in a southwestern state, gifted education candidates are placed in local school programs for the gifted and/or other school-based classroom settings that are conducive to working with the gifted. A traditional clinical observation schedule consisting of three observations over the course of the semester is followed and a gifted education teacher observation scale is used to rate observed lessons; however, candidates are observed in real time using Skype® VOIP software. Teacher candidates and the university supervisor are required to connect via Skype using a tablet device or computer. The candidate places the tablet at an optimal location in the room or uses a SWIVL robotic mobile device that allows the tablet to rotate 360 degrees (allowing for full view of the classroom). In efforts to observe authentic student learning behaviors and to avoid becoming a distraction to Pre-K–12 students, the university supervisor suppresses her live action Skype image on the webcam (students cannot see the university supervisor on the tablet/computer). More interestingly, teacher candidates are also equipped with a Bug-in-the-Ear (BIE) Bluetooth device, allowing the university supervisor to provide live on-demand corrective feedback (coaching) using minimally intrusive short phrases to redirect poor instructional practices. The BIE device also provides live debriefing opportunities following the observed lesson. Simultaneously, the university supervisor uses Pamela® Video Recording Software for Skype (a software add-on that works in conjunction with Skype) that allows the university supervisor to record the observed lessons and share the videos with candidates for reflection purposes.

The research associated with the university's implementation of the virtual observation project has demonstrated early promise in improving teacher candidates' instructional practices (via on-demand corrective feedback/coaching). Furthermore, the innovation has decreased supervisor travel time and budgets, and has diminished the barrier of distance associated with traveling to conduct face-to-face clinical experiences (Benson & Cotabish, 2014; Cotabish & Benson, 2014).

Capturing Candidate Outcomes: Face-to-Face and Online Gifted Education Programs

Candidate outcomes should reflect a summative product from the practicum experience. The product might be a portfolio documenting the candidate experiences for each standard, candidate reflections on his or her competency to teach toward the standard, and candidate's impact on student learning. Many institutions may wish to initiate e-portfolios as opposed to paper ones as a means to document the progress of their candidates over time. Free online digital portfolio websites such as LiveBinder (http://www.livebinder.com) are becoming increasingly popular options for candidates to house and share their work. These types of multipurpose digital libraries allow candidates to document their proficiencies in the university program of study, store content over the course of their program, and continue to contribute resources (e.g., websites, documents, Power Points, conference presentations, curriculum, technology, instructional strategies, etc.) beyond the completion of their program of study. Thus, the digital portfolio serves as an evolving, transformative "live" binder to house candidates' valuable curriculum and instructional materials over the course of their teaching careers.

Some programs use a more complete version of the portfolio for evidence of program completion. Minimally, practicum portfolios should document the implementation of planned differentiated curriculum experiences with the student populations of interest, provide evidence of the nature and extent of their learning in the unit, and address issues and problems encountered in helping all students learn the desired material. A 45-minute recording of a lesson taught during the practicum might be included (video can be uploaded and shared with the university supervisor through an online "cloud" storage infrastructure such as Google Drive or Dropbox) along with a candidate critique of the lesson using the same structured observation form used to observe their teaching by the supervisor and administrator. To more fully align with the CAEP requirement of demonstrating candidate impact on student learning, selected lesson plans and student products should be highlighted to illustrate the standards addressed and learner impact. A daily log of reflections might be considered, as well as documentation of candidate practicum hours. Typically, the candidates would reflect upon their strengths and weaknesses in terms of their daily teaching of gifted and advanced learners, document their impressions with regard to the day's lessons, assess the extent to which the day's objectives were met, and set goals to improve their teaching.

Candidates exiting the practicum experience in gifted education should have met the following outcomes (Johnsen et al., 2008):

* gained competence in the skills delineated in the seven CAEP standards related to working with gifted learners,
* demonstrated efficacy in the selected settings of the practicum,
* provided evidence of growth over time in planning for and teaching gifted learners,
* demonstrated a reflective orientation to professional improvement,
* articulated issues and concerns in appropriate venues and showed evidence of effective problem-solving skills to address them, and
* documented and analyzed student impact.

Other outcomes seen as desirable by individual programs should be added to the list above.

Practicum experiences should be personalized to provide each candidate the necessary background for effectively addressing the needs of gifted learners. These experiences should be tailored to individual and cohort needs.

Increasing Collaboration and Partnership Efforts Within the Pre-K–12 Gifted Community

The nature of Pre-K–12 gifted programming has historically been grounded in collaborative activities. Beginning with the identification process, gifted education personnel often tap potential talent in whole-group enrichment classes as early as Pre-K–2. In the later grades, identification procedures often involve a student nomination process sought from stakeholder groups. In many school districts, nominations are accepted from parents, community members, teachers, students, and other school personnel. Although research documents outreach efforts to include multiple stakeholders in the identification process (Ford & Webb, 1994; Hunsaker, Finley, & Frank, 1997; Miller, 2005; Siegle & Powell, 2004), it has long been noted that teachers are the "gatekeepers" to identification for programming services (Ford & Webb, 1994; Miller, 2005; Swanson, 2006). Increasing participation of diverse stakeholders (beyond teachers) in the nomination process will require increased communication and forward-thinking strategies. For example, many school districts require parent representation on their gifted identification advisory board. The parent representative plays a role during the screening process, providing valuable input in the identification process. Although an important role, one parent representative on one gifted and talented committee is not sufficient to represent adequately the "voice" of all parents of gifted learners. Other avenues to increase involvement need to be explored. For example, some school districts have a parent/community group affiliated with their state's gifted and talented organization that functions as a PTO/PTA organization within the school/district. These affiliate members often meet quarterly, discuss important concerns regarding gifted programming and services, assist with programming activities (e.g., spelling bee, chess, quiz bowl), and can serve as an advocacy voice when needed. The affiliate group can be an important component to consider, and can potentially increase communication and participation of parents and other interested individuals within the district and community at large.

Social media outlets can also increase communication and expand collaboration efforts. Creating and utilizing a school-based Twitter, Facebook, listserv, and other electronic social media accounts can potentially increase communication, and possibly, the participation of gifted and talented stakeholder groups. Many, if not all, social media outlets report user-friendly analytics (metric tools) that allow account holders to generate reports that summarize the contributions and participation of targeted audiences. With the advent of such communicative tools that are within easy grasp of many, using social media as a communication tool to strengthen partnerships in gifted programming is one to be considered.

Other Types of Partnership Activities to Consider

Beyond the partnership activities that have been mentioned thus far, other types of partnership activities warrant consideration. Student mentorship and shadowing opportunities can be negotiated across any and all partnership agencies. Students wanting to shadow higher education faculty (e.g., engineering, nursing, business, etc.), and professionals in local industries (e.g., manufacturing facility personnel, bankers, marketers, etc.), among others, would be one way mentorships might enhance student learning and outcomes. Other activities might target parent partnerships. For example, parents might be allowed to assist with identifying their children's interests (for programming and mentorship opportunities) and be involved in the process of developing individual student plans for gifted program planning and instructional purposes. School competitions such as history day, science fairs, and Destination Imagination could be a catalyst to negotiate a student mentorship opportunity with a partner, and involve local businesses, parents, and higher education faculty to inform and even judge student work. Although these are only a couple of examples highlighting the types of activities that can be facilitated across partnership agencies, they demonstrate the strategic involvement that is necessary to increase buy-in and promote shared accountability among all involved.

Summary

Partnerships in gifted education are not egocentric in nature. They are not to be limited to clinical relationships between the EPP and schools/districts. Partnerships should be a cyclical relationship involving EPPs, Pre-K–12 schools/districts, and the larger community to support a continuum of services to gifted education candidates and high-ability students. A number of partnership activities and examples have been discussed in this section, and all support CAEP Standard 2 and the 2013 NAGC-CEC Teacher Preparation Standards (in particular, NAGC-CEC Standards 6 and 7). It is important to note that as education and technology advance, so do the opportunities for partnerships. Long gone are the days of static education and antiquated technology. It is wise to keep one's ear to the ground and involve those who can assist with our mission of continuous and sustained improvement in the quality of current and future teaching forces. Strategic partners can support that mission by sharing their expertise and resources and also by assisting with the latest technology advancements. It is equally important to note that our vision to facilitate partnerships on behalf of our gifted education candidates goes beyond preparing them to serve the differentiated learning needs of gifted students—we are also molding them to be our future partners.

CHAPTER 3

INTEGRATING GIFTED EDUCATION STANDARDS INTO EDUCATION PREPARATION PROVIDERS' PROGRAMS

DEBBIE DAILEY AND ALICIA COTABISH

Introduction

Included in this chapter is information on how to integrate gifted education standards into teacher preparation programs. It is necessary for Education Preparation Providers (EPPs) and specific teacher preparation programs to establish and share a common vision. This partnership is often demonstrated through the EPP's conceptual framework. To visualize the relationship between EPPs and gifted educator preparation programs, we provide an example conceptual framework, which is aligned to the 2013 NAGC-CEC Teacher Preparation Standards for Gifted Education and applicable measures of evidence. Additionally in this chapter, we discuss the integration of gifted standards into undergraduate teacher education programs. Because gifted students are in all classrooms and current teacher preparation programs provide little exposure to teacher candidates, we suggest EPPs include the NAGC Knowledge and Skills Standards in Gifted Education for All Teachers in teacher preparation coursework. These standards, drawn from the NAGC-CEC Teacher Preparation Standards, present the essential information needed concerning issues, learning differences, and appropriate strategies for teachers to make informed decisions about gifted student learning. We also provide three sample syllabi and a description of how the course syllabi and assessments meet the NAGC Knowledge and Skills Standards for All Teachers.

Relationship of Education Preparation Providers' Conceptual Framework to Gifted Education Standards

A well-developed conceptual framework establishes a shared vision among stakeholders who contribute to preparing educators to work in Pre-K–12 schools. The framework conveys the vision and mission of the EPP and provides direction for the program, curriculum, instruction, and assessment. Additionally, it is aligned with professional and state standards and articulates the EPP's professional commitment to raise the bar in educator preparation.

The following example demonstrates how a program for preparing teachers of gifted and talented students is linked to the EPP's conceptual framework (see Figure 3.1).

In Table 3.1, the Conceptual Framework Attributes (University of Central Arkansas College of Education, n.d.) are aligned with the 2013 NAGC-CEC Teacher Preparation Standards and applicable measures of evidence. CAEP (2014) recommended EPPs create a "culture of evidence . . . gather data on all aspects of their preparation programs and use them for continuous improvement" (p. 4). The measures of evidence in the following table are recommended by CAEP but can be useful for all universities seeking accreditation and continuous improvement.

The eight attributes found in the conceptual framework are integrated systematically into the courses and learning experiences of all teacher education candidates, including educators of gifted and talented students. There are, however, distinct differences in coursework for gifted and talented educators. When considering instructional planning and strategies, coursework emphasizes knowledge of how gifted students learn and presents multiple strategies

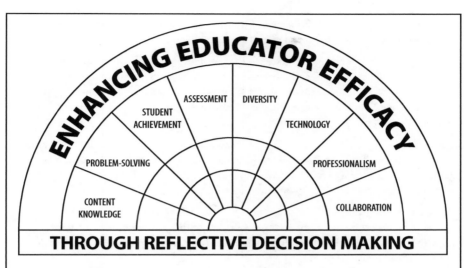

Enhancing educator efficacy through reflective decision making is the focusing agent for the EPP and is manifested through eight attributes.

In a synthesized and targeted way, efficacy provides a rationale for the conceptual framework—for both classroom teachers and other school professionals. In the realm of reflective decision making, efficacy is the reason why we reflect—it represents our ownership of the learning environment and achievement of all learners. The degree to which PEU candidates demonstrate efficacy directly correlates to their attainment of the knowledge, skills, and dispositions necessary to positively impact the learning of all learners. The eight attributes within the Conceptual Framework represent our view of the ideal educator.

Content Knowledge—Educators demonstrate knowledge of the central concepts and modes of inquiry in their disciplines. They use this knowledge to support effective practice so that all students may achieve.

Problem Solving—Educators implement reflective and systematic problem solving strategies based upon empirical science. They actively seek solutions that benefit all constituencies and create a fertile learning environment for all students.

Student Achievement—Educators plan, design, and deliver instruction and other services in a manner that engages and respects students, enhances academic and social-emotional outcomes, and fosters positive interactions. They employ alternative multiple pedagogical approaches to ensure that all students learn.

Assessment—Educators align assessments with the curriculum and instruction and provide a variety of ways for students to express knowledge, skills, and/or abilities. They use

FIGURE 3.1. Example conceptual framework from the College of Education at the University of Central Arkansas. From *UCA Conceptual Framework: Enhancing Educator Efficacy Through Reflective Decision-Making, n.d., University of Central Arkansas College of Education, n.d.*, retrieved from http://candidate.coe.uca.edu/NCATE/documents/ Conceptual%20Framework/Conceptual%20Framework%20FINAL. pdf. Reprinted with permission.

assessment data to inform their practice of what students know and can do, as well as where students need additional support to meet learning outcomes.

Diversity—Educators are open-minded to the possibility and validity of different values, beliefs, cultural/ethnic norms, and learning preferences. They are committed to the notion that all students can learn; therefore, they acknowledge and accommodate diversity, infuse multiple perspectives into their practice, and strategically plan to meet the needs of diverse student populations.

Technology—Educators integrate technology responsibly as a tool to enhance the learning environment for all students. They use technology to engage students in instruction, to gather and analyze data to foster student success, to extend the technological literacy of students, and to more effectively communicate with constituencies.

Professionalism—Educators seek continual professional growth, advocate and model ethical standards, and serve as effective ambassadors of the profession. They act to preserve the standards and integrity of their profession, and willingly accept responsibility for the learning of all students.

Collaboration—Educators promote and utilize a collaborative approach to professional responsibilities and activities. They forge partnerships with others in order to assist in effective decision-making and provide the richest environment for the learning and development of all students. (University of Central Arkansas College of Education, n.d., p. 1–3)

FIGURE 3.1. Continued.

to engage and challenge gifted learners effectively. For example, to challenge gifted learners, educators may need to move beyond grade-level standards and accelerate (Colangelo, Assouline, & Gross, 2004; Rogers, 1992, 2002; Steenberger-Hu & Moon, 2011) or compact the curriculum (Renzulli, Smith, & Reis, 1982). Addressing diversity issues, gifted educators must learn to recognize learning characteristics of culturally diverse gifted students and be prepared to differentiate the content or instructional methods to best meet their needs (Castellano & Frazier, 2010; Ford & Trotman, 2001). Regarding assessment, gifted educators need a comprehensive background in assessment—not only for making instructional decisions, but also for selecting and using adequate and fair assessments to identify gifted and talented students among all populations (VanTassel-Baska, Johnson, & Avery, 2002; VanTassel-Baska & Stambaugh, 2005).

The conceptual framework presented (University of Central Arkansas College of Education, n.d.) emphasized reflective decision making as the driving force to increase educator efficacy. To increase efficacy and improve teaching, teachers and teacher candidates from all fields and content areas should use reflection to critically self-assess their teaching practices. The practice of reflection enables teachers to continuously develop and refine their teaching. To assist in reflection and further assess teaching, teachers should seek

Table 3.1

Alignment Between EPP Conceptual Framework Attributes, NAGC–CEC Teacher Preparation Standards in Gifted Education, and Measures of Evidence

Conceptual Framework Attributes	2013 NAGC-CEC Teacher Preparation Standards in Gifted Education	Measures of Evidence (2013 CAEP Commission Recommendations to the CAEP Board of Directors)
Content Knowledge	3. Curricular Content Knowledge	• Standardized capstone assessments (e.g., Praxis specialty field) • College GPA in specialty field and in professional preparation courses
Problem Solving	5. Instructional Planning and Strategies	• Assessments and rubrics used to assess teaching practice at key points along a developmental continuum • Analysis of video-recorded lessons with review and evaluation based on rubrics and raters
Student Achievement	5. Instructional Planning and Strategies	• Student performance on valid, reliable assessments aligned with instruction during clinical practice experiences • Value-added student growth measures where available from the state
Assessment	4. Assessment	• Candidate designed assessments used in clinical practice experiences with Pre-K–12 students
Diversity	1. Learner Development and Individual Learning Differences	• Case study of the effectiveness of diverse field experiences on candidates' instructional practices • Evidence of differentiated instruction in response to student test data (formative and/or summative)
Technology	2. Learning Environments	• Evidence that candidates integrate technology into their planning and teaching and use it to differentiate instruction
Professionalism	6. Professional Learning and Ethical Practice	• Using self-assessments, mentor, and supervisor assessments, candidates provide a professional growth plan targeting areas of improvement • Candidates reflect on personal biases, access appropriate resources to deepen their understanding and use this information and related experiences to build stronger relationships with Pre-K–12 learners, and adapt their practices to meet the needs of each learner

Table 3.1, *Continued*

Conceptual Framework Attributes	2013 NAGC-CEC Teacher Preparation Standards in Gifted Education	Measures of Evidence (2013 CAEP Commission Recommendations to the CAEP Board of Directors)
Collaboration	7. Collaboration	• Collaboration evidence indicating candidate commitment and dispositions such as (1) teaching, volunteerism, coaching, civic organizations, commitment to urban issues; (2) content-related, goal-oriented, data-driven contributions/value-add to current employer or organization; (3) mindsets/dispositions/characteristics such as coachability, empathy, teacher presence of "with-it-ness," cultural competency, collaboration, beliefs, that all children can learn; or (4) professionalism, perseverance, ethical practice, strategic thinking, abilities to build trusting, supportive relationships with students and families during preparation

feedback from others, such as coaches, mentors, or peers. Feedback is a critical component in reflective decision making and is essential to the ongoing refinement of teaching (Daniel, Auhl, & Hastings, 2013). With this in mind, it is necessary for teachers and teacher candidates to be coachable—to take constructive criticism and use it to improve their practice. Teachers who are coachable will take ownership of their instructional problems and not blame their struggles on outside sources such as poverty, parental involvement, and wavering administrative support (Ginsburg, 2012). To increase the *coachability* of teachers, it is important for teacher preparation programs to engage teacher candidates and potential gifted educators in reflective practice and critical dialogue (Daniel et al., 2013). Daniel and colleagues (2013) stated "the capacity to provide and receive critical and constructive feedback is fundamental to the growth of the teaching profession, and preservice teacher education is a most appropriate place for it to be investigated and enculturated" (p. 170).

Identifying diversity issues in schools and classrooms is an integral component of reflective decision making and is essential to understanding students and meeting their needs. Educator efficacy can only be achieved if teachers are able to recognize the characteristics of diverse learners and provide appropriate learning experiences that interest, engage, and challenge learners. With this in mind, teacher candidates in all programs, including gifted and talented programs, are expected to use multiple and bias-free assessments to make identification and learning progress decisions. Using the assessment results, teachers should be able to select appropriate instructional strategies to further the learning of *all* students. This includes designing optimal learning experiences for advanced learners that encourage creative and critical thinking, offer opportunities for real-world problem solving, and provide a greater depth and complexity in subject area domains (VanTassel-Baska, 1986; VanTassel-Baska & Little, 2003, 2011).

Integrating Gifted Education Into Undergraduate Course Syllabi and Related Key Assessments

The NAGC-CEC Teacher Preparation Standards in Gifted Education were approved by CAEP for the national accreditation process (NAGC-CEC, 2013b) and are appropriate for all teacher preparation programs regardless of accreditation. A challenge, however, is to integrate gifted standards into existing undergraduate teacher preparation courses. Typically, training in gifted education culminates in a master's degree in gifted education or a gifted certificate as an add-on endorsement to an initial teacher licensure program. Despite students with gifts and talents being in most Pre-K–12 classrooms, teachers who do not seek a gifted certificate or degree often enter the classroom with little knowledge about the nature and needs of students with gifts and talents (Archambault et al., 1993; Bangel, Moon, & Capobianco, 2010; Berman, Schultz, & Weber, 2012; Hansen & Feldhusen, 1994). It would be beneficial to all students with gifts and talents to be in classrooms with teachers who have an understanding of these students and a repertoire of strategies to individualize their learning. To address this issue, NAGC developed the NAGC Knowledge and Skill Standards in Gifted Education for All Teachers. The Knowledge and Skills standards, which were drawn from the 2013 NAGC-CEC Teacher Preparation Standards in Gifted Education, were developed for use in general education preparation programs and teacher inservice professional development. NAGC recommends that all teachers:

(1) recognize the learning differences, developmental milestones, and cognitive/affective characteristics of gifted and talented students, including those from diverse cultural and linguistic backgrounds, and identify their related academic and social-emotional needs;

(2) design appropriate learning and performance modifications for individuals with gifts and talents that enhance creativity, acceleration, depth and complexity in academic subject matter and specialized domains; and

(3) select, adapt, and use a repertoire of evidence-based instructional strategies to advance the learning of gifted and talented students. (NAGC, 2014, para. 3)

To ensure that all teachers have awareness of the characteristics of students with gifts and talents and have strategies to support them, we suggest teacher preparation course syllabi and key assessments address the NAGC Knowledge and Skill Standards in Gifted Education for All Teachers in addition to the traditional teacher preparation and content standards. The Knowledge and Skills Standards are closely aligned with the InTASC Model Core Teaching Standards, which are found in CAEP's Standard 1 (Content and Pedagogical Knowledge and Skills).

As a concerted effort, EPPs can simply integrate the Knowledge and Skills Standards into existing teacher preparation courses. To provide an example, the NAGC Professional Standards Committee collaborated with three university faculty members—Cotabish, Hughes, and Shaunessy-Dedrick—to develop or revise undergraduate teacher preparation syllabi to include the Knowledge and Skill Standards. The three syllabi are included in Appendix C.

The Science Methods course (Cotabish, 2015) is for preservice science teachers seeking to complete requirements for a secondary science teaching degree. The course emphasizes instructional methods, curricula, and materials needed to teach all learners in a secondary science classroom. The course syllabus has been modified to address the Knowledge and Skills Standards. The modifications require teacher candidates to consider the needs of advanced and gifted learners and to suggest appropriate strategies to meet their needs. For example, the course's key assessment involves students creating a 5E curriculum unit. In this unit, teacher candidates are to include plans to accommodate advanced learners and at least two lessons should be linked to a problem and project-based learning experience. Teacher candidates also create an electronic LiveBinder that includes exemplar examples of differentiated instructional strategies, lessons, content, and technology resources.

The Survey of Children With Exceptionalities course (Hughes, 2015) introduces teacher candidates to various and diverse student exceptionalities and their impact on student learning in grades Pre-K–8. Making course revisions with gifted and advanced students in mind, teacher candidates explore multiple strategies that include "academic acceleration, enrichment, and differentiation" (Hughes, 2015, para. 3). Assessments and activities in this course include the creation of sample lesson plans that include specific instructional strategies for advanced learners. Additionally, teacher candidates collect field observation notes and choose one exceptional student (a gifted child or one with disabilities) to observe and evaluate. Using the collected data, teacher candidates interpret the data and make recommendations for appropriate teaching strategies to help the student grow and develop. As the course's final assessment, teacher candidates use the knowledge procured in the course and develop Individualized Education Plans (IEPs) for both gifted and struggling learners.

The Linking Literacy Assessment to Instruction course (Shaunessy-Dedrick, 2015) "prepares preservice teachers to use multiple assessment measures to assess students' strengths and needs in literacy learning" (para. 3). As a course modification, teacher candidates evaluate assessment data and learning profiles to design instructional experiences for all learners, including gifted and advanced learners. A key assessment in this course is an analysis of case study reports, including one that addresses the needs of a gifted learner with advanced reading abilities. Using diagnostic information, teacher candidates create an instructional plan to implement with the case study students. Gifted education standards are seamlessly integrated in this course with the concentration on using assessments and diagnostic data to make instructional decisions.

The syllabi examples provide multiple methods for integrating gifted education standards into existing teacher preparation courses. All three course syllabi require teacher candidates to consider specific instructional strategies appropriate for gifted and advanced learners. Furthermore, key assessments are aligned to each—demonstrating the necessary first steps to educate teacher candidates on the differentiated learning needs of gifted and advanced students. Table 3.2 provides a comparison of these courses with a traditional syllabi and syllabi with integrated gifted education standards.

Summary

In summary, we provided a brief overview of how to integrate the NAGC Knowledge and Skills Standards in Gifted Education for All Teachers into EPPs' undergraduate course syllabi and their related key assessments. Because most children with gifts and talents in the elementary and middle school grades, whether formally identified or not, remain within a heterogeneous classroom setting for much of the instructional day, many may not be receiving optimal educational opportunities to meet their needs. To address this critical issue, EPPs should consider integrating the Knowledge and Skills Standards into undergraduate teacher preparation programs. This small, but important step will help improve educational opportunities for gifted and advanced students.

Table 3.2
Comparison of Traditional Syllabi and Syllabi With Integrated Gifted Education Standards

Course Syllabi Examples	Traditional Syllabi	Syllabi With Integrated Gifted Education
Science Methods (Cotabish, 2015)		
Standards	Next Generation Science Standards, InTASC	Next Generation Science Standards, InTASC, NAGC Knowledge and Skills Standards in Gifted Education for All Teachers
Assignment: Curriculum Unit	Each lesson must describe how students will demonstrate that they have achieved the lesson objective.	Each lesson must describe how students will demonstrate that they have achieved the lesson objective and should include accommodations for advanced learners.
Survey of Children With Exceptionalities (Hughes, 2015)		
Standards	Council for Exceptional Children, InTASC	Council for Exceptional Children, InTASC, NAGC Knowledge and Skills Standards in Gifted Education for All Teachers
Assignment: Modified Lesson Plan	Prepare a lesson that has been modified for students with exceptional needs.	Prepare a lesson that has been modified for students with exceptional needs. Include strategies of differentiation for advanced learners.
Assignment: Field Observation Journal	Describe changes in the lesson-planning process that are made to meet the needs of one or more specific children.	Describe changes in the lesson planning process that are made to meet the needs of one or more specific children. Include descriptions of how advanced students are accommodated.
Assignment: Case Study	Choose an exceptional student from your field placement classroom to observe and evaluate.	Choose an exceptional student from your field placement classroom to observe and evaluate. The exceptional student can be a gifted child.
Assignment: Individualized Education Plan (IEP) or Gifted Individualized Education Plan (GIEP)	In a simulated IEP meeting, teams will determine appropriate goals and objectives for an exceptional student.	In a simulated GIEP meeting, teams will determine appropriate goals and objectives for a gifted student.

Table 3.2, *Continued*

Linking Literacy Assessment to Instruction (Shaunessy-Dedrick, 2015)		
Standards	International Reading Knowledge, InTASC	International Reading Knowledge, InTASC, NAGC Knowledge and Skills Standards in Gifted Education for All Teachers
Assignment: Case Study	Complete a case study for a student not identified as gifted who does not have advanced reading abilities. Include in the report reading levels, strengths, areas of need, and instructional recommendations. Also, create three lesson plans based on the case study findings.	Complete a case study for a gifted learner with advanced reading abilities. Include in the report reading levels, strengths, areas of need, and instructional recommendations. Also, create three lesson plans based on the case study findings.
Assignment: Article on effective reading intervention programs or strategies	Locate and read two articles on a reading intervention program or strategies.	Locate and read two articles on a reading intervention program or strategies, including one designed for advanced readers.

CHAPTER 4

DEVELOPING COURSES THAT INCORPORATE THE NATIONAL TEACHER PREPARATION STANDARDS IN GIFTED EDUCATION

ANN ROBINSON AND JENNIFER L. JOLLY

Introduction

The purpose of this chapter is to provide guidance to university program faculty in developing graduate, undergraduate, and online courses related to the joint standards of the National Association for Gifted Children (NAGC) and the Council for Exceptional Children (CEC) for preparing educators to work with students with gifts and talents.

The chapter includes textual explanation and exemplar syllabi. The textual explanation sections focus on the application of the evidence base to course design and on best practices in clinical practices. The exemplar syllabi in this chapter include a graduate survey course in gifted education, an undergraduate course on differentiated instruction, and an online course on the topic of creative behavior. The chapter includes an example case analysis assessment with its accompanying rubric in the graduate survey course syllabus and rubrics for evaluating a differentiated unit of instruction and a differentiated lesson plan in the undergraduate course syllabus.

Application of Evidence Base to Course Design

The standards and the underlying research, literature, and practice base are available from the National Association for Gifted Children (NAGC) and the Council for Exceptional Children (CEC) websites and in Appendix B in this book.

In developing new or revising existing course syllabi and outlines to align with the revised standards, the evidence base can be used in several ways.

1. The references should be integrated into the bibliographies of course syllabi and outlines.

2. Candidate products and artifacts can be designed to focus on background readings from the evidence base. A focus on the consensus evidence base supporting the standards would be particularly desirable for the assignments, products, and artifacts related to the six to eight key assessments required for CAEP program recognition, but all course assignments would benefit from being anchored in the evidence base.

3. Instructional strategies or curricular approaches from the evidence base that are effective for students with gifts and talents could be integrated into course design. Whether the course is delivered in a face-to-face, online, or hybrid format, evidence-based instructional strategies, such as inquiry, problem-based learning, or primary source analysis, can be selected and modeled throughout the course.

4. Course developers and instructors could also use the evidence base in course design itself. For example, an important and evidence-based best practice for students with gifts and talents is preassessment prior to instruction. Thus, each course in gifted education should begin with a preassessment and modify instruction based on the results. An additional example of using the evidence base on gifted education in course design would be allowing candidates choice in the format of products used to fulfill course requirements.

5. When candidates participate in their clinical placements, they can guide their school colleagues, the families of students with gifts and talents,

Graduate Introduction to Gifted Education Syllabus[1]
University of Arkansas at Little Rock
College of Education and Health Professions

Course prefix and number: GATE XXXX
Course title: Introduction to Gifted Education
Credit: 3 Hours

Course Description

Upon completion of this course, the candidate will understand the characteristics and needs of gifted children and youth, procedures used to identify gifts and talents, types of programs available to gifted children and youth, the historical and philosophical foundations required of professionals in the field, and the history of the gifted child movement.

National Association for Gifted Children (NAGC)-Council for Exceptional Children (CEC) Standards

This course is designed to enhance candidates' knowledge and skills as they relate to the NAGC-CEC Teacher Preparation Standards in Gifted Education.

State Program Standards

This course is designed to enhance teachers' knowledge and skills as they relate to the state principles of licensure that are based on the InTASC standards.

Principle #1: The teacher understands the central concepts, tools of inquiry, and structures of the discipline(s) he or she teachers, can create learning experiences that make these aspects of subject matter meaningful for students, and can link the discipline(s) to other subjects.

Principle #2: The teacher plans curriculum appropriate to the students, to the content, and to the course objectives.

Principle #3: The teacher plans instruction based upon human growth and development, learning theory, and the needs of students.

Principle #4: The teacher exhibits human relations skills that support the development of human potential.

Principle #5: The teacher works collaboratively with school colleagues, parents/guardians, and the community to support students' learning and well-being.

Major Emphases

1. When asked, the candidate will identify and discuss the rationale for specialized educational services for gifted students, including definitions, identification criteria, and program philosophy. (NAGC/CEC 6.2).
2. When asked, the candidate will identify the major historical foundations, classic studies, and multiple philosophical trends that have influenced the field of gifted education. (NAGC/CEC 6.2).
3. When asked, the candidate will discuss the contributions of influential thinkers in the psychology and education of individuals with gifts and talents. (NAGC/CEC 6.2).

FIGURE 4.1. Graduate introduction to gifted education syllabus.

4. Given case documents of individuals, candidates will identify intellective and nonintellective factors associated with giftedness and talent development, including special populations of individuals with gifts and talents. (NAGC/CEC 1.2).

5. Given case documents of individuals, candidates will identify potential participants in school programs and services with respect to the enrichment and acceleration needs of the students with gifts and talents, including diverse learners. (NAGC/CEC 1.2; 2.4).

6. Given interest inventories, behavioral checklists, and assessment data, the candidate will write a case analysis of a talented child or adolescent. (NAGC/CEC 4.1).

7. When asked, the candidate will identify factors related to social and emotional development in talented young people. (NAGC/CEC 1.2).

8. Given examples of school identification plans, referral policies, and placement procedures, the candidate will analyze and critique the plans with regard to the relevant state program approval standards. (NAGC/CEC 6.3).

9. Given information about major school adaptations for the gifted (acceleration, grouping, enrichment, guidance, mentorships, and community-based service learning), candidates will be able to discuss these adaptations, including the enrichment and acceleration needs of gifted learners as compared with the needs of the general population of learners, and evaluate these adaptations for feasibility in their own school or work setting (NAGC/CEC 2.4; 5.4).

Methods

This course will be structured to allow participants to become actively involved. Methods include weekly online readings and assignments, lectures, discussion, simulations, small-group work, and student presentations.

Texts, Readings, and Instructional Resources

Required Texts

There is no required text for this course. Required weekly readings are provided on the university electronic delivery system.

State Program Approval Standards: Download the most recent version from the Department of Education website.

Electronic portfolio accounts for licensure candidates and master's candidates should be purchased at the bookstore. If you already have your portfolio account, be certain it has not expired.

Recommended Texts

There are two recommended texts for this course:

Callahan, C. M., & Hertberg-Davis, H. (2013). *Fundamentals of gifted education.* New York, NY: Routledge.

Davis, G. A., Rimm, S. B., & Siegle, D. (2011). *Education of the gifted and talented* (6th ed.). Boston, MA: Pearson.

Supplemental Reading

Supplemental readings are designed to give you an "extra boost" background for course assignments and for the information you need to master in order to do well on the Gifted

FIGURE 4.1. Continued.

Education Praxis Examination that is required by the state. Many of these readings are drawn from the evidence base supporting the NAGC/CEC Standards on which your course objectives are based. Some of the supplemental readings are classics in the field; others are related to your course assignments and to the key assessment for this course: Helping Juan. This list of supplemental readings differs from the extensive bibliography in a subsequent section of the syllabus. The bibliography is more extensive and should inform your general professional reading; the supplemental readings should appear in the citations related to various written course assignments.

Books, book chapters, and monographs.

Angelelli, C., Enright, K., & Valdes, G. (2002). *Developing the talents and abilities of linguistically gifted bilingual students.* Storrs: University of Connecticut, The National Research Center on the Gifted and Talented.

Aronson, J., & Juarez, L. (2012). Growth mindsets in the laboratory and the real world. In R. F. Subotnik, A. Robinson, C. M. Callahan, & E. J. Gubbins (Eds.), *Malleable minds: Translating insights from psychology and neuroscience to gifted education* (pp. 19–36). Storrs: University of Connecticut, The National Research Center on the Gifted and Talented.

Bloom, B. S. (1985). *Developing talent in young people.* New York, NY: Ballantine Books.

Csikszentmihalyi, M., Rathunde, K. & Whalen, S. (1993). *Talented teenagers: The roots of success and failure.* New York, NY: Cambridge University Press.

Robinson, A., & Jolly, J. (2014). *A century of contributions to gifted education: Illuminating lives.* New York, NY: Routledge.

Torrance, E. P. (1984). The role of creativity in identification of the gifted and talented. In J. S. Renzulli (Ed.), *Identification of students for gifted and talented programs* (pp. 17–24). Thousand Oaks, CA: Corwin.

Articles.

Bloom, B., & Sosniak, L. (1981). Talent development vs. schooling. *Educational Leadership, 39,* 86–94.

Borland, J. H., & Wright, L. (1994). Identifying young, potentially gifted, economically disadvantaged students. *Gifted Child Quarterly, 38,* 164–171.

DuBois, W. E. B. (1903). *The talented tenth.* Retrieved from http://teachingamericanhistory.org/library/document/the-talented-tenth

Gagne, F. (1985). Giftedness and talent: Reexamining a reexamination of the definitions. *Gifted Child Quarterly, 29,* 103–112.

Maker, C. J. (1996). Identification of gifted minority students: A national problem, needed changes, and a promising solution. *Gifted Child Quarterly, 40,* 41–50.

Pierson, E. E., Kilmer, L. M., Rothlisberg, B. A., & McIntosh, D. E. (2012). Use of brief intelligence tests in the identification of giftedness. *Journal of Psychoeducational Assessment, 30*(1), 10–24.

Renzulli, J. S. (1978). What makes giftedness? Reexamining a definition. *Phi Delta Kappan, 59,* 180–184.

Robinson, A., & Clinkenbeard, P. R. (1998). Giftedness: An exceptionality examined. *Annual Review of Psychology, 49,* 117–139.

FIGURE 4.1. Continued.

Topical Outline

1. Definitions and conceptualizations of giftedness
2. Cognitive and affective characteristics of children and adolescents with gifts and talents
3. The gifted individual in society
4. Talent development: Processes and performance
5. Role of the teacher in talent development
6. Role of the family and community in talent development
7. Identifying the gifted learner
8. Giftedness among twice-exceptional, low-income, and culturally diverse populations: Impacts and implications
9. Major school adaptations for the gifted: Enrichment, acceleration, grouping, and guidance and counseling programming options
10. Professional and ethical practice: Fostering professional collaboration and advocacy

Assignments, Evaluation Procedures, and Grading Policy

Course Requirements

1. **Class participation:** Each candidate is expected to read assigned materials prior to class and participate in class discussions both face-to-face and online as appropriate to course format. *See also Absence From Class Policy.*
2. **Projects/Weekly Assignments:**
   a. *Case Analysis.* Helping Juan case study and analysis. This is a key assessment uploaded to your electronic portfolio.
   b. *What Happens in Your World? Program Description and Analysis.* A description and analysis of the programs and services currently in place in your district. If your district does not identify or serve students with gifts and talents, you may locate an example from another district within your state or an example from a district outside your state. Instructor approval required.
   c. *Weekly Assignments/Discussion Board.* Twelve weekly assignments and/or discussion board activities related to the readings or to other resources for the course topics.

Electronic Portfolio

Each candidate will be evaluated on the basis of his or her performance on course assignments. Candidates are required to upload the required major assignment to the appropriate rubrics in the electronic portfolio and to publish them to the instructor for assessment. Instructions for uploading assignments are provided by the TECH Lab, as well as on the electronic portfolio site.

Candidates in School Personnel Preparation programs, including certificate programs, are expected to purchase the designated electronic portfolio account and to load major assignments into their portfolio as directed by the course instructor. These assignments will be uploaded to specific rubrics/standards and will be assessed by class/field instructors. Failure to complete key assessments in the electronic portfolio can preclude completion of your licensure or degree program.

The Introduction to Gifted Education course includes one key assessment for program accreditation, as well as a measure of your learning. The key assessment is the case analysis, Helping Juan.

FIGURE 4.1. Continued.

Grading

1. The course has a total of 200 points. Grades are assigned on the basis of percentages. The following scale is used to assign letter grades:

   90% to 100% = A
   80% to 89% = B
   70% to 79% = C
   60% to 69% = D
   Less than 60% = F

2. Summary of points:

   120 points: Weekly Assignments/Discussion Board (12 assignments in total, including bio and conference)

   80 points: Case Study/Analysis: Key Assessment uploaded into the electronic portfolio (Helping Juan)

   50 points: Identification/Programs/Services Description/Analysis (What Happens in Your World?)

Evaluation

Students will be evaluated on their performance on projects, examinations (if applicable), and weekly class participation and assignments detailed in the syllabus.

Expectations and Evaluation

Class participation and attendance. Class participation is considered vital to the successful completion of the course. Class activities typically will include topical lectures, class discussion/discussion boards, review of current news items, guest speakers or Internet sources, simulations, and oral reports. Students are expected to make constructive contributions to class discussions, demonstrate a willingness to participate in class activities, and share examples from their professional experiences that illustrate the concepts and content explored in class to receive full credit for participation. Academic integrity and honesty is expected in compliance with the Student Handbook, Code of Student Rights, Responsibilities, and Behavior. *In the event of absence from a face-to-face class meeting or nonparticipation in an online activity, the student will be responsible for submitting a 5-page paper discussing the topics associated with the missed class session/assignments.* Course materials shared on the student password-protected course shell site are meant for student learning use only and are not to be either given to or sold to anyone else at any location.

- Please respect the rights, feelings, values, beliefs, and unique backgrounds of one another.
- Please hold confidential information that is shared during class activities and assignments.
- Please silence cell phones, television, and electronic devices while you are engaged in class activities.
- Please do not multitask while you are participating in online class assignments. Research indicates that multitasking affects your performance negatively.

Each Monday, the weekly assignments will be opened. Weekly assignments are due on Sunday night at 11:59 p.m.

FIGURE 4.1. Continued.

Semester Class Schedule

Week 1	**Assignments** 1. Course welcome message from instructor and short video 2. Pretest (formative only): Send completed pretest to instructor's course shell e-mail 3. Conceptualizations of giftedness: Then and now PowerPoint lecture 4. Assignment 1: Your course bio. Discussion board post **Readings** 1. History of gifted education 2. Chapter or article of your choice on a key figure in gifted education (chapter and article choices are in the Key Figures in Gifted Education Readings folder in Week 1)
Week 2	**Assignments** 1. Characteristics and needs of students with gifts and talents: PowerPoint lecture 2. Overview of case analysis, Helping Juan documents 3. Overview of case analysis rubric **Readings** 1. Chapter 2 (Characteristics) from Davis, Rimm, and Siegle 2. Robinson and Clinkenbeard chapter from Pfeiffer handbook in your readings folder in Week 2
Week 3	**Assignments** 1. Extreme performers from the videos folder 2. Discussion board post about the video **Reading** 1. Feldman article in your readings folder in Week 3
Week 4	**Assignments** 1. The gifted individual in society 2. Discussion board post about the role of the talented individual in society **Reading** 1. Mead article in your readings folder in Week 4
Week 5	**Assignments** 1. Jigsaw discussion groups: Special populations of talented learners 2. Jigsaw summary of your chapter from your expert group **Readings** 1. One chapter of your choice on a special population of individuals with gifts and talents: 2. Culturally diverse populations 3. Talented learners with disabilities 4. Talented learners living in poverty 5. Boys, girls, and/or rural and geographically isolated talented students
Week 6	**Assignments** 1. Issues and procedures in identification PowerPoint lecture 2. Discussion board post on identification issues **Readings** 1. Chapter 3 (Identification) from Davis, Rimm, and Siegle 2. Chapter 10 (Traditional Perspectives on Identification) by Johnsen from Callahan and Hertberg-Davis

FIGURE 4.1. Continued.

Week 7	**Assignment** 1. Identification and programming description **Readings** 1. Your district identification and programming materials (found at your district office or online) 2. Identification articles in readings folder for Week 7
Week 8	**Assignments** 1. What do gifted programs look like?: Overview of the major service delivery approaches 2. Acceleration: Issues and tools **Reading** 1. Chapter 5 (Acceleration) from Davis, Rimm, and Siegle
Week 9	**Fall Break**
Week 10	**Assignments** 1. Understanding an acceleration staffing conference 2. Iowa Acceleration Scale (IAS)—Case #2 3. Discussion board post on Iowa Acceleration Scale (IAS)—Case #2 **Reading** 1. Iowa Acceleration Scale description
Week 11	**Assignments** 1. Jigsaw discussion groups: Program models 2. Jigsaw summary of your chapter for your group **Readings** 1. Chapter 6 (Grouping, Differentiation, and Enrichment) from Davis, Rimm, and Siegle 2. Chapter 22 (Cluster Grouping Programs and the Total School Grouping Model) by Gentry and Fugate from Callahan and Hertberg-Davis 3. Chapter 17 (Understanding and Counseling Gifted Students) from Davis, Rimm, and Siegle
Week 12	**Assignments** 1. Role of the teacher PowerPoint lecture 2. Discussion post on the role of the teacher in talent development **Readings** 1. Fernandez, Gay, Lucky, and Gavilan article in your readings folder for Week 12 2. Robinson and Kolloff chapter in your readings folder for Week 12
Week 13	**Assignments** 1. Role of the family 2. Discussion: What can we learn from Juan's family? **Readings** 1. Strip and Hirsch article in your readings folder for Week 1 2. Hertzog and Bennett article in your readings folder for Week 13
Week 14	**Assignments** 1. Complete, polish, and apply rubric for self-evaluation of the Helping Juan case analysis 2. Purchase and establish your electronic portfolios 3. Upload Helping Juan case analysis to your electronic portfolio

FIGURE 4.1. Continued.

Week 15	**Assignments** 1. Face-to-face or Skype final conferences with your instructor/electronic portfolio check-off
Week 16	**Please remember to submit your course evaluation to the college course evaluation link. Thank you.**

Bibliography

Bernal, E. (2002). Three ways to achieve a more equitable representation of culturally and linguistically different students in GT programs. *Roeper Review, 24,* 82–88.

Clinkenbeard, P. R. (1996). Research on motivation and the gifted: Implications for identification, programming, and evaluation. *Gifted Child Quarterly, 40,* 220–221.

Feldman, D. H. (2003). A developmental, evolutionary perspective on giftedness. In J. H. Borland (Ed.), *Rethinking gifted education* (pp. 9–33). New York, NY: Teachers College Press.

Feldhusen, J. F. (1997). Secondary services, opportunities, and activities for talented youth. In N. Colangelo and G. A. Davis (Eds.). *Handbook of gifted* (2nd ed., pp. 189–197). Boston, MA: Allyn & Bacon.

Feldhusen, J. F., & Jarwan, F. A. (2000). Identification of gifted and talented youth for educational programs. In K. A. Heller, F. J. Mönks, R. J. Sternberg, & R. F. Subotnik (Eds.), *International handbook of giftedness and talent* (2nd ed., pp. 271–282). Amsterdam, The Netherlands: Elsevier.

Fishkin, A. S., & Johnson, A. S. (1998). Who is creative? Identifying children's creative abilities. *Roeper Review, 21,* 40–46.

Gagné, F. (2011). Academic talent development and the equity issue in gifted education. *Talent Development & Excellence, 1*(3), 3–22.

Gallagher, J. J. (2000). Changing paradigms for gifted education in the United States. In K. A. Heller, F. J. Mönks, R. J. Sternberg, & R. F. Subotnik (Eds.), *International handbook of giftedness and talent* (3rd ed., pp. 681–694). Amsterdam, The Netherlands: Elsevier.

Gardner, H. (1993). *Creating minds: An anatomy of creativity seen through the lives of Freud, Picasso, Stravinsky, Eliot, Graham, and Gandhi.* New York, NY: Basic Books.

Hertzog, N., & Bennett, T. (2004). In whose eyes? Parents' perspectives on the learning needs of their gifted children. *Roeper Review, 26,* 96–104.

Lohman, D. F. (2006). *Identifying academically talented minority students* (RM05216). Storrs: University of Connecticut, The National Research Center on the Gifted and Talented.

Maker, C. J. (1996). Identification of gifted minority students: A national problem, needed changes and a promising solution. *Gifted Child Quarterly, 40,* 41–50.

Matthews, M. S., & Castellano, J. (Eds.). (2014). *Talent development for English language learners: Identifying and developing potential.* Waco, TX: Prufrock Press.

Moon, T. R., & Callahan, C. M. (2001). Curricular modifications, family outreach, and a mentoring program: Impacts on achievement and gifted identification in high-risk primary students. *Journal for the Education of the Gifted, 24,* 305–321.

Olszewski-Kubilius, P. (2008). The role of the family in talent development. In S. I. Pfeiffer (Ed.), *Handbook of giftedness in children: Psycho-educational theory, research, and best practices* (pp. 13–31). New York, NY: Springer.

FIGURE 4.1. Continued.

Reis, S. M., Colbert, R. D., Hébert, T.P. (2005). Understanding resilience in diverse, talented students in an urban high school. *Roeper Review, 27,* 110–120.

Renzulli, J. S. (1978). What makes giftedness? Reexamining a definition. *Phi Delta Kappan, 59,* 180–184.

Rogers, K. B. (2006). *A menu of options for grouping gifted students.* Waco, TX: Prufrock Press.

Robinson, A. (1990). Does that describe me? Adolescent acceptance of the gifted label. *Journal for the Education of the Gifted, 13,* 245–255.

Robinson, A., & Clinkenbeard, P. R. (1998). Giftedness: An exceptionality examined. *Annual Review of Psychology, 49,* 117–139.

Robinson, A., & Clinkenbeard, P. R. (2008). History of giftedness: Perspectives from the past presage modern scholarship. In S. I. Pfeiffer (Ed), *Handbook of giftedness in children: Psycho-educational theory, research, and best practices* (pp. 13–31). New York, NY: Springer.

Simonton, D. K. (2009). *Genius 101.* New York, NY: Springer.

Subotnik, R., Robinson, A., Callahan, C., & Johnson, P. (Eds.). (2014). *Malleable minds: Insights from psychology and neuroscience.* Storrs: University of Connecticut, The National Research Center on the Gifted and Talented.

Tannenbaum, A. J. (2000). A history of giftedness in school and society. In K. A. Heller, F. J. Mönks, R. J. Sternberg, & R. F. Subotnik (Eds.), *International handbook of giftedness and talent* (2nd ed., pp. 23–53). Amsterdam, The Netherlands: Elsevier.

VanTassel-Baska, J. (2005). *Acceleration strategies for teaching gifted learners.* Waco, TX: Prufrock Press.

VanTassel-Baska, J., Feng, A. X., Quek, C., & Struck, J. (2004). A study of educators' and students' perceptions of academic success for underrepresented populations identified for gifted program. *Psychology Science, 46,* 363–378.

Yoon, S., & Gentry, M. (2009). Racial and ethnic representation in gifted programs: Current status of and implications for gifted Asian American students. *Gifted Child Quarterly, 53,* 121–136.

FIGURE 4.1. Continued.

Helping Juan

Juan is acting out in his third-grade classroom. His classroom teacher, Mrs. Bryant, notes that he alternates between dreamy, withdrawn episodes, and angry outbursts during seatwork sessions. He appears to be particularly frustrated by mathematics seatwork. Mrs. Bryant is concerned because Juan is viewed as a leader by several of his peers in her classroom. Both boys and girls in the class seek Juan out during group work to get his help on problems in mathematics and to find information in reference sources across a wide variety of topics during library time. Mrs. Bryant does not want students to imitate his angry episodes, and she is aware of his leadership potential.

According to the school counselor, Mr. Lopez, Juan comes from a bilingual home. His parents speak both English and Spanish, but prefer Spanish. Juan's grandmother who lives in the home speaks Spanish exclusively. The counselor notes that Juan takes the lead in communicating for his family whenever they come to the school and will translate from English to Spanish on the spot. He also noted that Juan tends to fill out his own forms and asks his parents to sign "on the dotted line." Juan has one younger sibling, Carmelita, who has just entered first grade and (like Juan) is fluent in both English and Spanish.

Juan is an omnivorous reader and chooses nonfiction when given the choice. His last selections from the library were biographies of Edmund Halley and Neil deGrasse Tyson. Mrs. Bryant noted that Juan drew and labeled his own scientific illustrations to Halley's biography.

At the request of Mrs. Bryant and Mr. Lopez, Juan was nominated for services offered to students with gifts and talents offered by the district. The following assessment data were available: a norm-referenced test battery that included an overall composite score at the 97th percentile using national norms. His reading scores were at the 99th percentile, his language composite (which includes spelling and grammar) was at the 89th percentile, his mathematics problem solving score was again at the 99th percentile. Based on his high achievement scores, his bilingual skill, and his observed outbursts, district administrators decided to undertake additional testing. On an individually administered brief form of an aptitude test, the K-BIT and using the relevant standard errors of measurement, Juan received a Performance IQ in the range of 138–144, a Verbal IQ of 130–140, and an overall IQ of 131–139. No further test or observational data are currently available, but the district gifted and talented coordinator is pursuing Juan's case.

Read through this case several times, reflect on what you have read, heard, and learned so far in this course. Make notes that will help you develop a written case analysis of Helping Juan.

- What is going on in this case?
- What additional information do we need about Juan, his family, and his school?
- How might we interpret Juan's test score information?
- How might we respond to Juan's academic, social, and emotional needs?
- What do you recommend as a course of action to plan an educational program for Juan?

FIGURE 4.2. Prompt for case analysis: Helping Juan.

The Beginning Gifted Education Professional . . .	Developing	Competent	Proficient
Individual Differences (40 points)	*0–9 points*	*10–30 points*	*31–40 points*
Uses understanding of development and individual differences and language, culture, economic status, family background, and/or area of disability to respond to the needs of individuals with gifts and talents (NAGC/CEC Standard #1, 1.1,1.2; Standard #6, 6.3).	The influence of language and culture, poverty, or disability on the development of talent is described; however, the analysis includes stereotypical thinking about individuals with gifts and talents. No reference is made to any evidence-based readings to support the description.	The influence of language, culture, poverty, or disability on the development of talent is described. The implications of these influences are noted in terms of meeting the affective and cognitive needs of individuals with gifts and talents. Reference is made to evidence-based readings from the course.	The influence of language, culture, poverty, or disability on the development of talents is described. The understanding of family influences on the development of talent is included in the description. Reference is made to evidence-based articles, chapters, or books outside the assigned readings for the course.
Assessment for Identification (10 points)	*0–2 points*	*3–7 points*	*8–10 points*
Understands that some groups of individuals with gifts and talents have been underrepresented in gifted education programs; selects and interprets technically sound formal and informal assessments that minimize bias (NAGC/CEC Standard #4, 4.1).	Assessments are described; however, the limitations of the assessments are not recognized, particularly if the limitations are related to the underrepresentation of some groups of individuals with gifts and talents.	Assessments are described. Limitations of the assessments are reviewed with respect to the student(s) described in the case analysis. Both formal and informal assessments related to educators and the schools are included. Informal assessments from peers or family are included.	Assessments are described. Limitations, strengths, and alternatives are reviewed. Both formal and informal assessments related to teachers, the school, parents, and community are included. The description includes reference to a staffing meeting between school officials and the family.
Assessment for Developing an Individual Plan (10 points)	*0–2 points*	*3–7 points*	*8–10 points*

FIGURE 4.3. Case analysis rubric and scoring guide using NAGC-CEC Teacher Preparation Standards in Gifted Education (2013).

The Beginning Gifted Education Professional . . .	Developing	Competent	Proficient
Uses assessment results to develop long- and short-range goals and objectives that take into consideration an individual's abilities and needs, including diversity (NAGC/CEC #4, 4.4).	A description of a plan for the student includes goals that address the cognitive area only with classroom activities the responsibility of a single educator. The plan relates to the assessment data. The plan is not shared with the student, other educators, or the family.	A description of a plan for the student includes short- and long-term goals in cognitive, affective, and social areas. Activities include multiple teachers, parents, and the student. The plan is based on both qualitative and quantitative data and includes input from multiple stakeholders.	A description of a plan for the student includes short- and long-term goals in cognitive, affective, and social and linguistic areas with specific activities in multiple environments that involve both specialist and general classroom teachers, and other school personnel. The plan relates to qualitative and quantitative assessment data and is developed after input from the student, parents, teachers, administrators, a gifted and talented coordinator, and a counselor.
	0–4 points	*5–15 points*	*16–20 points*
Learning Environments (20 points) Understands multiple environments that are part of a continuum of services for individuals with gifts and talents (NAGC/CEC #2, 2.4).	Describes multiple learning environments, but does not understand the continuum of services.	Describes multiple learning environments and the advantages and disadvantages each presents for the student with gifts and talents.	Describes multiple learning environments and the advantages and disadvantages each presents for the student with gifts and talents. Describes the implications of the continuation of services for educational and career development.

FIGURE 4.3. Continued.

Undergraduate Differentiated Instruction Syllabus[1]

Course Description

Admission to the teacher education program is required. This course provides information about the historical, philosophical, and theoretical background of curriculum differentiation and specific strategies that adapt instruction for individual student differences. Empirical research that addresses issues and trends will be presented to examine the best practices in differentiation. Specific differentiation strategies that relate to student differences in rate, content, and preference will be applied in the classroom setting.

Goals and Objectives of the Course

The teacher candidate's knowledge about historical, philosophical, and theoretical background of curriculum differentiation and specific strategies and program models (e.g., AP, IB, schoolwide enrichment, acceleration) that adapt instruction for individual student differences, particularly within a whole classroom setting, and empirical research that addresses issues and trends in differentiation. The teacher candidate's dispositions, benchmarks, and relationships to other standards for each of the benchmark areas are listed below.

Creating a Positive Learning Environment

Disposition. Routines and procedures for the management of classroom time, space, materials, and activities promote efficiency and safety.

Knowledge.
- Development and maintenance of progress records that assist in differentiating curriculum (NAGC-CEC Standard 4; ACEI 3.2)
- Empirical research that relates to the formation of flexible instructional groups and independent activities (NAGC-CEC Standard 2; ACEI 3.2)
- Development and management of multilevel activities that are based on achievement, developmental levels, and interest levels of students (NAGC-CEC Standard 2; ACEI 3.2, 3.4)

Skills.
- Organizes the learning environment for differentiation (NAGC-CEC Standards 2, 4, and 5; ACEI 3.2, 3.4)
- Prepares and manages materials and activities that are based on individual student's interests, achievement, and developmental levels (NAGC-CEC Standards 2 and 5; ACEI 1.0, 3.2, 3.4)
- Keeps progress records to match and adapt the curriculum to the characteristics of each student (NAGC-CEC Standard 4; ACEI 3.2)
- Forms flexible instructional groups based on progress records with independent activities matched to students' achievement and developmental levels (NAGC-CEC Standards 2 and 4; ACEI 1.0, 3.2, 3.4)
- Paces lessons and develops activities based on achievement, developmental levels, and interest levels of the students (NAGC-CEC Standard 5; ACEI 1.0, 3.2, 3.4)

FIGURE 4.4. Undergraduate differentiated instruction course syllabus.

Assessment

Disposition. Assessment assists in grouping students for instruction.

Knowledge.

- Assessment methods that match type of knowledge (declarative, procedural and strategic; NAGC-CEC Standard 4; ACEI 4.0)
- Types of assessment such as curriculum-based methods, criterion- and norm-referenced tests, and alternative assessments that are based on students' achievement, cultural background, exceptionalities, and developmental levels (NAGC-CEC Standard 4; ACEI 3.2, 4.0)
- Informal assessment activities that connect to student's experiences, cultural background, exceptionalities, and/or developmental levels (NAGC-CEC Standard 4; ACEI 4.0)

Skills.

- Develops and/or matches assessment method to knowledge and students' achievement, cultural background, exceptionalities, and developmental levels (NAGC-CEC Standard 4; ACEI 3.2, 4.0)
- Develops and/or matches assessment activities to students' experiences and considers cultural background, exceptionalities, and/or developmental levels of each student (NAGC-CEC Standard 4; ACEI 3.2, 4.0)
- Adapts instruction for an individual student or a group of students based on continuous assessment (NAGC-CEC Standard 4; ACEI 3.2, 4.0)

Curriculum Planning and Instruction

Disposition. A range of instructional methods promotes and develops high academic achievement.

Knowledge.

- Historical, philosophical, and theoretical background of program models and curriculum differentiation and their effects on current issues and trends (NAGC-CEC Standard 6)
- Methods for organizing curriculum (NAGC-CEC Standard 3 and 5; ACEI 2.0)
- Specific differentiation methods that address student differences in rate, content, and preference (NAGC-CEC Standards 1, 3, 4, and 5; ACEI 3.1, 3.2)

Skills.

- Organizes information and the instructional method to the type of knowledge and characteristics of the student (NAGC-CEC Standard 5; ACEI 1.0, 3.1, 3.2, 3.4)
- Uses the students' responses to match the instructional method to each student (NAGC-CEC Standard 5; ACEI 3.1, 3.2, 3.3, 4.0)
- Adapts instructional activities for each student in the group and/or classroom; (NAGC-CEC Standard 5; ACEI 3.1, 3.2, 3.3, 3.4, 4.0)
- Teaches students to use information independently; students learn about their interests and strengths through the curriculum (NAGC-CEC Standard 2; ACEI 3.1, 3.2, 3.3, 3.4)

Professional Development and Communication

Disposition. A teacher is part of a larger professional community, which is nurtured through collegial relationships and contributions to the systems as a whole.

FIGURE 4.4. Continued.

Knowledge.

- *Written/oral communication.* How to use verbal, nonverbal, and written language effectively (NAGC-CEC Standard 6; ACEI 3.5, 5.1, 5.2)
- *Punctuality/dependability.* Practices within the CEC Code of Ethics and other standards of the profession (NAGC-CEC Standard 6; ACEI 5.1)
- *Response to feedback.* How to reflect on one's practice to improve instruction and guide professional growth (NAGC-CEC Standard 6; ACEI 5.1)
- *Appearance.* Practices within the CEC Code of Ethics and other standards of the profession (NAGC-CEC Standard 6; ACEI 5.1)
- *Professional development.* How to maintain knowledge of research and literature in special and gifted education and participates in activities of professional organizations, (NAGC-CEC Standard 6; ACEI 5.1)
- Strategies for collaborating with families that engage them in their child's learning process (NAGC-CEC Standard 7; ACEI 5.2)
- Strategies for collaborating with other professionals and the community that engage them in developing programs for individual students (NAGC-CEC Standard 7; ACEI 5.2)

Skills.

- Demonstrates professional qualities by managing and taking care of teaching materials, being punctual, meeting with the classroom teacher as needed, planning and preparing lessons, dressing appropriately, seeking assistance and resources, accepting and using feedback (NAGC-CEC Standard 6; ACEI 5.1)
- Plans instructional programs for students with parents and other professionals (NAGC-CEC Standard 7; ACEI 5.2)
- Uses self-evaluation and reflective practice to improve instruction and guide professional growth (NAGC-CEC Standard 6; ACEI 5.1)

Required Texts

Karnes, F. A., & Bean, S. M. (Eds.). (2015). *Methods and materials for teaching the gifted* (4th ed.). Waco, TX: Prufrock Press.

Roberts, J. L., & Inman, T. F. (2015). *Strategies for differentiating instruction: Best practices for the classroom* (3rd ed.). Waco, TX: Prufrock Press.

Winebrenner, S., & Brulles, D. (2012). *Teaching gifted kids in today's classroom.* Minneapolis, MN: Free Spirit Publishing.

Texas Education Agency. (2009). *Texas state plan for the education of gifted/talented students.* Retrieved from http://www.tea.state.tx.us/index2.aspx?id=6420

Tentative Agenda

Class 1	Overview of syllabus *Readings*: Chapters 1, 2, and 3 from Roberts and Inman; Chapter 1 from Winebrenner and Brulles; Chapters 1, 2, and 3 from Karnes and Bean
Class 2	Key philosophies, theories, and models of differentiation *Readings*: Chapter 4 from Karnes and Bean

FIGURE 4.4. Continued.

Class 3	Designing a differentiated unit—organizing content; identifying themes, generalizations, key words, content outline *Readings*: Chapter 8 from Karnes and Bean **Due: Theme and times when you plan to implement your classroom unit**
Class 4	Designing the unit framework and learner objectives to fit within the unit framework that guide the lesson planning *Readings for process skills*: Chapters 5, 6, and 8 from Roberts and Inman; Chapters 5, 10, 11, 12, 13, and 14 from Karnes and Bean; Chapter 6 from Winebrenner *Readings for product skills*: Chapter 5 from Roberts and Inman; Chapter 6 from Karnes and Bean; Chapter 5 from Winebrenner and Brulles **Due: Generalizations, key words, and content outline**
Class 5	Designing lesson plans; instructional strategies *Readings*: Chapter 8 and Section IV from Karnes and Bean; Chapters 7 and 8 from Roberts and Inman **Due: Unit framework and learner objectives**
Class 6	Designing lesson plans; instructional strategies (continued) *Readings*: Chapter 8 and Section IV from Karnes and Bean; Chapters 7 and 8 from Roberts and Inman
Class 7	Designing assessments for the unit *Readings*: Chapters 4 and 10 from Roberts and Inman; Chapter 9 from Karnes and Bean; Chapter 8 from Winebrenner and Brulles **Due: Unit lesson plans**
Class 8	Designing a differentiated unit—managing the classroom environment *Readings*: Chapter 9 from Roberts and Inman; Chapter 7 from Karnes and Bean; Chapters 7 and 9 from Winebrenner and Brulles **Due: Assessments for the unit**
Class 9	Presentation of draft units **Due: Units**
Class 10	Unit feedback from instructors
Class 11	**Mini-test** Federal and state laws related to gifted and talented education *Readings:* Texas State Plan
Class 12	Discussion of current implementation of units and adaptations
Class 13	Reflections of unit and class **Due: Implemented units with student assessment data**

Grading Scale
    A = 176–190
    B = 158–175
    C = 139–157
    D = 120–138

FIGURE 4.4. Continued.

Requirements

I. **One mini-test on state rules and regulations (10 points).**

II. **Differentiated unit (will be modified based upon school requirements) with reflections and mentor/BU instructor observations (180 points).** *Be sure that you include for the lessons: student assessment data for each lesson, your adaptations of the lesson based on assessments, mentor/faculty supervisor observations, and reflections for each lesson.*

    a. *Planning for the unit* (10 points): Planning shows your understanding of the key philosophies, theories, models, and/or research and will be determined by your rationale and assignments that you turn in throughout the course.

    b. *Rationale for unit* (10 points): The rationale should show applications that have long-term relevance to the gifted learner, relate to standards, and differences in student characteristics, including the role of families and communities.

    c. *Theme or problem or issue* (5 points): The theme/problem/issue should be broad and allow for the integration of a variety of disciplines and student interests.

    d. *Generalizations* (10 points): Generalizations should be statements that are significant in giving meaning to different disciplines, may be proved or disproved, and include the theme as well as possibilities for interdisciplinary studies.

    e. *Content outline* (10 points): This outline includes key words (main headings), relates to the generalizations, and addresses the subject matter of the discipline(s) that will be addressed in the unit and includes main topics, subtopics, and independent study options. The subject matter provides for the full range of differences.

    f. *Overall framework of content, processes, and products* (30 points): This matrix includes the subject matter, the thinking skills (critical, creative, essential elements, research) that will be addressed during the unit, and possible products that the students will produce. The sequence is logical and relates to the content outline and generalizations.

    g. *Preassessment* (15 points): The preassessment identifies individual student performance on the unit objectives and shows how you adapted the framework and lessons.

    h. *Learner objectives and lesson plans* (45 points; see rubric).

    i. *Evaluation* (15 points): The assessments provide data that describes individual student progress on the unit objectives and determines the adaptation of lesson plans.

    j. *Management Plan* (30 points): The plan for implementation includes behavior management, materials organization, scheduling, room arrangement, and record keeping.

Differentiated Unit Rubric (180 points)

Characteristics (Standard)	Developing	Competent	Proficient
Planning (10 points)	*0–2 points*	*3–7 points*	*8–10 points*
(NAGC-CEC Standards #1, 1.1, 1.2; #6, 6.2; #7, 7.3) Based on foundational knowledge, plans a unit that considers	Planning does not consider key philosophies, theories, models, research, and issues and is partially consistent with developmental	Planning does not explicitly consider but is consistent with key philosophies, theories, models, research, and issues and is	Planning is explicitly based on key philosophies, theories, models, research, and issues with citations included in the

FIGURE 4.4. Continued.

Characteristics (Standard)	Developing	Competent	Proficient
developmental and individual differences of students with gifts and talents and collaborates to involve their families.	expectations for diverse learners. Families and cultural background are not considered.	consistent with developmental expectations for diverse learners. Families and cultural background are consulted.	planning section of the unit. It is designed with developmental expectations for diverse learners and includes culturally responsive communication and involvement with families.
Rationale for the Unit (10 points)	*0–2 points*	*3–7 points*	*8–10 points*
(NAGC-CEC Standards #1, 1.2; #3, 3.4; #4, 4.4) Based on the development and individual differences, modifies the curriculum and develops long- and short-range goals and objectives that considers the learning environment, families, and communities.	Relates to the grade level and state standards but not to the wide range of advanced knowledge and performance levels among students in the classroom.	Relates to standards, advanced knowledge and performance levels, and other student characteristics* and their development but focuses on short-term goals only.	Has goals that have long-term relevance to the learners, relates to standards, and differences in students' characteristics* and their development, including the role of the learning environment, families, and communities.
Theme/Problem/Issue (5 points)	*0–1 points*	*2–4 points*	*5 points*
(NAGC-CEC Standard #3, 3.1) Based on their understanding of the role of central concepts and cross-disciplinary skills, identifies a major theme, problem, or issue.	The unit is organized around a topic, not a central concept, theme, problem, or issue.	The central concept, theme, problem, or issue is driven by a single discipline and relates to a narrow range of student interests.	The central concept, theme, problem, or issue is broad, challenging, and allows for the integration of a variety of disciplines and student interests.
Generalizations (10 points)	*0–2 points*	*3–7 points*	*8–10 points*

FIGURE 4.4. Continued.

Characteristics (Standard)	Developing	Competent	Proficient
(NAGC-CEC Standard #3, 3.1) Based on their understanding of the structure of the discipline, identifies significant generalizations that provide opportunities for cross-disciplinary studies and skill development.	Statements give meaning to the topic, organize knowledge, and may be proved or disproved, but do not provide opportunities for interdisciplinary studies.	Statements are significant in giving meaning to one discipline; relate to the central concept, theme, problem, or issue; may be proved or disproved; organize knowledge, but do not provide opportunities for cross-disciplinary studies and skill development.	Statements are significant in giving meaning to different disciplines; may be proved or disproved; relate to the central concept, theme, problem, or issue; organize knowledge and provide opportunities for cross-disciplinary studies and skill development.
Content Outline (10 points)	*0–2 points*	*3–7 points*	*8–10 points*
(NAGC-CEC Standard #3, 3.1, 3.2) Based on their understanding of the structure of the discipline, constructs an outline with topics and subtopics that provides opportunities for creativity, acceleration, and depth and complexity.	The outline includes the topic and subtopics that will be addressed in the unit.	The outline includes main topics and subtopics and relates to the generalizations and subject matter of the discipline that will be addressed in the unit. The subject matter provides opportunities for creativity, acceleration, and depth and complexity.	The outline relates to the generalizations and addresses subject matter of the disciplines that will be addressed in the unit and includes main topics, subtopics, and independent study options. The subject matter provides opportunities for creativity, acceleration, and depth and complexity.
Framework (30 points)	*0–8 points*	*9–23 points*	*24–30 points*
(NAGC-CEC Standards #3, 3.1, 3.2; #5, 5.1) Based on their understanding of the discipline, develops a logical learning progression related to the	Includes a learning progression of the content, processes, and products that will be addressed in each lesson, but the logic is not clear. Lessons are not aligned with the	Includes a logical learning progression of lessons that enhance creative and critical thinking, problem solving, acceleration, depth, and complexity, but they do not relate to	Includes a logical learning progression of lessons that enhance creative and critical thinking, acceleration, problem solving, depth, and complexity and that relate to the

FIGURE 4.4. Continued.

Characteristics (Standard)	Developing	Competent	Proficient
content outline that enhances creative and critical thinking, acceleration, problem solving, depth, and complexity.	content outline and generalizations.	the content outline and generalizations.	content outline and generalizations.
Preassessment (15 points)	*0–4 points*	*5–11 points*	*12–15 points*
(NAGC–CEC Standards #3, 3.3; #4, 4.4) Uses preassessment results to adapt the framework for individual students' abilities and needs.	The unit is planned independent of knowledge about the students. Preassessment is not conducted or not used for the development and adaptation of the unit framework.	Preassessment identifies group performance on unit objectives with information used to plan the framework and small-group work. It does not consider an individual's abilities and needs.	Preassessment identifies individual student performance on unit objectives, and the individual's abilities and needs that determine the development and adaptation of the framework.
Learner Objectives and Lesson Plans (45 points)	*0–9 points*	*10–35 points*	*36–45 points*
See lesson plan rubric.	See lesson plan rubric.	See lesson plan rubric.	See lesson plan rubric.
Evaluations (15 points)	*0–4 points*	*5–11 points*	*12–15 points*
(NAGC–CEC Standard #4, 4.4) Uses assessment results to describe student progress and determine adaptations of lessons for individual students' abilities and needs.	Assessments are not implemented or not used to change or adapt lesson plans for subsequent days.	Assessments provide data indicating group's performance on unit's objectives with information used to adapt the lesson plans to meet abilities and needs of small groups.	Assessments provide data that describe individual student progress on unit objectives and determine the adaptation of lesson plans to meet abilities and needs of individuals within small and large groups.
Management Plan (30 points)	*0–8 points*	*9–23 points*	*24–30 points*
(NAGC–CEC Standards #2, 2.1)	The instructional management plan	The instructional management plan	Includes behavior management,

FIGURE 4.4. Continued.

Characteristics (Standard)	Developing	Competent	Proficient
Creates a safe, inclusive, culturally responsive environment that allows for differentiation.	creates a safe, inclusive, culturally responsive learning environment that attends to behavior management, materials organization, scheduling, room arrangement, and record keeping by the teacher only. The management plan does not show how the learner will be involved in assessing his or her own progress.	creates a safe, inclusive, culturally responsive learning environment that attends to behavior management, materials organization, scheduling, room arrangement, and student and teacher record keeping that creates a positive learning environment that respects cultural differences, but does not allow for differentiation of lessons within the unit.	materials organization, scheduling, room arrangement, and record keeping that creates a safe, inclusive, positive learning environment that respects cultural differences and allows for differentiation of lessons within the unit.
Total	**0–42 points**	**43–135 points**	**136–180 points**

* Note that student characteristics include cognitive, affective, aesthetic, social, and linguistic differences, as well as differences of culture, language, sexuality, socioeconomic status, gender, disability, and ethnicity.

Rubric for Lesson Plan (45 points)

Characteristic (Standard)	Developing	Competent	Proficient
Texas/National Standard (1 point)	*0 points*	*1 point*	*1 point*
(NAGC-CEC Standard #3) Uses knowledge of general curriculum to identify objective.	Lists number or statement. Does not relate to the objective.	Lists the number or statement. Relates to the objective.	Lists the number and the statement; relates to the objective.
Objective (5 points)	*0–1 points*	*2–4 points*	*5 points*
(NAGC-CEC Standard #3, 3.2, #5, 5.1) Describes content, process, and product that enhances creative and critical	Describes two of the components of the objective. Does not describe type of knowledge. Objective does not provide	Describes content, process, and product that relate to TEKS. Objective does provide opportunities that enhance creative and critical	Describes content, process, and product that relate to the TEKS and provides varied opportunities that enhance creative and

FIGURE 4.4. Continued.

Characteristic (Standard)	Developing	Competent	Proficient
thinking, problem solving, acceleration, depth, and complexity for individual students.	opportunities that enhance creative and critical thinking, problem solving, acceleration, depth and complexity	thinking, problem solving, acceleration, depth, and complexity. Type of knowledge is not described.	critical thinking, problem solving, acceleration, depth, and complexity for individual students. Type of knowledge (declarative, procedural, conditional) is challenging and identified.
Materials (4 points)	*0–1 points*	*2–3 points*	*4 points*
(NAGC-CEC Standard #3, 3.3) Selects and adapts materials and resources to address individual student differences.	Materials for students and teachers relate to the objective. Materials and resources are the same for all students.	Materials and resources for students and teachers relate to the objective and the student differences. The curriculum is adapted for groups of students.	Materials and resources for students and teachers are varied, relate to the objective, and can be differentiated to address individual student differences.
Procedure (5 points)	*0–1 points*	*2–4 points*	*5 points*
(NAGC-CEC Standards #5, 5.1) Uses procedures that are authentic, sequenced, and differentiated for advanced and typical students so that each student is challenged and has opportunities for independent research.	Is organized beginning with what is to be learned but does not have a closure. Is sequenced inductively or deductively. It does not use authentic methods and include higher level questions. Focus is primarily on activities, not teaching new knowledge.	Is organized for typical and advanced students so that each group is challenged at an appropriate level. It begins with what is to be learned and closes with a summary of what was learned. It is sequenced inductively or deductively and uses authentic methods. Uses some higher level questions. Uses examples, but not nonexamples to teach new knowledge.	Is organized for typical and advanced students so that individuals within each group are challenged at an appropriate level. It begins with what is to be learned and closes with a summary of what was learned. It is sequenced inductively or deductively and uses authentic methods that allow for independent research. Includes many higher level questions and examples/nonexamples to teach new knowledge.

FIGURE 4.4. Continued.

Characteristic (Standard)	Developing	Competent	Proficient
Differentiation (10 points)	*0–2 points*	*3–7 points*	*8–10 points*
(NAGC-CEC Standards #5, 5.1, 5.2) Using assessments, varies materials, including technologies, that consider abilities and multicultural backgrounds.	Variation occurs in materials used, but does not appear to be related to prior assessment. All groups use the same materials.	Is linked to prior assessment and paced according to student differences with some students exploring content in greater depth and other students acquiring the knowledge. No acceleration is noted. Variation also occurs in materials including technologies used with different students and/or groups and considers multicultural backgrounds.	Is linked to prior assessment with some students accelerating and exploring content in greater depth and other students acquiring the knowledge. Variation also occurs in materials including technologies used with different students and/or groups and considers multicultural backgrounds.
Assessments and Records (10 points)	*0–2 points*	*3–7 points*	*8–10 points*
(NAGC-CEC Standard #4, 4.4, 4.5) Using assessment results, develops long- and short-range goals and objectives that relate to students' progress records.	Teacher assessments are not related to all components of the objective. Records show grades but not specific characteristics.	Teacher assessments are related to all components of the objective and are used to develop long- and short-range goals and objectives. Characteristics are listed with related rubrics but are not observable behaviors. Records show the performance of the students on vague descriptors.	Teacher and student assessments are related to the objective and are used to develop long- and short-range goals and objectives. The content, process, and product characteristics are listed with related rubrics and are clearly observable behaviors. Records show the performance of the students using the assessments.
Reflection (10 points)	*0–2 points*	*3–7 points*	*8–10 points*

FIGURE 4.4. Continued.

Characteristic (Standard)	Developing	Competent	Proficient
(NAGC-CEC Standard #6, 6.4) Using reflections that accurately incorporate observations, identifies strengths and weaknesses in the lesson and ways to improve its effectiveness with students.	Identifies strengths and weaknesses of the instructor that accurately reflects observations.	Identifies strengths and weaknesses of the instructor that accurately reflect observations, and how the instructor will change future lessons. Reflection relates to previous feedback. While effect on the student is described, instructor's strengths and weaknesses are not clearly linked to student performance.	Describes the effect on the students, how the lesson might be changed to improve the effect on students, and what lessons need to be taught next. Based on effects on students, identifies strengths and weaknesses of the instructor that accurately reflect observations and how the instructor will change future lessons. Reflection relates to previous feedback.
Total	0–9 points	10–33 points	34–45 points

FIGURE 4.4. Continued.

Clinical Experiences in Gifted Education

Clinical experiences in gifted education are essential in making the connection between theory and practice, allowing for a demonstration of the relationship between the two. Each experience or collection of experiences should allow candidates to practice and exhibit aptitude and understanding of NAGC-CEC Teacher Preparation Standards in Gifted and Talented Education. These include learner development and individual learning differences, learning environments, curricular content knowledge, the use of assessment and data sources in making educational decisions about identification and student learning, instructional planning and strategies, professional learning and ethical practice, and collaboration.

Practica or clinical experiences need to represent a range of settings that candidates might encounter when working with students with gifts and talents. These necessitate working with diverse learners that not only exemplify different ethnicities, but also include varying socioeconomic strata and students with other exceptionalities. Candidates' ability to encounter students from diverse backgrounds should build on the discussions of diversity presented in course-work. For example, supporting culturally and linguistically different learners with gifts and talents may require curricular choices and/or activities that are culturally responsive, in addition to meeting the students' advanced readiness level or interests. Other considerations may include cultural mores while inter-acting with parents and/or caregivers and the need for certain documents to be sent home in more than one language.

Various learning environments most often include university-offered Saturday or weekend programs, summer camps, or school-based services for students with gifts and talents. Multiple placements can be embedded in sev-eral different courses or in one course depending on the nature of the course, the scope of the activities assigned, and the length of the clinical experience. Strategically connecting candidates with quality experiences is as important as the type.

Regardless of the type of experience, reflective practice must be incorpo-rated as part of the practicum. The university supervisor or an instructor should facilitate discussions situated in the standards with candidates in the practicum as to the strengths and challenges of the experience. These discussions can also include artifacts from the practicum, creating a purposeful connection from the academic and theoretical to the work done in the practitioner setting. These discussions can take place at the experience site, at the university campus, or in an online discussion board. All experiences should incorporate preassess-ment data that captures where students are before the experiences begin so that the activities and products and/or assessments during the camp, Saturday program, or school-based service can be differentiated based on readiness level. Summer camps and Saturday programming will most likely already be differ-entiated according to interest, based on the students signing up for the course. These environments should also offer candidates the opportunity to observe each other. A formal observation by the course instructor should be conducted as part of the assessment protocol to determine if a candidate has met a previ-ously agreed upon level of proficiency delineated by criteria outlined in a rubric that are based on the teacher preparation standards. After the observation, the course instructor and candidate should reflect on the observation with the rubric as a common reference point of understanding.

Example of clinical experiences might include the following:

* *Summer camps/programming*: University-based summer programs for students with gifts and talents can provide candidates with an inten-sive experience working with groups of gifted children in an interest area of their choosing.

* *Saturday programming*: A number of universities host Saturday pro-gramming for students with gifts and talents on a variety of topics or

interest areas. These courses are typically taught by teachers with previous training and experience in gifted education. Depending on the objective of the clinical experience, the candidate may be paired with the veteran teacher or may plan and teach the class on his or her own. As this type of programming may only cover one Saturday, it will not likely be long enough for a student to present a proficient understanding and practice of the compendium of standards.

❋ *School-based programming*: School-based programs may offer the most varied types of clinical experiences for candidates. These experiences must take into consideration school schedules including testing dates, school holidays, shortened schedules, etc. Depending on the grade level or subject, the school may offer pull-out or self-contained classes, AP courses, dual-enrollment, or designated subject-specific courses for the students with gifts and talents.

A capstone or summative assessment of the clinical experience(s) could include a portfolio of the candidate's work over the course of the placement. Items for the portfolio might include observations of students with gifts and talents during the experience while they are at free time or at lunch, videos of the candidate teaching, lesson plans indicating differentiated instruction, student work samples, feedback from observation made by the instructor, and candidate reflections of his or her teaching.

Clinical experiences are an important part of the series of courses in preparing teachers to work with students with gifts and talents. Preparing and working with students with gifts and talents allows the theoretical and academic knowledge to be applied in settings where feedback can be provided to help the candidates refine their practice with students with gifts and talents.

Online Learning Options in Gifted Education

The past decade has witnessed an exponential growth in online learning, with 7.1 million students currently enrolling in at least one course online (Allen & Seaman, 2014). Online courses are defined as those where 80% or more of the content is delivered online. There are also web-facilitated courses and blended/hybrid courses that incorporate web technology with traditional face-to-face course meetings (Allen & Seaman, 2014). Gifted education has been part of this online learning revolution with numerous institutions offering certificate, endorsement, or entire master's degree programs using web technology to facilitate learning. In preparing to move a course online or revising an already existing online course the following best practices based on the Checklist for Online Interactive Learning (COIL; Hanover Research Council, 2009) are offered as reflective tools to help improve the experience for both instructor and student (see Figure 4.5).

Regardless of the delivery method, the development of new or the revision of existing online courses should maintain alignment to the new NAGC-CEC Teacher Preparation Standards in Gifted and Talented Education, as shown in the syllabus in Figure 4.6. The quality of the individual courses and of the preparation program in gifted education is more likely to be maintained when highly qualified university faculty use the standards to develop them.

Summary

The NAGC-CEC standards provide university faculty the foundations from which to build course content and assessment activities. The standards themselves are derived from empirical evidence, which supports their use and implementation in gifted education coursework. The standards are flexible enough to build in the reading and content that best suits the needs of candidates in a particular region or institution. The standards can be used in both undergraduate and graduate contexts and in face-to-face and online environments. This is especially important as a significant number of gifted education programs offer a portion or all of their coursework online. Finally, the exemplar assessments engage candidates and the coordinating rubrics aid in capturing candidate performance.

Standards are the underpinnings of gifted education programs in higher education. The syllabi, assessments, and rubrics included in this chapter are another tool in helping maintain and build these programs, offered to help overlay content that best meets the needs of the particular students in your institution or region.

✓	COIL Categories
	Category 1: Student Behaviors Meet Criterion
	Demonstrate their prerequisite technology skills at beginning are adequate for hardware, software, and website use.
	Seek opportunities to, and support for, interacting with instructor and other students.
	Actively participate in all online activities.
	Actively involved through writing and interaction in web-based courses (improves student writing performance).
	Use a variety of communication techniques to enhance online learning.
	Personalize themselves by publishing online biographies and photographs to allow other members of the class to visualize them.
	Seek assistance in understanding and mastering different learning strategies.
	Demonstrate prerequisites and become more proficient in technology communication skills.
	Category 2: Faculty-Student Interactions
	Provide clear and adequate guidance.
	Use action research regularly to evaluate the success/failure of the course and meet student concerns.
	Personalize communications by/with student-student and student-teacher.
	Use variety of communication techniques to provide for greater empathy and personal approach than e-mail and website alone.
	Plan for increased time for student interactions as compared to traditional courses.
	Clearly delineate institutional policy on cheating and plagiarism at start of course.
	Maintain separate e-mail account for web courses.
	Forward responses to frequently asked questions to all students to avoid duplication.
	Give faculty reduced load and increased support to develop course materials.
	Provide students with continuous, frequent support, and feedback.
	Scaffold virtual discourse construction.
	Emphasize importance of good study skills throughout course.
	Closely monitor each student's progress.
	Create opportunities to coach and facilitate student construction of knowledge.
	Give negative comments to students privately, preferably by phone.
	Clearly delineate course requirements.
	Category 3: Technology Support
	Ensure a low level of technological difficulties in accessing website and communication.
	Provide adequate, friendly, easy, continuous technical support.

FIGURE 4.5. Checklist for Online Interactive Learning (COIL).

✓	COIL Categories
	Category 4: Learning Environment
	Use structured activities to provide an effective framework for online learning.
	Mandate smaller class size for online courses to give faculty appropriate time to deliver quality instruction board.
	Use flexible deadlines to motivate students, maintain communication, and allow for technical problems.
	Create social interaction through group collaboration to facilitate high achievement.
	Use streaming audio for reading online.
	Present course content in a manner that hierarchically structures the sequence of information.
	Organize website to enable student to interact with the content, other students, and instructor.
	Create a welcoming, safe, nurturing online environment.
	Present problem-solving situations in realistic context.
	Provide opportunities for students to question instructor to ensure accuracy of understanding.
	Create opportunities for students to communicate with each other to share understanding of course content.
	Provide opportunities to construct knowledge collaboratively based on multiple perspectives, discussion, and reflection.
	Provide opportunities for students to articulate and revise their thinking to ensure accuracy of knowledge construction.
	Ensure an equitable learning environment exists for all.
	Allow time for reflection at the end of the course.
	Include "warm-up" period with lighthearted exercises aimed to help students get to know one another.
	Ensure an equitable environment exists for gender differences in learning styles, reduction of barriers to participation, and communication.
	Start online course with all students together at the same time.
	Provide equal access to the shared conversation in the course.
	Provide discussion forums encouraging open and honest dialogue.
	Use computer conferencing to develop overall critical thinking skills.

FIGURE 4.5. Continued.

Online Course Syllabus[1]
Creative Behavior

Course Description

Nature and analysis of creative behavior; appraisal and implementation of specific processes designed to encourage creative productivity.

Course Goals and Objectives

The purpose of this course is to provide you with an opportunity to investigate selected factors related to the nature of the creative process and the procedures used to develop creativity in a wide variety of learning situations. The course will deal with both theoretical and empirical analyses of creativity, as well as practical applications of theories and research in multicultural instructional settings. Consideration of creativity within the field of gifted education will be a major focus.

Students will:

- Develop a knowledge and awareness of the nature of creative behavior and specific research relating to it.
- Utilize and interpret measures of divergent production.
- Examine and plan lessons utilizing techniques of developing creativity.
- Develop a product that represents a creative contribution to the theory of creative behavior and/or the practice of creativity assessment or training.

Required Course Texts

Beghetto, R. A., & Kaufman, J. C. (Eds.). *Nurturing creativity in the classroom.* New York, NY: Cambridge University Press.

Gardner, H. (1993). *Creating minds.* New York, NY: Basic Books.

American Psychological Association. (2009). *Publication manual of the American Psychological Association* (6th ed.). Washington, DC: Author.

Taking the tutorial for the APA Style Guide is **strongly** encouraged. It can be can be found at http://flash1r.apa.org/apastyle/basics/index.htm

We will also be using Turnitin to submit several of the assignments (Turnitin assignments will be submitted in through the Moodle platform). For more information about Turnitin see http://turnitin.com/en_us/training/student-training.

Other selected readings and videos are posted to Moodle. Some articles are provided. Citations are provided in other cases, and you will have to find the article on your own.

Course Requirements and Evaluation

Class Participation

As this is a graduate-level class, it is expected that you will actively participate in class discussions with thoughtful commentary on class readings and your fellow classmates' points of view.

---

1   Course adapted from Rita Culross, Louisiana State University, & Michael S. Matthews, University of North Carolina, Charlotte.

FIGURE 4.6. Online course on creative behavior syllabus.

As our class meetings will be in an online format, you will be expected to respond to discussion questions posted on Moodle based on readings, videos, etc., for the week's topic. Your formal posts should be approximately 400–600 words in length. This means they generally should not be longer than 2 pages, double-spaced, font size 12, if composed in Microsoft Word. They should not be much shorter than a page and a half. I recommend that you compose essays using MS Word or another word processor, edit and revise as needed, check your work for length and spelling/grammar, and then copy and paste your work into the discussion board dialogue box. One nice feature of Word is that it automatically provides a word count at the bottom of the page. By composing in a word processor before posting your work, you will be able to keep the document on file in case you need to draw upon it later, and you also will be less likely to lose your work if your Internet connection or Moodle are interrupted while you are typing. Please post responses as text (copy and paste from your Word file into the text window) rather than an attached file.

Your responses to your classmates will also be considered in determining the class participation of the course grade. Points will be awarded, taking into account your post's thoroughness and grammatical correctness, as well as your use of references to support your statements; points will also reflect the quality of your responses to your classmates, and whether you have kept up with the thread of comments. Posts are formal in nature and should be written as such. Instructor comments (on selected topics) sometimes will be posted. Not all posts will receive specific feedback, but some will. You will also be required to respond to at least two other posts by your classmates (250 words each). Posts are due each Wednesday when there is an assigned topic (by 4:30 p.m.). Responses are due by the Friday of that same week by 4:30 p.m. **(52 points/2 points per original post and 1 point per response to classmates)**

Lesson Plans

Develop a set of lesson plans for encouraging creative behavior in the classroom. The plans should encompass one week's instruction. Include in your plans the student objectives, a description of the learners, a list of any curriculum materials to be used, instructional strategies, and an evaluation component with rubric. Feel free to employ the lesson plan format used in your current teaching assignment. Integrating the lessons within an existing subject, such as social studies, is encouraged. (Rubric posted to Moodle.) **(25 points)**

Creative Project

Create your own project! Your creative product can take any form you would like; you are encouraged to explore a variety of formats and media. The essential characteristic is that the project must be original on your part—unique in the sense that it consists of material you have not produced prior to enrollment in this course. In addition to your project, please submit a write-up that includes a description of your creative project, how its creation contributed to your understanding of creativity, and the creative persons studied. (Rubric posted to Moodle.) Separately, you will need to post a picture(s), video, link, etc., of your project and 250-word description of your project to Moodle as a forum post to share with your classmates. **(25 points)**

Lifespan Creativity Paper

See direction posted to Moodle. **(25 points)**

FIGURE 4.6. Continued.

Midterm Exam

The midterm will be essay in nature and is designed to demonstrate synthesis of the readings and class information. It will cover the topics prior to the midterm. **(25 points)**

Final Exam

The final will be given according to the date and time on the final exam schedule. The exam will be essay in nature and is designed to demonstrate synthesis of the topics covered since the midterm. **(25 points)**

Grading Scale

93%–100% = A
83%–92% = B
78%–82% = C
69%–77% = D
0%–68% = F

Course Information

Assignments

All course assignments will be turned in on Moodle.

There are written assignments throughout the semester. It is important that you are able to critically reflect and convey your ideas in writing. All assignments submitted should be typed (using Times or Times New Roman 12 pt. font), double-spaced, pages consecutively numbered, and where appropriate follow APA (6th ed.) style guidelines. Assignments not following any of these guidelines will be returned and asked to be redone with a grade reduction of 20%.

If you believe a grading error has occurred, you may request a re-grade in writing within one week of the grade being posted on Moodle. For assignments due the last week of classes, re-grades must be requested by 4:30 p.m. on the Friday of exam week. A re-grade may result in a lower grade.

Technology

Technological challenges are a part of the modern era, but are not a suitable excuse for late or missing assignments. At the beginning of the term you should identify an alternate computer and alternate source of Internet access (a public library, for example) in case you experience technical difficulties with your home computer or Internet service provider. You also should make regularly scheduled electronic backups of your completed work and your work in progress. Late work due to computer difficulties will only be accepted in cases when the problems are due to the university's servers or Moodle being down. If this happens, I will e-mail a note to everyone or post an announcement in Moodle extending the due date as appropriate.

I expect you to read your university e-mail account and respond using your university e-mail account. I will not send e-mail to alternative e-mail addresses. There have been issues with e-mails not being received or sent to junk mail folders when using nonuniversity addresses. I will try to respond to your e-mail with in 24 hours. When you e-mail a classmate, or me please be sure to include the course number or name in the subject line of your message. It is

FIGURE 4.6. Continued.

important to follow good practice in your e-mail communications by including a salutation, as well as a signature line (first and last name at minimum).

Our means of communication will be via e-mail and discussion forum posts within the Moodle platform. Other features such as online chats may also be utilized as needed. Please become familiar with the various components of this platform. You must have a reliable computer and Internet service; high-speed access such as provided via a dedicated cable modem or fiber optic link is strongly recommended.

Time Issues

Successful completion of online classes will require the same time commitment as face-to-face classes: approximately twice as much time away from class as in class ought to be spent. Consequently, as a 3-credit course, you should plan for this class to occupy a *minimum* of 10 hours of your time each and every week during the fall semester session. One-third of these hours come from the time the class would meet, which in this case represent the time you will spend reading and responding to posts by your classmates and instructor. *You should read all discussion posts and follow-up message posts unless instructed otherwise.* The remaining two-thirds of these hours will involve the work you do on your own to prepare for class, including completing course readings, composing your own postings, and working on long-range course projects such as the lifespan paper. Some weeks will make different demands upon you, and you will find that more or fewer hours are needed. But please, arrange your schedule so that you will have sufficient time to complete the requirements for this class. If you must travel while class is in session, please be sure you have planned for the time and Internet access you will need in order to keep up in class. One thing that does happen to some online learners—especially in their first online class—is they lose track of the time and the nature of the work and fall behind. Please don't let that happen to you, as it can be difficult, if not impossible, to recover once you have fallen behind.

Course Schedule

	Topic	Readings/Assignments Due
Week 1	Overview	Read Syllabus/Moodle Post
Week 2	Definitions of Creativity Pt. 1 NAGC-CEC #1 and #4	NCC Ch. 3 and Moodle Readings/ Moodle Post
Week 3	Definitions of Creativity Pt. 2 NAGC-CEC #1 and #4	CM Ch. 1 and 2 Moodle Readings/ Moodle Post
Week 4	Teaching Creativity NAGC-CEC #3 and #5	NCC Ch. 1 and 2/Moodle Readings/ Moodle Post
Week 5	Teaching Creative Thinking vs. Teaching Creatively NAGC-CEC #2 and #5	NCC Ch. 8 and 9/Moodle Readings/ Moodle Post
Week 6	Motivation and Creativity NAGC-CEC #2	NCC Ch. 16/Moodle Readings/ Moodle Post Creative Lesson Plans Due
Week 7	Midterm Exam	Mid-Term Due

FIGURE 4.6. Continued.

	Topic	Readings/Assignments Due
Week 8	Creativity Assessment NAGC-CEC #8	NCC Ch. 12/Moodle Readings/ Moodle Post
Week 9	Creative People NAGC-CEC #1	CM Ch. 5, 6, and 7/Moodle Readings/Moodle Post
Week 10	Creative People Pt. II NAGC-CEC #1	CM Ch. 3, 4, and 9/Moodle Readings/Moodle Post
Week 11	Creative Project Due	Creative Project Due/Moodle Post
Week 12	Technology and Creativity NAGC-CEC #2 and #5	Moodle Readings/Moodle Post
Week 13	Creativity in the Workplace NAGC-CEC #7	Moodle Readings/Moodle Post Lifespan Creativity Paper Due
Week 14	Thanksgiving Holiday	No Class
Week 15	Creativity & Talent Development NAGC-CEC #1, #2, and #8	Moodle Reading/Moodle Post
Week 16	Final Exam	Final Exam Due

Note. With respect to the readings, NCC = Beghetto and Kaufman book and CM = Gardner book.

Rubric for Creative Lesson Plan

	Exceeds Expectation	Meets Expectations	Below Expectations
Instructional Planning (7 points)	*6–7 points*	*3–5 points*	*0–2 points*
NAGC-CEC #3, 3.1, 3.2, 3.4; #5, 5.2	Includes CCSS and ISTE technology standards that apply appropriate technologies to support instructional assessment, planning, and delivery that are pertinent to content and skills covered in the lesson. Provides objectives that use knowledge of general and specialized curricula to advance learning for individuals with gifts and talents including critical/creative thinking; provides opportunities for acceleration, independent study, problem solving, and content mastery as indicated by preassessment data.	Includes CCSS and ISTE technology standards that are consistent to content and skills covered in the lesson. Provides objectives that address critical/creative thinking and content mastery as indicated by preassessment data.	Includes two CCSS and/or ISTE technology standards. Provides objectives that address critical/creative thinking and content mastery, but are not based on preassessment data.

FIGURE 4.6. Continued.

	Exceeds Expectation	Meets Expectations	Below Expectations
Learner Characteristics (4 points)	*4 points*	*2–3 points*	*0–1 points*
NAGC-CEC # 1, 1.1, 1.2; #2, 2.1	Learner characteristics are described and incorporated taking into consideration how language culture, economic status, family background, and/or disability can influence the learning of individuals with gifts and talents. Special consideration is given for safe, inclusive and culturally responsive learning environments.	Learner characteristics are not described but are incorporated into the development of the lesson. Special consideration for diversity is only considered in the area of culture.	Learner characteristics are not described or incorporated into the development of the lesson. Special consideration for diversity is not considered.
Instructional Strategies (10 points)	*8–10 points*	*3–7 points*	*0–2 points*
NAGC-CEC #3, 3.3, #4, 4.2, and #5, 5.1	Differentiation strategies are based on preassessments to guide educational decisions in order to select, adapt, and create materials, including a repertoire of instructional strategies to enhance the learning of critical and creative thinking, problem-solving, and performance skills of individuals with gifts and talents.	Differentiation strategies based on preassessments are used, include two of the following—critical thinking, high-level questioning strategies, inquiry learning, creative thinking, and/or independent learning.	Differentiation strategies are not based on preassessments, and do not include critical, high-level questioning strategies, inquiry learning, creative thinking, and/or independent learning and are the same for all learners.
Personal Reflection (4 points)	*4 points*	*2–3 points*	*0–1 points*
NAGC-CEC #6, 6.4	Modifications are consistently made based on reflection and self-evaluation and professionals are aware of their own learning needs.	Modifications are not consistently made based on reflection and self-evaluation.	No modifications are made and reflection and self-evaluation is not employed.

FIGURE 4.6. Continued.

CHAPTER 5

PREPARATION OF THE SPECIALIZED PROFESSIONAL ASSOCIATION (SPA) REPORT FOR NATIONAL RECOGNITION

SUSAN K. JOHNSEN, JOYCE VANTASSEL-BASKA, AND JANE CLARENBACH

Introduction

This chapter is intended to assist faculty in preparing a specialized professional association (SPA) report in gifted education that will be submitted to the Council for the Accreditation of Teacher Preparation (CAEP). It will describe some of the central issues that faculty will encounter in the preparation of the report with respect to selecting and aligning assessments and reporting assessment results. Examples of real data findings and how they might be represented in the report are included where appropriate.

The CAEP national accreditation process for institutions of higher educa-tion (and others) that prepare teachers includes a review of individual specialty area teacher preparation programs, such as mathematics, early education, spe-cial education, and gifted education. Based on agreements between states and CAEP, programs provide evidence through data derived from 6–8 key assess-ments that demonstrate how their teacher candidates have mastered the spe-cialty area standards, as detailed (in the case of gifted education) in 7 standards made up of 28 individual elements. The program report as a whole is designed to focus faculty on using the data for program improvement. Programs that successfully demonstrate candidate mastery of the standards are awarded national recognition status. (Details regarding how national recognition status is awarded may be found in Appendix E.)

The specific details of submitting program reports are determined by CAEP. However, what follows is guidance for programs that are submitting reports for review in gifted education, including examples for writing Sections II and III of the program report, the selection of assessments and their rela-tionship to the gifted education teacher preparation standards; and Section IV, a description of the assessment and its alignment to the standards' elements. This chapter also addresses strategies for developing rubrics, as well as report-ing and interpreting the assessment results.

A team approach may be useful in constructing needed assessments. Although some assessment tools already exist that are useful for this task (see Appendix F), program coordinators may want to construct their own and establish the validity and reliability of the scales. A team approach may make that task easier, both through collaboration in the piloting of the instruments, as well as their initial design. Certainly a group discussion of the assessments selected and their administration and interpretation should be conducted across all faculty, including adjunct faculty who are often the frontline teachers of these courses.

Process for Report Preparation

The process of preparing the report involves the collection of program data and corresponding assessment data across two applications (i.e., administra-tions of an assessment) for initial submissions and one application for revised report submissions. Although it is necessary to select key assessments to illus-trate candidate competencies, the choice of assessments must be made carefully and include different types of data to make a convincing case. For example, the following types of data may be most effectively employed to demonstrate competency in the areas of the gifted education standards.

Portfolios

Using portfolios, candidates are able to show their self-efficacy in understanding the standards' elements by providing written evidence such as exemplary lesson plans, program plans, and reflection journals. The collection of these artifacts is useful when candidates' reflections about their work indicate their understanding of their growth in specific knowledge and skill areas.

Pre-Post Assessments of Content Learning

This form of assessment documentation provides a growth model that allows reviewers to see actual gains made by candidates on relevant content. Pre- and postmeasures related to the nature and needs of gifted learners in psychological and academic areas are one dimension of the standards that might be addressed in this way. Instructor-developed assessments or textbook-based assessments might be used for this purpose.

Products for Use in Classrooms

Taken individually, products that constitute a significant aspect of work with gifted learners may be excellent indicators of competency within key domains of the standards such as a curriculum unit that demonstrates competency in curriculum planning and delivery. A curriculum unit that is carefully laid out, using standard design principles (i.e., goals, outcomes, activities, resources, assessments) that are differentiated for gifted students provides a convincing artifact in the area of planning. Resulting pre- and postassessment data might then be collected in the classroom to see the unit's effects on Pre-K–12 gifted students.

Aligning Assessments to Gifted Education Standards

The selected assessments, taken as a whole, must demonstrate the candidate's mastery of each of the seven NAGC-CEC Teacher Preparation Standards. In completing Section II of the program report, faculty need to list the assessment that will be used for each of the following areas and when it is administered (end of licensure courses; during practicum, upon completing internship, junior or senior year, etc.):

1. *Licensure Test*: If the state requires a licensure test for gifted education (e.g., Praxis 5358), the pass rate for the program's candidates must be reported. For national program recognition, CAEP requires that *80% of program completers* receive a passing score on the required licensure exam. If there is no required license test, some form of content knowledge assessment substitutes for this key assessment.

2. *Content Knowledge*: Content knowledge assessments (other than the licensure test) such as gifted education comprehensive exams and portfolios that demonstrate the content knowledge of gifted education found in the teacher preparation standards for gifted education.

3. *Candidate's Ability to Plan*: This is demonstrated in assessments such as lessons and unit plans, Individualized Educational Plans, and student learning profiles.

4. *Field or Clinical Assessment*: This could include student teaching, an internship, or a practicum assessment. It could be assessed in ways such as classroom observations or videos of classroom teaching, using a structured observation guide that is completed by the candidate and the supervisor.

5. *Candidate Effect on Student Learning*: This includes case studies, teacher work samples, pre-post learning assessments, Functional Behavior Assessment, and student portfolios.

6. *Another Required Assessment*: This could be program evaluations, action research projects, reflection papers, and critiques of classroom practice or student work.

7. (and 8.) *Optional Assessments*: Although not required, other assessments may be added depending on the need for addressing the candidate's mastery of each of the seven NAGC-CEC Teacher Preparation Standards.

To complete Section III of the program report, these assessments then need to be aligned to the specific standards and to the elements in each (see Table 5.1).

In Table 5.1, each of the assessments addresses two or more standards but no more than four with the exception of the licensure test in gifted education, which has multiple sections to assess the content knowledge in each of the standards. Generally, assessments that attempt to address a great number of standards are too broad to address the individual standard knowledge and skill elements and typically are not useful in determining candidates' strengths and

Table 5.1

Alignment of Assessments to Standards

Standard	Assessment							
	1 Licensure Test	2 Content Exam	3 Products Such as Unit With Lesson Plans	4 Classroom Observation	5 Case Study	6 Assessment Evidence of Student Learning	7 Action Research	8 Portfolio
1. Learner Development and Individual Differences	✓	✓	✓				✓	
2. Learning Environments		✓		✓		✓	✓	
3. Curricular Content Knowledge	✓	✓	✓		✓	✓		✓
4. Assessment	✓	✓	✓		✓	✓		✓
5. Instructional Planning and Strategies		✓	✓	✓		✓	✓	✓
6. Professional Learning and Ethical Practice	✓	✓						
7. Collaboration					✓		✓	

needs. At the same time, the same assessment, if it is comprehensive enough, may be used for at least two or more standards. For example, an action research project may address learner development and individual differences (Standard 1), learning environments (Standard 2), instructional planning (Standard 5), and collaboration (Standard 7) by the candidate's collaboration with coteachers and parents in improving a student's performance in the classroom.

Issues of Concern With Some Assessments

The following issues of concern need to be considered when choosing assessments:

1. The assessment format does not align to the type of required assessment. For example, a paper/pencil test will not be appropriate for determining observable performances in the classroom. It is important to select assessments that truly reflect the desired learning of candidates.

2. The assessments are aligned to standards from the state or from InTASC, not the NAGC-CEC standards. It is critical that the current governing standards for a given SPA are the basis for assessment choices. For many institutions, new or revised standards will require alterations from earlier work.

3. The alignment is made to the overall standard and not to the specific elements of the standards. Addressing elements results in assessments that are aligned clearly to the vocabulary of the specific standards and to the comprehensive intent of that standard as well.

4. The assessment is too broad, attempting to assess too many standard elements. For example, a practicum observation form may include several delivery approaches but results often focus only on a few. It is critical that faculty develop a strategy to ensure that all core strategies named in the standard are specifically addressed in the assessment.

5. The assessments are used from courses that are not required for all candidates in the program. Elective courses or special seminars on topics of interest may not be used as evidence of candidate mastery even though they may enrich the program of studies at a given institution.

6. Assessments for which course grades are submitted do not include all of the components required by CAEP: the grading policies used by the institution or program, the minimum expectation for candidate grades, a brief description of the courses, a description of how the course aligns with specific SPA standards, a rationale for the selection of this particular set of courses as evidence of meeting the standards, and an analysis of grade data.

7. Candidate self-assessments must include a component where results are reviewed and discussed with the faculty or supervising teacher. Although candidate and peer reflections are useful, they lack objectivity and are not suitable for evaluating proficiency levels in the absence of a supervisor's commentary on the reflection.

8. Candidates should not have a choice of the components within an assessment. If candidates have choices, it is not possible to determine whether all of the candidates have met the same standards. For example, candidates must respond to all questions on a comprehensive exam. Choices on essay exams must also be avoided. Although choice represents best practice in the field, it interferes with the comprehensive assessment coverage needed for the SPA report.

In summary, faculty need to identify 6–8 key and distinct assessments that relate to content and pedagogical knowledge. The assessment formats need to fulfill a required area and need to focus on all of the specific standards' elements. In Section IV, each of the assessments needs to be discussed further to provide evidence for meeting the standards: a brief description of the assessment and its scoring guide, the current validity and reliability data about the assessment, and an analysis and interpretation of the data.

Writing Descriptions of Assessments

The narrative about each assessment (Section IV) should include the context (i.e., when and where and with whom the data are collected), a description of the assessment and its relationship to the standards, and how the assessment is used (see the case study assessment example below).

Case Study Assessment

During the final course, all candidates are required to select a gifted student who is also at-risk (e.g., lower income, special education, ethnic minority, underachiever, female with science/math interest). The classroom setting may be in a resource room for gifted students or in the general education classroom with a cluster of gifted students. Once they have selected the student, they acquire parent permission and then collect data. They identify and describe the assessments they will use, summarizing technical information that will influence the interpretation of the assessment (see Standard Element

4.1). Data include both quantitative (formal, see Standard Element 4.1) and qualitative (informal, see Standard Elements 4.1 and 4.3) assessments. In collecting the informal assessment data, they need to collect information from multiple sources (see Standard Elements 4.1 and 7.3) and in multiple settings (see Standard Element 7.3) during the instructional process to minimize bias (see Standard Element 4.3) and build opportunities for collaboration (see Standard Elements 4.3 and 7.3). Part of the informal data collected includes a dynamic assessment where the candidates reflect on the student's response to a set of six lessons that are differentiated for the student (see Standard Element 3.3). Following the data collection, the candidates summarize and interpret the results, making recommendations for services (see Standard Element 4.2). These recommendations are shared with the student's parent, teachers, other supportive personnel, and the student himself or herself (see Standard Elements 4.4 and 4.5). Together they collaborate in developing an individual plan that outlines short- and long-term goals (see Standard Elements 7.1 and 7.3). This case study builds on the candidates' previous knowledge about assessments used for identification, differentiating lessons, and collaboration. The product is used to determine the candidates' ability to synthesize and interpret data, collaborate, and make decisions about services for a gifted student who is also identified as at risk.

From this description of a case study assessment, the reviewer understands the context (i.e., during the final course in the program, the data are collected in a classroom with a student who may be at risk), the components of the assessment and each one's relationship to standard element(s), and how the information is used regarding the candidates' strengths and needs.

Issues of Concern With Some Assessment Descriptions

The following issues of concern need to be considered when writing descriptions of assessments:

1. The narrative does not include a description of the assessment and its alignment to the standards, the context, and/or its use in examining the candidate's strengths and needs.
2. The description does not clearly describe what the candidate is expected to do. For example, the narrative might state simply, "the candidates are required to do a case study in their final course."
3. The narrative does not include a description of how the assessment is aligned to the standards and the standards' elements. For example, "the

candidates review tests that are in the student's cumulative folder" does not describe the types of tests or how the candidate uses knowledge of measurement principles to interpret the tests.

In summary, the assessment needs to be described clearly so that the reviewer understands its distinctiveness, how it contributes to the program and relates to the standards, and how it will be used to examine each candidate's strengths and needs in making overall program improvements.

Developing Rubrics and a Scoring Guide

The program report requires that the rubrics used for each key assessment be submitted for review along with a scoring guide. Rubrics are a tool for communicating clear performance or product expectations by listing the essential criteria and describing performance at each level in relation to each of these criteria. Rubrics provide the teacher candidates with information about how they performed and what they need to do to be successful. The benefit of rubrics is that they are able to assess multidimensional and complex performances and products. They also can be used formatively to show baseline application of knowledge and a candidate's growth toward mastering particular standard(s) or element(s). In this way, candidates know how to improve their performances or products. As a summative tool, they also can be used to identify the overall strengths and weaknesses of a course or overall program and help instructors make changes to improve candidates' application of content and pedagogical knowledge. In developing the criteria for the rubric, instructors need to identify the essential criteria of the performance or product, how they are aligned to the assessment and standard elements, and specific observable performance levels for each criterion.

Once the criteria are identified for each performance level, instructors then develop a scoring guide, deciding how many points will be assigned to each criterion and at each level. In this way, the rubric along with its guide provides consistency so that products and performances are scored fairly and equitably. It is useful if the rubric can be piloted on selected artifacts to adjust the descriptions and scoring assignments as needed. Grades can then be assigned based on the number of available points given.

Identifying Major Components and Criteria for the Performances or Products

In identifying the major components and essential criteria, instructors need to consider what they would like the candidates to exhibit in their final products or performances. These will vary depending on the type and format of assessment. For example, the components and criteria for a program evaluation—a product—would be different from the components and criteria for a classroom observation—a teaching performance. In the former case, the components of the written product, which might address elements in Standards 6 (Professional Learning and Ethical Practice) and 7 (Collaboration), might include criteria for an ideal program and compare this ideal program with the candidate's school's program goals and objectives, identification, curriculum, teacher qualifications, program design, and program management. On the other hand, the components and criteria for a classroom observation, which might address elements in Standards 2 (Learning Environments) and 5 (Instructional Planning and Strategies), might include curriculum planning and delivery; accommodations for individual differences; strategies for problem solving, critical thinking, creative thinking, and research; and student engagement (see VanTassel-Baska & Little, 2003).

Aligning Criteria to Standard Elements

Once the major components and criteria are identified for each of the assessments, the criteria need to be elaborated so that each relates to the most essential aspects of the standards' elements. For example, criteria related to developing a differentiated lesson plan to assess the candidate's pedagogical knowledge in planning classroom instruction (i.e., required for Assessment #3), might include their use of assessments and instructional strategies that enhance critical and creative thinking and problem-solving skills, because these are parts of the elements for Standards 4 (Assessment) and 5 (Instructional Planning and Strategies). Note that although the format of the lesson plan and its organization may also be important to the instructor, these criteria would be peripheral and should either be included in another part of the course syllabus or given a much lower weight when compared to the criteria related to the standard elements. Teacher candidate performance on the peripheral qualities of general classroom criteria may not be used as evidence of meeting the standards for differentiation in a classroom where students with gifts and talents are the focus of the intervention.

In the case study example below (see Table 5.2), the components address "assessment for identification and services" (see Standard Elements 4.1 and 7.3), "collaboration" (see Standard Elements 4.3, 7.1, and 7.3), "curricular con-

Table 5.2
Case Study Rubric Example[1]

Select a student who has gifts and talents and is also identified as exceptional and/or at-risk (e.g., twice exceptional, gifted student from low income background, etc.)

The beginning gifted education professional . . .	Developing	Competent	Proficient
Formal Assessment for Identification and Services (10 points)	*0–3 points*	*4–7 points*	*8–10 points*
Selects and uses quantitative (formal) assessments that minimize bias to identify students for gifted programs and services (NAGC/CEC Standard #4, 4.1).	The purpose of the assessment is described; however, the assessment may not be appropriate for gifted students because of possible ceiling effects. Limitations of the assessment are not described. The summary of the educational implications for the student with gifts and talents is not related to the assessment's purpose or the student.	The purpose of the assessment, its technical qualities, scores, and range of student performance as outlined in the technical manual or a review of the tests are summarized. The educational implications for the student with gifts and talents are based on the quantitative data and interpretation of the test results. Equity and bias issues are included within the summary.	The purpose of the assessment, its technical qualities, scores, and range of student performance as outlined in the technical manual or a review of the tests are summarized. The educational implications for the student with gifts and talents are based on the quantitative data and interpretation of the test results. Equity and bias issues that might influence the student's performance are included within the summary as suggested by the validity studies in the technical manual and the target student's characteristics.*
Informal Assessment for Identification and Services (10 points)	*0–3 points*	*4–7 points*	*8–10 points*

Table 5.2, *Continued*

The beginning gifted education professional . . .	Developing	Competent	Proficient
Selects, collaborates, and uses multiple qualitative (informal) assessments that minimize bias across settings to identify students for gifted programs and services and identify the ways of promoting the well-being of the student (NAGC/CEC Standard #4, 4.1, 4.2; Standard #7, 7.3).	Characteristic checklists are collected from parents and teachers but are summarized quantitatively—not qualitatively. Anecdotal summaries of observations are made during the instructional process, but are not descriptive of the interactions between the candidate and the student. Summary is unclear regarding student characteristics and services.	Characteristic checklists are collected from parents and teachers that provide qualitative information about the student's strengths and needs. Anecdotal summaries collected across 2 weeks of observations in one classroom are made during the instructional process and describe objectively the interactions between the candidate and the student and the student's responses to the interactions. A summary of student characteristics and recommendations for services relate to the observations, to the anecdotal information derived from the checklists, and the collaboration with teachers and families.	Characteristic checklists are collected from parents and teachers in multiple settings that provide qualitative information about the student's strengths and needs. Anecdotal summaries collected across 2 weeks of observations across settings are made during the instructional process and describe objectively the interactions between the candidate and the student and the student's responses to the interactions. Equity and bias issues that might influence the student's performance are included within the summary. A summary of student characteristics and recommendations for services relate to observations and progress records, and the collaboration with teachers and families.
	0–3 points	*4–7 points*	*8–10 points*
Collaboration (10 points)			
Collaborates with colleagues and families in using qualitative (informal) assessments to make decisions and to promote student well-	Interviews with teachers are completed describing the student's achievements, but not social interactions and emotional strengths/needs.	Interviews with the student, teachers, and parents or guardians are completed and relate to information that describes the student's achievements,	Interviews with the student, teachers, and parents or guardians are completed and relate to information that describes the student's achievements,

Table 5.2, *Continued*

The beginning gifted education professional . . .	Developing	Competent	Proficient
being across settings and experiences (NAGC/CEC Standard #4, 4.3; Standard #7, 7.1, 7.3).	Summary relates to the interviews but does not describe similarities and differences among the perspectives. Collaboration is apparent in supporting the student's academic needs within the school only.	social interactions, emotional strengths/needs, or interests. Summary describes similarities and differences among the perspectives. Collaboration is apparent in supporting the student's academic needs in both school and outside-of-school activities.	social interactions, emotional strengths/weaknesses and interests. Summary describes similarities and differences among the perspectives and educational implications and future opportunities for collaboration. Collaboration is apparent in supporting the student's academic and social and emotional needs in both school and outside-of-school academic activities.
Curricular Content Knowledge (*10 points*)	*0–3 points*	*4–7 points*	*8–10 points*
Use assessments and their reflections to select, adapt, and create materials to differentiate instructional strategies and curriculum to challenge effectively individuals with gifts and talents (NAGC/CEC Standards #3, 3.3).	A random set of lesson plans show standards, objectives, materials, procedures, and assessments that differentiate for the student in academic areas. Reflections regarding general effects on all students in the classroom are included for each lesson.	A sequence of lesson plans show standards, objectives, materials, procedures, and assessments that clearly differentiate for the student in academic, affective, and social areas and relate to the progress data, but do not change the trajectory of the student's performance. Reflections regarding specific effects on the case study student are included for each lesson.	A sequence of six lesson plans show standards, objectives, materials, procedures, and assessments that clearly differentiate for the student in academic, affective, and social areas and address the qualitative and quantitative assessment data. Reflections regarding the specific short- and possible long-term effects on the case study student are included for each lesson.

Table 5.2, Continued

The beginning gifted education professional . . .	Developing	Competent	Proficient
Development of the Individual Plan (20 points)	*0–6 points*	*7–15 points*	*16–20 points*
Uses assessment results to develop goals and objectives, taking environment and diversity factors into account and involves the student, parents, and other support personnel in the planning (NAGC/CEC Standard #4, 4.4, 4.5; Standard #7, 7.1, 7.3).	A description of a program for the student that includes short- and long-term goals addresses the cognitive area only with specific activities that involve teachers and the student. The plan relates to the academic and cognitive assessment data. The plan is shared with the student only after it is developed.	A description of a program for the student addresses short- and long-term goals in the cognitive, affective, and social areas; activities involve teachers, parents, and the student in the implementation. The plan relates to quantitative and qualitative assessment data and was developed after input from the student and parents.	A description of a program for the student addresses short- and long-term goals in cognitive, affective aesthetic, social and linguistic areas with specific activities in multiple environments that involve teachers, parents, the student, and evidence of collaboration with other supportive personnel within the school and the community as needed. The plan relates to quantitative and qualitative assessment data and was developed after input from the student, parents, and other support personnel.
Total	**0 to 22 points**	**23 to 47 points**	**48 to 60 points**

* Student characteristics include cognitive, affective, aesthetic, social, and linguistic differences as well as differences of culture, language, sexuality, socioeconomic status, gender, disability, and ethnicity.

[1]*Note.* All of the characteristics for this case study may or may not be used depending on course requirements and the context for data collection. This particular case study was used with candidates who were interning in classrooms with gifted education mentor teachers. They were collecting data on a gifted student who might be viewed or was labeled at-risk for performing at potential based on different characteristics such as poverty, ethnicity, race, disability, linguistic difference, behavior challenge, or gender. They collected both qualitative and quantitative data and shared the results with their mentor teacher, parents, and/or the student. Quantitative data consisted of assessments that were available in the school setting such as identification instruments, state-required assessments, grades, reading and math inventories, etc.; qualitative data included interviews and reflections made regarding the targeted student's responses to a series of differentiated lessons—a more dynamic assessment. Your candidates may be in different settings such as clinics, their own classrooms, or a variety of settings and may not have opportunities to collect information derived from implemented lessons over a 2-week period. Moreover, the program may address some of these standards in other assessments.

tent knowledge" (see Standard Element 3.3), and the "development of the individual plan" (see Standard Elements 4.4, 4.5, 7.1, and 7.3). Within each of the component areas, criteria essential to the standards' elements are listed. For example, within the component of "Assessment for Identification and Services," the criterion "Selects and uses quantitative (formal) assessments that minimize bias to identify students for gifted education programs and services" is directly related to Standard Element 4.1, "Selects and uses technically sound formal and informal assessments that minimize bias." The language relates closely to Standard 4's elements. The performance levels then elaborate specific candidate expectations related to the criterion.

Developing Performance Levels

Continuing with the case study example, each criterion was elaborated into specific performance expectations and proficiency levels. Performance expectations included the candidate's reviews of quantitative assessments, collection of data from multiple sources and across different settings (e.g., interviews, observations, dynamic assessments during lessons), interpretation of quantitative and qualitative assessment results, collaboration with other professionals and families, and the development of a plan related to the qualitative and quantitative assessment information.

Each of these performance expectations was elaborated further into observable and measureable behaviors and then divided into distinct levels of candidate performance. For example, the performance, "review of quantitative assessments," included these observable and measureable behaviors: a review of the assessment and a summary from the technical manual of the purpose of the assessment, its technical qualities, scores, range of student performance and its appropriateness for gifted students, and equity and bias issues related to validity studies.

Distinct levels of performance were then determined by placing these behaviors into the categories of "developing," "competent," and "proficient." In this case, the instructor wanted all of the candidates to be able to select formal or quantitative assessments that minimize bias (see "competent" level) to meet Standard Element 4.1, but didn't expect all of the candidates to go beyond this level, reviewing validity studies and making inferences regarding the test's usefulness with the targeted student (see "proficient" level). For the "developing" level, the instructor identified those behaviors that candidates most often exhibited when they did not have sufficient content knowledge. In this case, they didn't consider the test's ceiling effects or how it might be interpreted for students with gifts and talents.

The easiest way to develop these distinct levels of performance is to review candidates' past products and/or performances. Sorting these into those that clearly met the course expectations from those that did not will help in identifying observable and measureable behaviors and developing distinct levels of candidate proficiency. These exemplars then may be used as further documentation for the choices made in scoring work at a particular level.

Developing a Scoring Guide for the Rubric

In the case study example, each of the components in the rubric receives a specific number of points. With the exception of the "Development of the Individual Plan," candidates may receive a maximum of 10 points for meeting all of the criteria within the "proficient" level (8 to 10 points). Fewer points would be allocated for the "competent" (4 to 7 points) and "developing" levels (0 to 3 points). The scoring guide needs to indicate how the assessment will be scored, including the number of points allocated to each rubric component at each performance level and the total points achieved at each level.

In the case study example, the instructor decides to weight or allocate more points to the "Development of the Individual Plan" component because it requires the candidate to synthesize all of the assessment information, write short- and long-term goals in multiple areas, and collaborate with all of the stakeholders. Similar to the other components, the instructor allocates fewer points for "competent" and "developing" levels.

Issues of Concern With Some Rubrics and Scoring Guides

Rubrics guide the understanding of what is expected of candidates, an essential component in determining whether they have mastered each of the NAGC-CEC standards. The scoring guide allows candidates to see, based on the allotted points, which areas of an assessment are deemed most important.

Below are issues with rubric descriptors and scoring guides that negatively impact a program review decision.

Rubrics

1. Behaviors and performances described are not observable, but rather reflect a general process being applied. Some examples include: "provides a plan," "includes appropriate accommodations," and "knows how students learn." These general descriptors are more process-oriented and do not document candidate growth.

2. The criteria are not related to the specific knowledge and skills included in the standards' elements. These are often general statements that might apply to any set of educational standards (e.g., "aligns aids and

materials within individual lessons"). They are not specific to the language of the teacher preparation standards in gifted education.

3. Rubric descriptors simply restate the language of the standard. For example, the "candidate understands the role of central concepts, structures of the discipline, and tools of inquiry of the content areas they teach" (see Standard Element 3.1). This statement does not define the intention of the standard nor does it explain the product or performance that demonstrates the candidate's understanding.

4. Rubrics include subjective qualifiers (most, some, exceptional, limited, adequate, extensive) instead of descriptions of candidate performance. For example, "candidate provides a limited amount of contextual information," "candidate provides an adequate amount of contextual information," and "candidate provides an exceptional amount of contextual information." The use of subjective qualifiers does not help the candidate know how to improve the contextual information. Instead, characteristics of the context should be provided, such as required products and performances, diversity within and across the groups, assessment information, and so on. These characteristics then should be linked to developing, competent, and proficient levels.

5. The levels of performance are distinguished based on quantitative measures (e.g., the candidates demonstrated more of the behaviors) but do not describe qualitative differences. For example, these candidate behaviors are listed: "questions are used to assess learner understanding," "options for student products are available," "opportunities for student self assessment are provided," and "a variety of assessment tools are used to evaluate." The candidates would then be considered competent if they met three of four criteria and proficient if they met all four. Instead, qualitative evidence for the first example, "questions are used to assess learner understanding," might address the level of questions asked, the effectiveness of the questions based on student responses, and the systematic use of question clusters to elevate discussion.

6. Descriptors of unacceptable or developing performance levels do not include nonexamples but simply an absence of behaviors. For example, "anecdotal summaries are not descriptive of the teaching-learning process" is preferable to "anecdotal summaries are not included."

7. The acceptable or competent level does not address all of the standard's elements. In other words, a candidate may be deemed to be "competent" even if he or she had not been evaluated on important elements of the standard (e.g., can use formal but not informal assessments). The burden of proof is on the program faculty to ensure that all elements of the standards are addressed in some way through the assessments applied and operationalized through the rubric.

Scoring Guides

1. The scoring guide does not indicate the number of points needed to achieve a final score, by each performance level.

2. The scoring guide does not include information about the points allocated to each rubric component at each performance level.

3. The guide allocates more points to areas that are not related to the standard or its elements. For example, an equal number of points might be allocated to the writing and organization of a lesson plan rather than to the standards elements such as the inclusion of differentiated, accelerated, and evidence-based practices (see Instructional Planning and Strategies Standard 5.1).

In summary, rubrics need to be aligned to their corresponding assessments, describe observable behaviors and performances, and provide distinct levels of candidate proficiency that are related to the standards' elements. The scoring guides need to clearly indicate the points that will be awarded by component and scoring level and the total number of points needed to receive a final score at each performance level. Total points for a key assessment may be assigned a grade or be aggregated with other products and performances for an overall grade in the course (e.g., adding the points across all assigned products and performances).

Reporting Assessment Results

The program report requires that the data derived from each key assessment are aligned to the rubric and disaggregated by candidate performance level, semester administered (and location if the program operates on more than one campus), and by program (e.g., graduate and undergraduate; masters and endorsement) in cases where candidates from more than one program take the same key assessments in a semester.

The primary purpose of a data table is to provide information to faculty regarding the performance of candidates on a specific assessment's components, which when compared to other key assessments, provides critical information about the relative strengths and weaknesses of the overall program. Returning to the case study example, notice in Table 5.3 how the data table is aligned to the rubric components: Formal Assessment, Informal Assessment, Collaboration, Curricular Content Knowledge, and Individual Plan. For clarity, each standard's elements are listed for each component.

Table 5.3

2011–2013 Candidates' Performance on Case Study Assessment

Component	Developing			Competent			Proficient		
	2010–2011 N = 12	2011–2012 N = 10	2012–2013 N = 9	2010–2011 N = 12	2011–2012 N = 10	2012–2013 N = 9	2010–2011 N = 12	2011–2012 N = 10	2012–2013 N = 9
Formal Quantitative Assessment Standard Element 4.1 (10 points)	17% n = 2				10% n = 1		83% n = 10 (M = 9.2; SD = 0.72; R = 8-10)	90% n = 9 (M = 9.3; SD = 0.71; R = 8-10)	100% N = 9 (M = 9.6; SD = 0.53; R = 9-10)
Informal Qualitative Assessments Standard Elements 4.1, 7.3 (10 points)	17% n = 2		11% n = 1			33% n = 3	83% n = 10 (M = 9.2; SD = 0.72; R = 8-10)	100% N = 10 (M = 9.2; SD = 0.79; R = 8-10)	56% n = 5 (M = 8.6; SD = 0.55; R = 8-9)
Collaboration Standard Elements 4.3, 7.1, and 7 (10 points)		30% n = 3			30% n = 3		100% N = 12 (M = 9.0; SD = 0.85; R = 8-10)	40% n = 4	100% N = 9 (M = 9.2; SD = 0.83; R = 8-9)
Curricular Content Knowledge Standard Element 3.3 (10 points)						11% n = 1	100% N = 12 (M = 9.2; SD = 0.72; R = 8-9)	100% N = 10 (M = 9.2; SD = 0.79; R = 8-10)	89% n = 8 (M = 9.1; SD = 0.64; R = 8-10)
Individual Plan Standard Elements 4.4, 4.5, 7.1, 7.3 (20 points)			11% n = 1		50% n = 5 (M = 12; SD = 1.6; R = 10-14)	11% n = 1	100% N = 12 (M = 18.2; SD = 1.4; R = 16-20)	50% n = 5 (M = 18.2; SD = 1.3; R = 17-20)	88% n = 8 (M = 18.5; SD = 1.2; R = 17-20)

Note. M = Mean; *SD* = Standard Deviation; *R* = Range; Means, standard deviations and ranges were not calculated for numbers less than 5.

For data collected in 2011–2012, the relative strength of the candidates in this gifted university program appears to be in the Curricular Content Knowledge component, where all but one candidate scored in the proficient range. The candidates appear to be able to select, adapt, and create materials to differentiate instruction (see Standard 3.3). All of the candidates' means across all three applications were greater than 9 points, which is at the top of the range of possible points assigned to that component. Their relative weak areas appear to be in collaboration (40% were proficient in 2011–2012), developing an individual plan (50% were proficient in 2011–2012), and using informal assessments (56% were proficient in 2012–2013). This information is useful in considering course objectives, time spent on specific components, and perhaps clinical placements—did candidates have field opportunities to collaborate and develop individual plans? Faculty would want to consider the small numbers of candidates, differences in candidates from year to year, and the consistency in interrater reliability before drawing any conclusions. Table 5.3 also shows the number of candidates for each application of this assessment, which relate to the number of candidates reported in Section 1 of the report.

In another example from the same data set (see Table 5.4), the candidates' greatest strengths across all applications of the assessment relate to Standard 3.1—they "understand the role of central concepts, structures of the discipline, and tools of inquiry." They are able to identify a major theme and generalizations and organize the content into a meaningful learning progression. On the other hand, one of the weakest components of their unit plan across all applications appears to be in the assessment area—the use of preassessment in planning the lesson (Standards 3.3 and 4.4), involving students in assessing their own learning (Standard 4.5), and evaluating the effectiveness of their lesson (Standard 4.4). The other weak component is in the area of planning. The candidates appear to need to learn more about the principles of differentiated and accelerated practice (Standard 5.1) and foundational knowledge in the education of students with gifts and talents (Standard 6.2). This information is helpful for instructors in designing and revising course content and in making decisions regarding the allocation of time to particular standards.

Table 5.4 also shows the number of candidates for each application of this assessment, which relate to the number of candidates reported in Section I of the report. This information is also useful in showing any improvements in the program. It appears that the candidates performed better in 2012–2013 in the area of planning than in the previous year, which may indicate changes in the program. However, given the small number and the differences in candidates from year to year, it would be difficult to make any final conclusions.

In both of these examples, the Table of Results should also include an interpretation of how the data provides evidence that the standard has been

Table 5.4

2010–2013 Candidates' Performance on Unit Plan Assessment

Component	Developing			Competent			Proficient		
	2010–2011 N = 12	2011–2012 N = 10	2012–2013 N = 9	2010–2011 N = 12	2011–2012 N = 10	2012–2013 N = 9	2010–2011 N = 12	2011–2012 N = 10	2012–2013 N = 9
Planning Standards 1.1, 1.2, 6.2, 7.3 *(10 points)*				17% n = 2	70% n = 7 (M = 5.9; SD = 1.1; R = 4–7)	33% n = 3	83% n = 8 (M = 8.9; SD = 0.8; R = 8–10)	30% n = 3	67% n = 6 (M = 8.7; SD = 8.2; R = 8–10)
Rationale Standards 1.2, 3.4, 4.4 *(10 points)*					10% n = 1		100% N = 12 (M = 9; SD = 0.74; R = 8–10)	90% n = 9 (M = 8.9; SD = 0.8; R = 8–10)	100% N = 9 (M = 8.9; SD = 0.9; R = 8–10)
Theme/Problem/Issue Standard 3.1 *(5 points)*							100% N = 12 (M = 5; SD = 0)	100% N = 10 (M = 5; SD = 0)	100% N = 9 (M = 5; SD = 0)
Generalizations Standard 3.1 *(10 points)*							100% N = 12 (M = 9; SD = 0.9; R = 8–10)	100% N = 10 (M = 8.9; SD = 0.8; R = 8–10)	100% N = 9 (M = 9; SD = 0.8; R = 8–10)
Content Outline Standard 3.1 *(10 points)*							100% N = 12 (M = 9; SD = 0.9; R = 8–10)	100% N = 10 (M = 8.9; SD = 0.8; R = 8–10)	100% N = 9 (M = 9; SD = 0.8; R = 8–10)

Table 5.4, *Continued*

Component	Developing			Competent			Proficient		
	2010–2011 N = 12	2011–2012 N = 10	2012–2013 N = 9	2010–2011 N = 12	2011–2012 N = 10	2012–2013 N = 9	2010–2011 N = 12	2011–2012 N = 10	2012–2013 N = 9
Framework Standard 3.1, 3.2 *(30 points)*						11% n = 1	100% N = 12 (M = 26.7; SD = 1.8; R = 24–30)	100% N = 10 (M = 26.8; SD = 1.8; R = 25–30)	89% n = 8 (M = 27.1; SD = 1.8; R = 25–30)
Preassessment Standard 3.1, 3.2, 5.1 *(15 points)*	8% n = 1		11% n = 1	17% n = 2	10% n = 1		75% n = 9 (M = 13.1; SD = 1.1; R = 12–15)	90% n = 9 (M = 13.6; SD = 1.1; R = 12–15)	89% n = 8 (M = 13.4; SD = 1.1; R = 12–15)
Lesson Plans and Reflections Standard 3.2, 3.3, 4.4, 4.5, 5.1, 5.2, 6.4 *(45 points)*							100% N = 12 (M = 40.5; SD = 2.5; R = 37–45)	100% N = 10 (M = 40.9; SD = 2.5; R = 38–45)	100% N = 9 (M = 41.2; SD = 2.4; R = 38–45)
Evaluation Standard 4.4 *(15 points)*				33% n = 4		11% n = 1	67% n = 8 (M = 13.5; SD = 1.2; R = 12–15)	100% N = 10 (M = 14.0; SD = 1.1; R = 12–15)	89% n = 8 (M = 13.9; SD = 1.1; R = 12–15)
Management Plan Standard 2.1 *(30 points)*					20% n = 2		100% N = 12 (M = 28.0; SD = 1.5; R = 25–30)	80% n = 8 (M = 27.8; SD = 1.7; R = 25–30)	100% N = 9 (M = 28.0; SD = 1.7; R = 25–30)

Note. M = Mean; SD = Standard Deviation; R = Range; Means, standard deviations and ranges were not calculated for numbers less than 5.

met. For example, the case study data table might have a corresponding narrative that states:

> Across all applications, the majority of candidates scored in the competent or proficient range on all of the case study components showing that the standards addressed in this assessment have been met. Their relative strength appears to be in the area of curricular content knowledge, where all of the candidates with the exception of one were proficient in selecting, adapting, and creating materials to differentiate instruction (see Standard 3.3). The relatively weak areas were in use of assessments and collaboration. The faculty addressed these areas with mentors supervising their clinical experiences and in their coursework. Improvements were noted in collaboration, discussing plans with stakeholders, and in using formal assessment information. While variations across candidates influenced the scores, faculty need to continue to monitor candidates in their use of informal assessment information.

Issues of Concern With Some Data Tables

The data tables indicate whether teacher candidates were able to master the expectations in the NAGC-CEC standards. These are examples of issues that negatively impact a program review decision:

1. The data table is not aligned to the rubric and the standards, but to individual candidates or by application. For example, "Candidate 1 scored 34 of the 40 possible points on the assessment" or "50 percent of the candidates achieved a target rating in the fall of 2014."

2. Often averages or means are reported for candidates without providing the context. Percentages, standard deviations, and range of scores need to be reported in addition to the mean. Reviewers need to understand the results in small programs where variations may be the norm rather than the exception. In small programs, means by themselves may disguise the magnitude of differences.

3. No interpretation is provided. Faculty need to describe how they interpret the candidates' relative strengths and weaknesses in each of the key areas measured by the assessment. Based on this analysis, faculty should also suggest actions to be taken in the area of program improvement where warranted.

4. The number of candidates taking a key assessment does not match the number of candidates enrolled in the program, as reported in Section I of the report. (*Note.* An explanation for the discrepancy should be provided.)

5.   All candidates are grouped together in the table and not separated by semester or assessment administration.

6.   Other assessment data, such as candidates from more than one program (e.g., graduate and undergraduate; masters program and endorsement) or candidates at more than one location are taking the same key assessment in a semester, are not disaggregated. Data from online courses, for example, should be reported and compared to on-campus courses.

7.   Data from only one application of the assessment are provided in an initial program report submission instead of two. (Note that this is typically semester-based data; it may take three or more semesters to obtain two applications of an assessment because of course rotations.) Two assessments results must be reported regardless of the time interval.

In summary, in reporting assessment results, instructors need to (a) create tables that relate to the major components of the rubric and the standards; (b) summarize data qualitatively and quantitatively for the number of candidates by assessment application, (c) disaggregate data by program and location where applicable, making sure that the number corresponds to the number of candidates reported in Section I of the report; and (d) interpret the results, noting how the data will be used for program improvement.

Conclusion

This chapter has provided important guidance for gifted program faculty to prepare their SPA report in compliance with the NAGC-CEC standards and CAEP requirements. The chapter has provided examples of types of assessments to be selected for data collection efforts, noting the issues commonly associated with poor selection and utilization, based on reviewer data examined over the past several years. The chapter also examines concerns for aligning the assessments to the core standards and the problems associated with doing so. Extending commentary to the assessment rubrics and issues associated with their construction and administration is also noted. Finally, there is discussion of the need to interpret in a fair and consistent way the results of assessments and how to describe the analysis of results for reporting purposes. Sample data tables, which represent real data collected on gifted education candidates in earlier years, are provided and discussed as exemplars for use by program faculty.

CHAPTER 6

ADVANCED STANDARDS IN GIFTED EDUCATION

CHERYLL ADAMS

Background

After mastering initial gifted education teacher preparation standards, many educators in gifted education continue their professional growth by pursuing advanced professional standards at the postbaccalaureate levels, including master, specialist, and doctoral degree programs, as well as nondegree advanced certificate programs. For some, this pursuit means deepening their understandings and expertise and adding new responsibilities for leadership within the classroom. Others in gifted education work toward assuming positions outside the classroom, moving into specializations, administering gifted education programs and services, or moving into teacher preparation and research roles.

Regardless of the specific role, educators in advanced roles share an array of functions and responsibilities in common. Reflecting this commonality, the Council for Exceptional Children, The Association for the Gifted, and the National Association for Gifted Children developed and validated Advanced Standards in Gifted Education for Teacher Preparation (Advanced Standards), which delineate the knowledge and skills that all individuals in gifted education should have mastered as a part of their preparation for advanced practice.

In 2009, starting from the CEC's Advanced Common Core Standards (ACCS), a committee including members from TAG and NAGC modified

the ACCS to reflect knowledge and skills that are necessary for gifted educators in advanced roles to know, understand, and be able to do. Content and
teacher preparation experts conducted an extensive study of advanced teaching standards, including National Board for Professional Teaching Standards,
state standards, knowledge and skill standards that are expected of all special
educators in advanced roles, and standards used by the National Council for
the Accreditation of Teacher Education (NCATE) as part of the accreditation process. In the beginning, 67 knowledge and skills statements (elements)
and six standards were developed. Through a validation process, 54 knowledge
and skills statements were kept, based on the field's sense of which ones were
essential.

    In 2012, both the Initial (i.e., NAGC-CEC Teacher Preparation Standards
in Gifted Education) and the Advanced Teacher Preparation Standards were
revised to meet the new CEC Preparation Standards that had been revised
to meet new CAEP requirements limiting professional standards to no more
than 7 standards and 28 elements (See Figure 6.1). The seven standards in
the revised, validated Advanced Standards in Gifted Education for Teacher
Preparation are Assessment; Curricular Content Knowledge; Programs,
Services, and Outcomes; Research and Inquiry; Leadership and Policy;
Professional and Ethical Practice; and Collaboration. The original research
base was revised to reflect current research that supports the 7 standards and
the 28 elements (see Appendix G). The Assessment standard stresses advanced
knowledge and skills in educational assessment that include being able to carry
out all facets of assessment, from selecting instruments that minimize bias to
being able to interpret the results, as well as monitoring and reporting progress.
Curricular Content Knowledge goes beyond just the development of curriculum and focuses on the ability to select, develop, implement, and provide access
to challenging curriculum based on diverse students' learning differences. The
Programs, Services, and Outcomes standard stresses research and evaluation to
improve programs that provide a continuum of services that address the social,
emotional, academic, cultural, and economic diversity of students with gifts
and talents. Standard 4 emphasizes the importance of research and inquiry in
guiding all facets of the professional practice of gifted educators in advanced
roles. The Leadership and Policy Standard encourages gifted educators in
advanced roles to hold high professional expectations for themselves and to
model ethical practices while creating a positive and productive work environment. The Professional and Ethical Practice Standard charges gifted leaders
to demonstrate lifelong learning, practice ethically, have advanced knowledge
of the field, and promote the advancement of the profession. The last standard
addresses collaboration with all stakeholders to improve every facet of services
and outcomes for learners with gifts and talents.

NAGC-CEC Advanced Standards in Gifted Education Teacher Preparation

Advanced Preparation Standard 1: Assessment

Gifted education specialists use valid and reliable assessment practices to minimize bias.

1.1	Gifted education specialists review, select, and interpret psychometrically sound, nonbiased, qualitative and quantitative instruments to identify individuals with gifts and talents and assess their abilities, strengths, and interests.
1.2	Gifted education specialists monitor the progress of individuals with gifts and talents in the general education and specialized curricula.

Assessment is critical to the advanced roles of gifted education specialists. Underlying assessment is the knowledge of systems and theories of educational assessment, along with skills in examining the technical adequacy of instruments and the implementation of evidence-based practices in assessment. It is critical that assessments that minimize bias are used in the selection of instruments, methods, and procedures for both programs and individuals. With respect to assessment of individuals with gifts and talents, gifted education specialists in advanced roles apply their knowledge and skill to all stages and purposes of assessment, including identification of abilities, strengths, and interests and in monitoring and reporting learning progress in the general education curriculum, as well as in the specialized curriculum in their gifted education placement.

Advanced Preparation Standard 2: Curricular Content Knowledge

Gifted education specialists use their knowledge of general[1] and specialized[2] curricula to improve programs, supports, and services at classroom, school, community, and system levels.

2.1	Gifted education specialists align educational standards to provide access to challenging curriculum to meet the needs of individuals with exceptionalities.
2.2	Gifted educators continuously broaden and deepen professional knowledge, and expand expertise with instructional technologies, curriculum standards, effective teaching strategies, and assistive technologies to support access to and learning of challenging content.
2.3	Gifted education specialists use understanding of diversity and individual learning differences to inform the selection, development, and implementation of comprehensive curricula for individuals with exceptionalities.

Gifted education specialists use their deep understanding of educational standards within and across domains to provide access to challenging curriculum to meet the needs of individuals with exceptionalities. Gifted education specialists continuously broaden and deepen their professional knowledge, and expand their expertise with technologies, curriculum standards, effective teaching strategies, and assistive technologies to support learning. Gifted education specialists know how individual learning differences and diversity inform the selection, development, and implementation of comprehensive and cohesive curricula for individuals with exceptionalities.

---

1 As used, "general" or the core curricula means the general academic content of the curricula including math, reading, English/language arts, science, social studies, and the arts.

2 As used, "specialized curricula" means the content of specialized interventions that are designed to address the unique needs of individuals with gifts and talents.

FIGURE 6.1. NAGC-CEC Advanced Standards in Gifted Education Teacher Preparation.

Advanced Preparation Standard 3: Programs, Services, and Outcomes

Gifted education specialists facilitate the continuous improvement of general and gifted education programs, supports, and services at the classroom, school, and system levels for individuals with exceptionalities.

3.1	Gifted education specialists design and implement evaluation activities to improve programs, supports, and services for individuals with exceptionalities.
3.2	Gifted education specialists use their understanding of cultural, social, and economic diversity and individual learner differences to inform the development and improvement of programs, supports, and services for individuals with exceptionalities.
3.3	Gifted education specialists apply knowledge of theories, evidence-based practices, relevant laws, and policies to advocate for programs, supports, and a continuum of services for individuals with exceptionalities.
3.4	Gifted education specialists design and develop systematic program and curriculum models for enhancing talent development in multiple settings.
3.5	Gifted education specialists evaluate progress toward achieving the vision, mission, and goals of programs, services, and supports for individuals with exceptionalities.

Effective gifted educators in advanced roles design and implement research activities to evaluate the effectiveness of instructional practices and to assess progress toward the organizational vision, mission, and goals of their programs. They develop procedures for continuous improvement management systems. They use their understanding of the effects of cultural, social, and economic diversity and variations of individual development to inform their development of programs and services for individuals with exceptional learning needs. Gifted educators in advanced roles apply their knowledge of cognitive science, learning theory, and instructional technologies to improve instructional programs at the schoolwide and system-wide levels. They provide for a continuum of services to ensure the appropriate instructional supports for individuals with exceptional learning needs. They use their deep understanding of educational standards to help all individuals with exceptional learning needs access challenging curriculum.

Advanced Preparation Standard 4: Research and Inquiry

Gifted education specialists conduct, evaluate, and use inquiry to guide professional practice.

4.1	Gifted education specialists evaluate theory, research, and inquiry to identify effective practices.
4.2	Gifted education specialists use knowledge of the professional literature to improve practices with individuals with exceptionalities and their families.
4.3	Gifted education specialists evaluate and modify instructional practices in response to ongoing assessment data and engage in the design and implementation of research and inquiry.

Research and inquiry inform the decisions of gifted educators in advanced roles in guiding professional practice. Gifted educators in advanced roles know models, theories, philosophies, and research methods that form the basis for evidence-based practices in gifted education. This knowledge includes information sources, data collection, and data analysis strategies.

FIGURE 6.1. Continued.

Gifted educators in advanced roles evaluate the appropriateness of research methodologies in relation to practices presented in the literature. They use educational research to improve instructional techniques, intervention strategies, and curricular materials. They foster an environment supportive of continuous instructional improvement and engage in the design and implementation of action research. Gifted educators in advanced roles are able to use the literature to resolve issues of professional practice and help others understand various evidence-based practices.

Advanced Preparation Standard 5: Leadership and Policy

Gifted education specialists provide leadership to formulate goals, set and meet high professional expectations, advocate for effective policies and evidence-based practices, and create positive and productive work environments.

5.1	Gifted education specialists encourage high expectations, model respect for, and use ethical practices with all individuals with exceptionalities.
5.2	Gifted education specialists support and use linguistically and culturally responsive practices.
5.3	Gifted education specialists create and maintain collegial and productive work environments that respect and safeguard the rights of individuals with exceptionalities and their families.
5.4	Gifted education specialists advocate for policies and practices that improve programs, services, and outcomes for individuals with exceptionalities.
5.5	Gifted education specialists advocate for the allocation of appropriate resources for the preparation and professional development of all personnel who serve individuals with exceptionalities.

Gifted educators in advanced roles promote high professional self-expectations and help others understand the needs of individuals with exceptional learning needs within the context of an organization's mission. They advocate laws based on solid evidence-based knowledge to support high-quality education for individuals with exceptional learning needs. They also advocate for appropriate resources to ensure that all personnel involved have effective preparation. Gifted educators in advanced roles use their knowledge of organizational theory and the needs of different groups in a pluralistic society to formulate organizational goals promoting evidence-based practices and challenging expectations for individuals with exceptional learning needs. They provide leadership to create procedures that respect all individuals and permit professionals to practice ethically. They create positive and productive work environments and celebrate accomplishments with colleagues.

Advanced Preparation Standard 6: Professional and Ethical Practice

Gifted education specialists use foundational knowledge of the field and professional ethical principles and Program Standards to inform gifted education practice, engage in lifelong learning, advance the profession, and perform leadership responsibilities to promote the success of professional colleagues and individuals with exceptionalities.

6.1	A comprehensive understanding of the history of gifted education, legal policies, ethical standards, and emerging issues informs gifted education specialist leadership.

FIGURE 6.1. Continued.

6.2	Gifted education specialists model high professional expectations and ethical practice, and create supportive environments that increase diversity at all levels of gifted and talented education.
6.3	Gifted education specialists model and promote respect for all individuals and facilitate ethical professional practice.
6.4	Gifted education specialists actively participate in professional development and learning communities to increase professional knowledge and expertise.
6.5	Gifted education specialists plan, present, and evaluate professional development focusing on effective and ethical practice at all organizational levels.
6.6	Gifted education specialists actively facilitate and participate in the preparation and induction of prospective gifted educators.
6.7	Gifted education specialists actively promote the advancement of the profession.

Gifted education specialists in advanced roles have a comprehensive knowledge of gifted education as an evolving and changing discipline based on philosophies, evidence-based principles and theories, relevant laws and policies, diverse and historical points of view, and issues that have influenced and continue to influence gifted education and the education of and services for individuals with exceptionalities both in school and in society. They are guided by professional ethics and practice standards. In their advanced roles, gifted educators have leadership responsibilities for promoting the success of individuals with exceptional learning needs, their families, and colleagues. They create supportive environments that safeguard the legal rights of students, families, and school personnel through policies and procedures that promote ethical and professional practice. Gifted educators in advanced roles continuously broaden and deepen their professional knowledge, and expand their expertise with instructional technologies, curriculum, effective teaching strategies, and assistive technologies to support access to learning. Gifted educators in advanced roles plan, present, and evaluate professional development based on models that apply adult learning theories and focus on effective practice at all organizational levels. They are actively involved in the preparation and induction of prospective gifted educators. Gifted educators in advanced roles model their own commitment to continuously improving their own professional practice by participating in professional development themselves and promote the advancement of the profession.

Advanced Preparation Standard 7: Collaboration

Gifted education specialists collaborate with stakeholders to improve programs, services, and outcomes for individuals with gifts and talents and their families.

7.1	Gifted education specialists use culturally responsive practices to enhance collaboration.
7.2	Gifted education specialists use collaborative skills to improve programs, services, and outcomes for individuals with exceptionalities
7.3	Gifted education specialists collaborate to promote understanding, resolve conflicts, and build consensus for improving program, services, and outcomes for individuals with exceptionalities.

Gifted educators in advanced roles have a deep understanding of the centrality and importance of consultation and collaboration to the roles within gifted education, and they use this

FIGURE 6.1. Continued.

deep understanding to improve programs, services, and outcomes for individuals with exceptional learning needs. They also understand the significance of the role of collaboration and apply their skill to promote understanding, resolve conflicts, and build consensus among both internal and external stakeholders to provide services to individuals with exceptional learning needs and their families. They possess current knowledge of research on stages and models in both collaboration and consultation and ethical and legal issues related to consultation and collaboration. Moreover, gifted educators in advanced roles have a deep understanding of the possible interactions of language, diversity, culture, and religion with contextual factors and how to use collaboration and consultation to enhance opportunities for individuals with exceptional learning needs.

Glossary for the Advanced Standards

Individuals with exceptionalities: Individuals with exceptionalities include individuals with sensory, physical, emotional, social, or cognitive differences; developmental delays; exceptional gifts and talents; and individuals who are or have been abused or neglected whose needs differ sufficiently so as to require personalized special education services in addition to or in tandem with regular educational services available through general education programs and other human service delivery systems.

Special education service: Special education services are personalized services that appropriately credentialed special educators provide directly or indirectly to individuals with exceptionalities.

FIGURE 6.1. Continued.

Using the Advanced Standards

Individuals who are responsible for planning and implementing advanced degree programs in gifted education and school personnel who wish to develop advanced competencies would benefit from using the advanced standards to guide development or revisions of existing programs aimed at preparing individuals who have completed their initial preparation program for advanced roles in gifted education. Thus, any credential in this area should be added to an initial gifted education teaching credential.

Over the last 25 years, many universities have moved toward credentialing gifted educators as part of a master's degree program, and in some cases, as part of a bachelor's degree. After several years of practice and as a part of career ladders, individuals often desire to deepen their knowledge and skills and add leadership skills. In addition, many school districts seek individuals with in-depth knowledge and skills in gifted education to serve in advanced roles (Sparks & Mainzer, 2007). These Advanced Standards were created for use in programs preparing experienced gifted educators who work with both general and gifted education teachers and other professionals (e.g., principals, school psychologists, behavior specialists; administrators) to ensure that effective programs are delivered for individuals with exceptional gifts and talents. These professionals will often be the lead person who facilitates the development, implementation, evaluation, and ongoing support for gifted education services. For example, a gifted education coordinator for an entire system might be charged with designing and implementing a systemwide evaluation of the curriculum used with gifted and advanced learners. Similarly, in conjunction with the state science curriculum expert, the state gifted education specialist might convene a committee to differentiate the Next Generation Science Standards to provide challenging curriculum to meet the needs of the state's gifted science students, K–12.

There are four standards that have the same name in both the Initial and the Advanced Standards: Assessment; Curricular Content Knowledge; Professional and Ethical Practice; and Collaboration. The standards unique to the Advanced Standards include Programs, Services, and Outcomes; Research and Inquiry; and Leadership and Policy, while only the Initial Standards address Learner Development and Individual Learning Differences; Learning Environments; and Instructional Planning and Strategies. A complete discussion of the Initial Standards is included in the first section of this book (Chapter 1) and will not be analyzed here except to show differences and commonalities between the two sets.

Comparison of Standards Common to Both Initial and Advanced Preparation Standards

Assessment

Knowledge and skills pertaining to assessment are found in both sets of standards. Beginning gifted educators are expected to use multiple methods of assessment and data sources when making educational decisions about the identification of individuals with gifts and talents. For example, they need to understand basic measurement theory, the limitations of different types of assessment, how to select and use quantitative and qualitative assessment to support their decisions, and how to engage gifted students in assessing their own learning and performance. Those who are in advanced specialist programs must develop a deeper understanding of assessment, using their knowledge and skills to choose valid and reliable quantitative and qualitative assessments to minimize bias in all stages of assessment, from identifying individuals with gifts and talents, to monitoring their progress in the general and specialized curricula at the school or system level. A gifted education specialist who is in charge of designing and implementing the school system's identification plan would need to use these advanced knowledge and skills to choose appropriate identification instruments to identify students from diverse backgrounds for the system's advanced math program at the middle school.

Curricular Content Knowledge

Beginning gifted education professionals gain knowledge and skills related to central concepts, structures of the disciplines, and tools of inquiry. They use these to plan lessons using both general and specialized curricula to integrate cross-disciplinary skills and develop meaningful learning progressions for their students with gifts and talents. Gifted education specialists are expected to go beyond the level of creating and planning lessons; they must be able to improve programs, supports, and services at the classroom, school, committee, and systems levels. It is essential that they accomplish these tasks with a clear understanding of diversity and individual learning differences, while deepening their professional knowledge and expanding their expertise. In other words, beginning gifted educators are generally working on curriculum at the classroom level, and advanced educators have a broader focus from classrooms to systems. At a gifted resource center, the director uses her advanced curricular knowledge and skills to select an array of research-based challenging language arts curricula that have been written for diverse gifted learners in grades K–3. Teachers in the area can then visit the resource center to meet with the director who can assist them in selecting an appropriate specialized curriculum that will meet the needs of their particular students.

Professional Learning and Ethical Practice

In this standard, both beginning and advanced professionals must use foundational knowledge in the field, ethical practices, and the NAGC Pre-K–Grade 12 Gifted Education Programming Standards (NAGC, 2010) to inform their practice, engage in lifelong learning, and to advance the profession. In addition, professionals in advanced roles are required to perform leadership responsibilities to promote the success of their professional colleagues and individuals with gifts and talents. They are prepared to plan, develop, present, and evaluate professional development focusing on professional practice and ethics. They are involved in both preparing and inducting beginning gifted educators into the profession. At a university that offers a licensure in gifted education, instructors with advanced knowledge and skills provide frequent venues for their students to gain real-world knowledge of the field through opportunities to shadow practicing professionals, observe case conferences, team teach in Saturday Enrichment Programs, attend professional conferences, and engage in informal discussions, thereby encouraging their students to gain an inside view of the field in addition to their coursework.

Collaboration

Because collaboration among gifted educators, other educators, other school professionals, families, and individuals with gifts and talents has been recognized as having a positive impact on individuals with gifts and talents, it is not surprising to find this standard in both sets. Beginning gifted educators learn to work with an array of service providers and personnel from community agencies in conjunction with families and gifted individuals to provide a wide range of opportunities and experiences that promote the well-being of their gifted students. Gifted educators in advanced roles work toward enhancing and improving programs, services, and outcomes for individuals with gifts and talents. Beyond this, they build consensus and resolve conflicts among all stakeholders. It is vital that they accomplish these tasks with a deep understanding of the interactions among language differences, culture, socioeconomic status, and religion. For example, a gifted educator with advanced knowledge and skills may be asked to facilitate a meeting between the fourth-grade teacher and the parents of a child whose first language is not English to address concerns of the parents who feel the child's gifts and talents in math and science are being ignored because of some language issues.

Preparation Standards Unique to
Advanced Roles in Gifted Education

Programs, Services, and Outcomes

This standard addresses the continuous improvement of general and gifted education programs at all levels. This includes evaluating programs and services, advocating for a continuum of services, and enhancing talents in multiple settings by using their understanding of cultural, social, and economic diversity, as well as of individual learning differences. For example, the gifted education specialist for the county appears before the board of education to advocate for a continuum of services from K–12 to replace the pull-out program in grades 3–5 that currently represents the county's gifted services.

Research and Inquiry

Gifted educators in advanced roles learn to conduct, evaluate, and use research and inquiry to guide their practice. They need to be able to read the research and judge its merits, translate good research into best practices, and use research to improve instructional practices, curriculum, and intervention practices. They are able to design and implement action research. For example, a gifted specialist may work with a classroom teacher to design an action research project to determine if tiered lessons have a positive effect in raising the achievement of students of all levels in the teacher's mathematics class.

Leadership and Policy

This standard outlines how gifted educators in advanced roles should provide leadership and promote high professional self-expectations. They are asked to be advocates for effective policies and practices that affect individuals with gifts and talents, to create and maintain work environments that foster collegiality, and to use linguistically and culturally responsive practices. The state gifted coordinator, for example, testifies before the state legislature, providing evidence of the need for monies to be allocated to provide the resources necessary to allow teachers of gifted students to have effective preparation through professional development to enable them to carry out their responsibility for the education of these students.

The three standards discussed here demonstrate knowledge and skills not required of beginning gifted educators. Together with the four previously discussed standards, these seven standards provide guidance for programs preparing gifted educators for advanced roles. With an emphasis on policy, leadership, and research, as well as advanced knowledge of curriculum, assessment, professional practices and ethics, and collaboration, the Advanced Standards are an obvious choice for those wanting to develop a program based on current research and best practices that will prepare gifted educators for advanced roles.

Summary

Advanced gifted education professional standards are the basis for professionally recognizing gifted education preparation programs that have demonstrated through their graduates' performance that the program successfully prepares candidates in various leadership roles in the classroom, the school district, the state, or the university levels. Individuals mastering the knowledge and skills identified for advanced roles, although not necessarily earning a specific state license, can enhance their resumes and the professional roles they assume. The Advanced Standards provide benchmarks to ensure that experienced gifted education professionals are able to practice at an accomplished level. Teacher preparation faculty may use the advanced gifted education professional standards as a guide in developing, evaluating, and improving the program. This set of Advanced Standards has been validated for the knowledge and skills sets that inform and differentiate the specific skills and contextual expertise expected of educators in advanced roles in gifted education; thus, programs preparing professionals for these roles should ensure their programs are aligned with these advanced role standards.

CHAPTER 7

CHALLENGES

JOYCE VANTASSEL-BASKA, ANN ROBINSON,
ALICIA COTABISH, AND SUSAN K. JOHNSEN

W e conclude this guide by sharing a few special challenges that the teacher preparation standards present for universities to consider. These challenges represent issues in teacher preparation programs in gifted education, including compliance with CAEP requirements; alignments between courses, standards, and assessments; a lack of human resources; and internal philosophical conflicts about gifted education. Given a fragmented state system of personnel preparation and the lack of a federal mandate in gifted education, educators involved in preparing future gifted teachers and providing professional development face many challenges.

Compliance With CAEP Requirements for University Programs in Gifted Education

The need to design detailed rubrics may be a challenge for many programs in gifted education. The case study example we provided in Chapter 5 illustrates the extensiveness necessary to demonstrate the comprehensiveness to which a standard is addressed. For each assessment to demonstrate that degree of specificity will require much work on the part of program faculty, and extensive piloting of the language used to designate the categories of "developing, competent, and proficient."

The interpretation of data is another area where university personnel may experience difficulty. Our sample data tables should prove very useful in providing a model for such interpretation. That said, the understanding of charts and graphs is not a strength of many university personnel who work in gifted education. If faculty feel it necessary, a consultant should be used to help with the preparation of data tables, a description of their results, and the interpretation of those results. Interpretation of results is further hampered by small numbers of candidates completing programs at any point in time. It is risky to make program changes based on an N of 5. However, 2 years of data ($N = 10$), even when the range of performance is small, may provide some evidence for needed changes. Piloting changes in a small program may be a sensible way to respond to limited data.

The use of multiple assessments that need to be redesigned to meet the alignment concerns for the gifted education standards is another area of challenge for program coordinators. Each time an assessment is altered, regardless of purpose, there is a need to pilot the new form and adjust as needed. This process takes time and energy to be done well. Program faculty must devote a significant amount of time to these assessment remodeling processes in order to meet CAEP requirements. Moreover, the process of remodeling needs to be collaborative so that there is synchrony in the administration of assessments across instructors in the program. The involvement of adjunct faculty in this process is also critical.

There is a real need to plan carefully for the preparation of the SPA report. The program coordinator must ensure the following: (a) that assessments used in the program meet specifications outlined in this book; (b) that all data points on relevant assessments can be administered, collected, and scored; (c) that interpretation of results are derived from careful analysis of data tables; and (d) that inferences drawn are warranted, given the limitations of the data. The program coordinator will want to collaborate not only with all faculty involved in the program, but also those who might provide statistical and technical support. This collaboration is not a last-minute effort—it requires ongoing effort to accomplish all of the requirements.

Because the gifted education program at most universities does not function according to the principles of economy of scale, the same processes must be done in program accreditation for five annual graduates as is done for 100. Consequently, the engagement of faculty, who often have responsibilities in other programs as well, is great and may seem overwhelming at times. Deployment of graduate assistant help and the assistance of the office for handling the assessment process for the schoolwide report will be critical to ensure that all aspects of the accreditation process gets completed and the planning, implementation, and postanalysis occurs with regularity. This will require multiple meetings, at least once every 2 weeks, on some aspect of the process, as well as many e-mail exchanges on written aspects of the process. Allocation of responsibility for different sections of the report would also seem to be advisable, with people reporting out their findings at a relevant meeting. The goal is to prepare sections of the report even as you are testing out new assessments or designing new rubrics. Do not wait until you have all data to begin writing the report.

Alignment of Course Objectives, Assignments, and Rubrics to the 2013 Standard Elements

One of the challenges presented by the 2013 standards is that fewer standards and fewer elements translate into more general language associated with the descriptive levels of performance for candidates. If course developers built their syllabi and assignments from the previous 10 standards and their accompanying 70 plus elements, then substantial revision is likely to be necessary for course objectives, which should now contain the 2013 standards and elements language. To ensure alignment, the 2013 standards and elements language should reappear in the rubrics used to evaluate candidate performance on course assignments. At the element level in the 2013 standards, many of the 28 elements are cohesive. Thus, rubric descriptors will "hang" together. For example, Element 1.2 states that, "Beginning gifted education professionals use understanding of development and individual differences to respond to the needs of individuals with gifts and talents." This element is cohesive because the two major concepts in the element, development and individual differences, fit together seamlessly. A single rubric descriptor can encompass both, and the course assignment that results in a candidate product or performance is unlikely to result in a candidate who demonstrates mastery of development, but no understanding of individual differences. Both concepts emanate from psychology, are linked together, and are frequently taught in the same course.

In contrast, some elements are more loosely coupled. For example, Element 2.2 states that, "Beginning gifted education professionals use communication and motivation and instructional strategies to facilitate understanding of subject matter and to teach individuals with gifts and talents how to adapt to different environments and develop ethical leadership skills." In this complex element, the major concepts driving the skills to be demonstrated by the candidate include communication, motivation, and instructional strategies. The concepts come from different areas of psychology and education. In turn, the candidate is to use these three complex concepts to help his or her students understand subject matter, to adapt to different environments, and to develop ethical leadership skills. These three areas of student accomplishment differ considerably from one another and range from the cognitive domain of school subjects to the affective domain of ethical leadership. A single course assignment permitting the teacher candidate to demonstrate mastery of all parts of Element 2.2 would need to be a complex task with a rubric possibly using a part of the element as its descriptor rather than the complete element. A candidate might be able to demonstrate that he or she used communication, motivation, and instructional strategies to foster subject matter understanding, but no evidence of developing ethical leadership skills is evident. Or, the candidate may have effectively demonstrated communication skills or motivational strategies in the assignment, but not instructional strategies. How then, is the candidate performance scored if the descriptive language for multiple domains appear in one rubric criterion?

The challenge of alignment could be addressed by developing rubrics that use both models of descriptors. Some rubrics could align the language in the rubric criterion with a single element or with multiple elements as we have seen in several example course syllabi, assignments, and accompanying rubrics found in this book. In some cases, however, the candidate performance may best be captured by rubric criteria that use a part of rather than the complete language found in a single element.

Alignment of Gifted Education Courses With EPP Standards and Assessments

Challenges may also occur when gifted education faculty try to align gifted education course content, EPP program assessments, NAGC-CEC Teacher Preparation Standards, and the CAEP standards. Based on circumstances that may be related to specific program (e.g., number of courses offered in gifted education program) and/or individual EPP requirements to collect specific assessment data, the degree to which gifted education faculty face these challenges will vary.

One of the challenges that university gifted program faculty may face is aligning the NAGC-CEC Teacher Preparation standards to EPP unit assessments. Generally, EPPs approach the collection of key program assessment data with specific CAEP-related criteria and standards in mind. Typically, they are associated with the following: content (CAEP Standard 1); clinical experiences (CAEP Standard 2); admission and recruitment (CAEP Standard 3); evidence of candidate impact on K–12 students (CAEP Standard 4); integration of technology; consideration of diverse learners; and the ability to use data to make decisions that drive instructional practice. For consistency and CAEP reporting purposes, many EPPs have common assessments across programs (allowing them to make "apples to apples" comparisons across programs and report one metric per standard). Due to the varying nature of specialized programs (e.g., reading, special education, gifted education, counseling) and their discipline-specific teacher preparation standards, utilizing common assessment rubrics across programs may not be feasible. It is much easier for university gifted program faculty to approach the integration of the NAGC-CEC Teacher Preparation Standards with autonomy. It is also important to note that CAEP emphasizes the collection of evidence that demonstrates teacher impact on student achievement. University gifted education program faculty will want to consider this emphasis when identifying and using key program assessments.

Course Requirements for Gifted Education Credentials

Although postsecondary degrees in gifted education are available in a majority of states, the number of course semester hours for credentialing varies among states and ranges from 6 to 36 hours (NAGC & Council of State Directors of Programs for the Gifted [CSDPG], 2013). Gifted education programs requiring five or more courses that culminate in a state gifted education teacher license or add-on endorsement make it easier for program faculty to address the teacher preparation standards without having to overload courses with program assessments. It also allows program content to be covered in greater detail (breadth versus depth) without risking program quality. When fewer course hours are available, program faculty will need to consider how they might integrate standards within other course content.

Another challenge with too few courses is addressing the knowledge and skills included in state assessments or the Praxis exam in gifted education (see Gifted Education 5358). For example, the newest version of the Praxis exam has a greater emphasis on identification and assessment of gifted students and less emphasis on creativity than the previous version of the exam. This shift in focus may affect university gifted education programs that have a stand-alone creativity course. In this case, faculty may need to rethink their course objectives, general course content, or even course sequences.

Lack of Human Resources Dedicated to Gifted Education

Many universities with programs in gifted education at the initial licensure level suffer from a paucity of resources devoted to the issue. (Visit http://www.nagc.org for an updated list of universities with teacher preparation programs in gifted education.) Many programs are operated predominantly by adjunct faculty who may have limited depth or background in the field. The program faculty problem operates in online and hybrid programs as well as in face-to-face program formats. In fact, some online programs rely heavily on instructional coaches without terminal degrees and with limited knowledge or experience in gifted education. In other instances, faculty are "retreaded" to work in this area even though they have little background in the theory, research, or practice arenas of gifted education. It is also not uncommon to find the delivery of the program falling on one faculty member who is also likely to have other teaching and administrative responsibilities. Thus full-time attention to the program at the university level is problematic. One solution might involve identifying faculty members within the general education program who might be interested in enhancing their knowledge about gifted education and integrating some of the standards content within their courses. Faculty interest might be encouraged by collaborating with gifted education faculty in research and joint presentations at the National Association for Gifted Children (NAGC) or the Council for Exceptional Children (CEC) conferences. Another solution might entail partnering with those who have resources in special education or general education to develop new dual-certificate programs. A third solution would be to secure grants or external funding that provides resources for hiring individuals with a gifted background who might teach in the program.

Collaboration With Faculty With Different Philosophies

In some cases, particularly at the undergraduate level, educators may encounter resistance in developing programs to prepare teachers in gifted and talented education from faculty who have different philosophies or who are in opposition to the provision of special services for students with gifts and talents. Questions may be raised about equality of access, equality of services, and equality of outcomes—elitism and favoritism (Sapon-Shevin, 2003). Aren't all students gifted? Doesn't gifted education privilege some groups over others? Shouldn't all students have access to the same curriculum? Isn't it undemocratic to remove some students from the general education program and provide them with special services? Won't acceleration options increase the achievement gap? The debate can become so heated that faculty members in some programs will attempt to undermine or discredit candidates who choose to specialize in gifted and talented education.

Concentrating on student outcomes, required by CAEP, may help in finding common ground between faculty members in different teacher education programs. Agreeing that the central focus for candidates should be the Pre-K–12 student, faculty members might reframe questions so that all students might benefit from an individually prescribed curriculum: How might candidates create classrooms where a wide range of learner differences can be accommodated? How might candidates use ongoing assessment so that each student is learning new knowledge and skills? How might candidates pace curriculum and instruction to adapt to learner differences and keep each student engaged?

Involving candidates and interested school or university faculty in action research is also another way of redirecting attention away from philosophical discussions to student learning. Joint inquiries might examine which curriculum adjustments, classroom arrangements, and/or instructional strategies produce the greatest gains in learning for individual students. Finding faculty members who are interested in student outcomes and the effectiveness of teaching strategies may build bridges across programs and eventually build support for gifted and talented education.

States Without Mandated Teacher Preparation Programs in Gifted Education

One problem the field of gifted education faces is the lack of consistent policies on teacher preparation to work with gifted students in each state. Of the 30 states that responded to an NAGC and CSDPG (2013) survey, only 17 states required gifted education credentials. Of these 17, only eight states have written competencies for teachers in gifted education programs. Of those that do mandate gifted education training, the number of hours required for certification range from 30 clock hours to 36 hours of coursework. In states where endorsement or certification is in place, universities are offering programs that may or may not have received national recognition in gifted education. Clearly, the teacher preparation standards in gifted education must make an impact on that situation if the field is to develop evenly across the country with gifted students having high-quality teachers able to meet their needs. Universities and state agencies might collaborate in using these standards to make legislators and policy-making boards in teacher education aware that national standards exist in gifted education. This approach is particularly helpful in states that mandate programs or services but not teacher certification. Stakeholders in gifted education might pursue these questions: How does the state ensure that teachers who teach gifted and talented students are qualified? How might these qualifications make a difference in outcomes for gifted and talented students? With a mandate that requires standards-aligned coursework, there is greater likelihood that qualified teachers will teach gifted and talented students.

Lack of Personnel Preparation Policies at the State Level That Feed University Preparation of Teachers

Another problem in this area rests with current state policies in gifted education that ignore the critical role that universities assume in standards-based personnel preparation and that place more emphasis on professional development that can be carried out by school districts and regional entities that do not need to adhere to a core set of national standards. Although some states have tied state policy in this area to university preparation (e.g., North Carolina), many others have limited impact over the systematic and rigorous preparation of teachers for the field. The rules and regulations governing the administration of programs in every state should involve teacher preparation through the use of the NAGC-CEC teacher preparation standards as a basic requirement for all personnel working with these learners, linked to university coursework. The standards might provide the impetus for building new collaborations across teacher preparation agencies (e.g., schools, regional centers, universities). All of these agencies might examine the alignment between current programs and the standards. The new collaborative might have a greater influence on changing personnel preparation programs than with single entities such as universities.

Competition With Alternative Preparation Programs That Don't Meet Standards

Alternative programs have grown rapidly across the United States because of concerns about teacher quantity (Feistritzer & Chester, 2000). In the Secretary of Education's latest report on teacher quality (U.S. Department of Education, 2013), states reported three types of teacher preparation programs, with 69% classified as traditional, 21% alternative route teacher preparation programs based at institutions of higher education (IHE), and 10% alternative route teacher preparation programs not based at IHEs. Alternative programs offered to noncertified candidates with bachelor's degrees range from master's degree programs offered at universities to a few weeks of training during the summer followed by a mentored teaching experience (e.g., Teach for America).

Although researchers have reported that teachers who enter through alternative routes feel significantly less prepared than those who experience a more traditional program and were significantly less committed to teaching as a profession (Darling-Hammond, Chung, & Frelow, 2002), competition will most likely persist as long as the demand is greater than the supply. How do programs in gifted education that meet national standards compete with alternatives that offer shortcuts?

One way of improving the quality is for universities to partner with schools, states, and other agencies that want to offer alternatives to traditional university programs. Courses that meet standards might be offered in school settings with a team of university and school personnel providing follow-up and mentoring of candidates pursuing the initial certificate in gifted education. Some of the courses might be offered online to provide flexibility for practicing teachers in acquiring research-based knowledge and skills identified in the standards. To encourage initial participation, universities might be able to offer tuition scholarships because courses are offered off campus. As graduates of the program are able to demonstrate greater skills of differentiating curriculum in the classroom, the district and, most importantly, the students would benefit.

Another way of implementing standards in states that do not require gifted education teacher preparation is to consider offering a dual certificate program in gifted *and* elementary or secondary education at the undergraduate level. This option allows the gifted education standards to be integrated into the general education program and benefits candidates in not only the gifted program but also the general education program. More graduates are prepared to teach gifted and talented students in general education classrooms where most gifted and talented students are served.

Working with the states' directors in gifted education and boards for teacher certification is another way to improve teacher preparation programs in gifted education. States that do not have mandates for preparing teachers in gifted education or that have only minimal requirements will want to examine the teacher preparation standards and use them as leverage to change inadequate rules and policies that undermine quality programs and services for gifted and talented students.

Finally, the field needs to conduct research that examines the effects of teacher preparation in gifted education on the services and performance of gifted and talented students. Are there differences in classroom practices between teachers who are prepared in gifted education and those who are not? Do these differences in classroom practices result in greater student performance? Results from these studies and others may then be used to encourage changes in federal and state teacher licensure mandates.

REFERENCES

Allen, I. E., & Seaman, J. (2014). *Grade change: Tracking online education in the United States.* Retrieved from http://www.onlinelearningsurvey.com/reports/gradechange.pdf

Archambault, F. X., Jr., Westberg, K. L., Brown, S. W., Hallmark, B. W., Zhang, W., & Emmons, C. L. (1993). Classroom practices used with gifted third and fourth grade students. *Journal for the Education of the Gifted, 16,* 103–119.

Bangel, N. J., Moon, S. M., & Capobianco, B. M. (2010). Preservice teachers' perceptions and experiences in a gifted education training model. *Gifted Child Quarterly, 54,* 209–221.

Benson, T., & Cotabish, A. (2014). Virtual bugs: An innovative peer coaching intervention to improve the instructional behaviors of teacher candidates. *Southeastern Regional Association of Teacher Educators Journal, 24,* 1–9.

Berman, K. M., Schultz, R. A., & Weber, C. L. (2012). A lack of awareness and emphasis in preservice teacher training. Preconceived beliefs about the gifted and talented. *Gifted Child Today, 35,* 19–26.

Castellano, J. A., & Frazier, A. D. (2010). *Special populations in gifted education: Understanding our most able students from diverse backgrounds.* Waco, TX: Prufrock Press.

Clinkenbeard, P. R. (2012). Neuroscience and young children: Implications for the diversity of gifted programming. In R. F. Subotnik, A. Robinson, C.

M. Callahan, & E. J. Gubbins (Eds.), *Malleable minds: Translating insights from psychology and neuroscience to gifted education* (pp. 197–207). Storrs: University of Connecticut, The National Research Center on the Gifted and Talented.

Colangelo, N., Assouline, S. G., & Gross, M. U. M. (2004). Introduction. In N. Colangelo, S. G. Assouline, & M. U. M. Gross (Eds.), *A nation deceived: How schools hold back America's brightest students.* Iowa City: University of Iowa, Belin-Blank International Center for Gifted Education and Talent Development.

Cotabish, A. (2015). *Integrating gifted pedagogy into university science syllabi.* Washington, DC: National Association for Gifted Children.

Cotabish, A., & Benson, T. (2014). *The interim effects of virtual peer coaching on the instructional behaviors of pre-service teacher candidates. Proceedings of the 2014 American Educational Research Association.* Washington, DC: American Educational Research Association.

Council for Exceptional Children. (2010). *Validation study resource manual.* Retrieved from http://www.cec.sped.org/~/media/Files/Standards/Profess ional%20Preparation%20Standards/Specialty%20sets/Validation% 20Studies%20Resource%20Manual.pdf

Council for the Accreditation of Educator Preparation. (n.d.). *Standard 2 components: Clinical partnerships and practice.* Retrieved from http://caepnet. org/standards/standard-2

Council for the Accreditation of Educator Preparation. (2013). *CAEP accreditation standards and evidence: Aspirations for educator preparation.* Retrieved from http://www.caepnet.org/standards/introduction

Council for the Accreditation of Educator Preparation. (2014, February). *CAEP evidence guide.* Retrieved from http://www.caepnet.org/~/media/ Files/caep/knowledge-center/caep-evidence-guide.pdf

Daniel, G. R., Auhl, G., & Hastings, W. (2013). Collaborative feedback and reflection for professional growth: Preparing first-year pre-service teachers for participation in the community of practice. *Asia-Pacific Journal of Teacher Education, 41,* 159–172.

Darling-Hammond, L., Chung, R., & Frelow, F. (2002). Variation in teacher preparation: How well do different pathways prepare teachers to teach? *Journal of Teacher Education, 53,* 286–302.

Feistritzer, E., & Chester, D. (2000). *Alternative teacher certification: A state-by-state analysis 2000.* Washington, DC: National Center for Education Information.

Ford, D. Y. (1998). The underrepresentation of minority students in gifted education: Problems and promises in recruitment and retention. *Journal of Special Education, 32,* 4–14.

Ford, D. Y., & Trotman, M. F. (2001). Teachers of gifted students: Suggested multicultural characteristics and competencies. *Roeper Review, 23,* 235–239.

Ford, D. Y., & Webb, K. S. (1994). Desegregation of gifted educational programs: The impact of Brown on underachieving children of color. *The Journal of Negro Education, 63,* 358–373.

Ginsburg, D. (2012, November 30). *Re: Coachability: A key to performing up to capability* [Web log message]. Retrieved from http://blogs.edweek.org/teachers/coach_gs_teaching_tips/2012/11/coachability_a_key_to_performing_up_to_capability.html

Hanover Research Council. (2009). *Best practices in online teaching strategies.* Retrieved from http://www.uwec.edu/AcadAff/resources/edtech/upload/Best-Practices-in-Online-Teaching-Strategies-Membership.pdf

Hansen, J. B., & Feldhusen, J. F. (1994). Comparison of trained and untrained teachers of gifted students. *Gifted Child Quarterly, 38,* 115–121.

Hughes, C. E. (2015). *Integrating gifted pedagogy into university introduction to exceptionalities syllabi.* Washington, DC: National Association for Gifted Children.

Hunsaker, S., Finley, V., & Frank, E. (1997). An analysis of teacher nominations and student performance in gifted programs. *Gifted Child Quarterly, 41,* 19–24.

Interstate Teacher Assessment and Support Consortium. (2013). *InTASC model core teaching standards.* Retrieved from http://www.ccsso.org/Resources/Publications/InTASC_Model_Core_Teaching_Standards_A_Resource_for_State_Dialogue_%28April_2011%29.html

Johnsen, S. K. (2008). Identifying gifted and talented learners. In F. A. Karnes & K. R. Stephens (Eds.), *Achieving excellence: Educating the gifted and talented* (pp. 135–153). Upper Saddle River, NJ: Pearson.

Johnsen, S. K., Haensly, P. A., Ryser, G. R., & Ford, R. F. (2002). Changing general education classroom practices to adapt for gifted students. *Gifted Child Quarterly, 46,* 45–63.

Johnsen, S. K., VanTassel-Baska, J., & Robinson, A. (2008). *Using the national gifted education standards for university teacher preparation programs.* Thousand Oaks, CA: Corwin Press.

Johnsen, S. K., Wisely, L. W., & Fearon, D. D. (2012). *An observation report of elementary cluster classroom in the Waco Independent School District.* Waco, TX: Baylor University, School of Education, Department of Educational Psychology.

Kinnelon Public Schools. (n.d.). *Understanding by Design review rubric.* Retrieved from http://www.kinnelonpublicschools.org/boe/Curric/writing/UBD_Review_Rubric_0607.doc

Matthews, M. S., & Shaunessy, E. (2008). Culturally, linguistically, and economically diverse gifted students. In F. A. Karnes & K. R. Stephens (Eds.), *Achieving excellence: Educating the gifted and talented* (pp. 99–115). Upper Saddle River, NJ: Pearson.

McKee, L. (2014). *Partnerships for practice: CAEP Standard 2* [PowerPoint Slides]. Retrieved from http://caepnet.files.wordpress.com/2014/10/breakout_vii_standard_2_linda_mckee.pdf

Miller, E. (2005). Studying the meaning of giftedness: Inspiration from the field of cognitive psychology. *Roeper Review, 27,* 172–177.

National Association for Gifted Children. (2010). *Pre-K–grade 12 gifted education programming standards.* Washington, DC: Author.

National Association for Gifted Children. (2014). *Knowledge and skill standards in gifted education for all teachers.* Retrieved from http://www.nagc.org/resources-publications/resources/national-standards-gifted-and-talented-education/knowledge-and

National Association for Gifted Children, & Council for Exceptional Children. (2006). *NAGC-CEC teacher preparation standards in gifted education.* Retrieved from http://www.nagc.org/sites/default/files/standards/NACG-CEC%20CAEP%20standards%20%282006%29.pdf

National Association for Gifted Children, & Council for Exceptional Children. (2013a). *NAGC-CEC teacher preparation standards in gifted education.* Retrieved from Retrieved from http://www.nagc.org/sites/default/files/standards/NAGC-%20CEC%20CAEP%20standards%20%282013%20final%29.pdf

National Association for Gifted Children, & Council for Exceptional Children. (2013b). *Using the NAGC-CEC Teacher Preparation Standards in the CAEP accreditation process.* Retrieved from http://www.nagc.org/resources-publications/resources/national-standards-gifted-and-talented-education/nagc-cec-teacher-1

National Association for Gifted Children, & Council of State Directors of Programs for the Gifted. (2013). *2012–2013 state of the states in gifted education: National policy and practice data.* Washington, DC: NAGC.

National Council for Accreditation of Teacher Education. (2010). *Transforming teacher education through clinical practice: A national strategy to prepare effective teachers.* Retrieved from http://www.caepnet.org/~/media/Files/caep/accreditation-resources/blue-ribbon-panel.pdf

National Council for Accreditation of Teacher Education Specialty Area Studies Board. (2004). *SASB guidelines on writing and approval of SPA program standards.* Washington DC: Author.

National Research Council. (2010). *Preparing teachers: Building evidence for sound policy.* Washington DC: The National Academies Press.

Renzulli, J. S., Smith, L., & Reis, S. M. (1982). Curriculum compacting: An essential strategy for working with gifted students. *The Elementary School Journal, 82,* 185–194.

Robinson, A. (2012). The case approach: Translating research to professional development. In R. F. Subotnik, A. Robinson, C. M. Callahan, & E. J. Gubbins (Eds.), *Malleable minds: Translating insights from psychology and neuroscience to gifted education* (pp. 189–195). Storrs: University of Connecticut, The National Research Center on the Gifted and Talented.

Rogers, K. B. (1992). *A best-evidence synthesis of research on acceleration options for gifted students.* Retrieved from http://www.davidsongifted.org/db/Articles_id_10004.aspx

Rogers, K. B. (2002). Effects of acceleration on gifted learners. In M. Neihart, S. M. Reis, N. M. Robinson, & S. M. Moon (Eds.), *The social and emotional development of gifted children: What do we know?* (pp. 3–12). Waco, TX: Prufrock Press.

Rogers, K. B. (2015). Academic, socialization, and psychological effects of acceleration: Research synthesis. In S. G. Assouline, N. Colangelo, J. VanTassel-Baska, & A. Lupkowski-Shoplik (Eds.), *A nation empowered: Evidence trumps the excuses holding back America's brightest students* (pp. 13–30). Iowa City: University of Iowa, Belin-Blank International Center for Gifted Education and Talent Development.

Ryser, G. R. (2011). Fairness in testing and nonbiased assessment. In S. K. Johnsen (Ed.), *Identifying gifted students: A practical guide* (2nd ed., pp. 63–74). Waco, TX: Prufrock Press.

Sapon-Shevin, M. (2003). Equity, excellence, and school reform: Why is finding common ground so hard? In J. Borland (Ed.), *Rethinking gifted education* (pp. 127–142). New York, NY: Teachers College Press.

Shaunessy-Dedrick, E. (2015). *Integrating gifted pedagogy into university literacy syllabi.* Washington, DC: National Association for Gifted Children.

Siegle, D. (2012). Recognizing both effort and talent: How do we keep from throwing the baby out with the bathwater? In R. F. Subotnik, A. Robinson, C. M. Callahan, & E. J. Gubbins (Eds.), *Malleable minds: Translating insights from psychology and neuroscience to gifted education* (pp. 233–243). Storrs: University of Connecticut, The National Research Center on the Gifted and Talented.

Siegle, D., & Powell, T. (2004). Exploring teacher biases when nominating students for gifted programs. *Gifted Child Quarterly, 48,* 21–29.

Sparks, S., & Mainzer, R. (2007). *CEC validation studies overview 2007.* Arlington, VA: Council for Exceptional Children.

Steenbergen-Hu, S., & Moon, S. M. (2011). The effects of acceleration on high-ability learners: A meta-analysis. *Gifted Child Quarterly, 55,* 39–53.

Swanson, J. (2006). Breaking through assumptions about low-income, minority gifted students. *Gifted Child Quarterly, 50,* 11–25.

Tomlinson, C. A., & Hockett, J. A. (2008). Instructional strategies and programming models for gifted learners. In F. A. Karnes & K. R. Stephens (Eds.), *Achieving excellence: Educating the gifted and talented* (pp. 154–169). Upper Saddle River, NJ: Pearson.

U.S. Department of Education. (2006). *Partnerships for reform: Changing teacher preparation through the Title II HEA Partnership Program: Final report.* Washington DC: Author.

U.S. Department of Education. (2013). *Preparing and credentialing the nation's teachers: The secretary's ninth report on teacher quality.* Retrieved from http://www2.ed.gov/about/reports/annual/teachprep/index.html

University of Central Arkansas College of Education. (n.d.). *Enhancing educator efficacy through reflective decision-making.* Retrieved from http://candidate.coe.uca.edu/NCATE/documents/Conceptual%20Framework/Conceptual%20Framework%20FINAL.pdf

VanTassel-Baska, J. (1986). Effective curriculum and instructional models for talented students. *Gifted Child Quarterly, 30,* 164–169.

VanTassel-Baska, J., Johnson, D., & Avery, L. D. (2002). Using performance tasks in the identification of economically disadvantaged and minority gifted learners: Findings from Project Star. *Gifted Child Quarterly, 46,* 110–123.

VanTassel-Baska, J., & Little, C. A. (Eds.). (2003). *Content-based curriculum for high-ability learners.* Waco, TX: Prufrock Press.

VanTassel-Baska, J., & Little, C. A. (Eds.). (2011). *Content-based curriculum for high-ability learners* (2nd ed.). Waco, TX: Prufrock Press.

VanTassel-Baska, J., & Stambaugh, T. (2005). Challenges and possibilities for serving gifted learners in the regular classroom. *Theory Into Practice, 44,* 211–217.

VanTassel-Baska, J., & Wood, S. (2008). Curriculum development in gifted education: A challenge to provide optimal learning experiences. In F. A. Karnes & K. R. Stephens (Eds.), *Achieving excellence: Educating the gifted and talented* (pp. 209–229). Upper Saddle River, NJ: Pearson.

Zeichner, K. (2010). Rethinking the connection between campus courses and field experiences in college- and university-based teacher education. *Journal of Teacher Education, 61,* 89–99.

COMPARISON OF 2006 NAGC-CEC TO 2013 NAGC-CEC TEACHER PREPARATION STANDARDS IN GIFTED AND TALENTED EDUCATION

2006 NAGC-CEC Teacher Preparation Standards in Gifted and Talented Education	2013 NAGC-CEC Teacher Preparation Standards in Gifted and Talented Education
Standard 1. Foundations	*Standard 6. Professional Learning and Ethical Practice (Primarily)*
GT1K1: Historical foundations	Element 6.2
GT1K2: Key philosophy/research	Element 6.2
GT1K3: Laws and policies	Element 6.2
GT1K4: Conceptions/identification	Element 4.1
GT1K5: Impact of dominant culture	Element 1.1
GT1K6: Factors that enhance/inhibit	Elements 1.1
GT1K7: Key issues and trends	Element 6.2
Standard 2. Development and Characteristics of Learners	*Standard 1. Learning Development and Individual Learning Differences (Primarily)*
GT2K1: Cognitive/affective	Element 1.2
GT2K2: Culture/environmental effects	Element 1.1

2006 NAGC-CEC Teacher Preparation Standards in Gifted and Talented Education	2013 NAGC-CEC Teacher Preparation Standards in Gifted and Talented Education
GT2K3: Role of families	Element 1.1
GT2K4: Advanced milestones	Element 1.2
GT2K5: Differences with general	Element 1.2
Standard 3. Individual Learning Differences	*Standard 1. Learning Development and Individual Learning Differences (Primarily)*
GT3K1: Influences of diversity	Element 1.1
GT3K2: Academic/affective	Element 1.2
GT3K3: Idiosyncratic learning patterns	Element 1.2
GT3K4: Beliefs, traditions, values influences on relationships	Element 1.1
GT3S1: Integrate perspectives in planning instruction	Element 1.1
Standard 4. Instructional Strategies	*Standard 5. Instructional Planning and Strategies (Primarily)*
GT4K1: Resources/differentiation	Element 5.1
GT4K2: Effective strategies	Element 5.1
GT4S1: Pedagogical content knowledge	Elements 5.1, 5.3, 5.5
GT4S2: Apply HLT/metacognitive models to content areas	Element 5.1
GT4S3: Explore, develop, and research areas of interest	Elements 5.1, 5.4
GT4S4: Preassess learning in domains and adjust using assessment	Element 3.3, Elements 4.3, 4.4
GT4S5: Pace curriculum and instruction consistent with needs	Element 5.1
GT4S6: Challenging, multicultural curriculum	Element 5.4
GT4S7: Assistive technologies	Element 5.2
Standard 5. Learning Environments/Social Interactions	*Standard 2. Learning Environments (Primarily)*
GT5K1: Stereotypes/discrimination	Element 2.3
GT5K2: Social/emotional development influences on relationships	Element 2.1
GT5S1: Opportunities that promote self-awareness/peer relations/intercultural/leadership	Element 2.2
GT5S2: Environments that promote self-awareness, self-efficacy, leadership, learning	Element 2.2, Element 4.4

2006 NAGC-CEC Teacher Preparation Standards in Gifted and Talented Education	2013 NAGC-CEC Teacher Preparation Standards in Gifted and Talented Education
GT5S3: Safe environments for independence/interdependence/positive relationships	Element 2.1
GT5S4: Intercultural experiences	Element 2.1
GT5S5: Social interaction/coping skills to address personal/social issues, including discrimination	Element 2.1
Standard 6. Language and Communication	*Standard 2. Learning Environments (Primarily)*
GT6K1: Forms and methods	Element 2.3
GT6K2: Impact of diversity	Element 1.1, Element 2.3
GT6K3: Implications of culture, behavior, language	Element 2.3
GT6S1: Resources/strategies to enhance advanced communication	Element 2.3
GT6S2: Advanced oral/written tools, including assistive technologies	Element 5.2
Standard 7. Instructional Planning	*Standard 5. Instructional Planning and Strategies and Standard 3. Curricular Content Knowledge (Primarily)*
GT7K1: Theories/research models that form basis of curriculum and instruction	Element 3.1
GT7K2: Differences between differentiated and general curriculum	Element 3.3
GT7K3: Curriculum emphases within domains	Element 3.1
GT7S1: Instructional plans aligned to standards	Element 5.2
GT7S2: Design learning plans	Element 5.2
GT7S3: Scope and sequence	Element 3.1
GT7S4: Resources/strategies/product options that respond to differences	Elements 5.1, 5.2, 5.3, 5.5
GT7S5: Advanced, conceptually challenging, in-depth, distinctive, complex curricula	Elements 3.2, 3.4
GT7S6: Academic/career guidance	Element 5.4
Standard 8. Assessment	*Standard 4. Assessment (Primarily)*
GT8K1: Identification	Element 4.1
GT8K2: Multiple assessments in different domains for identifying	Element 4.3

2006 NAGC-CEC Teacher Preparation Standards in Gifted and Talented Education	2013 NAGC-CEC Teacher Preparation Standards in Gifted and Talented Education
GT8K3: Uses and limitations of assessments for documenting growth	Elements 4.1, 4.3
GT8S1: Nonbiased and equitable	Elements 4.1, 4.3
GT8S2: Technically adequate for identification/placement	Element 4.1
GT8S3: Differentiated and curriculum-based for use in instruction	Elements 4.4, 4.5
GT8S4: Alternative assessments and technologies to evaluate learning	Element 4.3
Standard 9. Professional and Ethical Practice	*Standard 6. Professional Learning and Ethical Practice (Primarily)*
GT9K1: Personal/cultural frames of reference, including bias	Element 6.2
GT9K2: Relevant organizations and publications	Element 6.1
GT9S1: Personal skills and limitations	Element 6.4
GT9S2: Confidential communication	Element 6.1
GT9S3: Encourage/model respect	Element 6.3
GT9S4: Laws, policies, standards	Elements 6.1, 6.2
GT9S5: Continuous research-supported professional development	Element 6.4
GT9S6: Professional organizations	Element 6.1
GT9S7: Reflect on personal practice	Element 6.4
Standard 10. Collaboration	*Standard 7. Collaboration (Primarily)*
GT10K1: Culturally responsive	Element 4.3, Element 5.3, Element 7.3
GT10S1: Concerns of families	Element 4.3, Element 5.3, Element 7.3
GT10S2: Stakeholders outside school setting	Elements 7.1, 7.3
GT10S3: Advocate for benefit	Element 6.5
GT10S4: Families, general and special educators, school staff in comprehensive program	Elements 7.1, 7.3
GT10S5: Families, community, and professionals in assessment	Elements 7.1, 7.3
GT10S6: School personnel about characteristics	Elements 7.2

RESEARCH SUPPORT FOR THE 2013 TEACHER PREPARATION STANDARDS IN GIFTED AND TALENTED EDUCATION

Standard 1: Learner Development and Individual Learning Differences

Beginning gifted education professionals understand the variations in learning and development in cognitive and affective areas between and among individuals with gifts and talents and apply this understanding to provide meaningful and challenging learning experiences for individuals with exceptionalities.

ELEMENT 1.1

Beginning gifted education professionals understand how language, culture, economic status, family background, and/or area of disability can influence the learning of individuals with gifts and talents.

Research-Based References

Benbow, C. P., Lubinski, D., Shea, D. L., & Eftekhari-Sanjani, H. (2000). Sex differences in mathematical reasoning ability at age 13: Their status 20 years later. *Psychological Science, 11,* 474–480.

Callahan, C. M., & Dickson, R. K. (2014). Mentors and mentorships. In J. A. Plucker & C. M. Callahan (Eds.), *Critical issues and practices in gifted education* (2nd ed., pp. 413–426). Waco, TX: Prufrock Press.

Coleman, M. R. (2001). Surviving or thriving? *Gifted Child Today, 24*(3), 56–63.

Foley Nicpon, M., Allmon, A., Sieck, B., & Stinson, R. D. (2011). Empirical investigation of twice-exceptionality: Where have we been and where are we going? *Gifted Child Quarterly, 55,* 3–17.

Good, C., Aronson, J., & Inzlicht, M. (2003). Improving adolescents' standardized test performance: An intervention to reduce the effects of stereotype threat. *Journal of Applied Developmental Psychology, 24,* 645–662.

Grantham, T. C. (2004). Rocky Jones: Case study of a high-achieving Black male's motivation to participate in gifted classes. *Roeper Review, 26,* 208–216.

Hébert, T. P. (2000). Defining belief in self: Intelligent young men in an urban high school. *Gifted Child Quarterly, 44,* 91–114.

Hébert, T. P., & Neumeister, K. L. S. (2000). University mentors in the elementary classroom: Supporting the intellectual, motivational, and emotional needs of high-ability students. *Journal for the Education of the Gifted, 24,* 122–148.

Johnson, N. (1994). *Understanding gifted underachievers in an ethnically diverse population.* (ERIC Document Reproduction Services No. ED368101)

Kalbfleisch, M. L. (2014). Twice-exceptional learners. In J. A. Plucker & C. M. Callahan (Eds.), *Critical issues and practices in gifted education* (2nd ed., pp. 671–690). Waco, TX: Prufrock Press.

Kanevsky, L., & Keighley, T. (2003). To produce or not to produce? Understanding boredom and the honor in underachievement. *Roeper Review, 26,* 20–28.

Kerr, B., & Kurpius, S. (2004). Encouraging talented girls in math and science: Effects of a guidance intervention. *High Ability Studies, 15,* 85–102.

McCoach, D. B., & Siegle, D. (2003). Factors that differentiate underachieving gifted students from high achieving gifted students. *Gifted Child Quarterly, 47,* 144–154.

Neihart, M. (2007). The socioaffective impact of acceleration and ability grouping: Recommendations for best practice. *Gifted Child Quarterly, 51,* 330–341.

Peters, S. J., & Gentry, M. (2012). Group-specific norms and teacher rating scales: Implications for underrepresentation. *Journal of Advanced Academics, 23*, 125–144.

Peters, W. A. M., Grager-Loidl, H., & Supplee, P. (2000). Underachievement in gifted and talented students: Theory and practice. In K. A. Heller, F. J. Mönks, R. J. Sternberg, & R. F. Subotnik (Eds.), *International handbook of giftedness and talent* (2nd ed., pp. 609–620). Amsterdam, The Netherlands: Elsevier.

Peterson, J. S. (2002). A longitudinal study of post-high-school development in gifted individuals at risk for poor educational outcomes. *Journal of Secondary Gifted Education, 14*, 6–18.

Peterson, J. S., & Rischar, H. (2000). Gifted and gay: A study of the adolescent experience. *Gifted Child Quarterly, 44*, 231–246.

Reis, S. M., Colbert, R. D., & Hébert, T. P. (2005). Understanding resilience in diverse, talented students in an urban high school. *Roeper Review, 27*, 110–120.

Renzulli, J., & Park, S. (2002). *Giftedness and high school dropouts: Personal, family, and school related factors* (RM02168). Storrs: University of Connecticut, The National Research Center on the Gifted and Talented.

Sak, U. (2004). A synthesis of research on psychological types of gifted adolescents. *Journal of Secondary Gifted Education, 15*, 70–79.

Tieso, C. (2007). Patterns of overexcitabilities in identified gifted students and their parents: A hierarchical model. *Gifted Child Quarterly, 51*, 11–22.

Sternberg, R. J., Torff, B., & Grigorenko, E. L. (1998). Teaching triarchically improves school achievement. *Journal of Educational Psychology, 90*, 374–384.

VanTassel-Baska, J., Bass, G., Ries, R., Poland, D., & Avery, L. (1998). A national study of science curriculum effectiveness with high ability students. *Gifted Child Quarterly, 42*, 200–211.

Theory-Based References

Barkan, J. H., & Bernal, E. M. (1991), Gifted education for bilingual and limited English proficient students. *Gifted Child Quarterly, 35*, 144–147.

Cross, T. L. (2011). *On the social and emotional lives of gifted children* (4th ed.). Waco, TX: Prufrock Press.

Gagné, F. (2011). Academic talent development and the equity issue in gifted education. *Talent Development & Excellence, 1*(3), 3–22.

Gagné, F. (2007). Ten commandments for academic talent development. *Gifted Child Quarterly, 51*, 93–118.

Hébert, T. P. (2011). *Understanding the social and emotional lives of gifted students*. Waco, TX: Prufrock Press.

Lohman, D. F. (2006). *Identifying academically talented minority students* (RM05216). Storrs: University of Connecticut, The National Research Center on the Gifted and Talented.

Lovecky, D. (2003). *Gifted children with AD/HD*. Reston, VA: ERIC Clearinghouse on Disabilities and Gifted Education. (ERIC Document Reproduction Services No. ED439555)

Milgram, R. M., Dunn, R., & Price, G. E. (1992). Teaching and counseling gifted and talented adolescents: An international learning style perspective. Westport, CT: Praeger Publishing.

Ogbu, J. (1995). Understanding cultural diversity and learning. In J. A. Banks & C. A. M. Banks (Eds.), *Handbook of research on multicultural education*. New York, NY: Macmillan.

Renzulli, J. S. (1978). What makes giftedness? Re-examining a definition. *Phi Delta Kappa, 60*, 180–181.

Rogers, K. B. (2002). What else do you need to know about your gifted child? In *Reforming gifted education* (pp. 47–72). Scottsdale, AZ: Great Potential Press.

Winzer, M. A., & Mazurek, K. (1998). *Special education in multicultural contexts*. Upper Saddle River, NJ: Prentice Hall.

Practice-Based References

Castellano, J. A., & Pinkos, M. (2005). A rationale for connecting dual language programs with gifted education. In V. Gonzalez & J. Tinajero (Eds.), *Review of research and practice* (Vol. 3, pp. 107–124). Mahwah, NJ: Lawrence Erlbaum Associates.

Friedman, R. C., & Lee, S. W. (1996). Differentiating instruction for high-achieving/gifted children in regular classrooms: A field test of three gifted-education models. *Journal for the Education of the Gifted, 19*, 405–436.

Hébert, T. P. (1991). Meeting the affective needs of bright boys through bibliotherapy. *Roeper Review, 13*, 207–212.

Kanevsky, L., & Keighley, T. (2003). To produce or not to produce? Understanding boredom and the honor in underachievement. *Roeper Review, 26*, 20–28.

Kirschenbaum, R. J. (2004). Dynamic assessment and its use with underserved gifted and talented populations. In A. Baldwin & S. Reis (Eds.), *Culturally diverse and underserved populations of gifted students. Essential reading in gifted education* (pp. 49–62). Thousand Oaks, CA: Corwin Press.

Kitano, M. K., & Pedersen, K. S. (2002). Action research and practical inquiry: Multicultural content integration in gifted education: Lessons from the field. *Journal for the Education of the Gifted, 25,* 269–289.

Matthews, P. H., & Matthews, M. S. (2004). Heritage language instruction and giftedness in language minority students: Pathways toward success. *Journal of Secondary Gifted Education, 15,* 50–55.

Nugent, S. A. (2000). Perfectionism: Its manifestations and classroom-based interventions. *Journal of Secondary Gifted Education, 11,* 215–221.

Renzulli, J. S., & Richards, S. (2000). *Addressing the needs of gifted middle school students. Practitioners' guide A0023.* (ERIC Document Reproduction Services No. ED456574)

Siegle, D., & Schuler, P. A. (2000). Perfectionism differences in gifted middle school students. *Roeper Review, 23,* 39–44.

Subotnik, R. F., & Coleman, L. (1996). Establishing the foundations for a talent development school: Applying principles to creating an ideal. *Journal for the Education of the Gifted, 20,* 175–189.

ELEMENT 1.2
Beginning gifted education professionals use understanding of development and individual differences to respond to the needs of individuals with gifts and talents.

Research-Based References

Ablard, K. E., & Tissot, S. L. (1998). Young students' readiness for advanced math: Precocious abstract reasoning. *Journal for the Education of the Gifted, 21,* 206–223.

Carter, K. R., & Ormrod, J. E. (1982). Acquisition of formal operations by intellectually gifted children. *Gifted Child Quarterly, 26,* 110–115.

Cross, T. L., & Coleman, L. J. (1993). The social cognition of gifted adolescents: An exploration of the stigma of giftedness paradigm. *Roeper Review, 16,* 37–40.

Diaz, E. I. (1998). Perceived factors influencing the academic underachievement of talented students of Puerto Rican descent. *Gifted Child Quarterly, 42,* 105–122.

Ford, D. Y., & Harris, J., III. (1997). A study of the racial identity and achievement of Black males and females. *Roeper Review, 20,* 105–110.

Gottfried, A. W., Cook, C. R., Gottfried, A. E., & Morris, P. E. (2005). Educational characteristics of adolescents with gifted academic intrinsic motivation: A longitudinal investigation from school entry through early adulthood. *Gifted Child Quarterly, 49,* 172–186.

Gottfried, A. W., Gottfried, A. E., & Guerin, D. W. (2006). The Fullerton longitudinal study: A long-term investigation of intellectual and motivational giftedness. *Journal for the Education of the Gifted, 29,* 430–450.

Grantham, T., & Ford, D. (1998). A case study of the social needs of Danisha: An underachieving gifted African-American female. *Roeper Review, 21,* 96–101.

Hyde, J. S., Fennema, E., Ryan, M., Frost, L. A., & Hopp, C. (1990). Gender comparisons of mathematics attitudes and affect. *Psychology of Women Quarterly, 14,* 299–314.

Lupkowski-Shoplik, A. E., & Assouline, S. G. (1994). Evidence of extreme mathematical precocity: Case studies of talented youths. *Roeper Review, 16,* 144–151.

McLaughlin, S. C., & Saccuzzo, D. P. (1997). Ethnic and gender differences in locus of control in children referred for gifted programs: The effects of vulnerability factors. *Journal for the Education of the Gifted, 20,* 268–284.

Shaw, P., Greenstein, D., Lerch, J., Clasen, L., Lenroot, R., Gogtay, N., . . . Giedd, J. (2006). Intellectual ability and cortical development in children and adolescents. *Nature, 440,* 676–679.

Singh, H., & O'Boyle, M. W. (2004). Interhemispheric interaction during global/local processing in mathematically gifted adolescents, average ability youth and college students. *Neuropsychology, 18,* 371–377.

Stormont, M., Stebbins, M. S., & Holliday, G. (2001). Characteristics and educational support needs of underrepresented gifted adolescents. *Psychology in the Schools, 38,* 413–423.

Theory-Based References

Baum, S. M., & Olenchak, F. R. (2002). The alphabet children: GT, ADHD, and more. *Exceptionality, 10,* 77–91.

Berk, L. E. (2004). *Development through the lifespan.* Boston, MA: Pearson.

Cattell, R. B. (1971). *Abilities: Their structure, growth and action.* Boston, MA: Houghton Mifflin.

Callahan, C. M., & Hébert, T. P. (2014). Gender issues. In J. A. Plucker & C. M. Callahan (Eds.), *Critical issues and practices in gifted education* (2nd ed., pp. 267–280). Waco, TX: Prufrock Press.

Clinkenbeard, P. R. (2014). Motivation and goals. In J. A. Plucker & C. M. Callahan (Eds.), *Critical issues and practices in gifted education* (2nd ed., pp. 427–348). Waco, TX: Prufrock Press.

Csikszentmihalyi, M., & Wolfe, R. (2000). New conceptions and research approaches to creativity: Implications of a systems perspective for creativity in education. In K. A. Heller, F. J. Mönks, & A. Harry Passow (Eds.),

International handbook of research and development of giftedness and talent (pp. 81–93). New York, NY: Pergamon.

Dai, D. Y., Moon, S. M., & Feldhusen, J. F. (1998). Achievement motivation and gifted students: A social cognitive perspective. *Educational Psychologist, 33*(2/3), 45–63.

Ericcson, K. A., & Charness, N. (1994). Expert performance: Its structure and acquisition. *American Psychologist, 49,* 725–747.

Feldman, D. H. (2003). A developmental, evolutionary perspective on giftedness. In J. H. Borland (Ed.), *Rethinking gifted education* (pp. 9–33). New York, NY: Teacher's College Press.

Ford, D. Y., Moore, J. L., III, Milner, H. R. (2005). Beyond culture blindness: A model of culture with implications for gifted education, *Roeper Review, 27,* 97–103.

Gagné, F. (2005). From gifts to talents: The DMGT as a developmental model. In R. J. Sternberg & J. E. Davidson (Eds.), *Conceptions of giftedness* (2nd ed., pp. 98–119). New York, NY: Cambridge University Press.

Gross, M. U. M. (1993). The 'me' behind the mask: Intellectually gifted students and the search for identity. *Roeper Review, 20,* 167–174.

Guilford, J. P. (1967). *The nature of human intelligence.* New York, NY: McGraw-Hill.

Horowitz, F. D., Subotnik, R. F., & Matthews, D. J. (2009). *The development of giftedness and talent across the life span.* Washington, DC: American Psychological Association.

Plucker, J. A., Robinson, N. M., Greenspon, T. S., Feldhusen, J. F., McCoach, D. B., & Subotnik, R. F. (2004). It's not how the pond makes you feel, but rather how high you can jump. *American Psychologist, 59,* 168–269.

Nisbett, R. (2003). *The geography of thought: How Asians and Westerners think differently . . . and why.* New York, NY: Free Press.

Shade, B. J. (Ed.). (1997). *Culture, style, and the educative process: Making schools work for racially diverse students* (2nd ed.). Springfield, IL: Charles C. Thomas.

Siegle, D., & Reis, S. M. (1998). Gender differences in teacher and student perceptions of gifted students' ability and effort. *Gifted Child Quarterly, 42,* 39–47.

Silverman, L. K. (1997). The construct of asynchronous development. *Peabody Journal of Education, 72*(3&4), 36–58.

Spearman, C. (1904). "General intelligence," objectively determined and measured. *American Journal of Psychology, 15,* 201–293.

Subotnik, R. F., Olszewski-Kubilius, P., & Worrell, F. C. (2011). Rethinking giftedness and gifted education: A proposed direction forward based on psychological science. *Psychological Science in the Public Interest, 12,* 3–54.

Practice-Based References

Harmon, D. (2002). They won't teach me: The voices of gifted African American inner-city students. *Roeper Review, 24,* 68–75.

Hong, E., & Aqui, Y. (2004). Cognitive and motivational characteristics of adolescents gifted in mathematics: Comparisons among students with different types of giftedness. *Gifted Child Quarterly, 48,* 191–201.

Peterson, J. S. (2007). A developmental perspective. In S. Mendaglio & J. S. Peterson (Eds.), *Models of counseling gifted children, adolescents, and young adults* (pp. 97–126). Waco, TX: Prufrock Press.

Shade, B. J., Kelly, C., & Oberg, M. (1997). *Creating culturally responsive classrooms.* Washington, DC: American Psychological Association.

Swiatek, M. A. (1993). A decade of longitudinal research on academic acceleration through the study of mathematically precocious youth. *Roeper Review, 15,* 120–123.

Standard 2: Learning Environments

Beginning gifted education professionals create safe, inclusive, and culturally responsive learning environments so that individuals with gifts and talents become effective learners and develop social and emotional well-being.

ELEMENT 2.1
Beginning gifted education professionals create safe, inclusive, culturally responsive learning environments that engage individuals with gifts and talents in meaningful and rigorous learning activities and social interactions.

Research-Based References

Albert, R., & Runco, M. (1989). Independence and the creative potential of gifted and exceptionally gifted boys. *Journal of Youth and Adolescence, 18,* 221–230.

den Brok, P., Levy, J., Rodriguez, R., & Wubbels, T. (2002). Perceptions of Asian-American and Hispanic-American teachers and their students on teacher interpersonal communication style. *Teaching and Teacher Education, 18,* 447–467.

Dunn, R. (1990). Grouping students for instruction: Effects of learning style on achievement and attitudes. *Journal of Social Psychology, 130,* 485–494.

Gonzalez, V. (2005). Cultural, linguistic, and socioeconomic factors influencing monolingual and bilingual children's cognitive development. In V. Gonzalez & J. Tinajero, (Eds.), *Review of research and practice.* (Vol. 3, pp. 67–104). Mahwah, NJ: Lawrence Erlbaum Associates.

Kulik, J. A., & Kulik, C. C. (1992). Meta-analytic findings on grouping programs. *Gifted Child Quarterly, 36,* 73–77.

VanTassel-Baska, J., Feng, A. X., Quek, C., & Struck, J. (2004). A study of educators' and students' perceptions of academic success for underrepresented populations identified for gifted programs. *Psychology Science, 46,* 363–378.

Theory-Based References

Banks, J. A., & Banks, C. M. (Eds.). (2004). *Handbook of research on multicultural education* (2nd ed.). San Francisco, CA: Jossey-Bass.

Bernal, E. (2003). To no longer educate the gifted: Programming for gifted students beyond the era of inclusionism. *Gifted Child Quarterly, 47,* 183–191.

Bernal, E. (2002). Three ways to achieve a more equitable representation of culturally and linguistically different students in GT programs. *Roeper Review, 24,* 82–88.

Ford, D., & Harris, J. (2000). A framework for infusing multicultural curriculum into gifted education. *Roeper Review, 23,* 4–10.

Ford, D. Y., & Trotman, M. F. (2001). Teachers of gifted students: Suggested multicultural characteristics and competencies. *Roeper Review, 23,* 235–239.

Gay, G. (2002). Preparing for culturally responsive teaching. *Journal of Teacher Education, 53,* 106–116.

Grant, B., & Piechowski, M. (1999). Theories and the good: Toward child-centered gifted education. *Gifted Child Quarterly, 43,* 4–12.

Grybe, D. (1997). Mentoring the gifted and talented. *Preventing School Failure, 41,* 115.

Johnsen, S., & Goree, K. (2015). Teaching gifted students through independent study. In F. A. Karnes & S. M. Bean (Eds.), *Methods and materials for teaching the gifted and talented* (4th ed., pp. 445–478). Waco, TX: Prufrock Press.

Soto, L. D., Smrekar, J. L., & Nekcovei, D. L. (Spring, 1999). Preserving home languages and cultures in the classroom: Challenges and opportunities. *Directions in Language and Education, 13,* 1–9.

Practice-Based References

Betts, G. (2004). Fostering autonomous learners through levels of differentiation. *Roeper Review, 26,* 190–191.

Bishop, K. (2000). The research process of gifted students: A case study. *Gifted Child Quarterly, 44,* 54–64.

Christophersen, E., & Mortweet, S. (2003). Encouraging independent play skills. In R. Christophersen & S. Mortweet (Eds.), *Parenting that works: Building skills that last a lifetime* (pp. 195–205). Washington, DC: American Psychological Association.

Cross, T., Stewart, R. A., & Coleman, L. (2003). Phenomenology and its implications for gifted studies research: Investigating the Lebenswelt of academically gifted students attending an elementary magnet school. *Journal for the Education of the Gifted, 26,* 201–220.

Ford, D., Tyson, C., Howard, T., & Harris, J. J., III. (2000). Multicultural literature and gifted Black students: Promoting self-understanding, awareness, and pride. *Roeper Review, 22,* 235–240.

Hughes, L. (1999). Action research and practical inquiry: How can I meet the needs of the high-ability student within my regular education classroom? *Journal for the Education of the Gifted, 22,* 282–297.

Mackin, J. (1995). The science of a team approach: Coaching gifted and talented students to work cooperatively in completing scientific research. *Gifted Child Today, 18,* 14–17, 42.

Peterson, J. S. (2003). An argument for proactive attention to affective concerns of gifted adolescents. *Journal for Secondary Gifted Education, 14,* 62–71.

Poelzer, G. H., & Feldhusen, J. F. (1997). The international baccalaureate: A program for gifted secondary students. *Roeper Review, 19,* 168–171.

Robbins, R., Tonemah, S., & Robbins, S. (2002). Project Eagle: Techniques for multi-family psycho-educational group therapy with gifted American Indian adolescents and their parents. *American Indian and Alaska Native Mental Health Research, 10,* 56–74.

Roeper, A. (1992). Global awareness and the young child. *Roeper Review, 15,* 52–53.

Schillereff, M. (2001). Using inquiry-based science to help gifted students become more self-directed. *Primary Voices K–6, 10,* 28–32.

Terry, A. W. (2000). An early glimpse: Service learning from an adolescent perspective. *Journal of Secondary Gifted Education, 11,* 115–135.

Tookey, M. E. (1999/2000). The international baccalaureate. *Journal of Secondary Gifted Education, 11,* 52–66.

Wolfgang, A. (1991). Intercultural training of teachers and counselors for the year 2000. *Gifted International, 7,* 33–36.

ELEMENT 2.2

Beginning gifted education professionals use communication and motivational and instructional strategies to facilitate understanding of subject matter and to teach individuals with gifts and talents how to adapt to different environments and develop leadership skills.

Research-Based References

Assouline, S. G., Colangelo, N., VanTassel-Baska, J., & Lupkowski-Shoplik, A. (2015). *A nation empowered: Evidence trumps the excuses holding back America's brightest students.* Iowa City: University of Iowa, The Connie Belin and Jacqueline N. Blank International Center for Gifted Education and Talent Development.

Bain, S., & Bell, S. (2004) Social self-concept, social-attributions, and peer relationships in fourth, fifth, and sixth graders who are gifted compared to high achievers. *Gifted Child Quarterly, 48,* 167–178.

Cameron, P. (1995). The social context and developmental patterns of crystallizing experiences among academically talented youth. *Roeper Review, 17,* 197–200.

Castillo, L. C. (1998). The effect of analogy instruction on young children's metaphor comprehension. *Roeper Review, 21,* 27–31.

Daugherty, M., & White, S. C. (2008). Relationships among private speech and creativity in Head Start and low-socioeconomic status preschool children. *Gifted Child Quarterly, 52,* 30–39.

Hébert, T. P., & Neumeister, K. L. S. (2000). University mentors in the elementary classroom: Supporting the intellectual, motivational, and emotional needs of high-ability students. *Journal for the Education of the Gifted, 24,* 122–148.

Karnes, F. (1995). Perceptions of leadership held by young females. *Journal of Secondary Gifted Education, 6,* 113–119.

Kyburg, R. M., Hertberg-Davis, H., & Callahan, C. M. (2007). Advanced Placement and International Baccalaureate programs: Optimal learning environments for talented minorities? *Journal of Advanced Academics, 18,* 172–215.

Smyth, E., & Ross, J. (1999). Developing leadership skills of pre-adolescent gifted learners in small group settings. *Gifted Child Quarterly, 43,* 204–211.

Theory-Based References

Brody, L. (1999). The talent searches: Counseling and mentoring activities. In N. Colangelo & S. Assouline (Eds.), *Talent development III, Proceedings from The 1995 Henry B. and Jocelyn Wallace national research symposium on talent development* (pp. 153–157). Scottsdale, AZ: Great Potential Press.

Pleiss, M. K., & Feldhusen, J. F. (1995). Mentors, role models and heroes in the lives of gifted children. *Educational Psychologist, 30,* 159–169.

Siegle, D., & McCoach, D. G. (2005). Extending learning through mentorships. In F. A. Karnes & S. Bean (Eds.), *Methods and materials for teaching gifted* (2nd ed., pp. 473–518). Waco, TX: Prufrock Press.

Torrance, E. P. (1984). *Mentor relationships: How they aid creative achievement, endure, change and die.* Buffalo, NY: Bearly Limited.

Practice-Based References

Betts, G. (2004). Fostering autonomous learners through levels of differentiation. *Roeper Review, 26,* 190–191.

Bonner, F. A., II, Jennings, M. E., Marbley, A. F., & Brown, L.-A. (2008). Capitalizing on leadership capacity: Gifted African American males in high school. *Roeper Review, 30,* 93–103.

Choi, E. Y. (1998). Through another's eyes: Student fear number one. *Gifted Child Today, 21*(4), 30–31, 48.

Christophersen, E., & Mortweet, S. (2003). Encouraging independent play skills. In R. Christophersen & S. Mortweet (Eds.), *Parenting that works: Building skills that last a lifetime* (pp. 195–205). Washington, DC: American Psychological Association.

Feldhusen, J. F., & Kennedy, D. M. (1988). Preparing gifted youth for leadership roles in a rapidly changing society. *Roeper Review, 10,* 226–230.

Frey, C. P. (2000). A writer's workshop for highly verbal students. *Gifted Child Today, 23*(5), 38–43.

Hensel, N. H. (1991). Social leadership skills in young children. *Roeper Review, 14,* 4–6.

Ingram, M. A. (2003). Sociocultural poetry to assist gifted students in developing empathy for the lived experiences of others. *Journal of Secondary Gifted Education, 14*(2), 83–90.

Johnsen, S., & Goree, K. (2015). Teaching gifted students through independent study. In F. A. Karnes & S. M. Bean (Eds.), *Methods and materials for teaching the gifted and talented* (4th ed., pp. 445–478). Waco, TX: Prufrock Press.

Johnson, K. (2000). Affective component in the education of the gifted. *Gifted Child Today, 23,* 36–40.

Leshnower, S. (2008). Teaching leadership. *Gifted Child Today, 31*(2), 29–35.

Merriman, J. (1999). Leadership conference. *Gifted Child Today, 22,* 18–27.

Ross, J., & Smyth, E. (1995). Differentiating cooperative learning to meet the needs of gifted learners: A case for transformational leadership. *Journal for the Education of the Gifted, 19,* 63–82.

Smutny, J. F. (2001). *Creative strategies for teaching language arts to gifted students* (K–8) (ERIC Digest E612). Arlington, VA: ERIC Clearinghouse on Disabilities and Gifted Education.

ELEMENT 2.3
Beginning gifted education professionals adjust their communication to an individual's language proficiency and cultural and linguistic differences.

Research-Based References

Castillo, L. C. (1998). The effect of analogy instruction on young children's metaphor comprehension. *Roeper Review, 21,* 27–31.

Fernández, A. T., Gay, L. R., Lucky, L F., & Gavilan, M. R. (1998). Teacher perceptions of gifted Hispanic limited English proficient students. *Journal for the Education of the Gifted, 21,* 335–351.

Kitano, M. K., & Pedersen, K. S. (2002). Action research and practical inquiry: Teaching gifted English learners. *Journal for the Education of the Gifted, 26,* 132–147.

Meador, K. S. (1994). The effect of synectics training on gifted and nongifted kindergarten students. *Journal for the Education of the Gifted, 18,* 55–73.

Shaunessy, E., McHatton, P. A., Hughes, C., Brice, A., & Ratliff, M. A. (2007). Understanding the experiences of bilingual, Latino adolescents: Voices from gifted and general education. *Roeper Review, 29,* 174–182.

Valdes, G. (2002). *Understanding the special giftedness of young interpreters* (RM02158). Storrs: University of Connecticut, The National Research Center on the Gifted and Talented.

VanTassel-Baska, J., Johnson, D. T., Hughes, C. E., & Boyce, L. N. (1996). A study of language arts curriculum effectiveness with gifted learners. *Journal for the Education of the Gifted, 19,* 461–480.

VanTassel-Baska, J., Zuo, L., Avery, L. D., & Little, C. A. (2002). Curriculum study of gifted-student learning in the language arts. *Gifted Child Quarterly, 46,* 30–44.

Theory-Based References

Hébert, T. P. (1991). Meeting the affective needs of bright boys through biblio-therapy. *Roeper Review, 13*, 207–212.

Kolloff, P. B. (1996). Gifted girls and the humanities. *Journal for Secondary Gifted Education, 7*, 486–492.

Little, C. (2002). Reasoning as a key component of language arts curricula. *Journal of Secondary Gifted Education, 13*(2), 52–59.

Marquez, J. A., & Sawyer, C. B. (1994). Curriculum extension for the gifted and talented student with limited English proficiency. In L. M. Malave (Ed.), *Proceedings from the National Association for Bilingual Education annual conference journal* (pp. 15–21). Washington, DC: National Association for Bilingual Education.

Practice-Based References

Bermudez, A. B., Rakow, S. J., Marquez, J. M., Sawyer, C., & Ryan, C. (1993). Meeting the needs of the gifted and talented limited English proficient student: The UHCL Prototype. In L. M. Malave (Ed.), *Proceedings from the National Association for Bilingual Education annual conference journal* (pp. 115–133). Washington, DC: National Association for Bilingual Education.

Bisland, A. (2003). Student-created public relations for gifted education. *Gifted Child Today, 26*(2), 60–65.

Choi, E. Y. (1998). Through another's eyes: Student fear number one. *Gifted Child Today, 21*(4), 30–31, 48.

Matthews, M. S., & Castellano, J. (2013). *Talent development for English language learners: Identifying and developing potential.* Waco, TX: Prufrock Press.

Riley, T. L., & Brown, M. E. (1998). The magic of multimedia: Creating leaders of yesterday, today, and tomorrow. *Gifted Child Today, 21*(5), 20–22, 24–26.

Ring, L. M. (2000). The T in art is for thinking. *Gifted Child Today, 23*(3), 36–45, 53.

Schack, G. D. (1988). Experts-in-a-book: Using how-to books to teach the methodologies of practicing professionals. *Roeper Review, 10*, 147–150.

ELEMENT 2.3
Beginning gifted education professionals demonstrate understanding of the multiple environments that are part of a continuum of services for individuals with gifts and talents, including the advantages and disadvantages of various settings and teach students to adapt to these environments.

Research-Based References

Ablard, K. E., Mills, C. J., & Duvall, R. (1994). *Acceleration of CTY math and science students* (Tech. Rep. No. 10). Baltimore, MD: Johns Hopkins University, Center for Talented Youth.

Assouline, S. G., Colangelo, N., VanTassel-Baska, J., & Lupkowski-Shoplik, A. (2015). *A nation empowered: Evidence trumps the excuses holding back America's brightest students.* Iowa City: University of Iowa, The Connie Belin and Jacqueline N. Blank International Center for Gifted Education and Talent Development.

Davalos, R. A., & Haensly, P. A. (1997). After the dust has settled: Youth reflect on their high school mentored research experience. *Roeper Review, 19,* 204–207.

Gallagher, S. A., & Stepien, W. (1996). Content acquisition in problem-based learning: Depth versus breadth in American studies. *Journal for the Education of the Gifted, 19,* 257–275.

Gentry, M., Rizza, M. G., & Owen, S. V. (2002). Examining perceptions of challenges and choice in classrooms: The relationship between teachers and their students and comparisons between gifted students and other students. *Gifted Child Quarterly, 46,* 145–155.

Hébert, T. P. (1993). Reflections at graduation: The long-term impact of elementary school experiences in creative productivity. *Roeper Review, 16,* 22–28.

Kulik, J. A., & Kulik, C. C. (1992). Meta-analytic findings on grouping programs. *Gifted Child Quarterly, 36,* 73–77.

Lubinski, D., & Benbow, C. P. (1995). The study of mathematically precocious youth: The first three decades of a planned 50-year study of intellectual talent. In R. F. Subotnik & K. D. Arnold (Eds.), *Beyond Terman: Contemporary longitudinal studies of giftedness and talent* (pp. 255–289). Norwood, NJ: Ablex.

Moon, S. M., Feldhusen, J. F., & Dillon, D. R. (1994). Long-term effect of an enrichment program based on the Purdue Three-Stage Model. *Gifted Child Quarterly, 38,* 38–48.

Olszewski-Kubilius, P. (2014). Talent search. In J. A. Plucker & C. M. Callahan (Eds.), *Critical issues and practices in gifted education* (2nd ed., pp. 633–644). Waco, TX: Prufrock Press.

Olszewski-Kubilius, P., & Lee, S.-Y. (2004). Gifted adolescents' talent development through distance learning. *Journal for the Education of the Gifted, 28*, 7–35.

Theory-Based References

Renzulli, J. (1992). A general theory for the development of creative productivity through the pursuit of ideal acts of learning. *Gifted Child Quarterly, 36*, 170–183.

Renzulli, J., & Reis, S. (2009). The Schoolwide Enrichment Model: A focus on student strengths and interests. In J. S. Renzulli, E. J. Gubbins, K. S. McMillen, R. D. Eckert, & C. A. Little (Eds.), *Systems and models for developing programs for the gifted and talented* (2nd ed., pp. 323–352). Waco, TX: Prufrock Press.

Rogers, K. B. (2002). *Re-forming gifted education: Matching the program to the child.* Scottsdale, AZ: Great Potential Press.

Stephens, K. R. (1999). Parents of the gifted and talented: The forgotten partner. *Gifted Child Today, 22*(5), 38–43, 52.

VanTassel-Baska, J. (2005). *Acceleration strategies for teaching gifted learners.* Waco, TX: Prufrock Press.

Practice-Based References

Barbeau, E., & Taylor, P. J. (Eds.). (2009). *Challenging mathematics in and beyond the classroom: The 16th ICMI Study.* New York, NY: Springer.

Betts, G. T., & Neihart, M. (1986). Implementing self-directed learning models for the gifted and talented. *Gifted Child Quarterly, 30*, 174–177.

Cooper, H. (2001). *Summer school: Research-based recommendations for policymakers.* SERVE Policy Brief. (ERIC Document Reproduction Services No. ED456557)

Frey, C. P. (1998). Struggling with identity: Working with seventh-and eighth-grade gifted girls to air issues of concern. *Journal for the Education of the Gifted, 21*, 437–451.

Hughes, C. E., & Rollins, K. (2009). RtI for nurturing giftedness: Implications for the RtI school-based team. *Gifted Child Today, 32*(3), 31–39.

Olszewski-Kubilius, P. (2004). Talent searches and accelerated programming for gifted students. In N. Colangelo, S. G., Assouline, & M. U. M. Gross (Eds.), *A nation deceived: How schools hold back America's brightest students* (Vol. II, pp. 69–76). Iowa City: University of Iowa, The Connie Belin and

Jacqueline N. Blank International Center for Gifted Education and Talent Development.

Siegle, D., & McCoach, D. G. (2005). Extending learning through mentorships. In F. A. Karnes & S. M. Bean (Eds.), *Methods and materials for teaching gifted* (2nd ed., pp. 473–518). Waco, TX: Prufrock Press.

Strip, C., & Hirsch, G. (2001). Trust and teamwork: The parent-teacher partnership for helping the gifted child. *Gifted Child Today, 24*(2), 26–30, 64.

Zeidner, M., & Schleyer, E. J. (1999). Evaluating the effects of full-time vs. part-time educational programs for the gifted: Affective outcomes and policy considerations. *Evaluation and Program Planning, 22*, 413–427.

Standard 3: Curricular Content Knowledge

Beginning gifted education professionals use knowledge of general[5] and specialized curricula[6] to advance learning for individuals with gifts and talents.

ELEMENT 3.1
Beginning gifted education professionals understand the role of central concepts, structures of the discipline, and tools of inquiry of the content areas they teach, and use their understanding to organize knowledge, integrate cross-disciplinary skills, and develop meaningful learning progressions within and across grade levels.

Research-Based References

Assouline, S. G., Colangelo, N., VanTassel-Baska, J., & Lupkowski-Shoplik, A. (2015). *A nation empowered: Evidence trumps the excuses holding back America's brightest students.* Iowa City: University of Iowa, The Connie Belin and Jacqueline N. Blank International Center for Gifted Education and Talent Development.

Corazza, L., Gustin, W., & Edelkind, L. (1995). Serving young gifted math students. *Gifted Child Today, 18*(3), 20–21, 24–25, 40–41.

---

5   As used, "general curricula" means the academic content of the general curricula including math, reading, English/language arts, science, social studies, and the arts.

6   As used, "specialized curricula" means the content of specialized interventions or sets of interventions including, but not limited to academic, strategic, communicative, social, emotional, self-guided, and independent curricula.

Gallagher, S. A., & Stepien, W. (1996). Content acquisition in problem-based learning: Depth versus breadth in American studies. *Journal for the Education of the Gifted, 19,* 257–275.

Gavin, M. K., Casa, T., Adelson, J. L., Carroll, S. R., & Sheffield, L. J. (2009). The impact of advanced curriculum on the achievement of mathematically promising elementary students. *Gifted Child Quarterly, 53,* 188–202.

Gentry, M. (1999). *Promoting student achievement and exemplary classroom practices through cluster grouping: A research-based alternative to heterogeneous elementary classrooms.* Storrs: University of Connecticut, The National Research Center on the Gifted and Talented.

Hannah, C. L., & Shore, B. M. (1995). Metacognition and high intellectual ability: Insights from the study of learning-disabled gifted students. *Gifted Child Quarterly, 39,* 95–109.

Robinson, A., Dailey, D., Hughes, G. D., & Cotabish, A. (2014). The effects of a science-focused STEM intervention on gifted elementary students' science knowledge and skills. *Journal of Advanced Academics, 25,* 189–213.

Schillereff, M. (2001). Using inquiry-based science to help gifted students become more self-directed. *Primary Voices K–6, 10,* 28–32.

Stamps, L. (2004). The effectiveness of curriculum compacting in first grade classrooms. *Roeper Review, 27,* 31–41.

VanTassel-Baska, J., Avery, L. D., Little, C., & Hughes, C. (2000). An evaluation of the implementation of curriculum innovation: The impact of the William and Mary units on schools. *Journal for the Education of the Gifted, 23,* 244–272.

VanTassel-Baska, J., Bass, G., Ries, R., Poland, D., & Avery, L. D. (1998). A national study of science curriculum effectiveness with high ability students. *Gifted Child Quarterly, 42,* 200–211.

VanTassel-Baska, J., Johnson, D. T., Hughes, C. E., & Boyce, L. N. (1996). A study of language arts curriculum effectiveness with gifted learners. *Journal for the Education of the Gifted, 19,* 461–480.

Theory-Based References

Anderson, L. W., & Krathwohl, D. R. (Eds.). (2001). *A taxonomy for learning, teaching, and assessing: A revision of Bloom's taxonomy of educational objectives.* New York, NY: Longman.

Paul, R., & Elder, L. (2002). *Critical thinking: Tools for taking charge of your professional and personal life.* New York, NY: Prentice Hall.

Rogers, K. B. (2002). *Re-forming gifted education: Matching the program to the child.* Scottsdale, AZ: Great Potential Press.

Rogers, K. B. (1991). *The relationship of grouping practices to the education of the gifted and talented learner*. Storrs: University of Connecticut, The National Research Center on the Gifted and Talented.

Sheffield, L. (2003). *Extending the challenge in mathematics: Developing mathematical promise in K–8 students*. Thousand Oaks, CA: Corwin Press.

Steiner, H. H., & Carr, M. (2003). Cognitive development in gifted children: Toward a more precise understanding of emerging differences in intelligence. *Educational Psychology Review, 15*, 215–246.

Stronge, J. (2002). *Qualities of effective teachers*. Alexandria, VA: Association for Supervision and Curriculum Development.

Tomlinson, C. A. (Ed). (2004). *Differentiation for gifted and talented students*. Waco, TX: Prufrock Press.

VanTassel-Baska, J., & Little, C. A. (Eds.). (2003). *Content-based curriculum for gifted learners*. Waco, TX: Prufrock Press.

Practice-Based References

Angelelli, C., Enright, K., & Valdés, G. (2002). *Developing the talents and abilities of linguistically gifted bilingual students: Guidelines for developing curriculum at the high school level* (RM02156). Storrs: University of Connecticut, The National Research Center on the Gifted and Talented.

Carr, M., Alexander, J. M., & Schwanenflugel, P. J. (1996). Where gifted children do and do not excel on metacognitive tasks. *Roeper Review, 18*, 212–217.

Coates, D. L., Perkins, T., Vietze, P., Reyes Cruz, M., & Park, S. (2003). *Teaching thinking to culturally diverse, high ability, high school students: A triarchic approach* (RM03174). Storrs: University of Connecticut, The National Research Center on the Gifted and Talented.

Elder, L., & Paul, R. (2003). *Analytic thinking: How to take thinking apart and what to look for when you do*. Dillon Beach, CA: The Foundation for Critical Thinking.

Elder, L., & Paul, R. (2004). *The art of asking essential questions*. Dillon Beach, CA: The Foundation for Critical Thinking.

Elder, L., & Paul, R. (2004). *Guide to the human mind: How it learns, how it mislearns*. Dillon Beach, CA: The Foundation for Critical Thinking.

Renzulli, J. S., Leppien, J. H., & Hays, T. S. (2000). *The multiple menu model: A practical guide for developing differentiated curriculum*. Waco, TX: Prufrock Press.

Renzulli, J. S., & Reis, S. (2004). Curriculum compacting: A research-based differentiation strategy for culturally diverse talented students. In D. Boothe

& J. C. Stanley (Eds.), *In the eyes of the beholder: Critical issues for diversity in gifted education* (pp. 87–100). Waco, TX: Prufrock Press.

Tomlinson, C. A., & Cunningham-Eidson, C. (2003). *Differentiation in practice: A resource guide for differentiating curriculum, grades 5–9.* Alexandria, VA: Association for Supervision and Curriculum Development.

Winebrenner, S., & Brulles, D. (2012). *Teaching gifted kids in in today's classroom.* Minneapolis, MN: Free Spirit.

ELEMENT 3.2

Beginning gifted education professionals design appropriate learning and performance modifications for individuals with gifts and talents that enhance creativity, acceleration, depth, and complexity in academic subject matter and specialized domains.

Research-Based References

Gallagher, S. A., & Stepien, W. (1996). Content acquisition in problem-based learning: Depth versus breadth in American studies. *Journal for the Education of the Gifted, 19,* 257–275.

VanTassel-Baska, J., Bass, G., Ries, R., Poland, D., & Avery, L. D. (1998). A national study of science curriculum effectiveness with high ability students. *Gifted Child Quarterly, 42,* 200–211.

VanTassel-Baska, J., Johnson, D. T., Hughes, C. E., & Boyce, L. N. (1996). A study of language arts curriculum effectiveness with gifted learners. *Journal for the Education of the Gifted, 19,* 461–480.

Theory-Based References

Purcell, J. H., Burns, D. E., Tomlinson, C. A., Imbeau, M. B., & Martin, J. L. (2002). Bridging the gap: A tool and technique to analyze and evaluate gifted education curricular units. *Gifted Child Quarterly, 46,* 306–338.

Roberts, J. L., & Roberts, R. A. (2005). Writing units that remove the learning ceiling. In F. A. Karnes & S. M. Bean (Eds.), *Methods and materials for teaching the gifted* (2nd ed., pp. 179–210). Waco, TX: Prufrock Press.

Tomlinson, C. (1995). Differentiating instruction for advanced learners in the mixed-ability middle school classroom. (ERIC Digest E536)

VanTassel-Baska, J., & Stambaugh, T. (2006). *Comprehensive curriculum for gifted learners* (3rd ed.). Boston, MA: Allyn & Bacon.

Practice-Based References

Avery, L. D., & Zuo, L. (2003). Selecting resources and materials for high-ability learners. In J. VanTassel-Baska & C. A. Little (Eds.), *Content-based curriculum for high-ability learners* (pp. 259–278). Waco, TX: Prufrock Press.

Johnsen, S. K., Ryser, G. R., & Assouline, S. (2014). *A teacher's guide to using the Common Core State Standards for with mathematically gifted and advanced learners.* Waco, TX: Prufrock Press.

Johnsen, S. K., & Sheffield, L. J. (Eds.). (2013). *Using the Common Core State Standards for mathematics with gifted and advanced learners.* Waco, TX: Prufrock Press.

Kaplan, S. N. (2005). Layering differentiated curricula for the gifted and talented. In F. A. Karnes & S. M. Bean (Eds.). *Methods and materials for teaching the gifted* (2nd ed., pp. 107–136). Waco, TX: Prufrock Press.

Riley, T. R. (2005). Teaching on a shoestring: Materials for teaching gifted and talented students. In F. A. Karnes & S. M. Bean (Eds.), *Methods and materials for teaching the gifted* (2nd ed., pp. 657–700). Waco, TX: Prufrock Press.

Tomlinson, C. A., & Cunningham-Eidson, C. (2003). *Differentiation in practice: A resource guide for differentiating curriculum, grades 5–9.* Alexandria, VA: Association for Supervision and Curriculum Development.

Tomlinson, C. A., & Cunningham-Eidson, C. (2003). *Differentiation in practice: A resource guide for differentiating curriculum, grades K–5.* Alexandria, VA: Association for Supervision and Curriculum Development.

Winebrenner, S., & Brulles, D. (2012). *Teaching gifted kids in in today's classroom.* Minneapolis, MN: Free Spirit.

ELEMENT 3.3
Beginning gifted education professionals use assessments to select, adapt, and create materials to differentiate instructional strategies and general and specialized curricula to challenge individuals with gifts and talents.

Research-Based References

Ablard, K. E., Mills, C. J., & Duvall, R. (1994). *Acceleration of CTY math and science students* (Tech. Rep. No. 10). Baltimore, MD: Johns Hopkins University, Center for Talented Youth.

Feng, A. X., VanTassel-Baska, J., Quek, C., Bai, W., & O'Neill, B. (2005). A longitudinal assessment of gifted students' learning using the integrated

curriculum model (ICM): Impacts and perceptions of the William and
Mary language arts and science curriculum, *Roeper Review, 27,* 78–83.

Johnson, D. T., Boyce, L. N., & VanTassel-Baska, J. (1995). Science curriculum review: evaluating materials for high-ability learners. *Gifted Child
Quarterly, 39,* 36–45.

Reis, S. M., Westberg, K. L., Kulikowich, J. M., & Purcell, J. H. (1998).
Curriculum compacting and achievement test scores: What does the
research say? *Gifted Child Quarterly, 42,* 123–129.

Swiatek, M. A. (1993). A decade of longitudinal research on academic acceleration through the study of mathematically precocious youth. *Roeper
Review, 15,* 120–123.

VanTassel-Baska, J., Avery, L. D., Little, C., & Hughes, C. (2000). An evaluation of the implementation of curriculum innovation: The impact of the
William and Mary units on schools. *Journal for the Education of the Gifted,
23,* 244–272.

Theory-Based References

Johnsen, S. (2005). Within-class acceleration. *Gifted Child Today, 28*(1), 5.

Purcell, J. H., Burns, D. E., Tomlinson, C. A., Imbeau, M. B., & Martin, J. L.
(2002). Bridging the gap: A tool and technique to analyze and evaluate
gifted education curricular units. *Gifted Child Quarterly, 46,* 306–338.

Tomlinson, C. A. (2001). *How to differentiate instruction in mixed ability
classrooms* (2nd ed.). Alexandria, VA: Association of Supervision and
Curriculum Development.

Tomlinson, C. A. (2001). Differentiated instruction in the regular classroom:
What does it mean? How does it look? *Understanding Our Gifted, 14,* 3–6.

Tomlinson, C. A. (2002). Different learners, different lessons. *Instructor, 112,*
21, 24–26.

VanTassel-Baska, J. (2005). *Acceleration strategies for teaching gifted learners.*
Waco, TX: Prufrock Press.

VanTassel-Baska, J., & Stambaugh, T. (2006). Curriculum development processes. In *Comprehensive curriculum for gifted learners* (3rd ed., pp. 31–45).
Boston, MA: Allyn & Bacon.

Practice-Based References

Avery, L. D., & Zuo, L. (2003). Selecting resources and materials for high-ability learners. In J. VanTassel-Baska & C. A. Little (Eds.). *Content-based curriculum for high-ability learners* (pp. 259–278). Waco, TX: Prufrock Press.

Johnsen, S. K., Haensly, P. A., Ryser, G. R., & Ford, R. F. (2002). Changing general education classroom practices to adapt for gifted students. *Gifted Child Quarterly, 46,* 45–63.

Reis, S. M., Burns, D. E., & Renzulli, J. S. (1992). *Curriculum compacting: The complete guide to modifying the regular curriculum for high ability students.* Waco, TX: Prufrock Press.

Riley, T. R. (2005). Teaching on a shoestring: Materials for teaching gifted and talented students. In F. A. Karnes & S. M. Bean (Eds.), *Methods and materials for teaching the gifted* (2nd ed., pp. 657–700). Waco, TX: Prufrock Press.

Tomlinson, C. A., & Reis, S. (Ed). (2004). *Differentiation for gifted and talented students.* Thousand Oaks, CA: Corwin Press.

Winebrenner, S., & Brulles, D. (2012). *Teaching gifted kids in in today's classroom.* Minneapolis, MN: Free Spirit.

ELEMENT 3.4
Beginning gifted educators understand that individuals with gifts and talents demonstrate a wide range of advanced knowledge and performance levels and modify the general or specialized curriculum appropriately.

Research-Based References

Firmender, J. M., Reis, S. M., & Sweeny, S. M. (2012). Reading comprehension and fluency levels ranges across diverse classrooms: The need for differentiated reading instruction and content. *Gifted Child Quarterly, 57,* 3–14.

Friedman, R. C., & Lee, S. W. (1996). Differentiating instruction for high-achieving/gifted children in regular classrooms: A field test of three gifted-education models. *Journal for the Education of the Gifted, 19,* 405–436.

Moon, T. R., & Callahan, C. M. (2001). Curricular modifications, family outreach, and a mentoring program: Impacts on achievement and gifted identification in high-risk primary students. *Journal for the Education of the Gifted, 24,* 305–321.

Reis, S. M. (2009). How academically gifted elementary, urban students respond to challenge in an enriched, differentiated reading program. *Journal for the Education of the Gifted, 33,* 203–240.

Reis, S. M., Westberg, K. L., Kulikowich, J. M., & Purcell, J. H. (1998). Curriculum compacting and achievement test scores: What does the research say? *Gifted Child Quarterly, 42,* 123–129.

Swiatek, M. A. (1993). A decade of longitudinal research on academic acceleration through the study of mathematically precocious youth. *Roeper Review, 15,* 120–123.

Theory-Based References

Gentry, M. (2009). Myth 11: A comprehensive continuum of gifted education and talent development services: Discovering, developing, and enhancing young people's gifts and talents. *Gifted Child Quarterly, 53,* 262–265.

Gilman, B. (2004). *Empowering gifted minds: Educational advocacy that works.* Phoenix, AZ: Deleon Publishing.

Maker, C. J., & Nielson, A. G. (1996). *Curriculum development and teaching strategies for gifted learners* (2nd ed.). Austin, TX: Pro-Ed.

Renzulli, J. S., Leppien, J. H., & Hays, T. S. (2000). *The multiple menu model: A practical guide for developing differentiated curriculum.* Mansfield Center, CT: Creative Learning Press.

Renzulli, J. S., & Reis, S. M. (2003). The Schoolwide Enrichment Model: Developing creative and productive giftedness. In N. Colangelo & G. A. Davis (Eds.), *Handbook of gifted education* (3rd ed., pp.184–203). Boston, MA: Allyn & Bacon.

Rogers, K. (2002). *Re-forming gifted education: Matching the program to the child.* Scottsdale, AZ: Great Potential Press.

Southern, T., & Jones, E. (Eds.). (1991). *The academic acceleration of gifted children.* New York, NY: Teachers' College Press.

Practice-Based References

Reis, S. M., Burns, D. E., & Renzulli, J. S. (1992). *Curriculum compacting: The complete guide to modifying the regular curriculum for high ability students.* Waco, TX: Prufrock Press.

Rogers, K. (2002). *Re-forming gifted education: Matching the program to the child.* Scottsdale, AZ: Great Potential Press.

Treffinger, D. J., Young, G. C., Nassab, C. A., & Wittig, C. V. (2004). *Enhancing and expanding gifted programs.* Waco, TX: Prufrock Press.

VanTassel-Baska, J. (2004). Curricular diversity and the gifted. In D. Boothe & J. C. Stanley (Eds.), *In the eyes of the beholder: Critical issues for diversity in gifted education* (pp. 167–178). Waco, TX: Prufrock Press.

VanTassel-Baska, J. (2005). *Acceleration strategies for teaching gifted learners.* Waco, TX: Prufrock Press.

Winebrenner, S., & Brulles, D. (2012). *Teaching gifted kids in in today's classroom.* Minneapolis, MN: Free Spirit.

Standard 4: Assessment

Beginning gifted education professionals use multiple methods of assessment and data sources in making educational decisions about identification of individuals with gifts and talents and student learning.

ELEMENT 4.1

Beginning gifted education professionals understand that some groups of individuals with gifts and talents have been underrepresented in gifted education programs and select and use technically sound formal and informal assessments that minimize bias in identifying students for gifted education programs and services.

Research-Based References

Briggs, C. J., Reis, S. M., & Sullivan, E. E. (2008). A national view of promising programs and practices for culturally, linguistically, and ethnically diverse gifted and talented students. *Gifted Child Quarterly, 52,* 131–145.

Cunningham, C. M., Callahan, C. M., Plucker, J. A., Roberson, S. C., & Rapkin, A. (1998). Identifying Hispanic students of outstanding talent: Psychometric integrity of a peer nomination form. *Exceptional Children, 64,* 197–209.

Lohman, D. F. (2006). *Identifying academically talented minority students* (RM05216). Storrs: University of Connecticut, The National Research Center on the Gifted and Talented.

Masten, W., & Plata, M. (2000). Acculturation and teacher ratings of Hispanic and Anglo-American students. *Roeper Review, 23,* 45–46.

Naglieri, J. A., & Ford, D. Y. (2003). Addressing underrepresentation of gifted minority children using the Naglieri Nonverbal Ability Test (NNAT). *Gifted Child Quarterly, 47,* 155–160.

Reid, C., Romanoff, B., Algozzine, B., & Udall, A. (2000). An evaluation of alternative screening procedures. *Journal for the Education of the Gifted, 23,* 378–396.

Tomlinson, C. A., Callahan, C. M., & Lelli, K. M. (1997). Challenging expectations: Case studies of high-potential, culturally diverse young children. *Gifted Child Quarterly, 41,* 5–17.

VanTassel-Baska, J., Johnson, D., & Avery, L. D. (2002). Using performance tasks in the identification of economically disadvantaged and minority gifted learners: Findings from Project STAR. *Gifted Child Quarterly, 46,* 110–123.

Wyner, J. S., Bridgeland, J. M., & DiIulio, J. J. (2007). *The achievement trap.* Lansdowne, VA: The Jack Kent Cooke Foundation.

Yoon, S., & Gentry, M. (2009). Racial and ethnic representation in gifted programs: Current status of and implications for gifted Asian American students. *Gifted Child Quarterly, 53,* 121–136.

Theory-Based References

Ford, D. Y. (2004). *Intelligence testing and cultural diversity: Concerns, cautions, and considerations* (RM04204). Storrs: University of Connecticut, The National Research Center on the Gifted and Talented.

Ford, D. Y., & Trotman, M. F. (2000). The Office for Civil Rights and nondiscriminatory testing, policies, and procedures: Implications for gifted education. *Roeper Review, 23,* 109–112.

Joseph, L., & Ford, D. Y. (2006). Nondiscriminatory assessment: Considerations for gifted education. *Gifted Child Quarterly, 50,* 42–51.

Lohman, D. F. (2005b). An aptitude perspective on talent: Implications for identification of academically gifted minority students. *Journal for the Education of the Gifted, 28,* 333–360.

Naglieri, J. A., & Kaufman, J. C. (2001). Understanding intelligence, giftedness and creativity using the PASS theory. *Roeper Review, 23,* 151–156.

Peters, S. J. (2012). The importance of multi-group validity evidence in the identification of exceptionalities. *Gifted and Talented International, 26,* 99–104.

Ryser, G. R. (2011). Fairness in testing and nonbiased assessment. In S. K. Johnsen (Ed.), *Identifying gifted students: A practical guide* (2nd ed., pp. 63–72). Waco, TX: Prufrock Press.

Sternberg, R. J., Grigorenko, E. L., & Ferrari, M. (2004). *Giftedness and expertise* (RM04198). Storrs: University of Connecticut, The National Research Center on the Gifted and Talented.

Practice-Based References

Artiles, A. J., & Zamora-Duran, G. (Eds). (1997). *Reducing disproportionate representation of culturally diverse students in special and gifted education.* Arlington, VA: The Council for Exceptional Children.

Baldwin, A. Y. (2002). Culturally diverse students who are gifted. *Exceptionality, 10,* 139–147.

Castellano, J. A. (2002). Renavigating the waters: The identification and assessment of culturally and linguistically diverse students for gifted and talented education. In J. A. Castellano & E. I. Diaz (Eds.), *Reaching new horizons: Gifted and talented education for culturally and linguistically diverse students* (pp. 94–116). Boston, MA: Allyn & Bacon.

Cline, S. (1999). *Suggestions for screening entering kindergarten students to assist in the identification of possibly gifted children.* Solvay, NY: Advocacy for Gifted and Talented Education in New York State. (ERIC Document Reproduction Service No. ED 440489)

Hertzog, N. B. (2005). Equity and access: Creating general education classrooms responsive to potential giftedness. *Journal for the Education of the Gifted, 29,* 213–257.

Johnsen, S. K. (Ed.). (2011). *Identifying gifted students: A practical guide* (2nd ed.). Waco, TX: Prufrock Press.

McKenzie, J. A. (1986). The influence of identification practices, race and SES on the identification of gifted students. *Gifted Child Quarterly, 30,* 93–95.

Passow, A. H., & Frasier, M. M. (1996). Toward improving identification of talent potential among minority and disadvantaged students. *Roeper Review, 18,* 198–202.

Rizza, M. G., & Morrison, W. F. (2003). Uncovering stereotypes and identifying characteristics of gifted students and students with emotional/behavioral disabilities. *Roeper Review, 25,* 73–77.

ELEMENT 4.2
Beginning gifted education professionals use knowledge of measurement principles and practices to differentiate assessments and interpret results to guide educational decisions for individuals with gifts and talents.

Research-Based References

Baum, S., Owen, S. V., & Oreck, B. A. (1996). Talent beyond words: Identification of potential talent in dance and music in elementary students. *Gifted Child Quarterly, 40,* 93–101.

Clark, G. (2004). Screening and identifying students talented in the visual arts: Clark's drawing abilities test. In J. S. Renzulli (Ed.), *Identification of students for gifted and talented programs* (pp. 101–115). Thousand Oaks, CA: Corwin Press.

Feng, A. X., VanTassel-Baska, J., Quek, C., Bai, W., & O'Neill, B. (2005). A longitudinal assessment of gifted students' learning using the Integrated Curriculum Model (ICM): Impacts and perceptions of the William and Mary language arts and science curriculum (On teaching gifted students). *Roeper Review, 27,* 78–84.

McKenna, M. A., Hollingsworth, P. L., & Barnes, L. L. B. (2005). Developing latent mathematics abilities in economically disadvantaged students. *Roeper Review, 27,* 222–227.

Lee, S.-Y., & Olszewski-Kubilius, P. (2009). Follow-up with students after 6 years of participation in Project EXCITE. *Gifted Child Quarterly, 53,* 137–156.

Oakland, T., Falkenberg, B. A., & Oakland, C. (1996). Assessment of leadership in children, youth and adults. *Gifted Child Quarterly, 40,* 138–146.

Oreck, B. A, Owen, S. V., & Baum, S. M. (2003). Validity, reliability, and equity issues in an observational talent assessment process in the performing arts. *Journal for the Education of the Gifted, 27,* 62–94.

Reid, C., Romanoff, B., Algozzine, B., & Udall, A. (2000). An evaluation of alternative screening procedures. *Journal for the Education of the Gifted, 23,* 378–396.

Swiatek, M. A. (1993). A decade of longitudinal research on academic acceleration through the study of mathematically precocious youth. *Roeper Review, 15,* 120–123.

Williams, E. R., & Baber, C. R. (2007). Building trust through culturally reciprocal home-school-community collaboration from the perspective of African-American parents. *Multicultural Perspectives, 9*(2), 3–9.

VanTassel-Baska, J. (2002). Assessment of gifted student learning in the language arts. *Journal of Secondary Gifted Education, 13,* 67–72.

VanTassel-Baska, J., Bass, G., Ries, R., Poland, D., & Avery, L. (1998). A national study of science curriculum effectiveness with high ability students. *Gifted Child Quarterly, 42,* 200–211.

Theory-Based References

Assouline, S., Colangelo, N., VanTassel-Baska, J., & Lupkowski-Shoplik, A. (Eds.). (2015). *A nation empowered: Evidence trumps the excuses that hold back America's brightest students.* Iowa City: University of Iowa, The Connie Belin and Jacqueline N. Blank International Center for Gifted Education and Talent Development. Retrieved from http://www.accelerationinstitute. org/Nation_Empowered/Default.aspx

Feldhusen, J. F. (1996). Is it acceleration or simply appropriate instruction for precocious youth? *TEACHING Exceptional Children, 28,* 48–51.

Heritage, M. (2007). Formative assessment: What do teachers need to know and do? *Phi Delta Kappan, 89,* 140–145.

Rogers, K. (2002). *Re-forming gifted education: Matching the program to the child.* Scottsdale, AZ: Great Potential Press.

Torrance, E. P. (1984). The role of creativity in identification of the gifted and talented. In J. S. Renzulli (Ed.), *Identification of students for gifted and talented programs* (pp. 17–24). Thousand Oaks, CA: Corwin Press.

VanTassel-Baska, J. (2004). *Curriculum for gifted and talented students.* Thousand Oaks, CA: Corwin Press.

Practice-Based References

Feldhusen, J. F., Asher, J. W., & Hoover, S. M. (2004). Problems in the identification of giftedness, talent, or ability. In J. S. Renzulli (Ed.), *Identification of students for gifted and talented programs* (pp. 79–85). Thousand Oaks, CA: Corwin Press.

Gentry, M., & Ferriss, S. (1999). StATS: A model of collaboration to develop science talent among rural students. *Roeper Review, 21,* 316–320.

Heacox, D. (2001). *Differentiating instruction in the regular classroom: How to reach and teach all learners, grades 3–12.* Minneapolis, MN: Free Spirit Press.

Johnsen, S. K. (2008). Using portfolios to assess gifted and talented students. In J. VanTassel-Baska (Ed.), *Alternative assessments with gifted and talented students* (pp. 227–257). Waco, TX: Prufrock Press.

Johnsen, S. K. (Ed.). (2011). *Identifying gifted students: A practical guide* (2nd ed.). Waco, TX: Prufrock Press.

Joint Committee on Testing Practices. (2005). *Code of fair testing practices in education.* Washington, DC: American Psychological Association.

Kanevsky, L. (2000). Dynamic assessment of gifted learners. In K. A. Heller, F. J. Mönks, R. J. Sternberg, & R. F. Subotnik (Eds.), *International handbook of giftedness and talent* (2nd ed., pp. 283–295). New York, NY: Pergamon.

Mendaglio, S., & Pyryt, M. C. (1995). Self-concept of gifted students: Assessment-based intervention. *TEACHING Exceptional Children, 27*(3), 40–45.

Reis, S. M., Burns, D. E., & Renzulli, J. S. (1992). *Curriculum compacting: The complete guide to modifying the regular curriculum for high ability students.* Mansfield Center, CT: Creative Learning Press.

Siegle, D. (2002). Creating a living portfolio: Documenting student growth with electronic portfolios. *Gifted Child Today, 25*(3), 60–65.

Winebrenner, S., & Brulles, D. (2012). *Teaching gifted kids in in today's classroom.* Minneapolis, MN: Free Spirit.

> ## ELEMENT 4.3
> Beginning gifted education professionals collaborate with colleagues and families in using multiple types of assessment information to make identification and learning progress decisions and to minimize bias in assessment and decision making.

Research-Based References

Cunningham, C. M., Callahan, C. M., Plucker, J. A., Roberson, S. C., & Rapkin, A. (1998). Identifying Hispanic students of outstanding talent: Psychometric integrity of a peer nomination form. *Exceptional Children, 64,* 197–209.

Gentry, M., & Owen, S. V. (1999). An investigation of the effects of total school flexible cluster grouping on identification, achievement, and classroom practices. *Gifted Child Quarterly, 43,* 224–243.

Hertzog, N. B. (2005). Equity and access: Creating general education classrooms responsive to potential giftedness. *Journal for the Education of the Gifted, 29,* 213–257.

Hunsaker, S. L., & Callahan, C. M. (1995). Creativity and giftedness: Published instrument uses and abuses. *Gifted Child Quarterly, 39,* 110–114.

Pletan, M. D., Robinson, N. M., Berninger, V. W., & Abbot, R. D. (1995). Parents' observations of kindergartners who are advanced in mathematical reasoning. *Journal for the Education of the Gifted, 19,* 30–44.

Scroth, S. T., & Helfer, J. A. (2008). Identifying gifted students: Educator beliefs regarding various policies, processes, and procedures. *Journal for the Education of the Gifted, 32,* 155–179.

Swiatek, M. A., & Lupkowski-Shoplik, A. (2005). An evaluation of the elementary student talent search by families and schools. *Gifted Child Quarterly, 49,* 247–259.

Valencia, R. R., & Suzuki, L. A. (2001). *Intelligence testing and minority students.* Thousand Oaks, CA: Sage Publications.

Theory-Based References

Landrum, M. S. (2002). *Resource consultation and collaboration in gifted education.* Mansfield Center, CT: Creative Learning Press.

Matthews, D. J., & Foster, J. F. (2005). A dynamic scaffolding model of teacher development: The gifted education consultant as catalyst for change. *Gifted Child Quarterly, 49,* 222–230.

Practice-Based References

Johnsen, S. K. (2011). Making decisions about placement. In S. K. Johnsen (Ed.), *Identifying gifted students: A practical guide* (2nd ed., pp. 119–150). Waco, TX: Prufrock Press.

Kingore, B. (1995). Introducing parents to portfolio assessment: A collaborative effort toward authentic assessment. *Gifted Child Today, 18*(4), 12–13, 40.

Stephens, K. R. (1999). Parents of the gifted and talented: The forgotten partner. *Gifted Child Today, 22*(5), 38–43, 52.

ELEMENT 4.4

Beginning gifted education professionals use assessment results to develop long- and short-range goals and objectives that take into consideration an individual's abilities and needs, the learning environment, and other factors related to diversity.

Research-Based References

Little, C., Feng, A., VanTassel-Baska, J., Rogers, K., & Avery, L. (2007). A study of curriculum effectiveness in social studies. *Gifted Child Quarterly, 51*, 272–284.

Reis, S. M., Westberg, K. L., Kulikowich, J. M., & Purcell, J. H. (1998). Curriculum compacting and achievement test scores: What does the research say? *Gifted Child Quarterly, 42*, 123–129.

Stormont, M., Stebbins, M. S., & Holliday, G. (2001). Characteristics and educational support needs of underrepresented gifted adolescents. *Psychology in the Schools, 38*, 413–423.

Uresti, R., Goertz, J., & Bernal, E. M. (2002). Maximizing achievement for potentially gifted and talented and regular minority students in a primary classroom. *Roeper Review, 25*, 27–31.

VanTassel-Baska, J., Bass, G., Ries, R., Poland, D., & Avery, L. (1998). A national study of science curriculum effectiveness with high ability students. *Gifted Child Quarterly, 42*, 200–211.

VanTassel-Baska, J., & Brown, E. F. (2007). An analysis of the efficacy of curriculum models in gifted education. *Gifted Child Quarterly, 51*, 342–358.

VanTassel-Baska, J., Johnson, D. T., Hughes, C. E., & Boyce, L. N. (1996). A study of language arts curriculum effectiveness with gifted learners. *Journal for the Education of the Gifted, 19*, 461–480.

Theory-Based References

Anderson, L. W., & Krathwohl, D. R. (Eds.). (2001). *A taxonomy for learning, teaching, and assessing: A revision of Bloom's taxonomy of educational objectives.* New York, NY: Longman.

Callahan, C. M. (2005). Making the grade or achieving the goal? Evaluating learner and program outcomes in gifted education. In F. A. Karnes & S. M. Bean (Eds.), *Methods and materials for teaching the gifted* (2nd ed., pp. 211–246). Waco, TX: Prufrock Press.

Ogbu, J. U. (1994). Understanding cultural diversity and learning. *Journal for the Education of the Gifted, 17,* 355–383.

Shade, B. J., Kelly, C., & Oberg, M. (1997). *Creating culturally responsive classrooms.* Washington, DC: American Psychological Association.

Stiggins, R. (2008). *Assessment manifesto: A call for the development of balanced assessment systems.* Portland, OR: ETS Assessment Training Institute.

Practice-Based References

Castellano, J., & Frazier, A. D. (2011). *Special populations in gifted education.* Waco, TX: Prufrock Press.

Kirschenbaum, R. J. (1998). Dynamic assessment and its use with underserved gifted and talented populations. *Gifted Child Quarterly, 42,* 140–147.

Kitano, M. K., & Pedersen, K. S. (2002). Action research and practical inquiry: Multicultural-content integration in gifted education: Lessons from the field. *Journal for the Education of the Gifted, 26,* 269–289.

Nugent, S. A. (2005). Affective education: Addressing the social and emotional needs of gifted students in the classroom. In F. A. Karnes & S. M. Bean (Eds.), *Methods and materials for teaching the gifted* (2nd ed., pp. 409–438). Waco, TX: Prufrock Press.

Rollins, K., Mursky, C., Shah-Coltrane, S., & Johnsen, S. K. (2009). RtI models for gifted students. *Gifted Child Today, 32*(1), 20–30.

ELEMENT 4.5
Beginning gifted education professionals engage individuals with gifts and talents in assessing the quality of their own learning and performance and in setting future goals and objectives.

Research-Based References

Bain, S., & Bell, S. (2004). Social self-concept, social-attributions, and peer relationships in fourth, fifth and sixth graders who are gifted compared to high achievers. *Gifted Child Quarterly, 48,* 167–178.

Frey, C. P. (1998). Struggling with identity: Working with seventh-and eighth-grade gifted girls to air issues of concern. *Journal for the Education of the Gifted, 21,* 437–451.

VanTassel-Baska, J., Olszewski-Kubilius, P., & Kulieke, M. (1994). A study of self-concept and social support in advantaged and disadvantaged seventh and eighth grade gifted students. *Roeper Review, 16,* 186–191.

Theory-Based References

Greenspon, T. S. (1998). The gifted self: Its role in development and emotional health. *Roeper Review, 20,* 162–166.

Stiggins, R., Arter, J., Chappuis, J., & Chappuis, S. (2006). *Classroom assessment for student learning: Doing it right–using it well.* Portland, OR: ETS Assessment Training Institute.

VanTassel-Baska, J. (Ed.). (2008). *Alternative assessments with gifted and talented students.* Waco, TX: Prufrock Press.

Practice-Based References

Betts, G. T., & Neihart, M. (1986). Implementing self-directed learning models for the gifted and talented. *Gifted Child Quarterly, 30,* 174–177.

Chappuis, S., & Chappuis, J. (2007/2008). The best value in formative assessment. *Educational Leadership, 65*(4), 14–19.

Ford, D., Tyson, C., Howard, T., & Harris, J. J., III. (2000). Multicultural literature and gifted Black students: Promoting self-understanding, awareness, and pride. *Roeper Review, 22,* 235–240.

Heritage, M. (2007). Formative assessment: What do teachers need to know and do? *Phi Delta Kappan, 89,* 140–145.

Johnsen, S. K. (2008). Using portfolios to assess gifted and talented students. In J. VanTassel-Baska (Ed.), *Alternative assessments with gifted and talented students* (pp. 227–257). Waco, TX: Prufrock Press.

Standard 5: Instructional Planning and Strategies

Beginning gifted education professionals select, adapt, and use a repertoire of evidence-based instructional strategies[7] to advance the learning of individuals with gifts and talents.

ELEMENT 5.1

Beginning gifted education professionals know principles of evidence-based, differentiated, and accelerated practices and possess a repertoire of instructional strategies to enhance the learning of critical and creative thinking, problem-solving, and performance skills of individuals with gifts and talents.

Research-Based References

Assouline, S. G., Colangelo, N., VanTassel-Baska, J., & Lupkowski-Shoplik, A. (2015). *A nation empowered: Evidence trumps the excuses holding back America's brightest students.* Iowa City: University of Iowa, The Connie Belin and Jacqueline N. Blank International Center for Gifted Education and Talent Development.

Betts, G. T., & Neihart, M. (1986). Implementing self-directed learning models for the gifted and talented. *Gifted Child Quarterly, 30,* 174–177.

Carr, M., Alexander, J. M., & Schwanenflugel, P. J. (1996). Where gifted children do and do not excel on metacognitive tasks. *Roeper Review, 18,* 212–217.

Clark, G. (2004). Screening and identifying students talented in the visual arts: Clark's drawing abilities test. In J. S. Renzulli (Ed.), *Identification of students for gifted and talented programs* (pp. 101–115). Thousand Oaks, CA: Corwin Press.

Friedman, R. C., & Lee, S. W. (1996). Differentiating instruction for high-achieving/gifted children in regular classrooms: A field test of three gifted-education models. *Journal for the Education of the Gifted, 19,* 405–436.

Gallagher, S. A., & Stepien, W. (1996). Content acquisition in problem-based learning: Depth versus breadth in American studies. *Journal for the Education of the Gifted, 19,* 257–275.

Gavin, M. K., & Adelson, J. L. (2014). Mathematics gifted education. In J. A. Plucker & C. M. Callahan (Eds.), *Critical issues and practices in gifted education* (2nd ed., pp. 386–412). Waco, TX: Prufrock Press.

---

7   Instructional strategies, as used throughout this document include intervention used in academic and specialized curricula.

Gross, M. U. M. (1992). The use of radical acceleration in cases of extreme intellectual precocity. *Gifted Child Quarterly, 36,* 91–99.

Moon, S. M., Feldhusen, J. F., & Dillon, D. R. (1994). Long-term effects of an enrichment program based on the Purdue Three-Stage Model. *Gifted Child Quarterly, 38,* 38–48.

Reis, S. M., Westberg, K. L., Kulikowich, J. M., & Purcell, J. H. (1998). Curriculum compacting and achievement test scores: What does the research say? *Gifted Child Quarterly, 42,* 123–129.

Rostan, S. M., Pariser, D., & Gruber, H. E. (2002). A cross-cultural study of the development of artistic talent, creativity and giftedness. *High Ability Studies, 13,* 125–155.

Russo, C. F. (2004). A comparative study of creativity and cognitive problem-solving strategies of high IQ and average students. *Gifted Child Quarterly, 48,* 179–190.

Stamps, L. (2004). The effectiveness of curriculum compacting in first grade classrooms. *Roeper Review, 27,* 31–41.

Steenbergen-Hu, S., & Moon, S. M. (2010). The effects of acceleration on high-ability learners: A meta-analysis. *Gifted Child Quarterly, 20,* 39–53.

Sternberg, R. J., Torff, B., & Grigorenko, E. L. (1998). Teaching triarchically improves school achievement. *Journal of Educational Psychology, 90,* 374–384.

Swiatek, M. A. (2000). A decade of longitudinal research on academic acceleration through the study of mathematically precocious youth. *Roeper Review, 24,* 141–144.

VanTassel-Baska, J., Avery, L. D., Little, C., & Hughes, C. (2000). An evaluation of the implementation of curriculum innovation: The impact of the William and Mary units on schools. *Journal for the Education of the Gifted, 23,* 24–272.

Theory-Based References

Anderson, L. W., & Krathwohl, D. R. (Eds.). (2001). *A taxonomy for learning, teaching, and assessing: A revision of Bloom's taxonomy of educational objectives.* New York, NY: Longman.

Davis, G. A., Rimm, S. B., & Siegle, D. (2010). *Education of the gifted and talented* (6th ed.). Boston, MA: Allyn & Bacon.

Elder, L., & Paul, R. (2004). *The art of asking essential questions.* Dillon Beach, CA: The Foundation for Critical Thinking.

Gagné, F. (2005). From gifts to talents: The DMGT as a developmental model. In R. J. Sternberg & J. E. Davidson (Eds.), *Conceptions of giftedness* (2nd ed., pp. 98–119). New York, NY: Cambridge University Press.

Hartman, H. J. (Ed.). (2001). *Metacognition in learning and instruction: Theory, research and practice.* Dordrecht, The Netherlands: Kluwer Academic Publishers.

Rogers, K. B. (2002). *Re-forming gifted education: Matching the program to the child.* Scottsdale, AZ: Great Potential Press.

Sternberg, R. J. (2000). Giftedness as developing expertise. In K. A. Heller, F. J. Mönks, R. J. Sternberg, & R. F. Subotnik (Eds.), *International handbook of giftedness and talent* (pp. 55–66). New York, NY: Elsevier.

VanTassel-Baska, J. (2004). *Curriculum for gifted and talented students.* Thousand Oaks, CA: Corwin Press.

Practice-Based References

Betts, G. (2004). Fostering autonomous learners through levels of differentiation. *Roeper Review, 26,* 190–191.

Institute for Research and Policy on Acceleration, National Association for Gifted Children, & Council of State Directors of Programs for the Gifted. (2009). *Guidelines for developing an academic acceleration policy.* Iowa City: University of Iowa, Institute for Research and Policy on Acceleration.

Little, C., Feng, A., VanTassel-Baska, J., Rogers, K., & Avery, L. (2007). A study of curriculum effectiveness in social studies. *Gifted Child Quarterly, 51,* 272–284.

National Association for Gifted Children. (2010). *NAGC Pre-K–Grade 12 gifted programming standards: A blueprint for quality gifted education programs.* Washington, DC: Author.

NGSS Lead States. (2013). *Next Generation Science Standards: For states, by states.* Washington, DC: The National Academies Press.

National Governors Association Center for Best Practices, & Council of Chief State School Officers. (2010a). *Common Core State Standards for English language arts.* Retrieved from http://www.corestandards.org/the-standards

National Governors Association Center for Best Practices, & Council of Chief State School Officers. (2010b). *Common Core State Standards for mathematics.* Retrieved from http://www.corestandards.org/the-standards.

Parker, J. P., & Begnaud, L.G. (2003). *Developing creative leadership.* Gifted Treasury Series. Portsmouth, NH: Reed Elsevier.

Renzulli, J., & Reis, S. (2009). The Schoolwide Enrichment Model: A focus on student strengths and interests. In J. S. Renzulli, E. J. Gubbins, K. S. McMillen, R. D. Eckert, & C. A. Little (Eds.), *Systems and models for developing programs for the gifted and talented* (2nd ed., pp. 323–352). Waco, TX: Prufrock Press.

Schlichter, C. L., & Palmer, W. R. (Eds.). (1993). *Thinking smart: A premiere of the Talents Unlimited model.* Mansfield Center, CT: Creative Learning Press.

Tomlinson, C. A. (2002). Different learners, different lessons. *Instructor, 112*(2), 21, 24–26.

Tomlinson, C. A., & Cunningham-Eidson, C. (2003). *Differentiation in practice: A resource guide for differentiating curriculum, grades 5–9.* Alexandria, VA: Association for Supervision and Curriculum Development.

Tomlinson, C. A., Kaplan, S. N., Renzulli, J. S., Purcell, J. H., Leppien, J. H., Burns, D. E. . . . Imbeau, M. B. (2008). *The parallel curriculum* (2nd ed.). Thousand Oaks, CA: Corwin Press.

VanTassel-Baska, J., & Brown, E. F. (2007). An analysis of the efficacy of curriculum models in gifted education. *Gifted Child Quarterly, 51,* 342–358.

ELEMENT 5.2
Beginning gifted education professionals apply appropriate technologies to support instructional assessment, planning, and delivery for individuals with gifts and talents.

Research-Based References

Davalos, R., & Griffin, G. (1999). The impact of teachers' individualized practices on gifted students in rural, heterogeneous classrooms. *Roeper Review, 21,* 308–314.

Olszewski-Kubilius, P., & Lee, S.-Y. (2004). Gifted adolescents' talent development through distance learning. *Journal for the Education of the Gifted, 28,* 7–35.

Ravaglia, R., Suppes, P., Stillinger, C., & Alper, T. M. (1995). Computer-based mathematics and physics for gifted students. *Gifted Child Quarterly, 39,* 7–13.

Theory-Based References

Berger, S. (2003). Technology and gifted learners. In W. A. Owings & L. S. Kaplan (Eds.), *Best practices, best thinking, and emerging issues in school leadership* (pp. 177–190). Thousand Oaks, CA: Corwin Press.

Siegle, D. (2004). *Using media and technology with gifted learners.* Waco, TX: Prufrock Press.

Practice-Based References

Pyryt, M. C. (2003). Technology and the gifted. In N. Colangelo & G. A. Davis (Eds.), *Handbook of gifted education* (3rd ed., pp. 582–589). Boston, MA: Allyn & Bacon.

VanTassel-Baska, J., & Stambaugh, T. (2006). Using technology to supplement gifted curriculum. In J. VanTassel-Baska & T. Stambaugh (Eds.), *Comprehensive curriculum for gifted learners* (3rd ed., pp. 290–308). Boston, MA: Allyn & Bacon.

ELEMENT 5.3

Beginning gifted education professionals collaborate with families, professional colleagues, and other educators to select, adapt, and use evidence-based strategies that promote challenging learning opportunities in general and specialized curricula.

Research-Based References

Johnson, D. T., Boyce, L. N., & VanTassel-Baska, J. (1995). Science curriculum review: evaluating materials for high-ability learners. *Gifted Child Quarterly, 39,* 36–45.

Matthews, D., & Menna, R. (2003). Solving problems together: Parent/school/community collaboration at a time of educational and social change. *Education Canada, 43*(1), 20–23.

Tomlinson, C. A., Coleman, M. R., Allan, S., Udall, A., & Landrum, M. (1996). Interface between gifted education and general education: Toward communication, cooperation, and collaboration. *Gifted Child Quarterly, 40,* 165–171.

Theory-Based References

Johnsen, S. (2005). Within-class acceleration. *Gifted Child Today, 28*(1), 5.

Kaplan, S. N. (2005). Layering differentiated curricula for the gifted and talented. In F. A. Karnes & S. M. Bean (Eds.). *Methods and materials for teaching the gifted* (2nd ed., pp. 107–136). Waco, TX: Prufrock Press.

Karnes, F. A., & Bean, S. M. (Eds.). (2005). *Methods and materials for teaching the gifted* (2nd ed.). Waco, TX: Prufrock Press.

Landrum, M. S. (2002). *Resource consultation in gifted education: Teachers working together to serve students.* Mansfield, CT: Creative Learning Press.

Paul, R., & Elder, L. (2002). *Critical thinking: Tools for taking charge of your professional and personal life.* New York, NY: Prentice Hall.

Steiner, H. H., & Carr, M. (2003). Cognitive development in gifted children: Toward a more precise understanding of emerging differences in intelligence. *Educational Psychology Review, 15,* 215–246.

Treffinger, D. J., Isaksen, S. G., & Stead-Dorval, K. B. (2006). *Creative problem solving: An introduction* (4th ed.). Waco, TX: Prufrock Press.

VanTassel-Baska, J. (2004). *Curriculum for gifted and talented students.* Thousand Oaks, CA: Corwin Press.

VanTassel-Baska, J., & Little, C. A. (Eds.). (2003). *Content-based curriculum for gifted learners.* Waco, TX: Prufrock Press.

Practice-Based References

Coates, D. L., Perkins, T., Vietze, P., Reyes Cruz, M., & Park, S. (2003). *Teaching thinking to culturally diverse, high ability, high school students: A triarchic approach* (RM03174). Storrs: University of Connecticut, The National Research Center on the Gifted and Talented.

Coleman, M. R., & Johnsen, S. K. (Eds.). (2011). *RtI for gifted students.* Waco, TX: Prufrock Press.

Elder, L., & Paul, R. (2003). *Analytic thinking: How to take thinking apart and what to look for when you do.* Dillon Beach, CA: The Foundation for Critical Thinking.

Gentry, M., & Ferriss, S. (1999). StATS: A model of collaboration to develop science talent among rural students. *Roeper Review, 21,* 316–320.

Hughes, C., Kettler, T., Shaunessy-Dedrick, E., & VanTassel-Baska, J. (2014). *A teacher's guide to using the Common Core State Standards with gifted and advanced learners in the English language arts.* Waco, TX: Prufrock Press.

Johnsen, S. K. (Ed.). (2012). *NAGC pre-K–grade 12 gifted education programming standards: A guide to planning and implementing high-quality services.* Waco, TX: Prufrock Press.

Johnsen, S. K., & Goree, K. K. (2015). Teaching gifted students through independent study. In F. A. Karnes & S. M. Bean (Eds.), *Methods and materials for teaching the gifted* (4th ed., pp. 445–478). Waco, TX: Prufrock Press.

Johnsen, S. K., Ryser, G. R., Assouline, S. (2014). *A teacher's guide to using the Common Core State Standards with mathematically gifted and advanced learners.* Waco, TX: Prufrock Press.

Johnsen, S. K., Sulak, T., & Rollins, K. (2012). *Serving gifted students within an RtI framework.* Waco, TX: Prufrock Press.

Purcell, J. H., & Leppien, J. H. (1998). Building bridges between general practitioners and educators of the gifted: A study of collaboration. *Gifted Child Quarterly, 42,* 172–181.

Renzulli, J. S., Leppien, J. H., & Hays, T. S. (2000). *The multiple menu model: A practical guide for developing differentiated curriculum.* Waco, TX: Prufrock Press.

Winebrenner, S., & Brulles, D. (2012). *Teaching gifted kids in today's classroom.* Minneapolis, MN: Free Spirit.

ELEMENT 5.4

Beginning gifted education professionals emphasize the development, practice, and transfer of advanced knowledge and skills across environments throughout the lifespan leading to creative, productive careers in a multicultural society for individuals with gifts and talents.

Research-Based References

Hébert, T. P. (1993). Reflections at graduation: The long-term impact of elementary school experiences in creative productivity. *Roeper Review, 16,* 22–28.

Kerr, B., & Sodano, S. (2003). Career assessment with intellectually gifted students. *Journal of Career Assessment, 11,* 168–186.

Lee, S.-Y., & Olszewski-Kubilius, P. (2009). Follow-up with students after 6 years of participation in Project EXCITE. *Gifted Child Quarterly, 53,* 137–156.

Uresti, R., Goertz, J., & Bernal, E. M. (2002). Maximizing achievement for potentially gifted and talented and regular minority students in a primary classroom. *Roeper Review, 25,* 27–31.

VanTassel-Baska, J., Feng, A. X., Quek, C., & Struck, J. (2004). A study of educators' and students' perceptions of academic success for underrepresented populations identified for gifted programs. *Psychology Science, 46,* 363–378.

Wessel, L. E. (1999). *Career counseling for gifted students: Literature review and critique.* (ERIC Document Reproduction Services No. ED427267)

Theory-Based References

Berger, S. (1989). *College planning for gifted students.* Reston, VA: The Council for Exceptional Children.

Horowitz, F. D., Subotnik, R. F., & Matthews, D. J. (2009). *The development of giftedness and talent across the life span.* Washington, DC: American Psychological Association.

Renzulli, J. (1992). A general theory for the development of creative productivity through the pursuit of ideal acts of learning. *Gifted Child Quarterly, 36,* 170–183.

Renzulli, J. S., & Reis, S. M. (2003). The Schoolwide Enrichment Model: Developing creative and productive giftedness. In N. Colangelo & G. A. Davis (Eds.), *Handbook of gifted education* (3rd ed., pp. 184–203). Boston, MA: Allyn & Bacon.

Simonton, D. K. (1999). *Genius, creativity, and leadership: Historiometric inquiries.* Bloomington, IN: Universe.

Su, Y.-H. (2009). Idea creation: The need to develop creativity in lifelong learning practices. *International Journal of Lifelong Education, 28,* 705–717.

Practice-Based References

Adams, C. M., & Boswell, C. (2012). *Effective program practices for underserved gifted students.* Waco, TX: Prufrock Press.

Boothe, D., & Stanley, J. C. (Eds.). (2004). *In the eyes of the beholder: Critical issues for diversity in gifted education.* Waco, TX: Prufrock Press.

Ford, D. (1996). *Reversing underachievement among gifted Black students: Promising practices and programs.* New York, NY: Teachers College Press.

Ford, D., Tyson, C., Howard, T., & Harris, J. J., III. (2000). Multicultural literature and gifted Black students: Promoting self-understanding, awareness, and pride. *Roeper Review, 22,* 235–240.

Granada, J. (2002). Addressing the curriculum, instruction, and assessment needs of the gifted bilingual/bicultural student. In J. A. Castellano & E. I. Diaz (Eds.), *Reaching new horizons: Gifted and talented education for culturally and linguistically diverse students.* Boston, MA: Allyn & Bacon.

Hébert, T. P. (1993). Reflections at graduation: The long-term impact of elementary school experiences in creative productivity. *Roeper Review, 16,* 22–28.

Hertzog, N. B. (2005). Equity and access: Creating general education classrooms responsive to potential giftedness. *Journal for the Education of the Gifted, 29,* 213–257.

Peterson, J. S. (2007). A developmental perspective. In S. Mendaglio & J. S. Peterson (Eds.), *Models of counseling gifted children, adolescents, and young adults* (pp. 97–126). Waco, TX: Prufrock Press.

ELEMENT 5.5

Beginning gifted education professionals use instructional strategies that enhance the affective development of individuals with gifts and talents.

Research-Based References

Byers, J. A., Whitsell, S. S., & Moon, S. M. (2004). Gifted students' perceptions of the academic and social/emotional effects of homogeneous and heterogeneous grouping. *Gifted Child Quarterly, 48,* 7–23.

Cornell, D. G., Delcourt, M. A. B., Goldberg, M. D., & Bland, L. C. (1995). Achievement and self-concept of minority students in elementary school gifted programs. *Journal for the Education of the Gifted, 18,* 189–209.

Gentry, M. (2014). Cluster grouping. In J. A. Plucker & C. M. Callahan (Eds.), *Critical issues and practices in gifted education* (2nd ed., pp. 109–118). Waco, TX: Prufrock Press.

Gentry, M., & Owen, S. V. (1999). An investigation of the effects of total school flexible cluster grouping on identification, achievement, and classroom practices. *Gifted Child Quarterly, 43,* 224–243.

Peterson, J. S., & Norman, M. R. (2011). Student response to a small–group affective curriculum in a school for gifted children. *Gifted Child Quarterly, 55,* 167–180.

Theory-Based References

Dai, D. Y., Moon, S. M., & Feldhusen, J. F. (1998). Achievement motivation and gifted students: A social cognitive perspective. *Educational Psychologist, 33*(2/3), 45–63.

Peterson, J. S. (2003). An argument for proactive attention to affective concerns of gifted adolescents. *Journal for Secondary Gifted Education, 14,* 62–71.

Practice-Based References

Betts, G. T., & Neihart, M. (1986). Implementing self-directed learning models for the gifted and talented. *Gifted Child Quarterly, 30,* 174–177.

Cross, T. R., & Cross, J. R. (Eds.). (2012). *Handbook for counselors serving students with gifts and talents: Development, relationships, school issues, and counseling needs/interventions.* Waco, TX: Prufrock Press.

Nugent, S. A. (2005). Affective education: Addressing the social and emotional needs of gifted students in the classroom. In F. A. Karnes & S. M. Bean (Eds.), *Methods and materials for teaching the gifted* (2nd ed., pp. 409–438). Waco, TX: Prufrock Press.

Peterson, J. S. (2006). Addressing counseling needs of gifted students. *Professional School Counseling, 10,* 1, 43–51.

Mendaglio, S., & Peterson, J. S. (2007). *Models of counseling gifted children, adolescents, and young adults.* Waco, TX: Prufrock Press.

Standard 6: Professional Learning and Ethical Practice

Beginning gifted education professionals use foundational knowledge of the field and professional ethical principles and programming standards to inform gifted education practice, to engage in lifelong learning, and to advance the profession.

ELEMENT 6.1
Beginning gifted education professionals use professional ethical principles and specialized program standards to guide their practice.

Research-Based References

Keller, J. D. (1999). Deciphering teacher lounge talk. *Phi Delta Kappan, 81,* 328–329.

Klein, J. P., & Lugg, E. T. (2002). Nurturing young adolescents legally and ethically. *Middle School Journal, 34*(1), 13–20.

Theory-Based References

Copenhaver, J. (2002). *Primer for maintaining accurate special education records and meeting confidentiality requirements when serving children with disabilities—Family Educational Rights and Privacy Act (FERPA).* Logan: Utah State University, Mountain Plains Regional Resource Center.

Gallagher, J. (2002). *Society's role in educating gifted students: The role of public policy* (RM02162). Storrs: University of Connecticut, The National Research Center on the Gifted and Talented.

Kitano, M., Montgomery, D., VanTassel-Baska, J., & Johnsen, S. (2008). *Using the national gifted education standards for PreK–12 professional development.* Thousand Oaks, CA: Corwin Press.

Morehead, M. A. (1998). Professional behaviors for the beginning teacher. *American Secondary Education, 26*(4), 22–26.

Practice-Based References

Callahan, C., Cooper, C., & Glascock, R. (2003). *Preparing teachers to develop and enhance talent: The position of national education organizations.* (ERIC Document Services No. ED477882)

Council for Exceptional Children. (2010). *Special education professional ethical principles.* Retrieved from http://www.cec.sped.org/Standards/Ethical-Principles-and-Practice-Standards

Johnsen, S. K. (Ed.). (2012). *NAGC pre-K–grade 12 gifted education program-ming standards: A guide to planning and implementing high-quality services.* Waco, TX: Prufrock Press.

ELEMENT 6.2

Beginning gifted education professionals understand how foundational knowledge, perspectives, and historical and current issues influence professional practice and the education and treatment of individuals with gifts and talents in both school and society.

Research-Based References

Bain, S., Bourgeois, S., & Pappas, D. (2003). Linking theoretical models to actual practices: A survey of teachers in gifted education. *Roeper Review, 25,* 166–172.

Plucker, J. A., & Callahan, C. M. (Eds.). (2014). *Critical issues and practices in gifted education: What the research says* (2nd ed.). Waco, TX: Prufrock Press.

Renzulli, J. S. (1978). What makes giftedness? Reexamining a definition. *Phi Delta Kappan, 59,* 180–184.

Robinson, A., & Jolly, J. L. (2014). *A century of contributions to gifted education: Illuminating lives.* New York, NY: Routledge.

Theory-Based References

Carroll, J. B. (1993). *Human cognitive abilities: A survey of factor-analytical stud-ies.* New York, NY: Cambridge University Press.

Cattell, R. B. (1963), Theory of fluid and crystallized intelligence: A critical experiment. *Journal of Educational Psychology, 54,* 1–22.

Clarke, D., & Hollingworth, H. (2002). Elaborating a model of teacher profes-sional growth. *Teaching and Teacher Education, 18,* 947–967.

Dai, D. Y., & Chen, F. (2013). Three paradigms of gifted education: In search of conceptual clarity in research and practice. *Gifted Child Quarterly, 57,* 151–168.

Galton, F. (1865). Hereditary talent and character. *Macmillan's Magazine, 12,* 157–166, 318–327.

Gagné, F. (1985). Giftedness and talent: Reexamining a reexamination of the definitions. *Gifted Child Quarterly, 29,* 103–112.

Gardner, H. (1983). *Frames of mind: The theory of multiple intelligences.* New York, NY: Basic Books.

Guilford, J. P. (1967). *The nature of human intelligence.* New York, NY: McGraw Hill.

Joyce, B. R., & Showers, B. (2002). *Student achievement through staff development* (3rd ed.). Alexandria, VA: Association for Supervision and Curriculum Development.

National Association for Gifted Children. (2010). *Redefining giftedness for a new century: Shifting the paradigm* [Position statement]. Retrieved from http://www.nagc.org/sites/default/files/Position%20Statement/Redefining%20Giftedness%20for%20a%20New%20Century.pdf

Spearman, C. (1927). *The abilities of man: Their nature and measurement.* New York, NY: Macmillan.

Sternberg, R. J. (1985). *Beyond IQ: A triarchic theory of human intelligence.* New York, NY: Cambridge University Press.

Practice-Based References

Clark, C. M. (Ed.). (2001). *Talking shop: Authentic conversations and teacher learning.* New York, NY: Teachers College Press.

Johnsen, S. K. (Ed.). (2012). *NAGC pre-K–grade 12 gifted education programming standards: A guide to planning and implementing high-quality services.* Waco, TX: Prufrock Press.

Marland, S. P., Jr. (1972). *Education of the gifted and talented: Report to the Congress of the United States by the U.S. Commissioner of Education and background papers submitted to the U.S. Office of Education,* 2 vols. Washington, DC: U.S. Government Printing Office. (Government Documents, Y4.L 11/2: G36)

No Child Left Behind Act, 20 U.S.C. §6301 (2001).

U. S. Congress, Public Law 91-230, April 1970.

U. S. Department of Education. (1993). *National excellence: A case for developing America's talent.* Washington, DC: U. S. Government Printing Office.

ELEMENT 6.3

Beginning gifted education professionals model respect for diversity, understanding that it is an integral part of society's institutions and impacts learning of individuals with gifts and talents in the delivery of gifted education services.

Research-Based References

Gubbins, E. J., Westberg, K. L., Reis, S. M., Dinnocenti, S. T., Tieso, C. L., & Muller, L. M. . . . Burns, D. E. (2002). *Implementing a professional development model using gifted education strategies with all students* (RM02172).

Storrs: University of Connecticut, The National Research Center on the Gifted and Talented.

Masten, W. G., & Plata, M. (2000). Acculturation and teacher ratings of Hispanic and Anglo-American students. *Roeper Review, 23,* 45–46.

Theory-Based References

Boothe, D., & Stanley, J. C. (Eds.). (2004). *In the eyes of the beholder: Critical issues for diversity in gifted education.* Waco, TX: Prufrock Press.

Gallagher, J. (2002). *Society's role in educating gifted students: The role of public policy* (RM02162). Storrs: University of Connecticut, The National Research Center on the Gifted and Talented.

Practice-Based References

Bernal, E. M. (2000). The quintessential features of gifted education as seen from a multicultural perspective. In G. B. Esquivel & J. C. Houtz (Eds.), *Creativity and giftedness in culturally diverse students* (pp. 159–191). Cresskill, NJ: Harrington Press.

Ford, D. Y., & Trotman, M. F. (2001). Teachers of gifted students: Suggested multicultural characteristics and competencies. *Roeper Review, 23,* 235–239.

Harmon, D. (2002). They won't teach me: The voices of gifted African American inner-city students. *Roeper Review, 24,* 68–75.

ELEMENT 6.4
Beginning gifted education professionals are aware of their own professional learning needs, understand the significance of lifelong learning, and participate in professional activities and learning communities.

Research-Based References

Briggs, C. J., Reis, S. M., & Sullivan, E. E. (2008). A national view of promising programs and practices for culturally, linguistically, and ethnically diverse gifted and talented students. *Gifted Child Quarterly, 52,* 131–145.

Eyre, D., Coates, D., Fitzpatrick, M., Higgins, C., McClure, L., & Wilson, H. (2002). Effective teaching of able pupils in the primary school: The findings of the Oxfordshire Effective Teachers of Able Pupils project. *Gifted Education International, 16,* 158–169.

Garet, M. S., Porter, A. C., Desimone, L., Birman, B. F., & Yoon, K. S. (2001). What makes professional development effective? Results from a national sample of teachers. *American Educational Research Journal, 38,* 915–945.

Gentry, M. (1999). *Promoting student achievement and exemplary classroom practices through cluster grouping: A research-based alternative to heterogeneous elementary classrooms.* Storrs: University of Connecticut, The National Research Center on the Gifted and Talented.

Gubbins, E. J., Westberg, K. L., Reis, S. M., Dinnocenti, S. T., Tieso, C. L., & Muller, L. M. . . . Burns, D. E. (2002). *Implementing a professional development model using gifted education strategies with all students* (RM02172). Storrs: University of Connecticut, The National Research Center on the Gifted and Talented.

Han, K. S., & Marvin, C. (2000). A five-year follow-up study of the Nebraska Project: Still a long way to go . . . . *Roeper Review, 23,* 25–33.

Hanninen, G. E. (1988). A study of teacher training in gifted education. *Roeper Review, 10,* 139–144.

Higgins, T. E. (2006, April). *Pressures to participate: Factors influencing teachers' involvement in ongoing professional development programs.* Paper presented at the annual meeting of the American Educational Research Association, San Francisco, CA.

Hunsaker, S. L., Finley, V. S., & Frank, E. L. (1997). An analysis of teacher nominations and student performance in gifted programs. *Gifted Child Quarterly, 41,* 19–24.

Johnsen, S. K., Haensly, P. A., Ryser, G. R., & Ford, R. F. (2002). Changing general education classroom practices to adapt for gifted students. *Gifted Child Quarterly, 46,* 45–63.

Neumeister, K. L., Adams, C. M., Pierce, R. L., Cassady, J. C., & Dixon, F. A. (2007). Fourth-grade teachers' perceptions of giftedness: Implications for identifying and serving diverse gifted students. *Journal for the Education of the Gifted, 30,* 479–499.

Siegle, D., & Powell, T. (2004). Exploring teacher biases when nominating students for gifted programs. *Gifted Child Quarterly, 48,* 21–29.

Theory-Based References

Ancess, J. (2001). Teacher learning at the intersection of school learning and student outcomes. In A. Lieberman & L. Miller (Eds.), *Teachers caught in the action: Professional development that matters* (pp. 61–78). New York, NY: Teachers College Press.

Guskey, T. R. (2000). *Evaluating professional development.* Thousand Oaks, CA: Corwin Press.

Lave, J. (1991). Situated learning in communities of practice. In L. B. Resnick,
J. M. Levine, & S. D. Teasley (Eds.), *Perspectives on socially shared cognition*
(pp. 63–82). Washington, DC: American Psychological Association.
Wenger, E. (1998). *Communities of practice: Learning, meaning, and identity.*
New York, NY: Cambridge University Press.

Practice-Based References

Barab, S. A., Kling, R., & Gray, J. H. (Eds.). (2004). *Designing virtual communities in the service of learning.* New York, NY: Cambridge University Press.
Dettmer, P., & Landrum, M. (Eds.). (1998). *Staff development: The key to effective gifted education program.* Waco, TX: Prufrock Press.
Falk, J. K., & Drayton, B. (Eds.). (2009). *Creating and sustaining online professional learning communities.* New York, NY: Teachers College Press.

ELEMENT 6.5

**Beginning gifted education professionals advance the profession
by engaging in activities such as advocacy and mentoring.**

Research-Based References

Grantham, T. C. (2003). Increasing Black student enrollment in gifted programs: An exploration of the Pulaski County special school district's advocacy efforts. *Gifted Child Quarterly, 47,* 46–65.
Hébert, T. P., & Neumeister, K. L. S. (2000). University mentors in the elementary classroom: Supporting the intellectual, motivational, and emotional
needs of high-ability students. *Journal for the Education of the Gifted, 24,*
122–148.
Robinson, A., & Moon, S.M. (2003). A national study of local and state advocacy in gifted education, *Gifted Child Quarterly, 47,* 8–25.

Theory-Based References

Brody, L. (1999). The talent searches: Counseling and mentoring activities. In
N. Colangelo & S. Assouline (Eds.), *Talent development III, Proceedings
from The 1995 Henry B. and Jocelyn Wallace national research symposium on
talent development* (pp. 153–157). Scottsdale, AZ: Great Potential Press.
Feng, A. (2006). Developing personalized learning experiences: Mentoring
for talent development. In J. VanTassel-Baska (Ed.), *Serving gifted learners
beyond the traditional classroom* (pp. 189–212). Waco, TX: Prufrock Press.

Gallagher, J. J. (2004). No child left behind and gifted education. *Roeper Review, 26,* 121–123.

Hertzog, N. (2003). Advocacy: on the cutting edge. *Gifted Child Quarterly, 47,* 66–81.

Torrance, E. P. (1984). *Mentor relationships: How they aid creative achievement, endure, change and die.* Buffalo, NY: Bearly Limited.

Practice-Based References

Grybe, D. (1997). Mentoring the gifted and talented. *Preventing School Failure, 41,* 115.

Kitano, M. K. (2003). What's missing in gifted education reform? In J. Borland (Ed.). *Rethinking gifted education* (pp. 143–158). New York, NY: Teachers College Press.

Siegle, D., & McCoach, D. G. (2005). Extending learning through mentorships. In F. A. Karnes & S. M. Bean (Eds.), *Methods and materials for teaching gifted* (2nd ed., pp. 473–518). Waco, TX: Prufrock Press.

Troxclair, D., & Karnes, F. (1997). Public relations: Advocating for gifted students. *Gifted Child Today, 20*(3), 38–41, 50.

Standard 7: Collaboration

Beginning gifted education professionals collaborate with families, other educators, related-service providers, individuals with gifts and talents, and personnel from community agencies in culturally responsive ways to address the needs of individuals with gifts and talents across a range of learning experiences.

ELEMENT 7.1
Beginning gifted education professionals apply elements of effective collaboration.

Research-Based References

Matthews, D., & Menna, R. (2003). Solving problems together: Parent/school/community collaboration at a time of educational and social change. *Education Canada, 43,* 20–23.

Theory-Based References

Landrum, M. S. (2003). *Resource consultation in gifted education: Teachers working together to serve students.* Mansfield, CT: Creative Learning Press.

Practice-Based References

Gentry, M., & Ferriss, S. (1999). StATS: A model of collaboration to develop science talent among rural students. *Roeper Review, 21,* 316–320.

ELEMENT 7.2
Beginning gifted education professionals serve as a collaborative resource to colleagues.

Research-Based References

Tomlinson, C. A., Coleman, M. R., Allan, S., Udall, A., & Landrum, M. (1996). Interface between gifted education and general education: Toward communication, cooperation, and collaboration. *Gifted Child Quarterly, 40,* 165–171.

Theory-Based References

Landrum, M. S. (2001). An evaluation of the Catalyst Program: Consultation and collaboration in gifted education. *Gifted Child Quarterly, 45,* 139–151.
Landrum, M. S. (2003). *Resource consultation in gifted education: Teachers working together to serve students.* Mansfield, CT: Creative Learning Press.

Practice-Based References

Coleman, M. R., & Hughes, C. (2009). Meeting the needs of gifted students within the RtI framework. *Gifted Child Today, 32*(3), 14–19.
Coleman, M. R., & Johnsen, S. K. (Eds.). (2011). *RtI for gifted students.* Waco, TX: Prufrock Press.
Johnsen, S. K., Sulak, T., & Rollins, K. (2012). *Serving gifted students within an RtI framework.* Waco, TX: Prufrock Press.
Pereles, D. A., Omdal, S., & Baldwin, L. (2009). Response to intervention and twice-exceptional learners. A promising fit. *Gifted Child Today, 32*(3), 40–51.

Purcell, J. H., & Leppien, J. H. (1998). Building bridges between general practitioners and educators of the gifted: A study of collaboration. *Gifted Child Quarterly, 42*, 172–181.

ELEMENT 7.3

Beginning gifted education professionals use collaboration to promote the well-being of individuals with gifts and talents across a wide range of settings, experiences, and collaborators.

Research-Based References

Grantham, T. C. (2004). Rocky Jones: Case study of a high-achieving Black male's motivation to participate in gifted classes. *Roeper Review, 26*, 208–216.

Hébert, T. P., & Neumeister, K. L. S. (2000). University mentors in the elementary classroom: Supporting the intellectual, motivational, and emotional needs of high-ability students. *Journal for the Education of the Gifted, 24*, 122–148.

Hertzog, N., & Bennett, T. (2004). In whose eyes? Parents' perspectives on the learning needs of their gifted children. *Roeper Review, 26*, 96–104.

Jolly, J. L., Matthews, M. S., & Nestor, J. (2013). Homeschooling the gifted: A parent perspective. *Gifted Child Quarterly, 57*, 121–134.

Matthews, D., & Menna, R. (2003). Solving problems together: Parent/school/community collaboration at a time of educational and social change. *Education Canada, 43*(1), 20–23.

Olszewski-Kubilius, P., & Lee, S.-Y. (2004). Gifted adolescents' talent development through distance learning. *Journal for the Education of the Gifted, 28*, 7–35.

Olszewski-Kubilius, P., & Lee, S. (2004). Parent perceptions of effects of the Saturday Enrichment Program on gifted students' talent development. *Roeper Review, 26*, 156–165.

Pletan, M. D., Robinson, N. M., Berninger, V. W., & Abbot, R. D. (1995). Parents' observations of kindergartners who are advanced in mathematical reasoning. *Journal for the Education of the Gifted, 19*, 30–44.

Reis, S. M., Colbert, R. D., & Hébert, T. P. (2005). Understanding resilience in diverse, talented students in an urban high school. *Roeper Review, 27*, 110–120.

Williams, E. R., & Baber, C. R. (2007). Building trust through culturally reciprocal home-school-community collaboration from the perspective of African-American parents. *Multicultural Perspectives, 9*(2), 3–9.

Theory-Based References

Landrum, M. S. (2003). *Resource consultation in gifted education: Teachers working together to serve students.* Mansfield, CT: Creative Learning Press.

Ogbu, J. U. (1994). Understanding cultural diversity and learning. *Journal for the Education of the Gifted, 17,* 355–383.

Practice-Based References

Ford, D., & Grantham, T. (2003). Parenting gifted culturally diverse children: Focus on education-related issues and needs. *Understanding Our Gifted, 15,* 12–17.

Hughes, C. E., & Murawski, W. A. (2001). Lessons from another field: Applying coteaching strategies to gifted education. *Gifted Child Quarterly, 45,* 195–204.

Kingore, B. (1995). Introducing parents to portfolio assessment: A collaborative effort toward authentic assessment. *Gifted Child Today, 18*(4), 12–13, 40.

Limburg-Weber, L. (1999/2000). Send them packing: Study abroad as an option for gifted students. *Journal of Secondary Gifted Education, 11,* 43–51.

Melber, L. M. (2003). Partnerships in science learning: Museum outreach and elementary gifted education. *Gifted Child Quarterly, 47,* 251–258.

Olszewski-Kubilius, P., & Thomson, D. L. (2010). Gifted programming for poor or minority urban students: Issues and lessons learned. *Gifted Child Today, 33*(4), 58–64.

Pearl, P. (1997). Why some parent education programs for parents of gifted children succeed and others do not. *Early Child Development and Care, 130,* 41–48.

Roberts, J. L., & Jolly, J. L. (2013). *A teacher's guide to working with children and families from diverse backgrounds.* Waco, TX: Prufrock Press.

Siegle, D., & McCoach, D. G. (2005). Extending learning through mentorships. In F. A. Karnes & S. M. Bean (Eds.), *Methods and materials for teaching gifted* (2nd ed., pp. 473–518). Waco, TX: Prufrock Press.

Stephens, K. R. (1999). Parents of the gifted and talented: The forgotten partner. *Gifted Child Today, 22*(5), 38–43, 52.

Strip, C., & Hirsch, G. (2001). Trust and teamwork: The parent-teacher partnership for helping the gifted child. *Gifted Child Today, 24*(2), 26–30, 64.

Terry, A. W. (2003). Effects of service learning on young, gifted adolescents and their community. *Gifted Child Quarterly, 47,* 295–308.

Undergraduate Teacher Preparation Syllabi That Include the NAGC Knowledge and Skill Standards in Gifted Education for All Teachers

Syllabus Example 1: Science Methods

This syllabus was designed by Alicia Cotabish, Ed.D., for the National Association for Gifted Children.

Instructor: _____

Phone: _____

Office: _____

Office hours: By Appointment

Prerequisites

None

Course Description

This course is required for science teachers seeking to complete the requirements for secondary science teaching degrees. This course reviews instructional methods, curricula, and materials for secondary (middle and high school) science classrooms. The purpose of this course is to equip teachers with the pedagogical skills necessary to effectively instruct all learners in the secondary science classroom. Specifically, candidates will develop and apply an understanding of field, community, and cultural resources and develop family and community partnerships in a relevant science context. Different methodologies and philosophies regarding differentiated science teaching, as well as curriculum and instruction accommodations for advanced science learners will be examined, discussed, and modeled. In this course, teacher candidates develop a differentiated learning unit based on the 5E learning cycle. Candidates will utilize technology for science teaching by developing a LiveBinder for science content curation and employing Vernier probes in a laboratory setting.

Conceptual Framework

Enhancing educator efficacy through reflective decision making is the focusing agent for the EPP and is manifested through eight attributes. They are: (a) Content Knowledge, (b) Problem Solving, (c) Student Achievement, (d) Assessment, (e) Diversity, (f) Technology, (g) Professionalism, and (h) Collaboration. In a synthesized and targeted way, efficacy provides a rationale for the conceptual framework—for both classroom teachers and other school professionals. In the realm of reflective decision-making, efficacy is the reason why we reflect— it represents our ownership of the learning environment and achievement of all learners. The degree to which EPP candidates demonstrate efficacy directly correlates to their attainment of the knowledge, skills, and dispositions necessary to positively impact the learning of all learners. The eight attributes within the Conceptual Framework represent our view of the ideal educator.

Required Texts

Bybee, R., Powell, J. C., & Trowbridge, L. W. (2007). *Teaching secondary school science: Strategies for developing scientific literacy* (9th ed.). Columbus, OH: Pearson.

Adams, C., Cotabish, A., & Ricci, M. C. (2014). *Using the next generation science standards with advanced and gifted learners.* Waco, TX: Prufrock Press.

Other Resources

Adams, A., Cotabish, A., & Dailey, D. (2015). *A teacher's guide to using the Next Generation Science Standards with gifted and advanced learners.* Waco, TX: Prufrock Press.

Recommended Readings

National Academy of Sciences. (2007). *Rising above the gathering storm: Energizing and employing America for a brighter economic future.* Washington, DC: The National Academies Press.

National Academy of Sciences. (2010). *Rising above the gathering storm, revisited: Rapidly approaching category 5.* Washington, DC: The National Academies Press.

National Science Board. (2010). *Preparing the next generation of STEM innovators: Identifying and developing our nation's human capital.* NSB-10-33. Retrieved from http://www.nsf.gov/nsb/publications/pub_summ.jsp?ods_key=nsb1033

Pratt, H. (2007). Science education's 'overlooked ingredient': Why the path to global competitiveness begins in elementary school. *Education Week.* Retrieved from http://www.edweek.org/ew/articles/2007/10/10/07pratt.h27.html

Savery, J. R. (2006). Overview of problem-based learning: Definitions and distinctions. *The Interdisciplinary Journal of Problem-Based Learning, 1*(1), 9–20.

VanTassel-Baska, J. (1998). *Planning science programs for high ability learners.* Reston, VA: ERIC Clearinghouse on Disabilities and Gifted Education. Retrieved from http://www.ericdigests.org/1999-3/science.htm

Related Standards
National Association for Gifted Children Knowledge and Skill Standards for All Teachers:

All teachers should be able to:

1. recognize the learning differences, developmental milestones, and cognitive/affective characteristics of gifted and talented students, including those from diverse cultural and linguistic backgrounds, and identify their related academic and social-emotional needs;

2. design appropriate learning and performance modifications for individuals with gifts and talents that enhance creativity, acceleration, depth, and complexity in academic subject matter and specialized domains; and

3. select, adapt, and use a repertoire of evidence-based instructional strategies to advance the learning of gifted and talented students.

Interstate New Teacher Assessment and Support Consortium (INTASC) Standards:

Standard 2: The teacher understands how children learn and develop, and can provide learning opportunities that support a child's intellectual, social, and personal development.

Standard 3: The teacher understands how students differ in their approaches to learning and creates instructional opportunities that are adapted to diverse learners.

Next Generation Science Standards (NGSS):

The Next Generation Science Standards are arranged by disciplinary core ideas across grade levels. They contain the essential ideas in the major science disciplines that all students should understand during their K–12 experience. Science and engineering practices are used to construct the performance expectations utilizing grade bands arranged at the elementary, middle, and high school levels. Lastly, crosscutting concepts apply to one or more of the performance expectations noted in the Next Generation Science Standards. Because this course is a science methods course (not delving into the content of science), the following notations are used to denote the broader application of the NGSS to the assignments found in this course:

* Earth and Space Sciences (denoted as ES)
* Life Sciences (denoted as LS)
* Physical Sciences (denoted as PS)
* Science and Engineering Practices (denoted as ETS)

Course Outcomes (Goals and Objectives)

Throughout the course, the middle level and high school science content required by the National Science Education Standards and the State Curriculum Frameworks will be reviewed, with special emphasis placed on utilizing inquiry-driven, hands-on methods to teach this content. Special attention will also be focused on the use of technology in collecting and analyzing data in the science laboratory.

The course outcomes are:

1. Students will increase their understanding of technology integration as a tool for differentiation in articulating a concept-based science education curriculum product. (NAGC Standards, 1, 2, and 3; InTASC Standards 2 and 3; NGSS Standards ES, LS, PS, and ETS)
2. Students will be expected to read assigned literature relevant to science education and discuss, keep a reflective journal, and participate in activities related to the assigned reading. (NAGC Standards 1, 2, and 3; InTASC Standard 2; NGSS Standards ES, LS, PS, and ETS)
3. Students will research current literature related to a variety of science pedagogical methods and prepare a LiveBinder for content curation. (NAGC Standards 2 and 3; InTASC Standards 2 and 3; NGSS Standards ES, LS, PS, and ETS)
4. Students will develop a differentiated 5E Science Curriculum unit that integrates other disciplines with science. Students will present the unit to their peers using Prezi. (NAGC Standards 1, 2, and 3; InTASC Standards 2 and 3; NGSS Standards ES, LS, PS, and ETS)
5. Students will develop knowledge of the terminology, materials, and differentiated approaches to teaching science in grades 6–12. (NAGC Standards 1, 2, and 3; InTASC Standards 2 and 3; NGSS Standards ES, LS, PS, and ETS)
6. Students will obtain knowledge of the newly adopted Next Generation Science Standards. (NGSS Standards ES, LS, PS, and ETS)
7. Students will develop and apply higher order critical, creative thinking, and problem-solving skills through open-ended approaches in meeting specific course objectives and goals. (NAGC Standards 1, 2, and 3; InTASC Standards 2 and 3)
8. Students will engage in class discussions and assignments that require the integration of skills in content development, content delivery, and address teaching, learning, and assessments that respond to individual student needs. (NAGC Standards 1, 2, and 3; InTASC Standards 2 and 3; NGSS Standards ES, LS, PS, and ETS)

Assessment and Standards Alignment

Assignments to Be Assessed	Course Outcomes	NAGC Knowledge and Skills Standards	InTASC Standards	NGSS Standards
BIOL 6395				
Conduct a Review of the NGSS	1, 5, 6	3	2	ES, LS, PS, ETS
Interview a Science Teacher	5, 8	1	2, 3	ES, LS, PS. ETS
Reflective Journal	2, 8	1	2	ES, LS, PS, ETS
5E Unit	4, 5, 6, 7, 8	1, 2, 3	2, 3	ES, LS, PS, ETS
LiveBinder	3, 5, 7, 8	1, 2, 3	2, 3	ES, LS, PS, ETS

Student Evaluation

1. Conduct a Review of the NGSS **(170 Points Possible)**
2. Interview a Science Teacher **(50 Points Possible)**
3. Reflective Journal **(100 Points)**
4. Construct a 5E Unit **(200 Points Possible)**
5. Create a LiveBinder **(100 Points)**
    Total: 620 Points Possible

Grading Scale

558–620 = A
496–557 = B
434–495 = C
333–372 = D
Below 333 = F

Course Assignments

#1: Next Generation Science Standards Review (170 Points Possible).

Instructions. You are to conduct a review of the final draft of the Next Generation Science Standards for Achieve (the organization responsible for creating the standards). In a process managed by Achieve, Inc., a nonprofit education reform organization, 26 states, NSTA, and AAAS are currently leading the development of Next Generation Science Standards (NGSS). The standards are available online at http://www.nextgenscience.org. You will complete the review document about the NGSS. Your responses should be 3 to 4 sentences in length to answer each question. You may type directly on this form when responding to the questions. Each response is worth 5 points each; there are 34 questions. There are a total of 170 points possible.

Once completed, you will upload the review into the Blackboard assignment dropbox.

Section I directions. The questions in Section I require you to focus on a set of standards for your relevant grade level (either middle school or high school). You are to review all standards in your designated grade level when responding to the following questions. Please specify the set of standards you are reviewing (middle school or high school). If you refer to a specific set of standards, please note the standards code that can be found at the top of the standards page (e.g., HS-ESS2 Earth's Systems).

Section II directions. The following discussion questions require you to look across multiple sets of performance expectations at several different grade levels/spans. You are required to look across all Middle School (MS) and High School (HS) standards to find relevant sections and then review those sections in more detail to answer the questions.

Section III directions. The engineering design disciplinary core ideas have been integrated into the other three core ideas. The performance expectations that have been integrated are indicated with *. For these questions, focus on a particular set of core ideas for physical, life, or Earth and space sciences and review those performance expectations that are indicated with *.

Section IV directions. The nature of science has been included in both the practices and crosscutting concepts. For these questions, focus on a particular set of core ideas for physical, life, or Earth and space sciences and review those performance expectations that include nature of science ideas.

Rating rubric.

Element	Distinguished	Proficient	Novice
Section I (*85 Points*)	The candidate's response focuses on a particular set of core ideas for physical, life, or Earth and space sciences and provides an adequate review of performance expectations that include three to four sentences each.	The candidate's response somewhat focuses on a particular set of core ideas for physical, life, or Earth and space sciences and provides an adequate review of performance expectations that include three to four sentences each.	The candidate's response somewhat focuses on a particular set of core ideas for physical, life, or Earth and space sciences and provides a vague review of performance expectations.
Section II (*55 points possible*)	The candidate demonstrates an understanding through well-developed responses focused on performance expectations, scientific and engineering practices, disciplinary core ideas,	The candidate demonstrates an understanding through adequate responses focused on performance expectations, scientific and engineering practices, disciplinary core ideas,	The candidate somewhat demonstrates an understanding through responses focused on performance expectations, scientific and engineering practices, disciplinary core ideas,

Element	Distinguished	Proficient	Novice
Section II, *continued*	and cross-cutting concepts that span multiple middle and high school standards.	and cross-cutting concepts that span multiple middle and high school standards.	and cross-cutting concepts that span multiple middle and high school standards.
Section III *(15 points possible)*	The candidate focuses on a particular set of core ideas for physical, life, or Earth and space sciences and provides a well-developed review of the performance expectations that are indicated with an *.	The candidate focuses on a particular set of core ideas for physical, life, or Earth and space sciences and provides an adequate review of the performance expectations that are indicated with an *.	The candidate focuses on a particular set of core ideas for physical, life, or Earth and space sciences and provides a vague review of the performance expectations that are indicated with an *.
Section IV *(15 points possible)*	The candidate focuses on a particular set of core ideas for physical, life, or Earth and space sciences and provides a well-developed review of those performance expectations that include the nature of science ideas.	The candidate focuses on a particular set of core ideas for physical, life, or Earth and space sciences and provides an adequate review of those performance expectations that include the nature of science ideas.	The candidate focuses on a particular set of core ideas for physical, life, or Earth and space sciences and provides a vague review of those performance expectations that include the nature of science ideas.

#2: An Interview With a Science Teacher (50 Points Possible).

Instructions. You are to identify a person currently teaching in a public or private school to interview. Once you have identified this person and asked his or her permission to interview him or her, then you are to set up a time and a place to interview him or her. This can be done at his or her school or off-site, but must be in a safe and highly trafficked area. The questions have been predetermined. You are to stick with the questions, not veering off and asking your own questions. Why? This will maintain the standardization of the interviews and the information gained through them. You may either tape record—with the person's permission—the answers provided or you may write the words down as they are stated. If you choose to write the words down, then they must be word for word as spoken in the conversation. If you opt to tape record the conversation, then you are forced to transcribe the information. This requires you to play the conversation back bit by bit and write down each and every word said throughout. Once the interview has concluded, thank the person for his or her time and willingness to assist you in the course assignment.

The format of the written interview will be as follows: Question/Answer, Question/Answer, and so forth. You will leave a space between each subsequent question. You are to bold the questions and underline the answers for all throughout the written document. You are to also identify your teacher only by his or her first name and the grade he or she teaches. The school/district where he or she works *should not be identified.*

On a separate page, but attached to the interview document, you will complete a reflection of the process and the information gained. The first paragraph will be headed "Interview Process." This will solely provide your reflection of the interview process, the method of asking specific questions, listening and capturing the words, and then transcribing the information onto paper. The second paragraph will be headed, "Information Gained." This will focus on the information gained through the dialogue with the teacher and upon the transcription phase, as you reflect upon it and connect with our class.

The interview questions should include:

1. What is the science program in your school?
   a. How many courses are offered?
   b. What is the approximate enrollment in life science? Earth science? Physical science? What curriculum materials are used? Are they differentiated for advanced learners? If so, how?
   c. How is educational technology incorporated into each course? Is technology differentiated?
   d. How does the science program in your school relate to the rest of the science programs in the district?
   e. Does your school offer any special science courses (e.g., AP, gifted, honors)?
   f. Has the science program changed in the last 5 years? If so, how?
2. What do you see as the important trends and issues in science teaching?
   a. Have enrollments in science increased? Decreased? If so, what is the probable cause of the fluctuation?
   b. Has the science budget increased? Decreased? How much do you use the laboratory in science teaching? Do you introduce any science-related social issues? If so, what are they?
3. What are your concerns as a science teacher?
   a. Are your facilities adequate? Do you have materials for your program?
   b. Is student interest high? Low?
   c. Is maintaining discipline a problem?
4. What are your greatest rewards as a science teacher?
5. Why is science important?
6. What advice do you have for me as a potential science teacher?

Preparation activity. The interview will provide you with invaluable information from a current teacher in the area. It will also introduce you to the process of interviewing should you ever wish to conduct qualitative research. We will discuss the interview process in class prior to you going out and conducting your own.

Evaluation of the interview with a science teacher. The following criteria will be used to evaluate the work completed by each student.

1. *Grammar and Mechanics*: The entire document will be free from any grammatical or mechanical errors (10 Points Possible).

2. *Formatting*: The interview questions and answers will be formatted in accordance to the instructions above and discussed in class: Question/Answer, Question/Answer, and so forth. You will leave a space between each subsequent question. You are to bold the questions and underline the answers for all throughout the written document. You are to identify your teacher's first name and the grade he or she teaches (10 Points Possible).

3. *Capturing the Conversation*: The conversation is captured word for word as it occurred on the day of the interview. No changes will be made of anything spoken between you or the teacher being interviewed. If there are stumbling words, such as "uh" or "hum," they will also be included in the written conversation. The questions will be read exactly as they are worded for you and will be written on the document in the exact same format (10 Points Possible).

4. *Interview Process Reflection*: The reflective piece will focus solely on the process of the interview. You will deeply reflect upon your thoughts regarding the interview process, the method of asking specific questions, listening and capturing the words, and then transcribing the information onto paper (10 Points Possible).

5. *Information Gained Reflection*: The reflective piece will focus solely on the information gained through the interview and the transcription component of the interview. You will deeply reflect upon the words provided by the teacher and your connections made throughout the dialogue and the transcription process, as you directly connect the words with the content (10 Points Possible).

Rating rubric.

Element	Distinguished	Proficient	Novice
Grammar and Mechanics *(10 Points Possible)*	The entire document is free from any grammatical or mechanical errors.	The document contains minor (less than 10) grammatical and mechanical errors.	The document contains 10 or more grammatical and mechanical errors.

Element	Distinguished	Proficient	Novice
Formatting *(10 Points Possible)*	The interview questions and answers are formatted in accordance with the instructions.	The interview questions and answers partially adhere to the formatting in accordance with the instructions.	The interview questions and answers do not adhere to the formatting in accordance with the instructions.
Capturing the Conversation *(10 Points Possible)*	The conversation is captured word for word as it occurred on the day of the interview.	The conversation is adequately captured (but not word for word) as it occurred on the day of the interview.	The conversation was partially captured as it occurred on the day of the interview.
Interview Process Reflection *(10 Points Possible)*	The reflective piece focuses solely on the process of the interview. The candidate deeply reflects upon his or her thoughts regarding the interview process, the method of asking specific questions, listening and capturing the words, and then transcribing the information onto paper.	The reflective piece focuses solely on the process of the interview. The candidate somewhat reflects upon his or her thoughts regarding the interview process, the method of asking specific questions, listening and capturing the words, and then transcribing the information onto paper.	The reflective piece does not solely focus on the process of the interview. The candidate somewhat reflects upon his or her thoughts regarding the interview process, the method of asking specific questions, listening and capturing the words, and then transcribing the information onto paper.
Information Gained Reflection *(10 Points Possible)*	The reflective piece focuses solely on the information gained through the interview and the transcription component of the interview. The candidate deeply reflects upon the words provided by the teacher and the connections made throughout the dialogue and the transcription process, as the candidate directly connects the words with the content.	The reflective piece focuses solely on the information gained through the interview and the transcription component of the interview. The candidate somewhat reflects upon the words provided by the teacher and the connections made throughout the dialogue and the transcription process, as the candidate attempts to connect the words with the content.	The reflective piece does not solely focus on the information gained through the interview and the transcription component of the interview. The candidate somewhat reflects upon the words provided by the teacher and the connections made throughout the dialogue and the transcription process, as the candidate attempts to connect the words with the content.

#3: Reflective Journal (25 Points per Reflective Piece = 100 Points Possible).

Instructions. Throughout the semester, four mile markers will be given to you. These will be in the form of a reflective journal and will serve as an ongoing form of assessment. All questions will be focused on differentiated instruction, its purpose, and various strategies. Each journal entry is to be submitted to the Blackboard assignment dropbox by the indicated due date.

Preparation activity. The following writing prompts will be used for the journal writings and must be submitted to the assignment dropbox.

1. How will the Next Generation Science Standards shape your delivery of differentiated curriculum planning and instruction? What accommodations will you make for advanced science learners? How will you address NGSS cross-cutting concepts in your classroom?

2. Do you feel you received an adequate science education in your K–12 experiences? Explain your response.

3. What suggestions can you make regarding the argument that there is little time to teach science with the current national push for reading and mathematics?

4. In terms of the course readings, interviews, and observations you have conducted in this course thus far, what do you feel are the most pressing issues in science education and how will you address these issues as a science teacher?

Evaluation of the reflective journal. The following criteria will be used to evaluate the work completed by each student.

1. *Grammar and Mechanics*: The entire document will be free from any grammatical or mechanical errors (5 Points Possible).

2. *Clarity of Reflection*: You will provide a clear connection of the writing topic image with the notion of science instruction. You should use specific examples in an attempt to clarify your reflection (20 Points Possible).

Rating rubric.

Element	Distinguished	Proficient	Novice
Grammar and Mechanics *(5 points possible)*	The entire document is free from any grammatical or mechanical errors.	The document contains minor (less than five) grammatical and mechanical errors.	The document contains five or more grammatical and mechanical errors.
Clarity of Reflection *(20 points possible)*	A clear connection is made between the writing topic image and the notion of science instruction.	A clear connection is made between the writing topic image and the notion of science instruction.	A vague connection is made between the writing topic image and the notion of science instruction.

Element	Distinguished	Proficient	Novice
Clarity of Reflection, *continued*	Specific examples are used to clarify the reflection.	Vague examples are included and/or missing altogether.	Examples are not included.

#4: 5E Lesson Plan Unit (30 Points Possible per Day + Prezi = 200 Total Points Possible).

Instructions. This assignment is designed to assist you in learning how to research and gather information on curriculum that is relevant, challenging, integrative, and exploratory in secondary science. As a science teacher, you really must know the scope and sequence of the disciplines you teach in order to demonstrate that you understand the central concepts, tools of inquiry, and structures of the content in your teaching field so that you can create learning experiences that make aspects of subject matter meaningful for students.

In each lesson plan, you must demonstrate knowledge of the concepts, principles, and theories of a child's development including advanced learners. This knowledge must be supported by the research that you have learned throughout the course. The lesson plans presented must be proven and supported by research that shows it is relevant, challenging, integrative, and exploratory.

The assignment will allow you to assess the quality and appropriateness of materials, and resources based on the state instructional frameworks:

1. The major concepts, principles, theories, and research related to secondary science and assessment.
2. The major central concepts, tools of inquiry, standards, and structures of content in secondary science.
3. The major concepts, principles, theories, and research related to working collaboratively with family and community members.

Your job in this assignment is to create five lesson plans based on the 5E learning cycle—one for each day and for the grade level based on the NGSS. Two of the five lessons must be tied to a problem-based learning activity and a project-based learning activity (one lesson for each one; may include the ones developed in class). You will present an overview of each lesson by creating a Prezi (not PowerPoint) presentation. You can have a simple, single statement on each slide to prompt you to talk about each lesson. With this said, you will have a minimum of 10 slide exchanges (5 slides—one for each of your differentiated science lessons; 5 slides to present your differentiated assessments). You can sign up for a free Prezi account by visiting http://www.prezi.com.

Preparation activity. You will be provided reading materials and a lesson plan template in Blackboard. These will help to formulate key components found in the 5E Learning Cycle and how they work together to create a cohesive unit.

Formatting the 5E lesson plan unit. You will complete each section of the template found below as you create your 5E lesson plan unit. The Word-formatted template is located in Blackboard.

5E Lesson Plan

Teacher:
Date:
Subject area/course/grade level:
Materials:
NGSS/AR Frameworks:
Lesson objective(s):
Differentiation strategies to meet diverse learner needs:
ENGAGEMENT • Describe how the teacher will capture students' interest. • What kind of questions should the students ask themselves after the engagement?
EXPLORATION • Describe what hands-on/minds-on activities students will be doing. • List "big idea" conceptual questions the teacher will use to encourage and/or focus students' exploration.
EXPLANATION • Student explanations should precede introduction of terms or explanations by the teacher. What questions or techniques will the teacher use to help students connect their exploration to the concept under examination? • List higher order thinking questions that teachers will use to solicit student explanations and help them to justify their explanations.
ELABORATION • Describe how students will develop a more sophisticated understanding of the concept. • What vocabulary will be introduced and how will it connect to students' observations? • How is this knowledge applied in our daily lives?
EVALUATION • How will students demonstrate that they have achieved the lesson objective? (This should be embedded throughout the lesson as well as at the end of the lesson.)

Evaluation of the 5E lesson plan unit. The following criteria will be used to evaluate the work completed by each student.

1. *Standards/Objectives*: Each lesson plan will identify and align with at least one specific Next Generation Science Standards). The objective will be written in the format of "The student will . . ." and will strive to use the verbs found on the revised Bloom's taxonomy chart available at http://classic.icc.edu/innovation/PDFS/assessmentEvaluation/RevisedBloomsChart_bloomsverbsmatrix.pdf (25 Points Possible).

2. *Engagement*: Each lesson plan must describe how the teacher will capture students' interests (with attention paid to accommodating advanced learners), and describe the kind of questions that students should ask themselves after the engagement (25 Points Possible).

3. *Exploration*: Each lesson plan must describe the hands-on, minds-on activities students will be doing, and list "big idea" conceptual questions the teacher will use to encourage and/or focus students' exploration (25 Points Possible).

4. *Explanation*: Each lesson must include the questions or techniques to be used to help students (including advanced students) connect their exploration to the concept under examination, and list higher thinking questions that teachers will use to solicit student explanation and help them to justify their explanations (25 Points Possible).

5. *Elaboration*: Each lesson must describe how students will develop a more sophisticated understanding of the concept (including accommodations made for advanced learners), include the vocabulary that will be introduced and how it will connect to students' observations, and describe how the knowledge is applied in our daily lives (25 Points Possible).

6. *Evaluation*: Each lesson must describe how students will demonstrate that they have achieved the lesson objective and accommodate for differentiated learning, and be evident throughout the lesson as well as the end of the lesson (25 Points Possible).

7. *Presentation of unit using Prezi*: Includes a minimum of 10 slides (50 Points Possible).

Rating rubric.

Element	Distinguished	Proficient	Novice
Standards/ Objectives *(5 points each lesson; 25 points possible)*	The lessons identify and align with at least one specific Next Generation Science Standard. The objectives are written in the format of "The student will . . ." and use the verbs found on the revised Bloom's taxonomy chart.	The lessons identify and align with at least one specific Next Generation Science Standard. The objectives are not well developed.	Only some of the lessons identify and/ or align with at least one specific Next Generation Science Standard. The objectives are not well developed.
Engagement *(5 points each lesson; 25 points possible)*	Each lesson plan describes how the teacher will capture students' interests *(2 of the 5 lessons must be a project-based learning experience)* with attention paid to accommodating advanced learners; and describes the kind of questions that students should ask themselves after the engagement.	Each lesson plan describes how the teacher will capture students' interests and describes the kind of questions that students should ask themselves after the engagement. The lessons do not make concessions for accommodating advanced learners.	Only some of the lesson plans describe how the teacher will capture students' interests and describe the kinds of questions that students should ask themselves after the engagement. The lessons do not make concessions for accommodating advanced learners.
Exploration *(5 points each lesson; 25 points possible)*	Each lesson plan adequately describes the hands-on, minds-on activities students will be doing, and lists "big idea" conceptual questions the teacher will use to encourage and/or focus students' exploration.	Each lesson plan only partially describes the hands-on, minds-on activities students will be doing; the lesson lists "big idea" conceptual questions the teacher will use to encourage and/or focus students' exploration.	The lesson plan(s) do/ does not adequately describe the hands-on, minds-on activities students will be doing; may or may not list "big idea" conceptual questions the teacher will use to encourage and/or focus students' exploration.
Explanation *(5 points each lesson; 25 points possible)*	Each lesson includes the questions or techniques to be used to help students (including advanced students) connect their exploration to the concept under examination, and lists higher thinking	Each lesson includes the questions or techniques to be used to help students connect their exploration to the concept under examination, and lists higher thinking questions that teachers will use to	Each lesson includes the questions or techniques to be used to help students connect their exploration to the concept under examination; however, higher order thinking questions are not

Element	Distinguished	Proficient	Novice
Explanation, *continued*	questions that teachers will use to solicit student explanation and help them to justify their explanations.	solicit student explanation and help them to justify their explanations. The lessons do not make concessions for accommodating advanced learners.	included nor are concessions made for accommodating advanced learners.
Elaboration *(5 points each lesson; 25 points possible)*	Each lesson describes how students will develop a more sophisticated understanding of the concept (including accommodations made for advanced learners), includes the vocabulary that will be introduced and how it will connect to students' observations, and describes how the knowledge is applied in our daily lives.	Each lesson describes how students will develop a more sophisticated understanding of the concept, includes the vocabulary that will be introduced and how it will connect to students' observations, and describes how the knowledge is applied in our daily lives. The lessons do not make concessions for accommodating advanced learners.	Each lesson describes how students will develop a more sophisticated understanding of the concept and includes the vocabulary that will be introduced and how it will connect to students' observations; however, the lesson(s) fail to describe how the knowledge is applied in our daily lives nor are concessions made for accommodating advanced learners.
Evaluation *(5 points each lesson; 25 points possible)*	Each lesson describes how students will demonstrate that they have achieved the lesson objective and accommodated for differentiated learning; is evident throughout the lesson, as well as at the end of the lesson.	Each lesson describes how students will demonstrate that they have achieved the lesson objective and is evident throughout the lesson, as well as at the end of the lesson. The lessons do not make concessions for accommodating advanced learners.	The lesson plan(s) do/does not adequately describe how students will demonstrate that they have achieved the lesson objective, which is evident throughout the lesson as well as at the end of the lesson. The lessons do not make concessions for accommodating advanced learners.
Presentation *(5 points per Prezi slide; 50 points possible)*	The Prezi includes a minimum of 10 slides with adequate content to present the 5E unit including all 5E components in each lesson and accommodations for advanced learners.	The Prezi includes a minimum of 10 slides with adequate content to present the 5E unit including all 5E components in each lesson. The Prezi does not include accommodations for advanced learners.	The Prezi includes a minimum of 10 slides but does not include content to present the 5E unit including all 5E components in each lesson. The Prezi does not include accommodations for advanced learners.

#5: LiveBinders (100 Points Possible).

Instructions. LiveBinders is an online 3-ring binder that is housed on the web and allows you to create an online binder (digital library) for content curation. The purpose of this assignment is to create an invaluable resource that you can use for the duration of your teaching career. You will create a LiveBinder for this course that will consist of secondary science content, differentiated instructional strategies, and any other resources pertinent to science teaching. The content to be housed in your LiveBinder can be found through Internet sources, conferences, PowerPoints, etc., and can include your own personal science content collection (system allows you to upload your personal content). You must have a minimum of 25 resources in your LiveBinder separated into a minimum of five tabs (differentiated instructional strategies, differentiated lessons, differentiated content, technology, NGSS resources). You can set up a free account by visiting http://www.livebinders.com. You will share the link to your LiveBinder by copying and pasting the URL link into the Blackboard assignment dropbox field text box linked to this assignment.

Preparation activity. You can visit http://www.livebinders.com/welcome/learn_more for tutorials and additional information.

Evaluation of the LiveBinder. The following criteria will be used to evaluate the LiveBinder.

1. *Number of resources*: A minimum of 25 resources worth 3 points each (75 points possible).

2. *Organization*: Resources separated into five tabs (differentiated instructional strategies, differentiated lessons, differentiated content, technology, NGSS resources) with a minimum of five resources per tab. Each tab is worth 5 points each (25 points possible).

Rating rubric.

Element	Distinguished	Proficient	Novice
Number of Resources *(75 points possible)*	A minimum of 25 resources are included in the LiveBinder. The resources are highly relevant to science curriculum and instruction and advanced learning.	A minimum of 25 resources are included in the LiveBinder. The resources are adequately relevant to science curriculum and instruction and advanced learning.	A minimum of 25 resources are included in the LiveBinder. The resources are somewhat relevant to science curriculum and instruction and advanced learning.
Organization *(25 points possible)*	Electronic resources are organized and separated into five tabs (differentiated instructional strategies,	Electronic resources are organized and separated into five tabs (differentiated instructional strategies,	Electronic resources are somewhat organized into tabs (differentiated instructional strategies, differentiated lessons,

Element	Distinguished	Proficient	Novice
Organization, *continued*	differentiated lessons, differentiated content, technology, NGSS resources) with a minimum of five resources per tab.	differentiated lessons, differentiated content, technology, NGSS resources). Not all tabs contain a minimum of five resources.	differentiated content, technology, NGSS resources). Not all tabs contain a minimum of five resources.

Timeline/Activities/Homework

Date	Course Outcomes	In-Class Activity	Online Activity	Homework
Week 1	1, 3, 6, 8 NAGC K&S Standards 1, 2, and 3	Introductions, syllabus review, and Blackboard course shell and overview Introduction to the Next Generation Science Standards Introduce LiveBinders	Use of Blackboard for class materials Introductions using Blackboard discussion boards	Next Generation Science Standards review (Submit review document to Blackboard assignment dropbox)
Week 2	2, 3, 7 NAGC K&S Standards 1, 2, and 3	Introduction to project-based learning (PBL)	Seminars on science research	Read Chapter 1 in Bybee et al. text Interview with a science teacher
Week 3	2, 3, 7, 8 NAGC K&S Standards 1, 2, and 3	Class discussion over assigned reading Continue project-based learning Discuss: Interview with a science teacher	Seminars on science research—guided login using "demo" Research into project-based learning (PBL) science sites—links	Read Chapters 2 and 3 in Bybee et al. text Create a project-based learning activity to share at next face-to-face class
Week 4	2, 4, 5, 6, 7, 8 NAGC K&S Standards 1, 2, and 3	No face to face	**Reflective journal 1 due** Online discussion over course reading	Read pp. 1–22 in Adams et al. text Submit project-based learning activity to the Blackboard

Date	Course Outcomes	In-Class Activity	Online Activity	Homework
Week 4, continued			Online class only: 5E Learning Cycle and the Next Generation Science Standards	dropbox for peer review
Week 5	1, 2, 4, 5, 7, 8 NAGC K&S Standards 1, 2, and 3	Class discussion over assigned reading Overview of technology tools: Vernier probes, Prezi 5E Learning Cycle and differentiated curriculum class discussion (Discuss Adams et al.)	Class development of PBL	Identify PBL topic and share in class Continue working on PBL identification and project presentation Read pp. 23–62 in Adams et al. text
Week 6	1, 2, 8 NAGC K&S Standards 1, 2, and 3	Class discussion over assigned reading Continue project-based learning Conducting labs with Vernier probes		Read chapter 4 in Bybee et al. text
Week 7	1, 2, 5, 8 NAGC K&S Standards 1, 2, and 3	Class discussion over assigned reading Continue project-based learning Conducting labs with Vernier probes, continued	Research into project-based science sites—links **Reflective journal 2** due in Blackboard	Create a project-based learning activity to share at next face-to-face class
Week 8	2, 5, 7, 8 NAGC K&S Standards 1, 2, and 3	Online class only	Online discussion over course reading Class exercise: Look up 5E lessons	Read Chapter 5 in Bybee et al. text

Date	Course Outcomes	In-Class Activity	Online Activity	Homework
Week 8, continued			lessons and demonstrate ways the lessons could differentiated. Submit responses to designated discussion board.	
Week 9	2, 4, 8 NAGC K&S Standards 1, 2, and 3	Class discussion over assigned reading Curriculum unit and Prezi: Overview and rubrics Begin class development of final products		Read Chapter 6 in Bybee et al. text
Week 10	Break			
Week 11	2, 3, 8 NAGC K&S Standards 1, 2, and 3	Class discussion over assigned reading Class development of final products	**Reflective journal 3** due	Read Chapter 7 in Bybee et al. text Begin working on LiveBinder
Week 12	2, 3, 4, 7, 8 NAGC K&S Standards 1, 2, and 3	Class discussion over assigned reading Class development of final products		Read Chapter 8 in Bybee et al. text Continue working on LiveBinder Work on differentiated 5E curriculum unit and Prezi presentation
Week 13	2, 3, 7, 8 NAGC K&S Standards 1, 2, and 3	Online class only No face-to-face meeting	Online discussion over course reading	Read Chapter 9 in Bybee et al. text Continue working on LiveBinder

Date	Course Outcomes	In-Class Activity	Online Activity	Homework
Week 13, continued				Continue working on differentiated 5E curriculum unit and Prezi presentation
Week 14	1, 2, 3, 4, 8 NAGC K&S Standards 1, 2, and 3	Project and presentation preparation Presentation of LiveBinders		Read Chapter 10 in Bybee et al. text Continue working on LiveBinder Continue working on differentiated 5E curriculum unit and Prezi presentation
Week 15	1, 2, 4, 7, 8 NAGC K&S Standards 1, 2, and 3	Class discussion over assigned reading Submit 5E curriculum unit Class presentations (Prezi) begin	**Reflective journal 4** due	
Week 16	1, 4 NAGC K&S Standards 1, 2, and 3	Class presentations (Prezi), continued		

Syllabus Example 2: Survey of Children With Exceptionalities

This syllabus was designed by Claire E. Hughes, Ph.D., for the National Association for Gifted Children.

Instructor: _____

E-mail: _____

Phone: _____

Office: _____

Office hours: By Appointment

Prerequisites

Introduction to education; Multicultural education

Course Description

The course provides teacher candidates an opportunity to survey the specific exceptionalities and the impact they have on learning for students in grades Pre-K–8. Strategies for academic acceleration, enrichment, and differentiation; social skill development; assistive technologies; and behavior management, as well as federal and state legislation, will be presented. This course meets the certification requirements. Guided field experiences required in interrelated and inclusionary classrooms.

Conceptual Framework

Preservice teachers will have opportunities to construct knowledge concerning individuals with disabilities and with gifts and talents and develop appropriately differentiated lessons that will assist them in becoming effective teachers of all students.

Required Texts

1. Mastropieri, M., & Scruggs, T. (2013). *The inclusive classroom: Strategies for effective, differentiated instruction*. Upper Saddle River, NJ: Pearson.
2. Resources available via the NAGC website: http://www.nagc.org

Related Standards

University and program standards alignment (Adapt to local college standards).

College of Education conceptual framework.

1. Successful teacher candidates will demonstrate success in bringing all students from diverse cultural, ethnic, international, and socioeconomic groups to high levels of learning.
2. Successful teacher candidates will effectively use visual literacy technologies as tools for learning and exploring that meet the Georgia Technology Standards for Educators as required by the Georgia Professional Standards Commission.
3. Successful teacher candidates will use data on student learning and achievement to set benchmarks, monitor and plan for student progress toward continuous improvement, and communicate results with appropriate audiences.
4. Successful teacher candidates will differentiate instruction for individual students and groups of students that reflect students' own experiences, learning styles, interests, cultures, and special needs.

University-level learning objectives.

1. Successful teacher candidates will demonstrate knowledge of the philosophical, historical, sociological, and legal foundations of education and special education.
2. Successful teacher candidates will demonstrate a knowledge base of educational foundations, educational psychology, human development, human exceptionalities, and parental and family dynamics.
3. Successful teacher candidates will interact and communicate effectively with a range of audiences (students, parents, administrators, stakeholders, educational agency staff, and the general public).

National standards.
National Association for Gifted Children Knowledge and Skills Standards in Gifted Education for All Teachers

All teachers should be able to:

1. recognize the learning differences, developmental milestones, and cognitive/affective characteristics of gifted and talented students, including those from diverse cultural and linguistic backgrounds, and identify their related academic and social-emotional needs;
2. design appropriate learning and performance modifications for individuals with gifts and talents that enhance creativity, acceleration, depth, and complexity in academic subject matter and specialized domains; and
3. select, adapt, and use a repertoire of evidence-based instructional strategies to advance the learning of gifted and talented students.

Council for Exceptional Children standards.
Standard 1: Learner Development and Individual Learning Differences
Standard 2: Learning Environments
Standard 3: Curricular Content Knowledge
Standard 4: Assessment
Standard 5: Instructional Planning and Strategies
Standard 6: Professional Learning and Practice
Standard 7: Collaboration

Interstate New Teacher Assessment and Support Consortium (INTASC) standards
Standard 2: The teacher understands how children learn and develop, and can provide learning opportunities that support a child's intellectual, social, and personal development.
Standard 3: The teacher understands how students differ in their approaches to learning and creates instructional opportunities that are adapted to diverse learners.

Assessment and standards alignment.

Assessment SPED 3110	Course Outcomes	CEC Standards	NAGC Standards	InTASC Standards
Lesson Plan Modification	6, 7	5	3	2, 3
Tests Over Text and Required Readings	1–8	1	1	2
IEP Activity	3	4, 5	2, 3	2, 3
Case Study of Student	4	1	2	2
Field Observation Journals	1, 2	1, 2	1, 2	2
www for Educators	1, 8	5	1, 3	2
Active Participation	1, 2		1	2

Course Goals and Objectives
Each student will:
1. Develop an increased understanding of, and positive attitude toward, the diversity of learners and the uniqueness of each individual student, with an introduction to accommodations for learner differences and the historical development of policies regarding students with exceptionalities as demonstrated in dispositions in field experiences and exams.
2. Participate in the teaching-learning process in field placements, with appropriate written reflection of those experiences, to a successful level of completion as determined by course instructor and cooperating teacher.

3. Document understandings of state and federal laws regarding students with exceptionalities through a simulated Individualized Education Plan (IEP or Gifted IEP).
4. Describe basic characteristics of exceptional learners as assessed through a referral profile of a student.
5. Describe models of collaboration that occur within school settings through the application of coteaching models in a lesson plan.
6. Describe the use of a variety of teaching and learning strategies to improve student learning through the designation of tiered models in a lesson plan.
7. Design an individualized teaching plan to address a student with exceptional needs in a general education classroom through the development of a simulated IEP or Gifted IEP.
8. Describe resources that are accessible to support student learning as demonstrated through the use of web-based resources.

Course Requirements/Assignments

Tests	300 points
Lesson Plan Modification	150 points
www for Educators	100 points
Case Study of Student	100 points
Field Observation Journal	150 points
GIEP/IEP Activity (group)	100 points
Participation	100 points
Total	**1,000 points**

Assignments: Brief description.

Tests: 300 points. Two exams and a noncumulative final exam will be given on the dates assigned. The exams will be multiple choice, short answer, and essay in nature and will cover material from class and the textbook. A study guide will be provided one week ahead of time.

Modified lesson plan: 150 points. The student will develop two sample lesson plans that includes specific strategies of differentiation—both for advanced learners and learners who are struggling—along with justification of selected strategies.

IEP activity: 100 points. Each student will participate on a GIEP/IEP team for a twice-exceptional learner. Each team will receive specific information about a student and will determine appropriate goals and objectives for the student in a simulated meeting.

www for educators: 100 points. Develop a list of at least five Internet sites appropriate for teachers of particular exceptional students. You will need to complete the following information for *each* site:

* URL (the location of the site on the Internet)
* Description of the site
* Validity and timeliness of the site
* Selling points of the site
* Relation of site to course

Journal of field observations: 150 points. Each student is required to observe in a classroom that has students with learning differences during the course of the semester. In addition, students are required to keep journals regarding their experiences during observations. The purpose of the journal is to identify theories in practice and teaching strategies, and to state plans for incorporating these as a teacher. There will be three journal entries with each entry worth 50 points

Participation: 100 points.

Grading Policy

The total number of possible points is 1,000.

Grading Scale

A	90%–100%	900–1,000 points
B	80%–89.9%	800–899 points
C	70%–79.9%	700–799 points
D	60%–69.9%	600–699 points

Agenda/Schedule of Topics

Some variation may occur due to unforeseeable events (e.g., weather, illness). All changes will be presented either in person or electronically.

Date	Topics	Readings Due	Assignments Due
Week 1	Syllabus review; having an exceptionality	Chapter 1	
Week 2	Legalities: IDEA, TALENT Act, collaboration, RtI	Chapter 2	
Week 3	Quiz 1: Background Intellectual disabilities	Chapter 3	**Quiz 1** IDD websites review
Week 4	Labor Day: NO CLASS Emotional disabilities		Field journal 1 due EBD websites review
Week 5	Learning disabilities ADHD Autism; Communication Disorders	Chapter 4	SLD websites review Autism/CD websites review

Date	Topics	Readings Due	Assignments Due
Week 6	Physical and OHI/ Giftedness	Chapter 5	Deaf/blind websites review Gifted websites review
Week 7	CLD Quiz 2: Characteristics and needs	Chapters 3–5	Quiz 2 Field journal 2 due
Week 8	Differentiation: Up and down	Chapter 6	Case study due
Week 9	RTI and continuum of services	Chapter 7	
Week 10	Social skills and management Promoting inclusion: "It's not fair"	Chapters 8 and 9	
Week 11	Writing objectives Quiz 3	Chapters 6–9	Quiz 3
Week 12	Motivation/Underachievement	Chapter 10	Field journal 3 due
Week 13	Attention issues, study skills	Chapters 11 and 12	
Week 14	Assessment: Ceiling and floor effects Quiz 4	Chapters 10–13	Quiz 4
Week 15	Literacy strategies Math strategies Science/Social studies	Chapters 14–16	
Week 16	Lesson plan modification sharing		Lesson plan modifications due
	Final Exam	GIEP/IEP Activity	**Final Exam**: IEP (in class)

Detailed Assignment Descriptions

Tests: 300 points. Four noncumulative tests will be given on the dates assigned. The exams will be multiple choice, short answer, and essay in nature and will cover material from class and the textbook. A study guide will be provided one week ahead of time.

Modified lesson plans: 150 points. You are to prepare a 45-minute lesson that has been modified for students with exceptional needs.

Plan to have in your class:

* 2 children with gifts and talents in your content area,
* 2 children with reading disabilities,
* 1 child with mild intellectual and developmental disabilities,
* 1 child with cerebral palsy in a wheelchair, and
* 23 general education students.

You should plan on having a special education teacher in your class with whom you can coteach.

The lesson will need to start with an introduction that describes the:
* content that is being taught, and
* the context of the classroom—setting, nature of students, physical setup, and time of year.

The lesson will need to follow the following format:
1. Goal/Objective of Lesson
2. Materials and Resources Needed for Lesson
3. Motivating/Beginning Activity
   a. Background knowledge needed is specified
   b. Appropriate modifications and differentiations
   c. Justification for modification selected
   d. Coteaching model used

4. Questions to Ask and Information to Present
   a. Appropriate modifications and differentiations
   b. Justification for modification selected

5. Instructional Activities
   a. Appropriate modifications and differentiations
   b. Justification for modification selected
   c. Coteaching model used

6. Practice—Guided and Independent
   a. Appropriate modifications and differentiations
   b. Justification for modification selected
   c. Coteaching model used

7. Homework
   a. Appropriate modifications and differentiations
   b. Justification for modification selected

8. Form of Assessment
   a. Appropriate modifications and differentiations
   b. Justification for modification selected

At the conclusion of the unit, you will need to include a Reflection and Insights section. This section should include your reflection about the process of writing these lessons. You should describe:
* how you incorporated the elements of the course into the lesson,

* how you integrated the characteristics of students and their resultant needs,
* how you maintained the integrity of *all* students so that all of them learned something new, and
* what you learned from this process about teaming, consultation, and collaboration.

Evaluation. The lesson plan will be evaluated based on the following rubric.

Adapted Curriculum Rubric for Differentiated Lesson Plan

	Excellent	Fair	Poor
Student Learning	• Lesson plan requires students to interpret, evaluate, theorize, and/or synthesize information. • All enduring objectives clearly align with the state content standards, essential questions, the learning plan, and the assessment. • Lesson plan clearly addresses diverse learners including gifted and struggling students. • Questions include overarching essential questions as well as open-ended topical questions.	• Lesson plan requires students to analyze and apply information, solve problems, and/or make conclusions. • Some enduring objectives align with state content standards, essential questions, and learning plan. • Lesson plan provides weak support for diverse learners. • Essential questions are not clear.	• Lesson plan requires students to define, identify, describe, and/or summarize; very little higher order thinking is required to complete the learning objectives. • Relationship between enduring objectives and state content standards, but relationship to learning plan and essential questions is unclear. • Lesson plan does not accommodate a diversity of learners. • Questions do not include overarching essential questions.
Implementation	• Lesson plan is clearly written and provides details for implementation. • Lesson plan can be easily modified and implemented in a variety of classrooms.	• Lesson plan is clearly written, but lacks detail for implementation. • Lesson plan might be applicable to other classrooms.	• Lesson plan lacks clarity and is not an effective guide for implementation. • Lesson plan is limited to the teacher's own classroom implementation.

	Excellent	Fair	Poor
Student Assessment and Evaluation	• Instrument(s) for authentic assessment of all targeted objectives are included. • A strong relationship is evident between learning objective and assessment of student learning.	• Instrument(s) for assessment of most targeted objectives are included. • A weak relationship exists between learning objectives, student need, and assessment; assessments are all the same for all students, or do not take diverse student needs into consideration.	• Instrument(s) for assessment of targeted objective are not included or the assessment(s) does not match the targeted objectives. • Relationship between objectives and assessment tools is unclear. • Assessments do not take student needs into consideration.
Integration of Technology	• Proposed technology use is engaging, age appropriate, beneficial to student learning, and supportive of higher order thinking skills. • Technology is integral to the success of the lesson plan. • A strong relationship exists between the use of technology and student learning, and is exhibited through student samples. • Use of technology enhances the lesson plan by using the computer as a research tool, a publishing tool, or a communication device.	• Proposed technology use is engaging and age appropriate, but it is unclear as to how it enhances student learning. • Technology is important, but not integral to the lesson plan. • A weak relationship exists between the use of technology and student learning and is not clearly exhibited through student activities. • Use of technology is limited to using the computer as a publishing tool.	• Proposed technology is not age appropriate, nor engaging, and does not enhance student learning. • Importance of technology to the lesson plan is unclear. • No relationship between the use of technology and student learning is exhibited by the students' samples. • Lesson plan does not take advantage of research, publishing, and communication capabilities.

	Excellent	Fair	Poor
Observable Indicators: Differentiated Curriculum	• Lesson reflects a coherent design; content standards, big ideas, and essential questions are clearly aligned with assessments and learning activities. • There are multiple ways to take in and explore ideas. • Multiple forms of assessment allow students to demonstrate their understanding in various ways. • The teacher and students use a variety of resources; the textbook is only one resource among many; resources reflect different cultural backgrounds, reading levels, interests, and approaches to learning.	• Lesson reflects a coherent design; content standards, big ideas, and essential questions are somewhat aligned with assessments and learning activities. • Pathways to take in and explore ideas are limited. • Although resources may reflect different cultural backgrounds, reading levels, interests, and approaches to learning, a limited number of resources are included in the unit.	• Lesson does not reflect a coherent design; content standards, big ideas, and essential questions are not aligned with assessments and learning activities. • Pathways to take in and explore ideas are not considered. • Only one form of assessment to demonstrate student understanding is included. • The evaluation includes only paper and pencil evaluation instruments (i.e., tests, quizzes). • The textbook is the only resource; resources that reflect different cultural backgrounds, reading levels, interests, and approaches to learning are not considered.
Academic Language	• Language in reflection is academic and uses appropriate professional terminology in a clear and coherent manner. • Reflection indicates depth of thought by providing numerous examples of choices and logical reasons for exclusion of other options.	• Language in reflection is academic and uses appropriate professional terminology in a clear manner; some terminology may be confusing and unclear. • Reflection indicates depth of thought by providing one or two examples of choices and logical reasons for exclusion of one or two other options.	• Language in reflection is not academic and unprofessional; terminology is unclear and inappropriate for the meaning of the reflection. • Reflection indicates lack of depth of thought by providing no or inappropriate examples of choices and there is no discussion why options were excluded.

Note. Adapted from Kinnelon Public Schools (n.d.).

www for Educators: 100 points (each is worth 20 points). Develop a list of at least five Internet sites appropriate for teachers of exceptional students and make copies to share with the class. You will select your site and "claim" your site on a Blackboard posting. You will need to complete the following information for *each* site:

- ❋ URL (the location of the site on the Internet)
- ❋ Description of the site (4 points):
    - » What does the site look like?
    - » What kinds of information are included in the site? *Be specific!*

- ❋ Validity and timeliness of the site (4 points):
    - » Is the information contained within the site valid?
    - » Are sources cited? Are the sources credible?
    - » Is the information recent?

- ❋ Usefulness of the site (5 points):
    - » Why would this be an appropriate site for educators of exceptional students?
    - » How might an educator use this site in relation to the needs of exceptional students?

- ❋ Relation of site to course (7 points):
    - » How does this site relate to course material?
    - » What is your overall impression of the site?

Dates. The following schedule should be used when turning in the five sites for this assignment (choose five from the provided schedule).

Week 3	Intellectual Disabilities	Chapter 3	IDD Websites Review
	Emotional Disabilities		EBD Websites Review
Week 4	Learning Disabilities/ADHD		SLD Websites Review
	Autism; Communication Disorders	Chapter 4	Autism CD Websites Review
Week 5	Physical and OHI		Deaf Blind Websites Review
	Giftedness	Chapter 5	Gifted Websites Review

Note. Students may choose five websites focused on any five of the seven exceptionalities.

Field observation journals: 50 points each. Each student is required to observe and participate in a diverse classroom during the course of the semester. In addition, students are required to keep journals regarding their experiences during observations. The purpose of the journal is to identify theories in practice and teaching strategies, and to state plans for incorporating these as a teacher. There will be *two* journal entries with each entry worth 25 points.

Field journals should be written in double-spaced format, be about 2–3 pages long, and include:

1. Introduction: Placement, grade level, and teacher.
2. Describe in broad detail some of the activities or significant events that happened during the practicum experience.
3. Specific topic assignment, about a page long.
4. I am learning _____ (how to ..., about ..., when ...) so far. Make this personal and thoughtful.

Specific topics:

1. Describe some of the differences in learning abilities, communication, and behavioral abilities you see in class. Be sure to describe students who perform above and below the typical expectation.
2. What types of differentiation do you see in your classroom? What changes in the lesson planning process are made to meet the needs of one or more specific children? How are these children assessed? Be sure to describe how advanced students and struggling students are accommodated.
3. What assessment issues do you see in your classroom? Are students assessed on the same instrument? How is growth documented? How does the teacher use assessment to modify instruction?

Journals will be graded based on the criteria listed below.

Criteria	Possible	Received
Connection between course and experience with students is clearly stated.	10	
Analysis of specific topic is logical, clear, and thoughtful.	40	
Total for Field Journals	50	

Atypical case study: 100 points. As a teacher, you will be asked to formally and informally assess a specific student's progress and levels of achievement. An important part of this process is to learn to objectively observe a student, then more subjectively make conclusions about that student. This project will assist you in developing these skills, particularly with respect to students with disabilities.

You will engage in research, conduct surveys, and interview/elicit information from parents, teachers, and students for the purpose of exploring development and "fit" within their learning environments for exceptional children.

You will choose an exceptional student from your field placement classroom, either a gifted child or a child with disabilities, to observe and evaluate. You should ask your cooperating teacher about this student, obtaining as many details as the teacher is comfortable giving without violating the *student's right to privacy*. For example, you might ask the student's age, disability classification, level(s) of academic achievement, and strengths and weaknesses in terms of social and emotional behavior. This "background" information will be the Data section on your student. There are two important guidelines related to the teacher code of ethics that you need to follow when interviewing and writing the paper. They are: (a) use pseudonyms, you should not mention any name that may identify the student, parent, or school personnel; and (b) describe locations and/or schools, but do not use their names.

Data. Gather the following information about the student:

* age/race,
* socioeconomic status,
* linguistic development description,
* cognitive development description,
* emotional development description,
* reasoning and ethical development description,
* physical development description, and
* student's expectations for schooling/value orientation/personal expectations.

Gather the following information about the parents and community:

* parental involvement (what they say, what teachers say, what can be done to establish a participation model),
* important developmental issues for parents,
* parental expectations for schooling/value orientation, and
* community issues and demographics.

Gather the following information about the school:

* experience of teacher,
* important developmental issues faced by and understood by teacher, and
* make-up of the classroom (demographics, etc.).

Interpretation. The introductory Data section should then be followed by an Interpretation section of what you have observed about this student in your placement. *This summary should be very detailed and explanatory.* For example, you might note how your student responds to other students in the classroom, and give possible explanations for these interactions. If your student exhibits aggressive behaviors such as hitting or pushing, these behaviors likely interfere with positive peer relationships.

From your research, survey, interviews, and observations, teacher candidates should accomplish the following:

* Identify the student's
    » cognitive level,
    » social level,
    » linguistic level,
    » emotional level, and
    » physical characteristics and needs.

* Link to the data that validates your determination.
* Describe the impacts of the family, the culture, the community and the school on the development—socially, cognitively, physically, linguistically, and emotionally—of the student. Be careful not to be deficit in your thinking—describe the implications. This section should include significant connections to the texts and should be a discussion of specific developmental concepts/characteristics of your student's disability category and developmental aspects that are covered in your texts, handouts, and class discussion, and *how they relate to your students*. For example, if your student has a behavior disorder such as oppositional defiant disorder, how do your observations mesh with what your text says about this area of disability? What is in agreement? What is in disagreement? Be specific. Do not just comment that your student "has learning problems." What specific learning problems does your student exhibit, and are these similar to the ones listed in your textbook?
* Discuss how the child is alike and different from others of his or her age or disability label.

Teaching recommendations.

1. Be SPECIFIC in teaching strategies that will help this child grow and develop.
2. LINK the teaching strategies back to the data and the developmental level of the child.
3. HOW will you help this child continue to develop?

Be sure to look at the rubric and closely follow the guidelines for writing the paper. *Remember to keep your student's name and information confidential!*

It should be a professional document: size 12 font, double spaced, and written with correct grammar, punctuation, and spelling. The product should be between 7–9 pages in length. Charts are fine.

Evaluation. Case studies will be graded on the following rubric.

Element	Distinguished 90%–100%	Meets 70%–90%	Does Not Meet/ Needs Improvement <70%
Understanding of Human Development (20 points) • School of Education Conceptual Foundation Objective #2 • InTASC #2 • EdTPA #1 Planning—Using knowledge of students—Rubric 2	Extensive background knowledge that specifically demonstrates understanding of typical and atypical human growth and development. Extensive use of relevant data. Common developmental misconceptions specific to the individual are addressed.	Adequate background knowledge that specifically demonstrates understanding of typical and atypical human growth and development. Strong linkage to data. Common developmental misconceptions relevant to age group are addressed.	Little or no background knowledge that specifically demonstrates understanding of typical and atypical human growth and development. Little to no data provided. Common developmental misconceptions are poorly addressed.
Teaching Implications of Developmental Issues (30 points) • InTASC #2 • School of Education Conceptual Foundation ECSP Outcome #4 • EdTPA #1 Planning—Using knowledge of students—Rubric 3	Extensive relevant learning opportunities are described that support intellectual, social, and personal development, are clearly linked to identified developmental differences, and demonstrate high levels of expectations. Experiences clearly reflect the educational implications of characteristics of various exceptionalities. Justifies why learning tasks are appropriate using examples from prior learning and examples of personal assets.	Relevant learning opportunities are described that support intellectual, social, and personal development, are linked to identified developmental differences, and demonstrate high levels of expectations. Experiences reflect the educational implications of characteristics of various exceptionalities. Justifies why learning tasks are appropriate using examples from prior learning or examples of personal assets.	Few learning opportunities are described that support intellectual, social, and personal development, and/or are poorly linked to identified developmental differences, and/or demonstrate limited levels of expectations. Experiences do not reflect the educational implications of characteristics of various exceptionalities. Justification for learning tasks is either missing or represents a deficit view of students.

Element	Distinguished 90%–100%	Meets 70%–90%	Does Not Meet/ Needs Improvement <70%
Impacts on Development (20 points) • GA PSC 2-III, IV	Demonstrate extensive understanding of the characteristics and effects of the cultural and environmental milieu of the individual with exceptional learning needs and the family, and clearly explicates, using specific details, an understanding of family systems and the role of families in supporting development. Impact of parental and family dynamics on student development and achievement clearly discussed.	Demonstrates understanding of the characteristics and effects of the cultural and environmental milieu of the individual with exceptional learning needs and the family, and states a limited understanding of family systems and the role of families in supporting development. Impact of parental and family dynamics on student development and achievement discussed, but with few relevant details attached.	Limited understanding of the characteristics and effects of the cultural and environmental milieu of the individual with exceptional learning needs and the family, and/or limited understanding of family systems and the role of families in supporting development. Impact of parental and family dynamics on student development and achievement poorly discussed or only in generalities.
Compare and Contrast Between and Among Students (20 points) • GA PSC 2-V, VI	Clearly demonstrates awareness of similarities and differences among individuals with exceptional learning needs. Appreciation of human diversity is clearly demonstrated.	Demonstrates awareness of similarities and differences among individuals with exceptional learning needs. Appreciation of human diversity is demonstrated.	Demonstrates limited or judgmental awareness of similarities and differences among individuals with exceptional learning needs. Appreciation of human diversity is limited.
Mechanics (10 points)	Paper is professional and neat, with correct grammar, spelling, and punctuation.	Paper is professional, generally neat, with no more than five errors in grammar, spelling, or punctuation.	Paper lacks professional appearance and contains more than five errors in grammar, spelling, or punctuation.

Individualized Education Plan (IEP or Gifted IEP) activity (In-class final exam): 100 points. Each student will participate on an IEP team or a Gifted IEP team. Each team will receive specific information about a student and will determine appropriate goals and objectives for the student in a simulated IEP/GIEP meeting. Each person will then write an individual reflection on the process and the final product.

Evaluation. The IEP/Gifted IEP activity will be graded on the following rubric.

Element	Distinguished	Proficient	Novice
Demographics (5 points)	Demographics are complete.	Demographics are complete.	Demographics are incomplete.
PLOP (10 points)	Present Levels of Performance are adequately and appropriately described using data from classroom and testing performances; behavior is specific, measurable, and observable.	Present Levels of Performance are somewhat appropriately described using mostly data from classroom and testing performances; behavior is approximately 75% specific, measurable, and observable.	Present Levels of Performance are poorly described with minimal data from classroom and testing performances; behavior is not specific, less than 75% measurable, nor observable.
Special Factors (5 points)	Special factors are considered and, if appropriate, noted.	Special factors are considered and, if appropriate, noted.	Special factors are not considered, nor noted.
Goals and Objectives (10 points)	Goals and objectives are appropriately challenging, written in measurable and specific terms and linked to student performance.	Goals and objectives are somewhat challenging, written in measurable and specific terms, but appear unrelated to student performance.	Goals and objectives are not challenging, written in vague terms, and are not related at all to student performance.
Assessment of Goals and Communication Plan (10 points)	Assessments of the goals are linked to the goals and are measureable and specific; assessments provide opportunities for growth.	Assessments of the goals are loosely linked to the goals with incomplete sections of performance not noted, and are more than 75% measureable and specific.	Assessments of the goals are poorly linked to the goals and are less than 75% measureable; assessments are limited in range and do not allow for demonstrated growth.
Services Supports and Aids (10 points)	Support services and learning aids are specific and linked to goals.	Support services and learning aids are vague and loosely linked to goals.	Support services and learning aids are not specific and are not linked to goals.
Assessment Issues (5 points)	State testing accommodations are specified, specific, and appropriate.	State testing accommodations are vague, but appear appropriate to student need.	State testing accommodations are either not specified or not specific, nor appropriate.
Transition Plan (10 points)	Transition plan is present and reflects strengths of the student.	Transition plan is present but does not necessarily reflect individual strengths of the student but appears written for a "standard" student.	Transition plan is either not present or not focused on strengths of the student.

Element	Distinguished	Proficient	Novice
Mechanics (5 points)	There is use of appropriate grammar, mechanics, and spelling; product looks professional.	There is use of appropriate grammar, mechanics, and spelling; product looks professional.	There is inappropriate grammar, mechanics, or spelling; product does not look professional.
Individual Reflection			
Group Process (10 points)	Group process is described; individual contribution is appropriately assessed.	Group process is described; individual contribution is appropriately assessed.	Group process is poorly described; individual contribution is not appropriately assessed.
Usefulness and Validity (10 points)	Linkages between the written IEP and the student-documented needs are clearly explained.	Linkages between the written IEP and the student-documented needs are mostly explained.	Linkages between the written IEP and the student-documented needs are poorly explained.
Connections to Coursework Made (10 points)	Aspects of the course, such as cultural differences, • teaching/learning strategies, • classroom management, and • assessment strategies are made and linked to the IEP process.	Aspects of the course, such as cultural differences, • teaching/learning strategies, • classroom management, and • assessment strategies are made with 75% linkage and vaguely linked to the IEP process.	Aspects of the course, such as cultural differences, • teaching/learning strategies, • classroom management, and • assessment strategies are less than 75% linkages to the course content, but are not explicitly linked to the IEP process or are so vague that it is difficult to draw connections between the course and the IEP.

Syllabus Example 3: Linking Literacy Assessment to Instruction

Elizabeth Shaunessy-Dedrick, Ph.D., revised this syllabus for the National Association for Gifted Children. The original syllabus was created by Arleen P. Mariotti, Ph.D.

Instructor: _____

E-mail: _____

Phone: _____

Office: _____

Office hours: _____

Prerequisite Course/Concepts

Reading and Learning to Read/introductory coursework related to language acquisition, reading processes, and theories of reading, including reading comprehension, reading fluency, reading enjoyment, and the relationship of reading to achievement in school and beyond.

Course Description

This course will prepare preservice teachers to use multiple assessment measures to assess students' strengths and needs in literacy learning. Based on individual student profiles, preservice teachers will design instruction to enhance literacy development for students of varying reading abilities.

Conceptual Framework

The College of Education is dedicated to the ideals of Collaboration, Academic Excellence, Research, and Ethics/Diversity. These are key tenets in the Conceptual Framework of the College of Education. Competence in these ideals will provide candidates in educator preparation programs with skills, knowledge, and dispositions to be successful in the schools of today and tomorrow.

Required Text

Gillet, J. W., & Temple, C. (2011). *Understanding reading problems: Assessment and instruction* (8th ed.). Boston, MA: Allyn & Bacon.

Other Resources

Hughes, C. E., Kettler, T., Shaunessy-Dedrick, E., & VanTassel-Baska, J. (2014). *A teacher's guide to using the Common Core State Standards with gifted and advanced learners in the English language arts.* Waco, TX: Prufrock Press.

Little, C. A. (2011). Adapting language arts curricula for high-ability learners. In J. VanTassel-Baska & Little, C. A. (Eds.), *Content-based curriculum for high-ability learners* (pp. 151–186). Waco, TX: Prufrock Press.

National Association for Gifted Children. (2010). *2010 NAGC Pre-K–Grade 12 Gifted Programming Standards: Glossary of terms.* Retrieved from http://www.nagc.org/sites/default/files/standards/K-12%20standards%20glossary.pdf

Reis, S. M. (2009). *Joyful reading: Differentiation and enrichment for successful literacy learning, Grades K–8.* San Francisco: Jossey-Bass.

Southern, W. T., & Jones, E. D. (2004). Types of acceleration: Dimensions and issues. In N. Colangelo, S. G. Assouline, & M. U. M. Gross (Eds.), *A nation deceived: How schools hold back Americas brightest students* (Vol. 2, pp. 5–12). Iowa City: University of Iowa, The Connie Belin and Jacqueline N. Blank International Center for Gifted Education and Talent Development. Retrieved from http://www.accelerationinstitute.org/Nation_Deceived/ND_v1.pdf

VanTassel-Baska, J. (Ed.). (2013). *Using the Common Core State Standards for English language arts with gifted and advanced learners.* Waco, TX: Prufrock Press.

VanTassel-Baska, J., & Sher, B. T. (2011). Accelerating learning experiences in core content areas. In J. VanTassel-Baska & Little, C. A. (Eds.), *Content-based curriculum for high-ability learners* (pp. 49–69). Waco, TX: Prufrock Press.

Related Standards

National standards.

National Association for Gifted Children (NAGC) Knowledge and Skills Standards in Gifted Education for All Teachers. Gifted education standards for all teachers derived from the National Association for Gifted Children/Council for Exceptional Children Gifted Education Standards. *All teachers should be able to:*

1. recognize the learning differences, developmental milestones, and cognitive/affective characteristics of gifted and talented students, including those from diverse cultural and linguistic backgrounds, and identify their related academic and social-emotional needs;

2. design appropriate learning and performance modifications for individuals with gifts and talents that enhance creativity, acceleration, depth, and complexity in academic subject matter and specialized domains; and

3. select, adapt, and use a repertoire of evidence-based instructional strategies to advance the learning of gifted and talented students.

International Reading Association (IRA) standards.

※ *Standard 1: Foundational Knowledge.* Candidates understand the theoretical and evidence-based foundations of reading and writing processes and instruction.

※ *Standard 2: Curriculum and Instruction.* Candidates use instructional approaches, materials, and an integrated, comprehensive, balanced curriculum to support student learning in reading and writing.

※ *Standard 3: Assessment and Evaluation.* Candidates use a variety of assessment tools and practices to plan and evaluate effective reading and writing instruction.

※ *Standard 4: Diversity.* Candidates create and engage their students in literacy practices that develop awareness, understanding, respect, and a valuing of differences in our society.

※ *Standard 5: Literate Environment.* Candidates create a literate environment that fosters reading and writing by integrating foundational knowledge, instructional practices, approaches and methods, curriculum materials, and the appropriate use of assessments.

Interstate New Teacher Assessment and Support Consortium (INTASC) standards.

※ *Standard 1: Learner Development.* The teacher understands how learners grow and develop, recognizing that patterns of learning and development vary individually within and across the cognitive, linguistic, social, emotional, and physical areas, and designs and implements developmentally appropriate and challenging learning experiences.

※ *Standard 2: Learning Differences.* The teacher uses understanding of individual differences and diverse cultures and communities to ensure inclusive learning environments that enable each learner to meet high standards.

※ *Standard 3: Learning Environments.* The teacher works with others to create environments that support individual and collaborative learning, and that encourage positive social interaction, active engagement in learning, and self-motivation.

Course Goals and Objectives

1. Describe the relationship between instruction and assessment and identify ways to assess the literacy development of emergent, novice, transitional, fluent, and advanced readers and writers in the elementary classroom, including use of alternative assessments. (INTASC 2, 3; NAGC 2, 3; IRA 3, 5)

2. Demonstrate ability in matching and adapting materials for students having various levels of proficiency in reading, including materials for English learners and students with exceptionalities, including gifted/ advanced readers. (INTASC 2; NAGC 2, 3; IRA 2)

3. Demonstrate understandings of the similarities and differences in the literacy processes of beginning, skilled, and remedial readers. (INTASC 2; IRA 1, 2)

4. Give explanations of the causes of reading disabilities and how each impacts instructional decisions. (INTASC 2; IRA 1, 2)

5. Identify guidelines for developing literacy with elementary-level students who have varied ability levels, and who are from diverse cultural and linguistic backgrounds. (INTASC 2; NAGC 2, 3; IRA 1)

6. Describe instructional strategies and identify materials for facilitating the development of fluency and graphophonic cue system use with elementary-level remedial readers. (INTASC 1; IRA 1, 2)

7. Describe instructional strategies and identify materials for facilitating the development of fluency with elementary-level advanced readers. (INTASC 1; NAGC 2, 3; IRA 1, 2)

8. Describe the role of different assessment methods for determining student performance in literacy, including contrasting error analysis. (INTASC 1; IRA 3)

9. Explain strategies for developing students' ability to read for information in content text with varied expository structures. (INTASC 1; IRA 2)

10. Determine appropriate reading levels of instructional materials, including the leveling of trade books. (INTASC 1; NAGC 3; IRA 2)

11. Demonstrate ability in matching and adapting materials for students having various levels of proficiency in reading, including materials for ESOL learners and advanced readers. (INTASC 1, 2; NAGC 2, 3; IRA 2)

12. Plan for a variety of instructional formats, including grouping for guided reading lessons. (INTASC 2, 3; NAGC 2, 3; IRA 2)

Course Requirements

Assignment	Points
Case study report and assessments	100
Group presentation	20
Article on effective reading intervention programs or strategies	20
Midterm tests	40
Final exam	40

Assignment	Points
Homework	40
• Emergent literacy case	10
• Gifted reader case	10
• Grouping	10
• Grouping advanced readers	10
Class attendance	15
Participation in class	15
Total	**290**

Assignment descriptions.

1. **Case study report and assessments.** See rubric. Consists of original assessment records and a report addressing the needs of two students: a case study of a gifted learner with advanced reading abilities and a case study for a student not identified as gifted who does not have advanced reading abilities.

2. **Group presentation.** Groups will be assigned to a reading assessment and develop a class presentation outlining the approach and providing examples.

3. **Article on effective reading intervention programs or strategies.** Locate and read two articles on reading intervention programs or strategies, including one designed for advanced readers. Write a response on the log and present both articles to class.

4. **Tests.** Mid-term and final exam. Students will respond to questions regarding objectives addressed prior to each. Final is cumulative.

5. **Homework.**
   a. Cases: Emergent literacy case and gifted reader
   b. Grouping in general, grouping for advanced readers

6. **Attendance.** Two bonus points for perfect attendance.

7. **Participation.** In-class activities and discussions.

Assessments and Standards Alignment

National Association for Gifted Children/Council for Exceptional Children Gifted Education Standards for All Teachers	Activities
1. Understand the issues in definitions, theories, and identification of gifted and talented students, including those from diverse backgrounds.	Before class meeting: visit http://www.davidsongifted.org/db/StatePolicy.aspx and select three states. Determine how the definition of giftedness in each state is similar and different according to type of giftedness, grade levels included in the policy for the state, and the processes used for identifying giftedness. Note whether there are provisions for the inclusion of students from diverse backgrounds. In small groups of four in class, share the major similarities/differences you found across states and develop a trend statement about these policies to share with the class in a small-group presentation.
2. Recognize the learning differences, developmental milestones, and cognitive/affective characteristics of gifted and talented students, including those from diverse backgrounds, and identify their related academic and social-emotional needs.	In small groups, develop a sketch (mini-play) of a child reading on grade level and having a conversation with a classmate also on grade level about a text they are reading. Also create a sketch of a pair of advanced readers from the same grade level who are discussing a text that is two grade levels above the text discussed by the pair above. Then, one of your group members will debrief the class on the differences in vocabulary, reading comprehension, and concepts discussed by each pair. Discuss how K–12 classmates' perceptions of advanced students may be exhibited and how gifted learners may internalize or react to these perceptions.
3. Understand, plan, and implement a range of evidence-based strategies to assess gifted and talented students, to differentiate instruction, content, and assignments for them (including the use of higher order critical and creative thinking skills), and to nominate them for advanced programs or acceleration as needed.	Your fourth-grade class will soon begin a unit focused on the theme of identity. Four of the 18 students in the class read above grade level; all four also have an interest in science activities. Identify two books that may appeal to these four students that are written for readers in grades 5–6. Also identify two on-level texts for the 14 other students in the class. Provide a description of all of the texts you locate and a rationale for how these would address the unit's theme and the differentiated reading needs of this class.

Agenda/Schedule of Class Topics*

Date	Topic	Reading Assignment	Other Assignments Due
Aug. 26	Intro Literacy development stages Classroom model of assessment and diagnosis	pp. 8–27	
Sept 2	Correlates of reading problems ID struggling and advanced readers The interview Observations	pp. 362–379 and pp. 83–88	Sign-up for group presentation
Sept. 9	IRI administration: Finding reading levels Group meeting	pp. 32–61	Bring ARI to class **Due**: Research for group mtg
Sept. 16	IRI: Qualitative analysis	pp. 61–69	Bring ARI to class
Sept. 23	Evaluating word recognition and print skills Group meeting	pp. 71–74 and pp. 218–234	**Test 1** on IRI Begin work with child
Sept. 30	Assessing comprehension Cloze QAR	pp. 95–96 and pp. 251–270	Grp: Structural analysis
Oct. 7	Assessing emergent readers and advanced readers	pp. 170–209	Grp: Phonemic awareness
Oct. 14	Assessing fluency Motivation/Interests of emergent and advanced readers	pp. 234–245 pp. 280–296 pp. 300–312	**Due**: Homework on emergent reader case Grp: Metacognition
Oct. 21	Evaluating writing and spelling of emergent and gifted writers	pp. 296–330	Bring draft of case study Grp: Text structures
Oct. 28	Vocabulary assessment		Grp: Vocabulary
Nov. 4	Using formal assessments	Ch. 5 (all)	Grp: Inferencing, drawing conclusions
Nov. 18	Content area reading assessments	pp. 307–312	**Due**: Case Study Grp: Summarizing **Due**: Homework on grouping
Dec. 2	Intervention strategies Differentiation strategies for advanced readers Share articles	pp. 379–384; pp. 209–213	Grp: Visualization **Due**: Articles on intervention and advanced reading programs
Dec. 9	**Test 2**		

---

*   Subject to changes

Grading Policy

Grading will be based on quality of work and the demonstrated level of competence in meeting course objectives

A = 223–240 points
B = 204–222 points
C = 180–203 points
D = 156–179 points
F = Below 156 points

Note. The case study has been designated as a critical task to evaluate how well you are meeting professional and state competencies.

Students are required to earn a score of 3 or above on critical tasks in order for to pass the course. Students are required to revise assignments scored at 1 or 2 (see the Case Study Rubric). Please note that grades will reflect scores earned on the initial critical task attempt and these will be used to compute your final grade for the course.

Attendance Policy

You are expected to attend all classes and participate in class activities. There is no such thing as an "excused" absence. If you must miss a class, you should discuss the situation with the professor. After missing a second class, you must schedule an appointment with the professor to discuss your status in the course. *Absenteeism and/or infrequent or minimal class participation will result in the reduction of your course grade.*

Communications

All official class communications will be through university e-mail. *It is your responsibility to check your university e-mail account on a regular basis.* Announcements, assignments, and documents will also be posted on Blackboard.

Late Assignments

Late assignments will be accepted only in cases of extreme emergencies—and if you give notification of reasons for the lateness to the instructor. The decision to accept late work is solely the discretion of the instructor. Assignments that are turned in after the due date will have points deducted.

Cell Phones

Please silence cell phones, beepers, and similar gadgets during class meetings and put them **out of sight**. If an emergency signal is given, please quietly step outside of the classroom to address the matter. Please do not text during class time. If you are on your phone, then you're not attending to class information/activities.

Computers

You are encouraged to bring your computer to class for the purpose of taking class notes or referring to information posted on Blackboard. Please do not access your e-mails or other nonrelated websites during class.

Disability Statement

If you think that you have a disability that qualifies you under the Americans with Disabilities Act and requires accommodations, please visit the Office of Student Disabilities Services in order to receive special accommodations and services. Please give your professor written communication from this office regarding your special accommodations.

University Policy on Religious Observance

All students have a right to expect that the university will reasonably accommodate their religious observances, practices, and beliefs. Please notify the professor one week in advance *in writing* if you will be absent in accordance with this policy.

Academic Dishonesty

Plagiarism is defined as "literary theft" and consists of using an author's exact words of longer text without giving credit to the author. This offense includes using direct statements taken from Internet sources. The professor has the option of assigning a grade of F or FF to denote dishonesty.

Detection of Plagiarism

The university has an account with an automated plagiarism detection service that allows instructors to submit student assignments to be checked for plagiarism. You may be asked to submit an assignment as an electronic file in order to electronically submit assignments to Turnitin.com. Assignments are compared automatically with a huge database of journal articles, web articles, and previously submitted papers. The instructor receives a report showing exactly how a student's paper was plagiarized. For more information, go to http://www.turnitin.com.

Emergency Shut Down

In the event of an emergency, it may be necessary for the university to suspend normal operations. During this time, the university may opt to continue delivery of instruction through methods that include but are not limited to: Canvas, Elluminate, Skype, and e-mail messaging and/or an alternate schedule. It's the responsibility of the student to monitor course sites in Canvas for course-specific communication, and the main university, college, and department websites, e-mails, and MoBull messages for important general information.

Case Study

Materials: 1 clip and pocket folder

Your case study consists of the marked test forms (the original records) and a typed written report that *follows the outline below*; complete one case study for a gifted learner with advanced reading abilities and one case study for a student not identified as gifted who does not have advanced reading abilities:

1. Summary sheet (cover sheet)
2. Student background information
   a. Interview
      i. Interest
      ii. Attitudes
   b. Information from teacher/school (opt.)
      i. Grade/age
      ii. Achievement/classroom performance
      iii. Observations of child's behavior
3. Summary of testing
   a. List of tests administered
   b. Findings
      i. Reading levels
      ii. Strengths
      iii. Areas of need
4. Instructional recommendations (list format)
5. Three lesson plans based on the results of the assessment.

Tests that *must* be administered include:

IRI word lists and marked test passages, oral reading miscue analysis, Klesius-Homan Phonic Word Analysis Test, interview and writing sample
   OR
IRI word lists and marked test passages, oral reading miscue analysis, interview, emergent literacy assessments (CAP, Alphabet, etc.), and writing sample.

You MUST administer the IRI on your student, even if it's only the graded word lists and preprimer passage.

The typed report should be attached to the clips in the center of the folder and all test materials should be placed in the pockets.

Group Presentation

Background. The faculty of your school has decided to investigate several reading areas that they have determined to be student "need" areas. The faculty has been divided into small groups, each charged with the task of investigating the essential elements of the need area and making a presentation to the faculty on ways to effectively teach it.

Task. Your task is the following: Each member must research the area and bring his or her information to share with their group on _____.

The team then:

1. develops a common understanding of the area/concept,
2. selects at least three ways of teaching/reinforcing the concept,
3. determines the best way to present the information to the whole group,
4. designs a demonstration lesson for the whole group,
5. writes two test questions with their answers and posts these on Blackboard, and
6. writes a bibliography and all team members sign it.

Audience. The members of your class, who represent the faculty of a school, are your audience.

Performance and products. On the assigned day, your group will give a presentation to include:

* Presentation of concept
* Examples of how to teach (at least three different ways)
* Demonstration lesson
* Two typed test questions
* Typed bibliography of sources used for the presentation

Presentations should not last longer than 30 minutes and everyone in the group must participate.

Case Study Rubric: Linking Literacy Assessment to Instruction

Description. Preservice teachers will conduct two case studies about two students in a K–12 educational setting; one case study focused on a student identified as gifted with advanced reading abilities and the other focused on a learner not identified as a gifted reader. The case studies must include administration of individualized reading assessment, an interest inventory, and the collection of formal and informal reading measures collected from the K–12 students throughout the case study timeline. The diagnostic information must be synthesized and presented as an in-depth report interpreting the findings. Based upon the findings, create one instructional plan to implement with each of the case study students. The plans should organize and prioritize long-term and immediate instructional plans for the students and outline *how* the preservice teacher would instruct the students, including specific reading strategies based on each learner's reading abilities and interests.

Criterion #1: Maintenance of record system (NAGC/CEC Gifted Education Standard 2). The reading assessment shows evidence that the student has maintained observational and anecdotal records from various informal and standardized assessment procedures.

Score	Description
1 = Poor	The reading assessment shows no evidence that the student has maintained observational and anecdotal records from various informal and standardized assessment procedures.
2 = Basic	The reading assessment shows little evidence that the student has maintained observational and anecdotal records from various informal and standardized assessment procedures or that the student is able to interpret the data with some assistance.
3 = Proficient	The reading assessment shows evidence that the student has maintained observational and anecdotal records from various informal and standardized assessment procedures and is able to interpret the data with some assistance.
4 = Advanced	The reading assessment shows evidence that the student has maintained detailed observational and anecdotal records from various informal and standardized assessment procedures and is able to interpret the data independently.
5 = Exceptional	The reading assessment shows evidence that the student has maintained detailed observational and anecdotal records from various informal and standardized assessment procedures and is able to interpret the data with specific suggestions for the student's continuous growth as a reader.

Criterion #2: Interpretation of data (NAGC-CEC Gifted Education Standards 2 and 3). The reading assessment shows evidence that the student has interpreted reading data collected throughout the case study timeline, reflecting an accurate understanding of the developmental level(s) the K–12 student demonstrates at various time points during the case study, and provided specific recommendations for the K–12 student's continuous development as a reader as appropriate to his or her ability and interests in reading.

Score	Description
1 = Poor	The reading assessment shows no evidence that the student has interpret the data with some assistance. The interpretation does not reflect an understanding of the student's reading ability based on reading comprehension level, fluency, or interests in reading.

Score	Description
2 = Basic	The reading assessment shows little evidence that the student is able to interpret the data with some assistance. There is minimal evidence that the teacher candidate has used the reading data from the selected student to inform continued reading development planning with respect to comprehension, fluency, or interest.
3 = Proficient	The reading assessment shows evidence that the student is able to interpret the data with some assistance. Suggestions for addressing the student's growth as a reader are provided with multiple examples and are based on careful interpretation of comprehension, fluency, and student's interests.
4 = Advanced	The reading assessment shows evidence that the student is able to interpret the data without assistance, with general suggestions for instruction drawn from the interpretation. Suggestions addressing the student's growth as a reader are related to assessment results of comprehension, fluency, and student's interests.
5 = Exceptional	The reading assessment shows evidence that the student is able to interpret the data with specific suggestions for the student's continuous growth as a reader. Suggestions should be contextualized around the ongoing record system, infused throughout the case study experience, and discussed within the frame of the student's interests, comprehension, and fluency.

Criterion #3: Instructional plan (NAGC-CEC Gifted Education Standards 2 and 3). The teacher candidate provides an instructional plan that is specific to the instructional needs of the K–12 student and would be implemented following the case study experience pending feedback from the course instructor. The instructional plan will address reading interests, comprehension development, and appropriate instructional strategies (i.e., independent reading, book club, whole group) for the K–12 student. Objectives, activities, materials, and assessment(s) will be included, as well as a rationale for the various components of the lesson plan. Consideration of pacing, content complexity/depth, and other needs unique to the instruction of advanced readers are included.

Score	Description
1 = Poor	The instructional plan shows no evidence that the student can design a plan specific to the needs of an advanced reader. A rationale may be limited in its conception or the components of the lesson plan may be missing or underdeveloped.
2 = Basic	The instructional plan shows little evidence that the student can design a plan specific to the needs of an advanced reader. Neither the rationale nor the instructional plan components indicate the teacher candidate understands appropriate instruction for a learner with advanced reading ability.

Score	Description
3 = Proficient	The instructional plan shows evidence that the teacher candidate is able to design a reading lesson that addresses the interests and abilities of a K–12 student. A sound rationale for the objectives, activities, materials, and assignments is provided.
4 = Advanced	The instructional plan shows evidence that the teacher candidate is able to design a reading lesson that addresses the interests and abilities of a K–12 student. A well-developed, thoughtful rationale for instructional components (objectives, activities, materials, and assignments) is provided.
5 = Exceptional	The instructional plan shows extensive evidence that the teacher candidate is able to design a reading lesson that addresses the interests and abilities of a K–12 student. A detailed, insightful rationale of the instructional plan and its components (objectives, activities, materials, and assignments) is provided. A nuanced understanding of the components also reflects the teacher candidate's advanced understanding of instructional planning for the advanced reading abilities of the K–12 student and addresses pace, content depth/complexity, and other issues pertinent to the developing reading skills of an advanced learner.

EXEMPLAR CASES FOR ANALYSIS ALIGNED WITH NAGC-CEC STANDARDS

Case 1. Developing Programs for Young Gifted Children

Adapted from "Neuroscience and Young Children: Implications for the Diversity of Gifted Programming" by Pamela R. Clinkenbeard

Mary Jones is a Gifted and Talented Coordinator (one of several positions she holds at the school district level). Her district encompasses a mid-sized city in the Midwest with fairly stable enrollment numbers, significant budget challenges, and steadily increasing economic and cultural diversity in the student population. One of the district's main goals for GT programs and services is to increase the participation of students who are traditionally underrepresented in those programs.

The state mandates early identification of gifted and talented students, so Mary wants to work with Pre-K educators (within-district, Head Start, and private preschools) to expand the size and diversity of the pool of kindergarten children who might be considered for gifted and talented programming and services. She takes a talent development perspective; she prefers to offer high-level, open-ended thinking skill programming and activities to see what developmental levels all children can reach, rather than just identifying children who already have skills that are advanced for their age. However, she is also interested in working with early childhood educators to make sure that those children who are already advanced are receiving appropriately challenging curriculum.

To both challenge advanced preschoolers and to uncover and nurture hidden skills in diverse populations, Mary wants to select or develop a thinking skills program. She hopes to find a program or curriculum that promotes improvement in reasoning and executive function skills in particular, and one that has a solid research base. Although she acknowledges the great importance of literacy skills, she wants to find curriculum that has the broadest possible generalization to a variety of subject matter areas, including a tie-in to her district's emphasis on developing STEM (science, technology, engineering, and math) skills at an early age. She is aware of her state's early learning standards for mathematical and scientific thinking, which seem to have a high enough ceiling to accommodate gifted preschoolers. She has done some reading in the areas on the economic returns on investment in early childhood education. With her limited time and budget, she wants to know what kinds of curriculum and activities show clear evidence of improving young children's overall school readiness and performance. She also hopes to learn which kinds of thinking skills tend to characterize young children who are already identified as gifted, how those skills can be developed in other young children, and how those skills relate to real-world school readiness and success. Because Gifted Coordinator is only one of her jobs, she wants to embed her efforts in the broader early childhood education programming in her district.

As she prepares to meet with Pre-K educators and other stakeholders about her ideas, Mary is trying to anticipate some of the objections or barriers that she might encounter. She is open to a variety of structures for implementing some kind of a thinking skills curriculum, but obviously she has limited influence and authority with early childhood educators who work outside the school district. She hopes to construct a coherent grant proposal for her project ideas, but she must gain the cooperation and participation of outside agencies and programs.

There are three issues, in particular, for which she anticipates lively discussion. The first is that she is determined to introduce only curriculum or activities that have clear research evidence for their effectiveness, and she is concerned that some educators may not want to give up any of their favorite activities (some of which may have little demonstrated effectiveness) to find time to fit in a new thinking skills curriculum. The second issue is the use of the term "developmentally appropriate" in the early childhood community. She fears that some early childhood educators will see high-level, challenging thinking tasks as inappropriate for their young students. The third issue is that some of the Pre-K educators might balk at a program that is related to gifted education. They may feel that any special efforts should be focusing on the children who are the most educationally disadvantaged, rather than engaging in activities that could improve the achievement of the students who are already performing well at academic tasks in comparison to their peers. They may be concerned that the achievement gap will be widened due to improved performance of those who are already high achievers.

Instructions for the Course Developer

The following questions can be used to guide a discussion in a face-to-face or online course environment. The cases are open-ended, but suggested alignment with NAGC-CEC Teacher Preparation Standards in Gifted and Talented Education appear after each case analysis question.

* *What is going on in this case?* (Aligns with Standard #1 Learner Development and Individual Learning Differences; Element 1.1: Beginning gifted education professionals understand how language, culture, economic status, family background, and/or area of disability can influence the learning of individuals with gifts and talents and Element 1.2: Beginning gifted education professionals use understanding of development and individual differences to respond to the needs of individuals with gifts and talents. Aligns with Standard #6 Professional Learning and Ethical Practice; Element 6.3: Beginning gifted education professionals model respect for diversity, understanding that it is an integral part of society's institutions and impacts learning of individuals with gifts and talents in the delivery of gifted education services.)

* *What additional information do we need to help Mary Jones work through her plans for her school?* (Aligns with Standard #5 Instructional Planning and Strategies; Element 5.3: Beginning gifted education professionals collaborate with families, professional colleagues, and other educators to select, adapt, and use evidence-based strategies that promote challenging learning opportunities in general and specialized curricula.)

* *What are some suggestions for her next steps?* (Aligns with Standard #6 Professional Learning and Ethical Practice; Element 6.5: Beginning gifted education professionals advance the profession by engaging in activities such as advocacy and mentoring. Aligns with Standard #7 Collaboration; Element 7.1: Beginning gifted education professionals apply elements of effective collaboration; Element 7.2: Beginning gifted education professionals serve as a collaborative resource to colleagues.)

❋ *What do you recommend as her course of action for selecting an evidenced-based thinking skills curriculum for her school?* (Aligns with Standard #5 Instructional Planning and Strategies; Element 5.1: Beginning gifted educational professionals know principles of evidence-based, differentiated, and accelerated practices and possess a repertoire of instructional strategies to enhance the critical and creative thinking, problem-solving, and performance skills of individuals with gifts and talents.)

Case 2. Motivation in Middle School Advanced Academic Classes

Adapted from "Recognizing Both Effort and Talent: How Do We Keep From Throwing the Baby Out With the Bathwater?" by Del Siegle

The Malton School District is well known for having the highest test scores in the state on the state's mastery test. Based on sixth-grade test results, students in seventh grade are identified for a gifted and talented program that recognizes their advanced skills in mathematics. The students are selected for the program if their state achievement test scores are in the top 10%. Many, but not all, of the students who are selected for the advanced mathematics program have also participated in a pull-out program since they were in fourth grade. Malton's fourth-grade pull-out program has conservative, dated identification procedures, as opposed to the more current approach of using multiple criteria. In the district, teachers nominate students for the fourth-grade pull-out programs, and those students with an IQ score of 130 are placed in it. Some students who were in the pull-out program in fourth through sixth grades do not qualify for the advanced mathematics program.

Students in the advanced mathematics program work on mathematics curriculum that is 2 years above the curriculum most seventh-grade students receive, and the students understand that they have been selected for the class because of their advanced mathematics skills. At the beginning of the school year, Ms. Bon, the teacher, overhears several of her new students talking about people who are good at mathematics and those who are not good at mathematics. She is concerned that these students may have developed a fixed mindset and wonders how they will react to the more difficult mathematics curriculum they are about to encounter. She wants them to understand that the effort they put into their mathematics learning improves their mathematics skills as mathematicians. She is also concerned about the students who were formally identified as gifted in fourth grade who were not selected for the advanced mathematics program in seventh grade. She worries that those students in programs with a growth mindset may become discouraged by not being placed in the advanced mathematics class, may begin to believe that they have limitations on their skills, and may develop a fixed mindset. She also worries that not being placed in the advanced mathematics class will reinforce personal beliefs about limitations for students who already hold a fixed mindset.

Her initial efforts with students in the advanced class fail when she downplays the importance of mathematics ability and focuses on the importance of effort. Several of the students, some of whom she suspects have a fixed mindset, lose their confidence and begin questioning whether they should have been placed in the class. They believe if they have to work hard it probably means that they are not really good at mathematics. Some of the students who had been served in the fourth- through sixth-grade gifted program, but were not selected for the mathematics class, have approached her and asked why they are not in the advanced mathematics class and wonder whether this means they have lost their giftedness.

Instructions for the Course Developer

The following questions can be used to guide a discussion in a face-to-face or online course environment. The cases are open-ended, but suggested alignment with NAGC-CEC Teacher Preparation Standards in Gifted and Talented Education appear after each case analysis question.

* *What is going on in this case?* (Aligns with Standard #1 Learner Development and Individual Learning Differences; Element 1.2: Beginning gifted education professionals use understanding of development and individual differences to respond to the needs of individuals with gifts and talents. Aligns with Standard #2 Learning Environments; Element 2.4: Beginning gifted education professionals demonstrate understanding of the multiple environments that are part of a continuum of services for individuals with gifts and talents, including the advantages and disadvantages of various settings and teach students to adapt to these environments.)

* *What additional information do we need to understand Ms. Bon's concerns about her students' beliefs?* (Aligns with Standard #1 Learner Development and Individual Learning Differences; Element 1.2: Beginning gifted education professionals use understanding of development and individual differences to respond to the needs of individuals with gifts and talents.)

※ *How might we respond to Ms. Bon's concerns should she ask for advice?* (Aligns with Standard #2 Learning Environments; Element 2.2: Beginning gifted education professionals use communication and motivational and instructional strategies to facilitate understanding of subject matter and to teach individuals with gifts and talents how to adapt to different environments and develop ethical leadership skills. Aligns with Standard #3 Curricular Content Knowledge; Element 3.4: Beginning gifted education professionals understand that individuals with gifts and talents demonstrate a wide range of advanced knowledge and performance levels and modify the general or specialized curriculum appropriately.)

※ *What do you recommend to Ms. Bon as a course of action for meeting the affective needs of students in this academic setting?* (Aligns with Standard #4 Assessment; Element 4.5: Beginning gifted education professionals engage individuals with gifts and talents in assessing the quality of their own learning and performance and in setting future goals and objectives. Aligns with Standard #5 Instructional Planning and Strategies; Element 5.5: Beginning gifted education professionals use instructional strategies that enhance the affective development of individuals with gifts and talents.)

Note. These cases are adapted from *Malleable Minds: Translating Insights From Psychology and Neuroscience to Gifted Education* by R. F. Subotnik, A. Robinson, C. M. Callahan, and E. J. Gubbins, 2012, Storrs: University of Connecticut, The National Research Center on the Gifted and Talented. Copyright 2012 by NRCGT. Adapted with permission.

The work reported herein was supported under the Educational Research and Development Centers Program, PR/Award Number R305A060044, as administered by the Institute of Education Sciences, U.S. Department of Education. The findings and opinions expressed in this report do not reflect the position of policies of the Institute of Education Sciences or the U.S. Department of Education.

GUIDANCE FOR GIFTED EDUCATION PROGRAM REVIEWERS AND AUDITORS

Reviewing teacher preparation programs against the NAGC-CEC standards is a critically important part of the CAEP accreditation process; the feedback is also extremely helpful to the individual program leaders. In an effort to ensure that NAGC program review teams are as consistent as possible across teams, NAGC auditors have developed guidelines for determining when individual standards are met and in determining national program status. Below is a list of the elements within each standard to consider when reviewing a program submission.

1.   In determining whether an *individual standard* has been met, the auditors recommend the following:

   a.   To receive a "met" determination, all of the elements of the standard have been addressed and a preponderance of the evidence presented shows that the candidates are meeting the expectations of the standard.

   b.   To receive a "met with conditions" determination, all of the elements have been addressed, but there is insufficient evidence presented to determine that the candidates have met the expectations of the standard.

   c.   To receive a "not met" determination, there is little to no evidence that the candidates are meeting the expectations of the standard.

Note that on close decisions, reviewers should use their professional judgment in considering the evidence taken as a whole and the quality of the assessment to determine whether an individual standard is met.

2. In determining the *recognition status* for the program, the auditors recommend the following:

     a. To be "nationally recognized," all seven of the individual standards must be determined to be "met."

     b. To be "not nationally recognized" or "further development required," a program would have received "not met" on one or more individual standards.

     c. In all other cases, the status for the program would be "recognized with conditions."

Note that for programs that have received "met" on six standards and "met with conditions" on one standard, reviewers should use their professional judgment in considering the conditions for the seventh standard to determine whether national recognition status is appropriate.

NAGC-CEC Teacher Preparation Standards in Gifted and Talented Education (2013) 28 Elements by Standard

Standard 1: Learner Development and Individual Learning Differences

Candidates:

❋ understand how language, culture, economic status, family background, and/or area of disability can influence learning.

❋ use understanding of development and individual differences to respond to student needs.

Standard 2: Learning Environments

Candidates:

❋ create safe, inclusive, culturally responsive learning environments that engage individuals with gifts and talents in meaningful and rigorous learning activities and social interactions.

❋ use communication and motivational and instructional interventions to facilitate understanding of subject matter and to teach individuals with gifts and talents how to adapt to different environments and develop ethical leadership skills.

❋ adjust their communication to an individual's language proficiency and cultural and linguistic differences.

❋ demonstrate understanding of the multiple environments that are part of a continuum of services, including the advantages and disadvantages of various settings.

Standard 3: Curricular Content Knowledge

Candidates:

❋ understand the role of central concepts, structures of the discipline, and tools of inquiry of the content areas they teach, and use their understanding to organize knowledge, integrate cross-disciplinary skills, and develop meaningful learning progressions within and across grade levels.

❋ design appropriate learning and performance modifications that enhance creativity, acceleration, depth, and complexity in academic subject matter and specialized domains.

❋ use assessments to select, adapt, and create materials to differentiate instructional strategies and general and specialized curricula to challenge individuals with gifts and talents.

❋ understand that individuals with gifts and talents demonstrate a wide range of advanced knowledge and performance levels and modify the general or specialized curriculum appropriately.

Standard 4: Assessment

Candidates:

❋ understand that some groups of individuals with gifts and talents have been underrepresented in gifted education programs and select and use technically sound formal and informal assessments that minimize bias.

❋ use knowledge of measurement principles and practices to differentiate assessments and interpret results to guide educational decisions.

❋ collaborate with colleagues and families in using multiple types of assessment information to make identification and learning progress decisions and to minimize bias in assessment and decision making.

❋ use assessment results to develop long- and short-range goals and objectives that take into consideration an individual's abilities and needs, the learning environment, and other factors related to diversity.
❋ engage individuals with gifts and talents in assessing the quality of their own learning and performance and in setting future goals and objectives.

Standard 5: Instructional Planning and Strategies

Candidates:
❋ know principles of evidence-based, differentiated, and accelerated practices and possess a repertoire of instructional strategies to enhance critical and creative thinking, problem-solving, and performance skills.
❋ apply appropriate technologies to support instructional assessment, planning, and delivery.
❋ collaborate with families, professional colleagues, and other educators to select, adapt, and use evidence-based strategies that promote challenging learning opportunities in general and specialized curricula.
❋ emphasize the development, practice, and transfer of advanced knowledge and skills across environments throughout the lifespan leading to creative, productive careers in a multicultural society.
❋ use instructional strategies that enhance affective development.

Standard 6: Professional Learning and Ethical Practice

Candidates:
❋ use professional ethical principles and specialized program standards to guide their practice.
❋ understand how foundational knowledge, perspectives, and historical and current issues influence professional practice and the education and treatment of individuals with gifts and talents both in school and society.
❋ model respect for diversity, understanding that it is an integral part of society's institutions and impacts learning of individuals with gifts and talents in the delivery of gifted education services.
❋ are aware of their own professional learning needs, understand the significance of lifelong learning, and participate in professional activities and learning communities.
❋ advance the profession by engaging in activities such as advocacy and mentoring.

Standard 7: Collaboration

Candidates:

* apply elements of effective collaboration.
* serve as a collaborative resource for colleagues.
* use collaboration to promote the well-being of individuals with gifts and talents across a wide range of settings, experiences, and collaborators.

OBSERVATION TOOL: CLASSROOM OBSERVATION OF DIFFERENTIATION

SUSAN K. JOHNSEN

Description of the Instrument

This scale uses observable criteria to identify the characteristics of the learning task. After observing in math or English language arts from the beginning to the end of a lesson, the learning task is rated according to the presence or absence of 11 characteristics: theme, concept/generalization, problem-based lesson, method that is authentic to the subject area, independent study, variation in tasks, curriculum compacting, student-generated products, content beyond grade level, student interest, and choice. During the observation period, a sketch is made of the room arrangement (see Section I), the lesson is described (see Section I), the teacher and student questions are entered for small-group or whole-group interaction (see Section II), and student engagement is recorded for six students (see Section III). Following the data collection, the degree of differentiation is rated using the Classroom Instructional Practices Rating Scale (CIPS, see Section IV; Johnsen, Haensly, Ryser, & Ford, 2002). The CIPS examines the degree to which the teacher addresses individual differences in four areas: (a) the knowledge and skills that students need and want to learn (i.e., *content*); (b) the students' preferences or the most effective ways for them to learn the content (i.e., *preference*); (c) how quickly they learn (i.e., *rate*); and (d) the types of environments that enhance their learning (i.e., *environment*). For the most part, the CIPS is organized into learning progressions, beginning with the least adaptive classroom practice for individual differences and progressing to the most adaptive classroom practice. For example, within content, the lowest rating (C1) describes a content that is organized around the book's scope and sequence while C9 describes content organized around individual student interest. Within rate, an R1 rating means that the teacher provides the same amount of time for every student in the classroom to learn the content whereas an R9 rating means that the teacher uses preassessments to identify students who may need reteaching/recycling, in-depth study, enrichment, or acceleration and then provides for the varying needs of students in the classroom. Within environment, the lowest rating (E1) describes a classroom in which the teacher limits interactions between students and with learning materials; whereas an E6 rating describes a classroom where students learn from one another and use the community and the school as learning centers. Finally, within preference, at the lowest rating (P1), the student has no choice of learning materials and uses materials that have a similar format such as paper-pencil; at P5, the student may select or create varied learning activities.

Overall, the observation scale appears to be reliable. The percentage of agreement among 10 observers for coding teacher and student questions was 95% and for coding on-off task behaviors was 100%. This percentage indicates a high degree of consistency among individuals who were observing classrooms. The internal consistency, alpha coefficient, of the 11-point task scale was .795 for the learning task (Johnsen, Wisely, & Fearon, 2012).

References

Johnsen, S. K., Haensly, P., Ryser, G., & Ford, R. (2002). Changing general education classroom practices to adapt for gifted students. *Gifted Child Quarterly, 46,* 45–63.

Johnsen, S. K., Wisely, L. W., & Fearon, D. (2012). *An observation report of elementary cluster classrooms in the Waco ISD.* Waco, TX: WISD.

Agreed Upon Data Collection Procedures for Observers

1. Questioning
   a. When a teacher asks a multiple answer question, place a tick under the "R" category for each student response.
   b. When a teacher asks a question but doesn't pause for a student response, place a dash under the "R" category.
   c. When a teacher raises her voice after a statement, allowing for a student response, count the statement as a question (e.g., "Got it?").
   d. When a teacher asks a yes/no question, count it as a single answer question.
   e. When a teacher asks a multiple answer question, classify it under another category (e.g., CC, AC, process, evaluation/implications).
   f. Even if the teacher asks the same single answer question multiple times, count it each time.
   g. Only student-initiated questions should be placed under the student questions category.

2. Engagement
   a. Observers will look at the face of a student to determine engagement. If the student is following the rules for the majority of the time (e.g., looking at the task, the teacher or the group, working independently, etc.), she will be counted on task.
   b. If the student is moving but continues to be following the rules for the majority of the time, the student will be counted as engaged.
   c. These types of behaviors count as off task: looking at hands, thumbing through papers, talking about another topic, staring off into space, etc.
   d. If the student has her hand up during 5 seconds or more of the time period, she is waiting (W) and is not counted as being on or off task.
   e. Do not infer intent or label the child, just watch the behavior.

Brief Description of Lesson Using a School Example

The teacher had these objectives on the chalkboard: "sequence of events, write a declarative/interrogative sentence, round numbers to the nearest 10-100-1000."

The teacher began the lesson by discussing the importance of keeping a planner. She then asked if students had ever used a dictionary. Following this brief discussion, she described the tasks in each of the learning areas and groupings for the language arts period. One of the groups was going to begin by working with the teacher on dictionary skills, one was going to begin by working on a timeline with the student intern, and one was going to begin by creating a story with sequence picture cards. Those writing the story were able to resequence the picture cards as needed to create their story. The teacher described how the timeline was connected to what they were learning in social studies. During the morning, the student groups rotated from one activity to the next as the teacher directed. When the students rotated, the two teacher-directed activities changed to match the characteristics of the group. (Then you would describe how the content of the activities changed.)

Section I. Observation of Learning Task

Name of Teacher: _____ School: _____
Grade Level: _____ Number of Students in Class: _____
Date of Observation:_____ Observer: _____
Start and Ending Time of Observation:_____

Task Description. Obtained from lesson plan, observation, and student interviews, and relates to the lesson observed only.

- ❑ Is there explicit evidence of the use of a theme? (C7)
- ❑ Is there evidence of major concept/generalizations? (C7)
- ❑ Is the lesson problem-based? (C5)
- ❑ Is the method used authentic to the discipline? Process? (C5)
- ❑ Is there evidence of variation in activities or tasks within the unit? (P1–4)
- ❑ Is there evidence of student choice of tasks? (P5)
- ❑ Is there evidence of curriculum compacting/use of tests? (R4–R9)
- ❑ Is there evidence of student-generated products/performances? (C5, C7, P5)
- ❑ Is the content of student products/performances beyond grade level? (R6–R9)
- ❑ Does the lesson relate to student interest? (C9)
- ❑ Is there a positive environment that supports risk-taking?
  % Total

Room Arrangement. Sketch the physical arrangement below.

Brief Lesson Description. This should include purpose, instructional resources, and major activities (write on back). Do note if the task characteristics change for different groups (e.g., high group is more problem-based vs. low group).

Section II. Observation of Questioning Strategies

Name of Teacher: _____ School: _____
Number of Students in Group:_____
(low, medium, high) Subject: _____
Date of Observation:_____ Observer: _____
Start and Ending Time of Observation:_____

Teacher Questions	Code	R	Student Questions	Code
Total Number of Teacher Questions			**Total Number of Student Questions**	

Codes. Insert number of questions and percent of total number of questions in front of each.

# (%)		# (%)		# (%)	
	Single answer		Multiple answer		CConnections
	AConnections		Process		Evaluation/ Implications

Section III. Observation of Student Engagement

Teacher:_____ Date: _____

Observer:_____ Time: _____

	Setting	Type of Task	St. 1	St. 2	St. 3	St. 4	St. 5	St. 6
:30								
1:00								
1:30								
2:00								
2:30								
3:00								
3:30								
4:00								
4:30								
5:00								
5:30								
6:00								
6:30								
7:00								
7:30								
8:00								
8:30								
9:00								
9:30								
10:00								

Note. St. = Student. Every 30 seconds, observe each student for 5 seconds during the 30-second time period.

Codes.

%		+ =		On task—following directions, looking at teacher
%		- =		Off task—not engaged
%		W		Waiting—raising hand
%		S		Small group—smaller than the whole class
%		G		Whole group

Student #1		% on task		% off task
Student #2		% on task		% off task
Student #3		% on task		% off task
Student #4		% on task		% off task
Student #5		% on task		% off task

Glossary

Affective connections: question that asks the student to relate to his or her own personal experience (e.g., "Has something similar happened in your life?")

Authentic: the method that a professional would use in the discipline in creating knowledge (e.g., a historian would use primary and secondary sources)

Beyond grade level: depth or complexity of content is at a higher grade level (e.g., a second grader is doing third-grade work)

Cognitive connections: question that asks the student to relate to other disciplines/concepts, past or future learning; compare and contrast questions (e.g., "How are relationships like a pizza?")

Curriculum compacting: teacher uses pretests to determine if a student already knows the objectives, and if so, the student does alternative activities (e.g., one student is creating a map of another country while the rest of the students are learning about cities in the U.S.)

Evaluation/Implication: question that asks the student to evaluate or discuss implications; asks for reasons (e.g., "Why did you select that answer? What criteria did you use?")

Independent study: student is able to work alone on a topic of interest (e.g., student is studying favorite topic of black holes)

Major concept/generalization: relates to the theme and is the major point or purpose for teaching the lesson or unit (e.g., "Changes have positive and negative effects")

Multiple answer: question that allows for more than one correct answer (e.g., "What are some examples of prejudice?")

Problem-based: a problem initiates or is the focus of the lesson; students have opportunities to provide multiple answers or solve the problem in multiple ways (e.g., "These are the characters and the situation, what do you believe will occur in the story?")

Process: question that asks the student to describe the method or way he or she derived the answer; reflect (e.g., "How did you solve that problem?")

Risk-taking environment: the teacher supports different answers to questions and different types of methods or products/performances (e.g., Teacher makes supportive comments such as "Another good idea" or "I never thought about it that way" and never "puts down" a student idea)

Single answer: question can be answered by a yes/no; true or false, short phrase, or one correct answer (e.g., "Did the Little Red Hen get any help?")

Student-generated products/performances: students create the products instead of parents or teacher; products/performances include anything that is *not* a worksheet or workbook page (e.g., students are working on products/performances in the classroom—stories, debates, experiments)

Theme: broad-based so that it may be used authentically in different disciplines (e.g., structures, relationships, influences, change)

Variation in tasks/activities: students use different activities to learn the same objective or different activities are used throughout the same lesson (e.g., video, then discussion, then role play)

Section IV. Observation of Learning Task Classroom Instructional Practices Rating Scale

Observer:_____

Teacher:_____

Grade: _____ Number of Students: _____

School:_____Date Observed:_____

Discipline/Subject: _____

Start and Ending Time of Observation:_____

Content

- ❏   C1   Book or curriculum guide organizes content.
- ❏   C2   Focus is on procedural knowledge.
- ❏   C3   Focus is on concept learning.
- ❏   C4   Includes creative and critical thinking skills; higher level questions.
- ❏   C5   Authentic to discipline/problem-based.
- ❏   C6   Integration of multiple disciplines into discipline-based topics.
- ❏   C7   Interdisciplinary; broad-based themes; authentic methods.
- ❏   C8   Student's performance determines sequence.
- ❏   C9   Student's interest guides content.

Rate

- ❏   R1   Students have same/varied amount of time for tasks; early finishers do no assigned task.
- ❏   R2   Students have same/varied amount of time for tasks; early finishers do an unrelated task.
- ❏   R3   Students have same/varied time for completion of task; early finishers do a related task.
- ❏   R4   Postassessment at set times with no recycling.
- ❏   R5   Postassessment at varied times with no recycling.
- ❏   R6   Postassessment at set times with recycling and/or in-depth study/enrichment/acceleration.
- ❏   R7   Postassessment at varied times with recycling and/or in-depth study/enrichment/acceleration.
- ❏   R8   Pre- and postassessment at set times with recycling and/or in-depth study/enrichment/acceleration.
- ❏   R9   Pre- and postassessment at varied times with recycling and/or in-depth study/enrichment/acceleration.

Preference

☐ P1   No variation in tasks and/or response dimensions; not correlated.
☐ P2   Variation in tasks and/or response dimensions; not correlated.
☐ P3   No variation in tasks and/or response dimensions; correlated.
☐ P4   Variation in tasks and/or response dimensions; correlated.
☐ P5   Student choice of varied tasks and/or response dimensions; correlated.

Environment

☐ E1   Arrangement with limited student interaction; no interest or learning centers present.
☐ E2   Arrangement with limited student interaction; interest or learning centers present.
☐ E3   Arrangement with student interaction.
☐ E4   Arrangement with student interaction; interest centers present.
☐ E5   Arrangement with student interaction; learning centers present.
☐ E6   Use of school and/or community as learning centers.

RESEARCH SUPPORT FOR THE ADVANCED STANDARDS IN GIFTED EDUCATION FOR TEACHER PREPARATION

Advanced Preparation Standard 1: Assessment

Gifted education specialists use valid and reliable assessment practices to minimize bias.

ELEMENT 1.1
Gifted education specialists review, select, and interpret psychometrically sound, nonbiased, qualitative and quantitative instruments to identify individuals with gifts and talents and assess their abilities, strengths, and interests.

Research-Based References

Bermúdez, A. B., & Rakow, S. J. (1993). Examining identification and instruction practices for gifted and talented limited English proficient students. In L. M. Malave (Ed.), *Annual conference journal: Proceedings of the annual conference of the National Association for Bilingual Education* (pp. 99–114). Washington, DC: National Association for Bilingual Education. (ERIC Document Reproduction Service No. ED360871)

Borland, J. H. (1994). Identifying and educating young economically disadvantaged urban children: The lessons of Project Synergy. In N. Colangelo, S. G. Assouline, & D. L. Ambrose (Eds.), *Talent development: Proceedings of the second biennial Wallace Conference on Talent Development* (pp. 151–172). Dayton, OH: Ohio Psychology Press.

Burks, B. S., Jensen, D. W., & Terman, L. M. (1930). *The promise of youth: Follow-up studies of a thousand gifted children: Genetic studies of genius* (Vol. 3). Stanford, CA: Stanford University Press.

Esquivel, G. B., & Houtz, J. C. (Eds.). (2000). *Creativity and giftedness in culturally diverse students. Perspectives on creativity.* Cresskill, NJ: Hampton.

Frasier, M. M. (1997). Multiple criteria: The mandate and the challenge. *Roeper Review, 20,* A4–6.

Gentry, M., & Owen, S. V. (1999). An investigation of the effects of total school flexible cluster grouping on identification, achievement, and classroom practices. *Gifted Child Quarterly, 43,* 224–242.

Harris, B., Plucker, J. A., Rapp, K. E., & Martinez, R. S. (2009). Identifying gifted and talented English language learners: A case study. *Journal for the Education of the Gifted, 32,* 368–393.

Hunsaker, S. (2000). Documenting gifted program results for key decision-makers. *Roeper Review, 23,* 80–82.

Hunsaker, S. S. L., Finley, V. S., & Frank, E. L. (1997). An analysis of teacher nominations and student performance in gifted programs. *Gifted Child Quarterly, 31,* 19–24.

Johnson, S. T., Starnes, W. T., Gregory, D., & Blaylock, A. (1985). Program of assessment, diagnosis and instruction (PADI): Identifying and nurturing potentially gifted and talented minority students. *Journal of Negro Education, 54,* 416–430.

Kitano, M. K., & Espinosa, R. (1995). Language diversity and giftedness: Working with gifted English language learners. *Journal for the Education of the Gifted, 18,* 234–254.

Lohman, D. F., Korb, K. A., & Lakin, J. M. (2008). Identifying academically gifted English-Language Learners using nonverbal tests. *Gifted Child Quarterly, 52,* 275–296.

Naglieri, J. A., & Ford, D. Y. (2003). Addressing underrepresentation of gifted minority children using the Naglieri Nonverbal Ability Test (NNAT). *Gifted Child Quarterly, 47,* 155–160.

Patton, J. M., Prillaman, D., & VanTassel-Baska, J. (1990). The nature and extent of programs for the disadvantaged gifted in the United States and territories. *Gifted Child Quarterly, 34,* 94–96.

Shaklee, B. D. (1993). Preliminary findings of the Early Assessment for Exceptional Potential project. *Roeper Review, 16,* 105–109.

VanTassel-Baska, J. (2006). A content analysis of evaluation findings across 20 gifted programs: A clarion call for enhanced gifted program development. *Gifted Child Quarterly, 50,* 199–215.

Walters, J., Gardner, H., & Seidel, S. (2006). *APPLE project.* Retrieved from http://www.pz.gse.harvard.edu/apple_project.php

Theory-Based References

Arter, J., & McTighe, J. (2001). *Scoring rubrics in the classroom: Using performance criteria for assessing and improving student performance.* Thousand Oaks, CA: Corwin Press.

Artiles, A. J., & Zamora-Duran, G. (Eds.). (1997). *Reducing disproportionate representation of culturally diverse students in special and gifted education.* The Council for Exceptional Children: Arlington, VA.

Barab, S. A., & Plucker, J. A. (2002). Smart people or smart contexts? Cognition, ability and talent development in an age of situated approaches to knowing and learning. *Educational Psychologist, 37,* 165–182.

Buchanan, N., & Feldhusen, J. F. (Eds.). (1991). *Conducting research and evaluation in gifted education.* New York, NY: Teachers College Press.

Callahan, C. M. (Ed.). (2004). *Essential readings in gifted education: Program evaluation in gifted education* (Vol. 11). Thousand Oaks, CA: Corwin Press.

Callahan, C. M., & Caldwell, M. S. (1997). *A practitioner's guide to evaluating programs for the gifted.* Washington, DC: National Association for Gifted Children.

Callahan, C. M., Hunsaker, S. L., Adams, C. M., Moore, S. D., & Bland, L. C. (1995). *Instruments used in the identification of gifted and talented students* (RM95130). Storrs: University of Connecticut, The National Research Center on the Gifted and Talented.

Coleman, M. R. (2003). *The identification of students who are gifted.* (ERIC Document Reproduction Service ED480431)

Council for Exceptional Children, The Association for the Gifted. (2001). *Diversity and developing gifts and talents: A national action plan.* Reston, VA: Council for Exceptional Children.

Esquivel, G. B., & Houtz, J. C. (Eds.). (2000). *Creativity and giftedness in culturally diverse students. Perspectives on creativity.* Cresskill, NJ: Hampton.

Frasier, M. M., Garcia, J. H., & Passow, A. H. (1995). *A review of assessment issues in gifted education and their implications for identifying gifted minority students* (RM95204). Storrs: University of Connecticut, The National Research Center on the Gifted and Talented.

Johnsen, S. K. (Ed.). (2011). *Identifying gifted students: A practical guide* (2nd ed.). Waco, TX: Prufrock Press.

Kitano, M. K., & Espinosa, R. (1995). Language diversity and giftedness: Working with gifted English language learners. *Journal for the Education of the Gifted, 18,* 234–254.

Posner, G., Strike, K., Hewson, P., & Gertzog, W. (1982). Accommodation of a scientific conception: Towards a theory of conceptual change. *Science Education, 66,* 211–227.

Reynolds, C. R., & Kaiser, S. M. (1990). Bias in assessment of aptitude. In C. R. Reynolds & R. W. Kamphaus (Eds.), *Handbook of psychological and educational assessment of children: Intelligence and achievement* (pp. 611–653). New York, NY: Guilford.

Robinson, A., Shore, B. M., & Enersen, D. L. (2007). *Best practices in gifted education: An evidence-based guide.* Waco, TX: Prufrock Press.

Sternberg, R. J. (1999). Intelligence as developing expertise. *Contemporary Educational Psychology, 24,* 359–375.

Sternberg, R. J., & Davidson, J. E. (Eds.). (2005). *Conceptions of giftedness* (2nd ed.). New York, NY: Cambridge University Press.

Sternberg, R. J., & Grigorenko, E. L. (2002). *Dynamic testing: The nature and measurement of learning potential.* New York, NY: Cambridge University Press.

VanTassel-Baska, J. (2008). An overview of alternative assessment measures for gifted learners and the issues that surround their use. In J. VanTassel-Baska (Ed.), *Alternative assessments with gifted and talented students* (pp. 1–15). Washington, DC: National Association of Gifted Children.

VanTassel-Baska, J. (2008). Using performance-based assessments to document authentic learning. In J. VanTassel-Baska (Ed.), *Alternative assessments with gifted and talented students* (pp. 285–308). Washington, DC: National Association of Gifted Children.

Wiggins, G. (1993). *Assessing student performance: Exploring the purpose and limits of testing.* New York, NY: Jossey-Bass.

Practice-Based References

Avery, L., & VanTassel-Baska J. (2001). Investigating the impact of gifted education evaluation at state and local levels: Problems with traction. *Journal for the Education of the Gifted, 25,* 153–176.

Avery, L., VanTassel-Baska, J., & O'Neill, B (1997). Making evaluation work: One school district's model. *Gifted Child Quarterly, 41,* 28–37.

Belcher, R., & Fletcher-Carter, R. (1999). Growing gifted students in the desert: Using alternative, community-based assessment and an enriched curriculum. *Teaching Exceptional Children, 32,* 17–24.

Bohm, D. (2000, Fall). Gifted program evaluation in progress. *NRC/GT Newsletter,* 9–12.

Coleman, M. R., & Gallagher, J. J. (1994). *Updated report on state policies related to the identification of gifted students.* Chapel Hill: University of North Carolina, Gifted Education Policy Studies Program.

Green, J. E. (1993). *State academies for the academically gifted* (Fastback Series No. 349). Bloomington, IN: Phi Delta Kappa.

Hanna, G. S., & Dettmer, P. A. (2004). *Assessment for effective teaching: Using context-adaptive planning.* Boston, MA: Pearson.

Johnsen, S. K., & Ryser, G. R. (1997). The validity of portfolios in predicting performance in a gifted program. *Journal for the Education of the Gifted, 20,* 253–267.

Krisel, S. C., & Cowan, R. S. (1997). Georgia's journey towards multiple criteria identification of gifted students. *Roeper Review, 20,* A1–3.

Olszewski-Kubilius, P., & Kulieke, M. (2008). Using off-level testing and assessment for gifted and talented students. In J. VanTassel-Baska (Ed.). *Alternative assessments with gifted and talented students* (pp. 89–106). Waco, TX: Prufrock Press.

Renzulli, J. S., & Reis, S. M. (1986). The Enrichment Triad/Revolving Door Model: A schoolwide plan for the development of creative productivity. In J. S. Renzulli (Ed.) *Systems and models for developing programs for the gifted and talented* (pp. 215–266). Mansfield, CT: Creative Learning Press.

Reyes, E. I., Fletcher, R., & Paez, D. (1996). Developing local multidimensional screening procedures for identifying giftedness among Mexican American boarder population. *Roeper Review, 18,* 208–211.

VanTassel-Baska, J. Johnson, D., & Avery, L. D. (2002). Using performance tasks in the identification of economically disadvantaged and minority gifted learners: Findings from Project STAR. *Gifted Child Quarterly, 46,* 110–123.

Wright, L., & Borland, J. H. (1993). Using early childhood developmental portfolios in the identification and education of young, economically disadvantaged, potentially gifted students. *Roeper Review, 15,* 205–210.

Zorman, R. (1997). Eureka: The cross-cultural model for identification of hidden talents through enrichment. *Roeper Review, 20,* 54–61.

ELEMENT 1.2
Gifted education specialists monitor the progress of individuals with gifts and talents in the general education curriculum.

Research-Based References

Al-Hroub, A. (2010). Developing assessment profiles for mathematically gifted children with learning difficulties at three schools in Cambridgeshire, England. *Journal for the Education of the Gifted, 34,* 7–44.

Assouline, S. G., Foley Nicpon, M., & Whiteman, C. (2010). Cognitive and psychosocial characteristics of gifted students with written language disability. *Gifted Child Quarterly, 54,* 102–115.

Geary, D. C., & Brown, S. C. (1991). Cognitive addition: Strategy choice and speed-of-processing difference in gifted, normal, and mathematically disabled children. *Developmental Psychology, 27,* 398–406.

Theory-Based References

Coleman, M. R., & Johnsen, S. K. (Eds.). (2013). *Implementing RtI with gifted students: Service models, trends, and issues.* Waco, TX: Prufrock Press.

Kanevsky, L. (2000). Dynamic assessment of gifted learners. In K. A. Heller, F. J. Mönks, R. J. Sternberg, & R. F. Subotnik (Eds.), *International handbook of giftedness and talent* (2nd ed., pp. 283–295). New York, NY: Pergamon.

VanTassel-Baska, J. (2002). Assessment of gifted student learning in the language arts. *Journal of Secondary Gifted Education, 13,* 67–72.

Practice-Based References

Coleman, M. R., & Johnsen, S. K. (Eds.). (2011). *RtI for gifted students.* Waco, TX: Prufrock Press.

Johnsen, S. K., Sulak, T., & Rollins, K. (2012). *Serving gifted students within an RtI framework.* Waco, TX: Prufrock Press.

Reis, S. M., Burns, D. E., & Renzulli, J. S. (1992). *Curriculum compacting: The complete guide to modifying the regular curriculum for high ability students.* Waco, TX: Prufrock Press.

Advanced Preparation Standard 2: Curricular Content Knowledge

Gifted education specialists use their knowledge of general[8] and specialized[9] curricula to improve programs, supports, and services at classroom, school, community, and system levels.

ELEMENT 2.1
Gifted education specialists align educational standards to provide access to challenging curriculum to meet the needs of individuals with exceptionalities.

Research-Based References

Ford, D. Y., & Harmon, D. A. (2001). Equity and excellence: Providing access to gifted education for culturally diverse students. *Journal of Secondary Gifted Education, 12,* 141–148.

Johnson, D. T., Boyce, L. N., & VanTassel-Baska, J. (1995). Science curriculum review: Evaluating materials for high-ability learners. *Gifted Child Quarterly, 39,* 36–45.

Theory-Based References

Baker, E. L., & Schacter, J. (1996). Expert benchmarks for student academic performance: The case for gifted children. *Gifted Child Quarterly, 40,* 61–65.

Landrum, M. S., Callahan, C. M., & Shaklee, B. D. (2001). *Aiming for excellence: Gifted program standards.* Waco, TX: Prufrock Press.

National Association for Gifted Children. (2010). *NAGC pre-K–grade 12 gifted programming standards: A blueprint for quality gifted education programs.* Washington, DC: Author.

Renzulli, J. S. (2001). Standards and standards plus: A good idea or a new cage? *Journal of Secondary Gifted Education, 7,* 139–140.

VanTassel-Baska, J. (2005). *Acceleration strategies for teaching gifted learners.* Waco, TX: Prufrock Press.

---

8   As used, "general curricula" means the academic content of the general curriculum including math, reading, English/language arts, science, social studies, and the arts.

9   As used, "specialized curricula" means the content of specialized interventions or sets of interventions including, but not limited to academic, strategic, communicative, social, emotional, and independence curricula.

VanTassel-Baska, J., & Stambaugh, T. (2006). *Comprehensive curriculum for gifted learners* (3rd ed.). Boston, MA: Allyn & Bacon.

Practice-Based References

National Association for Gifted Children. (2010). *NAGC pre-K–grade 12 gifted programming standards: A blueprint for quality gifted education programs.* Washington, DC: Author.

Purcell, J. H., Burns, D. E., Tomlinson, C. A., Imbeau, M. B., & Martin, J. L. (2002). Bridging the gap: A tool and technique to analyze and evaluate gifted education curricular units. *Gifted Child Quarterly, 46,* 306–338.

Tomlinson, C. A. (2000). Reconcilable differences? Standards-based teaching and differentiation. *Educational Leadership, 58*(1), 6–11.

ELEMENT 2.2

Gifted educators continuously broaden and deepen professional knowledge, and expand expertise with instructional technologies, curriculum standards, effective teaching strategies, and assistive technologies to support access to and learning of challenging content.

Research-Based References

Colangelo, N., Assouline, S. G., & Gross, M. U. M. (2004). *A nation deceived: How schools hold back America's brightest students* (Vol. II). Iowa City: University of Iowa, The Connie Belin and Jacqueline N. Blank International Center for Gifted Education and Talent Development.

Lubinski, D., & Benbow, C. P. (1995). The study of mathematically precocious youth: The first three decades of a planned 50-year study of intellectual talent. In R. F. Subotnik & K. D. Arnold (Eds.), *Beyond Terman: Contemporary longitudinal studies of giftedness and talent* (pp. 255–289). Norwood, NJ: Albex.

Stamps, L. (2004). The effectiveness of curriculum compacting in first grade classrooms. *Roeper Review, 27,* 31–41.

Stronge, J. (2002). *Qualities of effective teachers.* Alexandria, VA: Association for Supervision and Curriculum Development.

Theory-Based References

Davis, G. A., Rimm, S. B., & Siegle, D. (2010). *Education of the gifted and talented* (6th ed.). Essex, England: Pearson Education Limited.

Karnes, F. A., & Bean, S. M. (2015). (Eds.). *Methods and materials for teaching the gifted* (4th ed.). Waco, TX: Prufrock Press.

Paul, R., & Elder, L. (2002). *Critical thinking: Tools for taking charge of your professional and personal life.* New York, NY: Prentice Hall.

Sheffield, L. (2003). *Extending the challenge in mathematics: Developing mathematical promise in K–8 students.* Thousand Oaks, CA: Corwin Press.

VanTassel-Baska, J., & Little, C. A. (Eds.). (2003). *Content-based curriculum for gifted learners.* Waco, TX: Prufrock Press.

Practice-Based References

Johnsen, S. K., & Sheffield, L. J. (Eds.). (2013). *Using the Common Core State Standards for mathematics with gifted and advanced learners.* Waco, TX: Prufrock Press.

Renzulli, J. S., Leppien, J. H., & Hays, T. S. (2000). *The multiple menu model: A practical guide for developing differentiated curriculum.* Waco, TX: Prufrock Press.

Renzulli, J. S., & Reis, S. (2004). Curriculum compacting: A research-based differentiation strategy for culturally diverse talented students. In D. Boothe & J. C. Stanley (Eds.), *In the eyes of the beholder: Critical issues for diversity in gifted education* (pp. 87–100). Waco, TX: Prufrock Press.

Tomlinson, C. A., & Cunningham-Eidson, C. (2003). *Differentiation in practice: A resource guide for differentiating curriculum, grades K–5.* Alexandria, VA: Association for Supervision and Curriculum Development.

Tomlinson, C. A., Kaplan, S. N., Renzulli, J., Burns, D. E., Leppien, J. H., & Purcell, J. H. (2001). *The parallel curriculum: A model for planning curriculum for gifted students and whole classrooms.* Thousand Oaks, CA: Corwin Press.

VanTassel-Baska, J. (Ed.). *Using the Common Core State Standards for English language arts with gifted and advanced learners.* Waco, TX: Prufrock Press.

ELEMENT 2.3
Gifted education specialists use understanding of diversity and individual learning differences to inform the selection, development, and implementation of comprehensive curricula for individuals with exceptionalities.

Research-Based References

Clasen, D. R. (2006). Project STREAM: A 13-year follow-up of a pre-college program for middle- and high-school underrepresented gifted. *Roeper Review, 29*, 55–63.

de Wet, C. F., & Gubbins, E. (2011). Teachers' beliefs about culturally, linguistically, and economically diverse gifted students: A quantitative study. *Roeper Review, 33*, 97–108.

Grantham, T. C. (2004). Rocky Jones: Case study of a high-achieving Black male's motivation to participate in gifted classes. *Roeper Review, 26*, 208–216.

Hannah, C. L., & Shore, B. M. (1995). Metacognition and high intellectual ability: Insights from the study of learning-disabled gifted students. *Gifted Child Quarterly, 39*, 95–109.

Kaylor, M., & Flores, M. M. (2007). Increasing academic motivation in culturally and linguistically diverse students from low socioeconomic backgrounds. *Journal of Advanced Academics, 19*, 66–89.

Theory-Based References

Anderson, L. W., & Krathwohl, D. R. (Eds.). (2001). *A taxonomy for learning, teaching, and assessing: A revision of Bloom's taxonomy of educational objectives.* New York, NY: Longman.

Ford, D. (1996). *Reversing underachievement among gifted Black students: Promising practices and programs.* New York, NY: Teachers College Press.

Steiner, H. H. & Carr, M. (2003). Cognitive development in gifted children: Toward a more precise understanding of emerging differences in intelligence. *Educational Psychology Review, 15*, 215–246.

VanTassel-Baska, J. (2003). *Content-based curriculum for low income and minority gifted learners* (RM03180). Storrs: University of Connecticut, The National Research Center on the Gifted and Talented.

Practice-Based References

Coates, D. L., Perkins, T., Vietze, P., Reyes Cruz, M., & Park, S. (2003). *Teaching thinking to culturally diverse, high ability, high school students: A triarchic approach* (RM03174). Storrs: University of Connecticut, The National Research Center on the Gifted and Talented.

Clark, G., & Zimmerman, E. (1997). *Project ARTS: Programs for ethnically diverse, economically disadvantaged, high ability, visual arts students in rural communities: Identification, curriculum, evaluation.* (ERIC Document Reproduction Service ED 419765)

Elder, L., & Paul, R. (2003). *Analytic thinking: How to take thinking apart and what to look for when you do.* Dillon Beach, CA: The Foundation for Critical Thinking.

Elder, L., & Paul, R. (2004). *The art of asking essential questions.* Dillon Beach, CA: The Foundation for Critical Thinking.

Granada, J. (2002). Addressing the curriculum, instruction, and assessment needs of the gifted bilingual/bicultural student. In J. A. Castellano & E. I. Diaz (Eds.). *Reaching new horizons: Gifted and talented education for culturally and linguistically diverse students.* Boston, MA: Allyn & Bacon.

Advanced Preparation Standard 3: Programs, Services, and Outcomes

Gifted education specialists facilitate the continuous improvement of general and gifted education programs, supports, and services at the classroom, school, and system levels for individuals with exceptionalities.

ELEMENT 3.1
Gifted education specialists design and implement evaluation activities to improve programs, supports, and services for individuals with exceptionalities.

Research-Based References

Henfield, M. S., Moore, J. L., & Wood, C. (2008). Inside and outside gifted education programming: Hidden challenges for African American students. *Exceptional Children, 74,* 433–450.

Matthews, D., & Kitchen, J. (2007). School-within-a-school gifted programs: Perceptions of students and teachers in public secondary schools. *Gifted Child Quarterly, 51,* 256–271.

Stahl, N. N., & Stahl, R. J. (1991). We can agree after all! Achieving consensus for a critical thinking component of a gifted program using the Delphi technique. *Roeper Review, 14,* 79–88.

Tyler-Wood, T. L., Mortenson, M., Putney, D., & Cass, M. A. (2000). An effective mathematics and science curriculum option for secondary gifted education. *Roeper Review, 22,* 266–269.

VanTassel-Baska, J., Bass, G., Ries, R., Poland, D., & Avery, L. D. (1998). A national study of science curriculum effectiveness with high ability students. *Gifted Child Quarterly, 42,* 200–211.

VanTassel-Baska, J., Zuo, L., Avery, L. D., & Little, C. A. (2002). A curriculum study of gifted-student learning in the language arts. *Gifted Child Quarterly, 46,* 30–44.

Vaughn, V. L., Feldhusen, J. F., & Asher, J. W. (1991). Meta-analyses and review of research on pull-out programs in gifted education. *Gifted Child Quarterly, 35,* 92–98.

Theory-Based References

Ford, D. Y., & Harris, J. J., III. (2000). A framework for infusing multicultural curriculum into gifted education. *Roeper Review, 23,* 4–10.

Jolly, J. (2009). A resuscitation of gifted education. *American Educational History Journal, 36,* 37–52.

Renzulli, J. S., & Reis, S. M. (1991). The reform movement and the quiet crisis in gifted education. *Gifted Child Quarterly, 35,* 26–35.

Treffinger, D. J., & Isaksen, S. G. (2005). Creative problem solving: The history, development, and implications for gifted education and talent development. *Gifted Child Quarterly, 49,* 342–353.

VanTassel-Baska, J. (Ed.). (2004). *Curriculum for gifted and talented students.* Thousand Oaks, CA: Corwin.

Practice-Based References

Gentry, M. (2009). Myth 11: A comprehensive continuum of gifted education and talent development services—Discovering, developing, and enhancing young people's gifts and talents. *Gifted Child Quarterly, 53,* 262–265.

Gentry, M. (with K. Ayers Paul, J. McIntosh, C. Matthew Fugate, & E. Jen). (2014). *Total school cluster grouping & differentiation: A comprehensive, research-based plan for raising student achievement & improving teacher practices.* Waco, TX: Prufrock Press.

VanTassel-Baska, J. (2006). A content analysis of evaluation findings across 20 gifted programs: A clarion call for enhanced gifted program development. *Gifted Child Quarterly, 50,* 199–215.

> ## ELEMENT 3.2
> **Gifted education specialists use their understanding of cultural, social, and economic diversity and individual learner differences to inform the development and improvement of programs, supports, and services for individuals with exceptionalities.**

Research-Based References

Byers, J. A., Whitsell, S. S., & Moon, S. M. (2004). Gifted students' perceptions of the academic and social/emotional effects of homogeneous and heterogeneous grouping. *Gifted Child Quarterly, 48,* 7–23.

Uresti, R., Goertz, J., & Bernal, E. M. (2002). Maximizing achievement for potentially gifted and talented and regular minority students in a primary classroom. *Roeper Review, 25,* 27–31.

Theory-Based References

Boothe, D., & Stanley, J. C. (Eds.). (2004). *In the eyes of the beholder: Critical issues for diversity in gifted education.* Waco, TX: Prufrock Press.

Ford, D. (1996). *Reversing underachievement among gifted Black students: Promising practices and programs.* New York, NY: Teachers College Press.

VanTassel-Baska, J. (2003). *Content-based curriculum for low income and minority gifted learners* (RM03180). Storrs: University of Connecticut, The National Research Center on the Gifted and Talented.

Winzer, M. A., & Mazurak, K. (2000). *Special education in multicultural contexts.* Upper Saddle River, NJ: Prentice Hall.

Practice-Based References

Clark, G., & Zimmerman, E. (1997). *Project ARTS: Programs for ethnically diverse, economically disadvantaged, high ability, visual arts students in rural communities: Identification, curriculum, evaluation.* (ERIC Document Reproduction Service ED 419765)

Granada, J. (2002). Addressing the curriculum, instruction, and assessment needs of the gifted bilingual/bicultural students. In J. A. Castellano & E. I. Diaz (Eds.), *Reaching new horizons: Gifted and talented education for cul-*

turally and linguistically diverse students (pp. 130–153). Boston, MA: Allyn & Bacon.

ELEMENT 3.3
Gifted education specialists apply knowledge of theories, evidence-based practices, and relevant laws to advocate for programs, supports, and services for individuals with exceptionalities.

Research-Based References

Grantham, T. C. (2003). Increasing Black student enrollment in gifted programs: An exploration of the Pulaski county special school district's advocacy efforts. *Gifted Child Quarterly, 47,* 46–65.

Robinson, A., & Moon, S. M. (2003). A national study of local and state advocacy in gifted education. *Gifted Child Quarterly, 47,* 8–25.

Theory-Based References

Gallagher, J. (2002). *Society's role in educating gifted students: The role of public policy* (RM02162). Storrs: University of Connecticut, The National Research Center on the Gifted and Talented.

Plucker, J. A., & Callahan, C. M. (Eds.). (2008). *Critical issues and practices in gifted education: What the research says.* Waco, TX: Prufrock Press.

Robinson, N. M. (2002). *Assessing and advocating for gifted students: Perspectives for school and clinical psychologists* (RM02166). Storrs: University of Connecticut, The National Research Center on the Gifted and Talented.

Zirkel, P. A. (2003). *The law on gifted education* (RM03178). Storrs: University of Connecticut, The National Research Center on the Gifted and Talented.

Practice-Based References

Berger, S. (2001). G + advocacy = gifted. *Understanding our Gifted, 13*(3), 25–28.

Hertzog, N. B. (2003). Advocacy: "On the cutting edge . . ." *Gifted Child Quarterly, 47,* 66–81.

Ridges, J. (2000). Advocate role in developing district policy for gifted students. *Roeper Review, 22,* 199–201.

ELEMENT 3.4
Gifted education specialists design and develop systematic program and curriculum models for enhancing talent development in multiple settings.

Research-Based References

Briggs, C. J., Reis, S. M., & Sullivan, E. E. (2008). A national view of promising programs and practices for culturally, linguistically, and ethnically diverse gifted and talented students. *Gifted Child Quarterly, 52*, 131–145.

Feng, A. X., VanTassel-Baska, J., Quek, C., Bai, W., & O'Neill, B. (2005). A longitudinal assessment of gifted students' learning using the integrated curriculum model (ICM): impacts and perceptions of the William and Mary language arts and science curriculum. *Roeper Review, 27*, 78–83.

Gentry, M., Hu, S., & Peters, S. (2008). Talented students in an exemplary career and technical education school. *Gifted Child Quarterly, 52*, 183–198.

Linn-Cohen, R., & Hertzog, N.B. (2007). Unlocking the GATE to differentiation: A qualitative study of two self-contained gifted classes. *Journal for the Education of the Gifted, 31*, 227–259.

Little, C. A., Feng, A. X., VanTassel-Baska, J., Rogers, K. B., & Avery, L. D. (2007). A study of curriculum effectiveness in social studies. *Gifted Child Quarterly, 51*, 272–284.

Moon, T. R., & Callahan, C. M. (2001). Curricular modifications, family outreach, and a mentoring program: Impacts on achievement and gifted identification in high-risk primary students. *Journal for the Education of the Gifted, 24*, 305–321.

VanTassel-Baska, J., Johnson, D. T., Hughes, C., & Boyce, L. N. (1996). A study of language arts curriculum effectiveness with gifted learners. *Journal for the Education of the Gifted, 19*, 461–480.

Theory-Based References

Dettmer, P. (1993). Gifted education: Window of opportunity. *Gifted Child Quarterly, 37*, 92–94.

Marsh, H. W., Seaton, M., Trautwein, U., Lüdtke, O., Hau, K. T., O'Mara, A. J., & Craven, R. G. (2008). The big-fish-little-pond-effect stands up to critical scrutiny: Implications for theory, methodology, and future research. *Educational Psychology Review, 20*, 319–350.

VanTassel-Baska, J. (1998). The development of academic talent: A mandate for educational best practice. *Phi Delta Kappan, 79*, 760–763.

VanTassel-Baska, J., & Feng, A. X. (Eds.). (2004). *Designing and utilizing evaluation for gifted program improvement.* Waco, TX: Prufrock Press.

Practice-Based References

Tomlinson, C. A. (2005). Quality curriculum and instruction for highly able students. *Theory into Practice, 44,* 160–167.

VanTassel-Baska, J., & Brown, E. (2007). Toward best practice: An analysis of the efficacy of curriculum models in gifted education. *Gifted Child Quarterly, 50,* 342–358.

VanTassel-Baska, J., & Stambaugh, T. (2005). Challenges and possibilities for serving gifted learners in the regular classroom. *Theory into Practice, 44,* 211–218.

ELEMENT 3.5
Gifted education specialists evaluate progress toward achieving the vision, mission, and goals of programs, services, and supports for individuals with exceptionalities.

Research-Based References

Hertzog, N. B., & Fowler, S. A. (1999). Perspectives: Evaluating an early childhood gifted education program. *Roeper Review, 21,* 222–227.

Johnsen, S. K. (2000). What the research says about accountability and program evaluation. *Tempo, 20*(4), 23–30.

Swiatek, M. A., & Lupkowski-Shoplik, A. (2005). An evaluation of the elementary student talent search by families and schools. *Gifted Child Quarterly, 49,* 247–259.

VanTassel-Baska, J. (2006). A content analysis of evaluation findings across 20 gifted programs: A clarion call for enhanced gifted program development. *Gifted Child Quarterly, 50,* 199–215.

VanTassel-Baska, J., Avery, L. D., Little, C., & Hughes, C. (2000). An evaluation of the implementation of curriculum innovation: The impact of the William and Mary units on schools. *Journal for the Education of the Gifted, 23,* 244–272.

Theory-Based References

Callahan, C., & Reis, S. (2004). *Program evaluation in gifted education.* Thousand Oaks, CA: Corwin Press.

Johnsen, S. K. (Ed.). (2012). *NAGC pre–K–grade 12 gifted education program-ming standards: A guide to planning and implementing high-quality services.* Waco, TX: Prufrock Press.

Practice-Based References

Callahan, C. M. (2005). Making the grade or achieving the goal? Evaluating learner and program outcomes in gifted education. In F. A. Karnes & S. M. Bean (Eds.), *Methods and materials for teaching the gifted* (2nd ed., pp. 211–246). Waco, TX: Prufrock Press.

Coleman, M. R., & Johnsen, S. K. (Eds.). (2011). *RtI for gifted students.* Waco, TX: Prufrock Press.

Johnsen, S. K., Sulak, T., & Rollins, K. (2012). *Serving gifted students within an RtI framework.* Waco, TX: Prufrock Press.

Purcell, J. H., Burns, D. E., Tomlinson C. A., Imbeau, M. B., & Martin, J. L. (2002). Bridging the gap: A tool and technique to analyze and evaluate gifted education curricular units. *Gifted Child Quarterly, 46,* 306–321.

Advanced Preparation Standard 4: Research and Inquiry

Gifted education specialists conduct, evaluate, and use inquiry to guide professional practice.

ELEMENT 4.1
Gifted education specialists evaluate research and inquiry to identify effective practices.

Research-Based References

Bain, S., Bourgeois, S., & Pappas, D. (2003). Linking theoretical models to actual practices: A survey of teachers in gifted education. *Roeper Review, 25,* 166–172.

Hansen, J. B., & Feldhusen, J. F. (1994). Comparison of trained and untrained teachers of gifted students. *Gifted Child Quarterly, 38,* 115–123.

Jatko, B. P. (1995). Action research and practical inquiry: Using a whole class tryout procedure for identifying economically disadvantaged students in three socioeconomically diverse schools. *Journal for the Education of the Gifted, 19,* 83–105.

Kitano, M. K., & Pedersen, K. S. (2002). Action research and practical inquiry: Multicultural-content integration in gifted education: Lessons from the field. *Journal for the Education of the Gifted, 26,* 269–289.

Kitano, M. K., & Pedersen, K. S. (2002). Action research and practical inquiry: Teaching gifted English learners. *Journal for the Education of the Gifted, 26,* 132–147.

Theory-Based References

Buchanan, N. K., & Feldhusen, J. F. (Eds.). (1991). *Conducting research and evaluation in gifted education: A handbook of methods and applications.* New York, NY: Teachers College Press.

Harris, A. (1998). Effective teaching: A review of the literature. *School Leadership and Management, 18,* 169–183.

Practice-Based References

Gubbins, E. J., Westberg, K. L., Reis, S. M., Dinnocenti, S. T., Tieso, C. L., & Muller, L. M., . . . Burns, D. E. (2002). *Implementing a professional development model using gifted education strategies with all students* (RM02172). Storrs: University of Connecticut, The National Research Center on the Gifted and Talented.

Kane, J., & Henning, J. E. (2004). A case study of the collaboration in mathematics between a fourth-grade teacher and a talented and gifted coordinator. *Journal for the Education of the Gifted, 27,* 243–266.

ELEMENT 4.2
Gifted education specialists use knowledge of the professional literature to improve practices with individuals with exceptionalities and their families.

Research-Based References

Friedman, R. C., & Lee, S. W. (1996). Differentiating instruction for high-achieving/gifted children in regular classrooms: A field test of three gifted-education models. *Journal for the Education of the Gifted, 19,* 405–436.

Gentry, M., & Owen, S. V. (1999). An investigation of the effects of total school flexible cluster grouping on identification, achievement, and classroom practices. *Gifted Child Quarterly, 43,* 224–243.

Reis, S. M., Westberg, K. L., Kulikowich, J. M., & Purcell, J. H. (1998). Curriculum compacting and achievement test scores: What does the research say? *Gifted Child Quarterly, 42*, 123–129.

Theory-Based References

Avery, L. D., & Zuo, L. (2003). Selecting resources and materials for high-ability learners. In J. VanTassel-Baska & C. A. Little (Eds.), *Content-based curriculum for high-ability learners* (pp. 259–278). Waco, TX: Prufrock Press.

Harris, A. (1998). Effective teaching: A review of the literature. *School Leadership and Management, 18*, 169–183.

Kirschenbaum, R. J. (2004). Dynamic assessment and its use with underserved gifted and talented populations. In A. Baldwin, & S. Reis (Eds.), *Culturally diverse and underserved populations of gifted students. Essential reading in gifted education* (pp. 49–62). Thousand Oaks, CA: Corwin Press.

Purcell, J. H., Burns, D. E., Tomlinson, C. A., Imbeau, M. B., & Martin, J. L. (2002). Bridging the gap: A tool and technique to analyze and evaluate gifted education curricular units. *Gifted Child Quarterly, 46*, 306–338.

Tomlinson, C. A. (1995). Action research and practical inquiry: An overview and an invitation to teachers of gifted learners. *Journal for the Education of the Gifted, 18*, 467–484.

Practice-Based References

Joffe, W. S. (2001). Investigating the acquisition of pedagogical knowledge: Interviews with a beginning teacher of the gifted. *Roeper Review, 23*, 219–225.

Kitano, M. K., & Pedersen, K. S. (2002). Action research and practical inquiry: Multicultural content integration in gifted education: Lessons from the field. *Journal for the Education of the Gifted, 25*, 269–289.

Kitano, M. K., & Pedersen, K. S. (2002). Action research and practical inquiry: Teaching gifted English learners. *Journal for the Education of the Gifted, 26*, 123–147.

Riley, T. R. (2005). Teaching on a shoestring: Materials for teaching gifted and talented students. In F. A. Karnes & S. M. Bean (Eds.), *Methods and materials for teaching the gifted* (2nd ed., pp. 657–700). Waco, TX: Prufrock Press.

ELEMENT 4.3
Gifted education specialists evaluate and modify instructional practices in response to ongoing assessment data and engage in the design and implementation of research and inquiry.

Research-Based References

Guskey, T. (1998, April). *Teacher efficacy measurement and change.* Paper presented at the annual meeting of the American Educational Research Association, San Diego, CA. (ERIC Document Reproduction Service No. ED422396)

Jolly, J. L., & Kettler, T. (2008). Gifted education research 1994–2003: A disconnect between priorities and practice. *Journal for the Education of the Gifted, 31,* 427–446.

Kulik, J. A., & Kulik, C. C. (1992). Meta-analytic findings on grouping programs. *Gifted Child Quarterly, 36,* 73–77.

Robinson, A., Shore, B. M., & Enersen, D. L. (2007). *Best practices in gifted education: An evidence-based guide.* Waco, TX: Prufrock Press.

Rogers, K. B. (1991). *The relationship of grouping practices to the education of the gifted and talented learner* (RBDM9102). Storrs: University of Connecticut, The National Research Center on the Gifted and Talented.

Shore, B. M., & Delcourt, M. A. (1996). Effective curricular and program practices in gifted education and the interface with general education. *Journal for the Education of the Gifted, 20,* 138–154.

Vaughn, V. L., Feldhusen, J. F., & Asher, J. W. (1991). Meta-analyses and review of research on pull-out programs in gifted education. *Gifted Child Quarterly, 35,* 92–98.

Theory-Based References

Asher, W. (2003). Meta-analysis and gifted education. *Journal for the Education of the Gifted, 27,* 7–19.

Bickman, L., & Rog, D. J. (Eds.). (1998). *Handbook of applied research methods.* Thousand Oaks, CA: Sage.

Colangelo, N., Assouline, S., & Gross, M. (2004). *A nation deceived: How schools hold back America's brightest students* (Vol. II). Iowa City: University of Iowa, The Connie Belin and Jacqueline N. Blank International Center for Gifted Education and Talent Development.

Dana, N. F., & Hoppey, D. Y. (2009). *The reflective educator's guide to classroom research* (2nd ed.). Thousand Oaks, CA: Corwin Press.

Koshy, V., & Welham, C. (2008). Nurturing young gifted and children: Teachers generating knowledge. *Perspectives in Education, 26*(2), 67–79.

Mendaglio, S. (2003). Qualitative case study in gifted education. *Journal for the Education of the Gifted, 26,* 163–183.

Patton, M. Q. (2002). *Qualitative research and evaluation methods* (3rd ed.). Thousand Oaks, CA: Sage.

Practice-Based References

Hughes, L. (1999). Action research and practical inquiry: How can I meet the needs of the high-ability student within my regular education classroom? *Journal for the Education of the Gifted, 22,* 282–297.

Jatko, B. P. (1995). Action research and practical inquiry: Using a whole class tryout procedure for identifying economically disadvantaged students in three socioeconomically diverse schools. *Journal for the Education of the Gifted, 19,* 83–105.

Stronge, J. (2002). *Qualities of effective teachers.* Alexandria, VA: ASCD.

Advanced Preparation Standard 5: Leadership and Policy

Gifted education specialists provide leadership to formulate goals, set and meet high professional expectations, advocate for effective policies and evidence-based practices, and create positive and productive work environments.

ELEMENT 5.1
Gifted education specialists encourage high expectations, model respect for, and use ethical practices with all individuals with exceptionalities.

Research-Based References

Cross, T. L., Stewart, R. A., & Coleman, L. (2003). Phenomenology and its implications for gifted studies research: Investigating the lebenswelt of academically gifted students attending an elementary magnet school. *Journal for the Education of the Gifted, 26,* 201–220.

den Brok, P., Levy, J., Rodriguez, R., & Wubbels, T. (2002). Perceptions of Asian-American and Hispanic American teachers and their students on teacher interpersonal communication style. *Teaching and Teacher Education, 18*, 447–467.

Landrum, M. (2001). An evaluation of the catalyst program: Consultation and collaboration in gifted education. *Gifted Child Quarterly, 45*, 139–151.

Purcell, J. H., & Leppien, J. H. (1998). Building bridges between general practitioners and educators of the gifted: A study of collaboration. *Gifted Child Quarterly, 42*, 172–181.

Scot, T. P., Callahan, C. M., & Urquhart, J. (2008). Paint-by-number teachers and cookie-cutter students: The unintended effects of high-stakes testing on the education of gifted students. *Roeper Review, 31*, 40–52.

Theory-Based References

Ambrose, D. (2003). Barriers to aspiration development and self-fulfillment: Interdisciplinary insights for talent discovery. *Gifted Child Quarterly, 47*, 282–294.

Castellano, J. A., & Pinkos, M. (2005). A rationale for connecting dual language programs with gifted education. In V. Gonzalez & J. Tinajero (Eds.), *Review of research and practice* (Vol. 3, pp. 107–124). Mahwah, NJ: Lawrence Erlbaum Associates.

Dweck, C. S., & Kamins, M. L. (1999). Person versus process praise and criticism: Implications for contingent self-worth and coping. *Developmental Psychology, 35*, 835–47.

Tomlinson, C., & Allan, S. (2000). *Leadership for differentiating schools and classrooms*. Alexandria, VA: Association for Supervision and Curriculum Development.

Practice-Based References

Cooper, C. R. (1998). For the good of humankind: Matching the budding talent with a curriculum of conscience. *Gifted Child Quarterly, 42*, 238–244.

Copenhaver, J. (2002). *Primer for maintaining accurate special education records and meeting confidentiality requirements when serving children with disabilities—Family Educational Rights and Privacy Act* (FERPA). Logan: Utah State University, Mountain Plains Regional Resource Center.

Klein, J. P., & Lugg, E. T. (2002). Nurturing young adolescents legally and ethically. *Middle School Journal, 34*(1), 13–20.

ELEMENT 5.2
Gifted education specialists support and use linguistically and culturally responsive practices.

Research-Based References

Harmon, D. (2002). They won't teach me: the voices of gifted African American inner-city students. *Roeper Review, 24,* 68–75.

Kitano, M. K., & Lewis, R. B. (2005). Resilience and coping: Implications for gifted children and youth at risk. *Roeper Review, 27,* 200–205.

Masten, W. G., & Plata, M. (2000). Acculturation and teacher ratings of Hispanic and Anglo-American students. *Roeper Review, 23,* 45–46.

Zirkel, S. (2008). The influence of multicultural educational practices on student outcomes and intergroup relations. *Teachers College Record, 110,* 1147–1181.

Theory-Based References

Bernal, E. M. (2000). The quintessential features of gifted education as seen from a multicultural perspective. In G. B. Esquivel & J. C. Houtz (Eds.), *Creativity and giftedness in culturally diverse students* (pp. 159–191). Cresskill, NJ: Harrington Press.

Boothe, D., & Stanley, J. C. (Eds.). (2004). *In the eyes of the beholder: Critical issues for diversity in gifted education.* Waco, TX: Prufrock Press.

Castellano, J. A., & Diaz, E. I. (2002). *Reaching new horizons: Gifted and talented education for culturally and linguistically diverse students.* Boston, MA: Allyn and Bacon.

Ford, D., Tyson, C., Howard, T., & Harris, J. J., III. (2000). Multicultural literature and gifted Black students: Promoting self-understanding, awareness, and pride. *Roeper Review, 22,* 235–240.

Practice-Based References

Coleman, L. (2006). Talent development in economically disadvantaged populations. *Gifted Child Today, 29*(2), 22–27.

Harper, S. R., & Antonio, A. (2008). Not by accident: Intentionality in diversity, learning and engagement. In S. R. Harper (Ed.), *Creating inclusive campus environments for cross-cultural learning and student engagement* (pp. 1–18). Washington, DC: National Association of Student Personnel Administrators.

Ingram, M. A. (2003). Sociocultural poetry to assist gifted students in developing empathy for the lived experiences of others. *Journal of Secondary Gifted Education, 14,* 83–90.

ELEMENT 5.3
Gifted education specialists create and maintain collegial and productive work environments that respect and safeguard the rights of individuals with exceptionalities and their families.

Research-Based References

Baker, B. D., & Friedman-Nimz, R. (2004). State policies and equal opportunity: The example of gifted education. *Education Evaluation and Policy Analysis, 26,* 39–64.

Brown, E., Avery, L., VanTassel-Baska, J., Worley, B., & Stambaugh, T. (2006). A five-state analysis of gifted education policies. *Roeper Review, 29,* 11–23.

Landrum, M. S., Katsiyannis, A., & DeWaard, J. (1998). A national survey of current legislative and policy trends in gifted education: Life after the National Excellence Report. *Journal for the Education of the Gifted, 21,* 352–371.

Robinson, A., & Moon, S. M. (2003). A national study by local and state advocacy in gifted education. *Gifted Child Quarterly, 47,* 8–25.

Theory-Based References

Gallagher, J. J. (2002). *Society's role in educating gifted students: The role of public policy* (RM02162). Storrs: University of Connecticut, The National Research Center on the Gifted and Talented.

Stephens, K. R. (2008). Applicable federal and state policy, law, and legal considerations in gifted education. In S. I. Pfeiffer (Ed.), *Handbook of giftedness in children: Psychoeducational theory, research, and best practice* (pp. 386–408). New York, NY: Springer Science+Business Media, LLC.

Practice-Based References

Clinkenbeard, P. R., Kolloff, P. B., & Lord, E. W. (2007). *A guide to state policies in gifted education* [CD-ROM]. Washington DC: National Association for Gifted Children.

Gallagher, J. J. (2004). No child left behind and gifted education. *Roeper Review, 26,* 121–123.

Stephens, K. R., & Karnes, F. A. (2000). State definitions for the gifted and talented revisited. *Exceptional Children, 66,* 219–238.

> ## ELEMENT 5.4
> **Gifted education specialists advocate for policies and practices that improve programs, services, and outcomes for individuals with exceptionalities.**

Research-Based References

Baker, B. D., & Friedman-Nimz, R. (2004). State policies and equal opportunity: The example of gifted education. *Education Evaluation and Policy Analysis, 26,* 39–64.

Brown, E., Avery, L., VanTassel-Baska, J., Worley, B., & Stambaugh, T. (2006). A five-state analysis of gifted education policies. *Roeper Review, 29,* 11–23.

Landrum, M. S., Katsiyannis, A., & DeWaard, J. (1998). A national survey of current legislative and policy trends in gifted education: Life after the National Excellence Report. *Journal for the Education of the Gifted, 21,* 352–371.

Robinson, A., & Moon, S. M. (2003). A national study by local and state advocacy in gifted education. *Gifted Child Quarterly, 47,* 8–25.

Theory-Based References

Gallagher, J. J. (2002). *Society's role in educating gifted students: The role of public policy* (RM02162). Storrs: University of Connecticut, The National Research Center on the Gifted and Talented.

Stephens, K. R. (2008). Applicable federal and state policy, law, and legal considerations in gifted education. In S. I. Pfeiffer (Ed.), *Handbook of giftedness in children: Psychoeducational theory, research, and best practice* (pp. 386–408). New York, NY: Springer Science+Business Media, LLC.

Practice-Based References

Clinkenbeard, P. R., Kolloff, P. B., & Lord, E. W. (2007). *A guide to state policies in gifted education* [CD-ROM]. Washington DC: National Association for Gifted Children.

Gallagher, J. J. (2004). No child left behind and gifted education. *Roeper Review, 26,* 121–123.

Grantham, T. C. (2003). Increasing Black student enrollment in gifted programs: An exploration of the Pulaski County special school district's advocacy efforts. *Gifted Child Quarterly, 47,* 46–65.

National Association for Gifted Children, & Council of State Directors of Programs for the Gifted. (2013). *2012–2013 state of the states in gifted education: National policy and practice data.* Washington, DC: Author.

ELEMENT 5.5

Gifted education specialists advocate for the allocation of appropriate resources for the preparation and professional development of all personnel who serve individuals with exceptionalities.

Research-Based References

Bain, S., Bourgeois, S., & Pappas, D. (2003). Linking theoretical models to actual practices: A survey of teachers in gifted education. *Roeper Review, 25,* 166–172.

Clark, C. M. (Ed.). (2001). *Talking shop: Authentic conversations and teacher learning.* New York, NY: Teachers College Press.

Garet, M. S., Porter, A. C., Desimone, L., Birman, B. F., & Yoon, K. S. (2001). What makes professional development effective? Results from a national sample of teachers. *American Educational Research Journal, 38,* 915–945.

Hansen, J. B., & Feldhusen, J. F. (1994). Comparison of trained and untrained teachers of gifted students. *Gifted Child Quarterly, 38,* 115–123.

Theory-Based References

Ancess, J. (2001). Teacher learning at the intersection of school learning and student outcomes. In A. Lieberman & L. Miller (Eds.), *Teachers caught in the action: Professional development that matters* (pp. 61–78). New York, NY: Teachers College Press.

Baker, B. D., & Friedman-Nimz, R. (2003). Gifted children, vertical equity, and state school finance policies and practices. *Journal of Education Finance, 28,* 523–555.

Clarke, D., & Hollingworth, H. (2002). Elaborating a model of teacher professional growth. *Teaching and Teacher Education, 18,* 947–967.

Practice-Based References

Callahan, C., Cooper, C., & Glascock, R. (2003). *Preparing teachers to develop and enhance talent: The position of national education organizations.* (ERIC Document Reproduction Services No. ED477882)

Falk, J. K., & Drayton, B. (Eds.). (2009). *Creating and sustaining online professional learning communities.* New York, NY: Teachers College Press.

Advanced Preparation Standard 6: Professional and Ethical Practice

Gifted education specialists use foundational knowledge of the field and professional Ethical Principles and Practice Standards to inform gifted education practice, engage in lifelong learning, advance the profession, and perform leadership responsibilities to promote the success of professional colleagues and individuals with exceptionalities.

ELEMENT 6.1
A comprehensive understanding of the history of gifted education, legal policies, ethical standards, and emerging issues informs gifted education specialist leadership.

Research-Based References

Baker, B. D., & McIntire, J. (2003). Evaluating state funding for gifted education programs. *Roeper Review, 25,* 173–179.

Karnes, F. A., & Marquardt, R. G. (2000). *Gifted children and legal issues: An update.* Scottsdale, AZ: Great Potential Press.

Moon, T. R., Brighton, C. M., & Callahan, C. M. (2003). State standardized testing programs: Friend or foe of gifted education. *Roeper Review, 25,* 49–60.

Theory-Based References

Hockett, J. A. (2009). Curriculum for highly able learners that conforms to general education and gifted education quality indicators. *Journal for the Education of the Gifted, 32,* 394–440.

Karnes, F. A., & Nugent, S. A. (2004). *Profiles of influence in gifted education: Historical perspectives and future directions.* Waco, TX: Prufrock Press.

Pfeiffer, S. I. (2003). Challenges and opportunities for students who are gifted: What the experts say. *Gifted Child Quarterly, 47,* 161–169.

Renzulli, J. S. (2002). Emerging conceptions of giftedness: Building a bridge to the new century. *Exceptionality, 10*(2), 67–75.

Sternberg, R. J., & Davidson, J. E. (Ed.). (2006). *Conceptions of giftedness.* New York, NY: Cambridge University Press.

Tannenbaum, A. (2000). A history of giftedness in school and society. In K. A. Heller, F. J. Mönks, R. J. Sternberg, & R. F. Subotnik (Eds.) *International handbook of giftedness and talent* (pp. 23–53). New York, NY: Elsevier.

Tomlinson, C. A., Coleman, M. R., Allan, S., Udall, A., & Landrum, M. (1996). Interface between gifted education and general education: Toward communication, cooperation, and collaboration. *Gifted Child Quarterly, 40,* 165–171.

Practice-Based References

Newman, J. L. (2008). Talents are unlimited: It's time to teach thinking skills again. *Gifted Child Today, 31*(3), 34–44.

ELEMENT 6.2
Gifted education specialists model high professional expectations and ethical practice, and create supportive environments that increase diversity at all levels of gifted and talented education.

Research-Based References

Grantham, T. C. (2004). Multicultural mentoring to increase Black male representation in gifted programs. *Gifted Child Quarterly, 48,* 232–245.

Speirs Neumeister, K. L., Adams, C. M., & Pierce, R. L. (2007). Fourth-grade teachers' perceptions of giftedness: Implications for identifying and serving diverse gifted students. *Journal for the Education of the Gifted, 30,* 479–499.

Theory-Based References

Baldwin, A. Y., & Vialle, W. (1999). *The many faces of giftedness: Lifting the mask.* Belmont, CA: Wadsworth.

Baum, S., & Owen, S. V. (2004). *To be gifted & learning disabled: Strategies for helping bright students with LD, ADHA, and more.* Mansfield Center, CT: Creative Learning Press.

Castellano, J. (2004). Empowering and serving Hispanic students in gifted education. In D. Boothe & J. C. Stanley (Eds.), *In the eyes of the beholder:*

Critical issues for diversity in gifted education (pp. 1–13). Waco, TX: Prufrock Press.

Ford, D. Y. (1996). *Reversing underachievement among gifted Black students.* New York, NY: Teachers College Press.

Ford, D. Y. (2003). Two other wrongs don't make a right: Sacrificing the needs of diverse students does not solve gifted education's unresolved problems. *Journal for the Education of the Gifted, 26,* 283–291.

Ford, D. Y., Grantham, T. C., & Milner, H. R. (2004). Underachievement among gifted African American students: Cultural, social, and psychological considerations. In D. Boothe & J. C. Stanley (Eds.), *In the eyes of the beholder: Critical issues for diversity in gifted education* (pp. 15–31). Waco, TX: Prufrock Press.

Ford, D. Y., Grantham, T. C., & Whiting, G. W. (2008). Culturally and linguistically diverse students in gifted education: Recruitment and retention issues. *Exceptional Children, 74,* 289–306.

Ford, D. Y., & Harris, J. J., III. (1999). *Multicultural gifted education.* New York, NY: Teachers College Press.

Ford, D. Y., & Trotman, M. F. (2001). Teachers of gifted students: Suggested multicultural characteristics and competencies. *Roeper Review, 23,* 235–239.

Gottfredson, L. S. (2004). Realities in desegregating gifted education. In D. Boothe & J. C. Stanley (Eds.), *In the eyes of the beholder: Critical issues for diversity in gifted education* (pp. 138–155). Waco, TX: Prufrock Press.

Klug, B. J. (2004). Children of the Starry Cope: Gifted and talented Native American students. In D. Boothe & J. C. Stanley (Eds.), *In the eyes of the beholder: Critical issues for diversity in gifted education* (pp. 49–71). Waco, TX: Prufrock Press.

Moore, J. L., Ford, D. Y., & Milner, H. R. (2005). Recruitment is not enough: Retaining African American students in gifted education. *Gifted Child Quarterly, 49,* 51–67.

Moore, J. L., Ford, D. Y., & Owens, D. (2006). Retention of African Americans in gifted education: Lessons learned from higher education. *Mid-Western Educational Researcher, 19*(2), 3–12.

National Research Council. (2002). *Minority students in special and gifted education.* Washington, DC: National Academy Press.

Renzulli, J. S., & Reis, S. M. (2004). Curriculum compacting: A research-based differentiation strategy for culturally diverse talented students. In D. Boothe & J. C. Stanley (Eds.), *In the eyes of the beholder: Critical issues for diversity in gifted education* (pp. 87–100). Waco, TX: Prufrock Press.

Sethna, B. N. (2004). An unconventional view of gifted children of Indian descent in the United States. In D. Boothe & J. C. Stanley (Eds.), *In the eyes of the beholder: Critical issues for diversity in gifted education* (pp. 101–117). Waco, TX: Prufrock Press.

Slocumb, P. D., & Payne R. K. (2000). *Removing the mask: Giftedness in poverty.* Highlands, TX: aha! Process.

Practice-Based References

Ford, D. Y., & Moore, J. L. (2004). Creating culturally responsive gifted education classrooms: Understanding "culture" is the first step. *Gifted Child Today, 27*(4), 34–39.

Matthews, D., Foster, J., Gladstone, D., Schieck, J., & Meiners, J. (2007). Supporting professionalism, diversity, and context within a collaborative approach to gifted education. *Journal of Educational & Psychological Consultation, 17,* 315–345.

Milner. H. R., & Ford, D. Y. (2005). Racial experiences influence us as teachers: Implications for gifted education curriculum development and implementation. *Roeper Review, 28,* 30–36.

Weber, C. L., Boswell, C., & Smith, D. (2008). Different paths to accountability: Defining rigorous outcomes for gifted learners. *Gifted Child Today, 31*(1), 54–65.

ELEMENT 6.3
Gifted education specialists model and promote respect for all individuals and facilitate ethical professional practice.

Research-Based References

Cross, T. L., Stewart, R. A., & Coleman, L. (2003). Phenomenology and its implications for gifted studies research: Investigating the lebenswelt of academically gifted students attending an elementary magnet school. *Journal for the Education of the Gifted, 26,* 201–220.

den Brok, P., Levy, J., Rodriguez, R., & Wubbels, T. (2002). Perceptions of Asian-American and Hispanic American teachers and their students on teacher interpersonal communication style. *Teaching and Teacher Education, 18,* 447–467.

Theory-Based References

Dweck, C. S., & Kamins, M. L. (1999). Person versus process praise and criticism: Implications for contingent self-worth and coping. *Developmental Psychology, 35,* 835–47.

Jackson, P. S. (2009). With Dabrowski in mind: Reinstating the outliers in support of full-spectrum development. *Roeper Review, 31,* 150–160.

Rogoff, B. (2003). *The cultural nature of human development.* New York, NY: Oxford University Press.

Practice-Based References

Copenhaver, J. (2002). *Primer for maintaining accurate special education records and meeting confidentiality requirements when serving children with disabilities—Family Educational Rights and Privacy Act (FERPA).* Logan: Utah State University, Mountain Plains Regional Resource Center.

Klein, J. P., & Lugg, E. T. (2002). Nurturing young adolescents legally and ethically. *Middle School Journal, 34*(1), 13–20.

ELEMENT 6.4
Gifted education specialists actively participate in professional development and learning communities to increase professional knowledge and expertise.

Research-Based References

Latz, A. O., Speirs Neumeister, K. L., Adams, C. A., & Pierce, R. L. (2009). Peer coaching to improve classroom differentiation: Perspectives from Project CLUE. *Roeper Review, 31,* 27–39.

VanTassel-Baska, J. (2006). A content analysis of evaluation findings across 20 gifted programs: A clarion call for enhanced gifted program development. *Gifted Child Quarterly, 50,* 199–210.

Theory-Based References

Dettmer, P., & Landrum, M. (Eds.). (1998). *Staff development: The key to effective gifted education programs.* Waco, TX: Prufrock Press.

Gubbins, E. J. (2008). Professional development. In J. Plucker & C. Callahan (Eds.), *Critical issues and practices in gifted education: What the research says* (pp. 535–562). Waco, TX: Prufrock Press.

Matthews, D. J., & Foster, J. F. (2005). *Being smart about gifted children.* Scottsdale, AZ: Great Potential Press.

Reis, S. M., & Westberg, K. L. (2003). The impact of staff development on teachers' ability to modify curriculum for gifted and talented students. *Gifted Child Quarterly, 38,* 127–135.

Strickland, C. A. (2009). *Professional development for differentiating instruction.* Alexandria, VA: Association for Supervision and Curriculum Development.

Tomlinson, C. A., & Allan, S. D. (2000). *Leadership for differentiating schools & classrooms.* Alexandria, VA: Association for Supervision and Curriculum Development.

Practice-Based References

Besnoy, K. (2007). Creating a personal technology improvement plan for teachers of the gifted. *Gifted Child Today, 30*(4), 44–48.

ELEMENT 6.5
Gifted education specialists plan, present, and evaluate professional development focusing on effective and ethical practice at all organizational levels.

Research-Based References

Bangel, N. J., Enersen, D., Capobianco, B., & Moon, S. M. (2006). Professional development of preservice teachers: Teaching in the Super Saturday Program. *Journal for the Education of the Gifted, 29,* 339–361.

Latz, A. O., Speirs Neumeister, K. L., Adams, C. A., & Pierce, R. L. (2009). Peer coaching to improve classroom differentiation: Perspectives from Project CLUE. *Roeper Review, 31,* 27–39.

Melber, L. M. (2003). Partnerships in science learning: Museum out-reach and elementary gifted education. *Gifted Child Quarterly, 47,* 251–285.

Olszewski-Kubilius, P., & Lee, S.-Y. (2004). Parent perceptions of effects of the Saturday Enrichment Program on gifted students' talent development. *Roeper Review, 26,* 156–165.

Pearl, P. (1997). Why some parent education programs for parents of gifted children succeed and others do not. *Early Child Development and Care, 130,* 41–48.

Theory-Based References

Karnes, F. A., & Shaunessy, E. (2004). The application of an individual professional development plan to gifted education. *Gifted Child Today, 27*(3), 60–64.

Kirschenbaum, R. J., Armstrong, D. C., & Landrum, M. (1999). Resource consultation model in gifted education to support talent development in today's inclusive schools. *Gifted Child Quarterly, 43,* 39–40.

Limburg-Weber, L. (1999/2000). Send them packing: Study abroad as an option for gifted students. *Journal of Secondary Gifted Education, 11,* 43–51.

Parker, J. P. (1996). NAGC standards for personnel preparation in gifted education: A brief history. *Gifted Child Quarterly, 40,* 158–164.

Stephens, K. R. (1999). Parents of the gifted and talented: The forgotten partner. *Gifted Child Today, 22*(5), 38–43, 52.

Wycoff, M., Nash, W. R., Juntune, J. E., & Mackay, L. (2003). Purposeful professional development: Planning positive experiences for teachers of the gifted and talented. *Gifted Child Today, 26*(4), 34–41.

Practice-Based References

Dettmer, P., Thurston, L. P., Knackendoffel, A., & Dyck, N. J. (2009). *Collaboration, consultation and teamwork for students with special needs* (6th ed.). Upper Saddle River, NJ: Pearson.

Hughes, C. E., & Murawski, W. A. (2001). Lessons from another field: Applying co-teaching strategies to gifted education. *Gifted Child Quarterly, 45,* 195–204.

Little, C. A. (2001). Probabilities and possibilities: The future of gifted education. *Journal of Secondary Gifted Education, 12,* 166–169.

Strip, C., & Hirsch. G. (2001). Trust and teamwork: The parent-teacher partnership for helping the gifted child. *Gifted Child Today, 24*(2), 26–30, 64.

Matthews, D. J., & Foster, J. F. (2005). A dynamic scaffolding model of teacher development: The gifted education consultant as catalyst for change. *Gifted Child Quarterly, 49,* 222–230.

ELEMENT 6.6
Gifted education specialists actively facilitate and participate in the preparation and induction of prospective special educators.

Research-Based References

Bain, S., Bourgeois, S., & Pappas, D. (2003). Linking theoretical models to actual practices: A survey of teachers in gifted education. *Roeper Review, 25,* 166–172.

Hébert, T. P., & Speirs Neumeister, K. L. (2000). University mentors in the elementary classroom: Supporting the intellectual, motivational, and emotional needs of high-ability students. *Journal for the Education of the Gifted, 24,* 122–148.

Joffe, W. S. (2001). Investigating the acquisition of pedagogical knowledge: Interviews with a beginning teacher of the gifted. *Roeper Review, 23,* 219–225.

Johnsen, S. K., Haensly, P. A., Ryser, G. R., & Ford, R. F. (2002). Changing general education classroom practices to adapt for gifted students. *Gifted Child Quarterly, 46,* 45–63.

Theory-Based References

Lave, J. (1991). Situated learning in communities of practice. In L. B. Resnick, J. M. Levine, & S. D. Teasley (Eds.), *Perspectives on socially shared cognition* (pp. 63–82). Washington, DC: American Psychological Association.

Wenger, E. (1998). *Communities of practice: Learning, meaning, and identity.* New York, NY: Cambridge University Press.

Practice-Based References

Callahan, C., Cooper, C., & Glascock, R. (2003). *Preparing teachers to develop and enhance talent: The position of national education organizations.* (ERIC Document Reproduction Services No. ED477882)

Falk, J. K., & Drayton, B. (Eds.). (2009). *Creating and sustaining online professional learning communities.* New York, NY: Teachers College Press.

Kitano, M., Montgomery, D., VanTassel-Baska, J., & Johnsen, S. (2008). *Using the national gifted education standards for PreK–12 professional development.* Thousand Oaks, CA: Corwin Press.

National Association for Gifted Children, & Council of State Directors of Programs for the Gifted. (2013). *2012–2013 state of the states in gifted education: National policy and practice data.* Washington, DC: Author.

ELEMENT 6.7
Gifted education specialists actively promote the advancement of the profession.

Research-Based References

Kennedy, D. M. (2003). Custer, South Dakota: "Gifted's" last stand. *Gifted Child Quarterly, 47,* 82–93.

Landrum, M., Katsiyannis, A., & DeWaard, J. (1998). A national survey of current legislative and policy trends in gifted education: Life after the national excellence report. *Journal for the Education of the Gifted, 21,* 352–371.

Larsen, M. D., Griffin, N. S., & Larsen, L. M. (1994). Public opinion regarding support for special programs for gifted children. *Journal for the Education of the Gifted, 17,* 131–142.

Robinson, A., & Moon, S. M. (2003). A national study of local and state advocacy in gifted education. *Gifted Child Quarterly, 47,* 8–25.

Todd, S. M., & Larson, A. (1992). In what ways might statewide advocates for gifted and talented education coordinate and focus their efforts? *Gifted Child Quarterly, 36,* 160–164.

Theory-Based References

Alvino, J. (1991). Media relations: What every advocate should know about the tricks of the trade. *Gifted Child Quarterly, 35,* 204–209.

Dettmer, P. (1991). Gifted program advocacy: Overhauling bandwagons to build support. *Gifted Child Quarterly, 35,* 165–172.

Irvine, D. J. (1991). Gifted education without a state mandate: The importance of vigorous advocacy. *Gifted Child Quarterly, 35,* 196–199.

Karnes, F. A., & Marquardt, R. (1997). *Know your legal rights in gifted education* (ERIC Digest E541). Reston, VA: ERIC Clearinghouse on Disabilities and Gifted Education.

Rash, P. K. (1998). Meeting parents' needs. *Gifted Child Today, 21*(5), 14–17.

Robinson, N. M. (2002). *Assessing and advocating for gifted students: Perspectives for school and clinical psychologists.* Storrs: University of Connecticut, The National Research Center on the Gifted and Talented.

Ross, P. O. (1991). Advocacy for gifted programs in the new educational climate. *Gifted Child Quarterly, 35,* 173–176.

Shaklee, B. D., Padak, N. D., Barton, L. E., & Johnson, H. A. (1991). Educational partnerships: Gifted program advocacy in action. *Gifted Child Quarterly, 35,* 200–203.

Zirkel, P. A. (2003). *The law on gifted education* (RM03178). Storrs: University of Connecticut, The National Research Center on the Gifted and Talented.

Practice-Based References

Berger, S. (2001). G + advocacy = gifted. *Understanding Our Gifted, 13*(3), 25–28.

Bisland, A. (2003). Student-created public relations for gifted education. *Gifted Child Today, 26*(2), 60–65.

Delcourt, M. A. B. (2003). Five ingredients for success: Two case studies of advocacy at the state level. *Gifted Child Quarterly, 47,* 26–37.

Advanced Preparation Standard 7: Collaboration

Gifted education specialists collaborate with stakeholders to improve programs, services, and outcomes for individuals with gifts and talents and their families.

ELEMENT 7.1
Gifted education specialists use culturally responsive practices to enhance collaboration.

Research-Based References

Landrum, M. S. (2001). An evaluation of the catalyst program: Consultation and collaboration in gifted education. *Gifted Child Quarterly, 45,* 139–151.

Williams, E. R., & Baber, C. R. (2007). Building trust through culturally reciprocal home-school-community collaboration from the perspective of African-American parents. *Multicultural Perspectives, 9,* 3–9.

Theory-Based References

Conzemius, A., & O'Neill, J. (2001). *Shared responsibility for student learning.* Alexandria, VA: Association for Supervision and Curriculum Development.

Shade, B. J., Kelly, C., & Oberg, M. (1997). *Creating culturally responsive classrooms.* Washington, DC: American Psychological Association.

Practice-Based References

Ford, D. Y. (2006). Creating culturally responsive classrooms for gifted students. *Understanding Our Gifted, 19*(1), 10–14.

Gentry, M., & Ferriss, S. (1999). StATS: A model of collaboration to develop science talent among rural students. *Roeper Review, 21,* 316–320.

Hertzog, N. B. (2005). Equity and access: Creating general education classrooms responsive to potential giftedness. *Journal for the Education of the Gifted, 29,* 213–257.

Kingore, B. (1995). Introducing parents to portfolio assessment: A collaborative effort toward authentic assessment. *Gifted Child Today, 18*(4), 12–13, 40.

Landrum, M. S. (2002). *Resource consultation and collaboration in gifted education.* Mansfield Center, CT: Creative Learning Press.

Tomlinson, C. A., Coleman, M. R., Allan, S., Udall, A., & Landrum, M. (1996). Interface between gifted education and general education: Toward communication, cooperation, and collaboration. *Gifted Child Quarterly, 40,* 165–171.

ELEMENT 7.2
Gifted education specialists use collaborative skills to improve programs, services, and outcomes for individuals with exceptionalities.

Research-Based References

Dansinger, S. (1998). Integrating gifted in special education services in the schools. *Gifted Child Today, 21*(3), 38–41.

Landrum, M. S. (2001). An evaluation of the catalyst program: Consultation and collaboration in gifted education. *Gifted Child Quarterly, 45,* 139–151.

Penney, S., & Wilgosh, L. (2000). Fostering parent-teacher relationships when children are gifted. *Gifted Education International, 14,* 217–229.

Terry A. W. (2003). Effects of service learning on young, gifted adolescents and their community. *Gifted Child Quarterly, 47,* 295–308.

Theory-Based References

Brighton, C. M. (2001). Stronger than apart: Building better models through collaboration and interconnection. *Journal of Secondary Gifted Education, 12,* 163–166.

McBee, M. T. (2004). The classroom as laboratory: An exploration of teacher research. *Roeper Review, 27,* 52–58.

VanTassel-Baska, J., & Johnsen, S. K. (2007). Teacher education standards for the field of gifted education: A division of coherence for personnel preparation in the 21st century. *Gifted Child Quarterly, 51,* 182–205.

Practice-Based References

Hébert, T. P., & Sergent, D. (2005). Using movies to guide: Teachers and counselors collaborating to support gifted students. *Gifted Child Today, 28*(4), 14–25.

Landrum, M. S. (2002). *Consultation in gifted education: Teachers working together to serve students.* Mansfield Center, CT: Creative Learning Press.

Renzulli, J. S., & Reis, S. M. (1985). *The Schoolwide Enrichment Model: A comprehensive plan for educational excellence.* Mansfield Center, CT: Creative Learning Press.

ELEMENT 7.3
Gifted education specialists collaborate to promote understanding, resolve conflicts, and build consensus for improving program, services, and outcomes for individuals with exceptionalities.

Research-Based References

Hertzog, N., & Bennett, T. (2004). In whose eyes? Parents' perspectives on the learning needs of their gifted children. *Roeper Review, 26,* 96–104.

Matthews, D., & Menna, R. (2003). Solving problems together: Parent/school/community collaboration at a time of educational and social change. *Education Canada, 43*(1), 20–23.

Melber, L. M. (2003). Partnerships in science learning: Museum outreach and elementary gifted education. *Gifted Child Quarterly, 47,* 251–258.

Moon, T. R., & Callahan, C. M. (2001). Curricular modifications, family outreach, and a mentoring program. *Journal for the Education of the Gifted, 24,* 305–321.

Solow, R. (2003). What parents want: In their own words. *Understanding Our Gifted, 15*(4), 3–7.

Theory-Based References

Chance, P. L. (1998). Meeting in the middle: Gifted education and middle schools working together. *Roeper Review, 21,* 133–138.

Landrum, M. S. (2003). *Consultation in gifted education: Teachers working together to serve students.* Mansfield, CT: Creative Learning.

Robinson, A. (2000, March). *Connecting the curriculum for excellence: English vertical teams.* Paper presented at the National Curriculum Network Conference, College of William & Mary, Williamsburg, VA.

Practice-Based References

Enersen, D. (2003). The art of bridge building: Providing for gifted children. *Gifted Child Quarterly, 47,* 38–45.

Johnsen, S. K. (2011). Assessing your school's RtI model in serving gifted students. In M. R. Coleman & S. K. Johnsen (Eds.), *RtI for gifted students* (pp. 105–120). Waco, TX: Prufrock Press.

Stephens, K. R. (1999). Parents of the gifted and talented: The forgotten partner. *Gifted Child Today, 22*(5), 38–43, 52.

Strip, C., & Hirsch, G. (2001). Trust and teamwork: The parent-teacher partnership for helping the gifted child. *Gifted Child Today, 24*(2), 26–30, 64.

Witte, M., & Johnsen, S. K. (2008). Collaborating with universities to provide special programs for gifted and talented students. *Tempo, 28*(3), 13–17.

About the Authors

Susan K. Johnsen, Ph.D., is a professor in the Department of Educational Psychology at Baylor University, where she directs the programs related to gifted and talented education. She is editor-in-chief of *Gifted Child Today*, coauthor of *Using the National Gifted Education Standards for University Teacher Preparation Programs*, *Using the National Gifted Education Standards for PreK–12 Professional Development*; and author of more than 200 articles, monographs, technical reports, and other books related to gifted education. She has also coauthored three tests used in identifying gifted students. She serves on the Board of Reviewers of the Council for Accreditation of Educator Preparation (CAEP) and is a reviewer and auditor of teacher preparation programs in gifted education. She is past president of The Association for the Gifted (TAG) and past president of the Texas Association for Gifted and Talented (TAGT). She has received awards for her work in the field of education, including NAGC's President's Award, CEC's Leadership Award, TAG's Leadership Award, TAGT's President's Award, TAGT's Advocacy Award, and Baylor University's Investigator Award, Teaching Award, and Contributions to the Academic Community. She may be reached at Department of Educational Psychology, School of Education, Baylor University, One Bear Place #97301, Waco, TX 76798, or Susan_Johnsen@baylor.edu.

Joyce VanTassel-Baska, Ed.D., is the Smith Professor Emerita at William & Mary where she developed a graduate program and a research and development center in gifted education. Formerly, she initiated and directed the Center for Talent Development at Northwestern University. She has also served as the state director of gifted programs for Illinois, as a regional director of a gifted service center in the Chicago area, as coordinator of gifted programs for the Toledo, OH, public school system, and as a teacher of gifted high school students in English and Latin. Dr. VanTassel-Baska has published widely, including 27 books and more than 500 refereed journal articles, book chapters, and scholarly reports. Her major research interests are on the talent development process and effective curricular interventions with the gifted.

Ann Robinson, Ph.D., is professor of educational psychology and founding director of the Jodie Mahony Center at the University of Arkansas at Little Rock, where she coordinates the graduate programs in gifted education. She is a former editor of *Gifted Child Quarterly,* is a past president of the National Association for Gifted Children, and received the Early Leader, the Early Scholar, the Distinguished Service, and the Distinguished Scholar awards from NAGC. Her coauthored article, "A National Study on Local and State Advocacy in Gifted Education" was juried as the *Gifted Child Quarterly* Paper of the Year. She was recognized as the Purdue University Alumna of Distinction for the College of Education, was honored by the William Jefferson Clinton Presidential Library for her public service, and has received the Faculty Excellence Award for Research twice from her university. Her collaborative Javits research and demonstration project, STEM Starters, was identified by the National Science Teachers Association as exemplary. Ann publishes and presents nationally and internationally on advocacy, biographical inquiry, and evidence-based interventions for teachers and students. Ann's most recent book, with coeditor Jennifer Jolly, is *A Century of Contributions to Gifted Education: Illuminating Lives.*

Alicia Cotabish, Ed.D., is an assistant professor in the Department of Teaching and Learning at the University of Central Arkansas, where she coordinates the gifted and talented education graduate program. She serves on the Professional Standards Committee for both the Council for the Accreditation of Educator Preparation (CAEP) and the National Association for Gifted Children (NAGC). She is an associate editor for the *Journal of Advanced Academics,* and the immediate past president of the Arkansas Association of Gifted Education Administrators (AAGEA).

Debbie Dailey, Ed.D., is an assistant professor in the Department of Teaching and Learning at the University of Central Arkansas. Formerly, Debbie was the associate director for the Jodie Mahony Center for Gifted Education at the University of Arkansas at Little Rock. Debbie also served as the curriculum coordinator and peer coach for a Javits-funded program, *STEM Starters*, which focused on improving science instruction in the elementary grades. Prior to moving to higher education, Debbie was a high school science teacher and gifted education teacher for 20 years.

Jennifer L. Jolly, Ph.D., is a senior lecturer in gifted education and a GERRIC Senior Research Fellow at the University of New South Wales in Sydney, Australia. Her research interests include the history of gifted education and parents of gifted children. Her work has been published in *Gifted Child Quarterly*, *Journal for the Education for the Gifted*, *Roeper Review*, and *Gifted Child Today*. Jennifer has written and edited several books, including *A Century of Contributions to Gifted Education: Illuminating Lives* with Ann Robinson and *Parenting Gifted Children*. She also served as editor of *Parenting for High Potential* from 2007 to 2012. Since 2010, she has served as a member of NAGC's Professional Standards Committee, contributing to *Using the Common Core State Standards for English Language Arts With Gifted and Advanced Learners*.

Jane Clarenbach, J.D., is the Director of Public Education at the National Association for Gifted Children. She coordinates NAGC's legislative and advocacy initiatives and promotes the needs of high achieving and high-potential children through her work with the media and state and national organizations. She also coordinates the reviews of teacher preparation programs in gifted and talented education as part of the national accreditation process through the Council for the Accreditation of Educator Preparation (CAEP).

Cheryll M. Adams, Ph. D., is the Director Emerita of the Center for Gifted Studies and Talent Development at Ball State University. She teaches online courses in gifted education for the University of Virginia and has presented widely at local, state, national, and international conferences. She is a former member of the Board of Directors of NAGC and is currently the Chair of the NAGC Professional Standards Committee. She contributed to the development, validation, and revision of the NAGC-CEC Advanced Standards in Gifted Education for Teacher Preparation. She is the series editor of the *NAGC Select* publications. In 2002, she received the NAGC Early Leader Award and in 2014, she received NAGC's Distinguished Service Award. She is Past President of the Indiana Association for the Gifted and of The Association for the Gifted, a division of the Council for Exceptional Children. She has many publications, including 12 coauthored books, 16 book chapters, and numerous other publications. She is an NCATE SPA reviewer and auditor. She contributed to the NAGC book, *Using the Common Core State Standards in Mathematics With Gifted and Advanced Learners*, and is a coauthor of *Using the Next Generation Science Standards With Gifted and Advanced Learners* and *A Teacher's Guide to Using the Next Generation Science Standards With Gifted and Advanced Learners*.